Innovative Marketing Communications
Strategies for the Events Industry

Other books in the Events Management series

The Management of Event Operations by Julia Tum, Philippa Norton and J. Nevan Wright

Events Management 2e by Glenn A J Bowdin, Johnny Allen, William O'Toole, Rob Harris and Ian McDonnell

Events Design and Experience by Graham Berridge

Event Feasibility by William O'Toole

Marketing and Selling Destinations and Venues: A Convention and Events Perspective by Tony Rogers and Rob Davidson

Innovative Marketing Communications

Strategies for the Events Industry

Guy Masterman
Assistant Professor in Sports Management
Tisch Center for Hospitality
Tourism and Sports Management
New York University, New York, USA

Emma H Wood
UK Centre for Events Management
Leeds Metropolitan University
Leeds, UK

ELSEVIER
BUTTERWORTH
HEINEMANN

AMSTERDAM • BOSTON • HEIDELBERG • LONDON • NEW YORK • OXFORD
PARIS • SAN DIEGO • SAN FRANCISCO • SINGAPORE • SYDNEY • TOKYO

Elsevier Butterworth-Heinemann
Linacre House, Jordan Hill, Oxford OX2 8DP
30 Corporate Drive, Burlington, MA 01803

First published 2006
Reprinted 2006

British Library Cataloguing in Publication Data
A catalogue record for this book is available from the British Library

Library of Congress Control Number: 2005925262
A catalogue record for this book is available from the Library of Congress

ISBN 0 7506 6361 8

For information on all Elsevier Butterworth-Heinemann
publications visit our website at www.books.elsevier.com

Working together to grow
libraries in developing countries

www.elsevier.com | www.bookaid.org | www.sabre.org

ELSEVIER   BOOK AID   Sabre Foundation
             International

Typeset by Newgen Imaging Systems (P) Ltd, Chennai, India
Printed and bound in Great Britain by MPG Books Ltd, Bodmin, Cornwall

Contents

List of Figures

List of Tables

Case Studies

Series Editors

Glenn A J Bowdin is Principal Lecturer in Events Planning at the UK Centre for Events Management, Leeds Metropolitan University where he has responsibility for managing events-related research. He is co-author of *Events Management*. His research interests include the area of service quality management, specifically focusing on the area of quality costing, and issues relating to the planning, management and evaluation of events. He is a member of the Editorial Boards for *Event Management* (an international journal) and *Journal of Convention & Event Tourism*, Chair of AEME (Association for Events Management Education), Charter Member of the International EMBOK (Event Management Body of Knowledge) Executive and a member of Meeting Professionals International (MPI).

Don Getz is a Professor in the Tourism and Hospitality Management Program, Haskayne School of Business, the University of Calgary. His ongoing research involves event-related issues (e.g. management, event tourism, events and culture) and special-interest tourism (e.g. wine). Recent books include *Event Management and Event Tourism* and *Explore Wine Tourism: Management, Development, Destinations*. He co-founded and is a member of the Editorial Board for *Event Management* (an international journal).

Professor Conrad Lashley is Professor in Leisure Retailing and Director of the Centre for Leisure Retailing at Nottingham Business School, Nottingham Trent University. He is also series editor for the Elsevier Butterworth Heinemann series on Hospitality Leisure and Tourism. His research interests have largely been concerned with service quality management, and specifically employee empowerment in service delivery. He also has research interest and publications relating to hospitality management education. Recent books include *Organisation Behaviour for Leisure Services, 12 Steps to Study Success, Hospitality Retail Management*, and *Empowerment: HR Strategies for Service Excellence*. He has co-edited, *Franchising Hospitality Services*, and *In Search of Hospitality: theoretical perspectives and debates*. He is the past Chair: of the Council for Hospitality Management Education. He is a Chair of the British Institute of Innkeeping's panel judges for the NITA Training awards, and is advisor to England's East Midlands Tourism network.

About the authors

Guy Masterman is Assistant Professor in Sports Management at the Tisch Center for Hospitality, Tourism and Sports Management at New York University. He was previously at the UK Centre for Events Management, Leeds Metropolitan University, where he helped found and then lead the first Masters Degree in Events Management. He has worked in the sports and events industries for over 25 years, the last 15 of which were spent as an independent consultant. Early in his career he was an international racquetball player and was involved in the development of that sport in the UK and internationally. His clients have included Coca-Cola, Pepsi, Nabisco, Capital Radio Group, Chelsea FC, Team Scotland, WCT Inc. and international governing bodies such as the ATP Tour, the International Yacht Racing Union and the International Stoke Mandeville Wheelchair Sports Federation. He has worked extensively for charity groups such as Muscular Dystrophy, Scope and Sparks and with sports stars Seb Coe, Jody Scheckter, Steve Backley and Lennox Lewis. His event work extends across all sectors of the industry and includes Euro '96, World Games, Coca-Cola Music Festival, Pepsi Extravaganza, Nabisco Masters Doubles and the promotion of concerts for Ray Charles, Santana, BB King, James Brown and Tony Bennett. His research focuses on strategic event planning and legacies and he sits on the editorial board of an international event research journal. His first book *Strategic Sports Event Management: An international approach* (Butterworth-Heinemann) was published in 2004.

Emma H Wood is Research Coordinator and Senior Lecturer in Events Marketing at the UK Centre for Events Management, Leeds Metropolitan University. She has considerable experience of marketing management within a range of industries and has worked in the UK, South-East Asia and Australia. She has been involved in numerous research projects that include the first national survey of small firms in the events sector and a comprehensive survey of local government use of events for destination marketing. Her consultancy work is specialized in the area of public sector events and has involved a number of social and economic impact studies for local government as well as audience development research and studies of event communication effectiveness. Her academic and consultancy research work is regularly disseminated at national and international conferences and through academic journals. She also sits on the editorial board of two industry-related periodicals.

Series Preface

The events industry, including festivals, meetings, conferences, exhibitions, incentives, sports and a range of other events, is rapidly developing and makes a significant contribution to business and leisure related tourism. With increased regulation and the growth of government and corporate involvement in events, the environment has become much more complex. Event managers are now required to identify and service a wide range of stakeholders and to balance their needs and objectives. Though mainly operating at national levels, there has been significant growth of academic provision to meet the needs of events and related industries and the organizations that comprise them. The English speaking nations, together with key Northern European countries, have developed programmes of study leading to the award of diploma, undergraduate and post-graduate awards. These courses focus on providing education and training for future event professionals, and cover areas such as event planning and management, marketing, finance, human resource management and operations. Modules in events management are also included in many tourism, leisure, recreation and hospitality qualifications in universities and colleges.

The rapid growth of such courses has meant that there is a vast gap in the available literature on this topic for lecturers, students and professionals alike. To this end, the *Events Management Series* has been created to meet these needs to create a planned and targeted set of publications in this area.

Aimed at academic and management development in events management and related studies, the *Events Management Series:*

- provides a portfolio of titles which match management development needs through various stages;
- prioritizes publication of texts where there are current gaps in the market, or where current provision is unsatisfactory;
- develops a portfolio of both practical and stimulating texts;
- provides a basis for theoretical and research underpinning for programmes of study;
- is recognized as being of consistent high quality;
- will quickly become the series of first choice for both authors and users.

Introduction

The Circus Maximus, Rome 2004. This serene, historical sight was once the venue for the Roman Empire's largest events. Some two thousand years ago, measuring approximately 530 metres long and 140 metres wide, this Great Circus staged events of such magnitude that up to 250 000 spectators would cram inside the structures that once stood there. In so doing, this venue provides an early example of the great capacity events have as communications tools.

The use of events as communications tools is not new. Indeed, the innovative use of sporting and culturally orientated activities for political purposes dates back to Greek and Roman times, at venues that even by today's standards were outstanding. Up to 50 000 people in the Coliseum and 250 000 in the Circus Maximus in ancient Rome at any one time, would gratefully receive the latest event provided at great expense by politically orientated nobility. The product was mass entertainment but the objectives were to secure the popular vote. Some 2000 years on, events are still staged for such communication purposes. However, in an age where customer expectations and choices increase simultaneously, an innovative approach for both event communications and the management of events as communications tools has perhaps become more critical. In presenting a strategic and innovative approach for communications in the events industry, this text is necessarily concerned with attaining and sustaining competitive advantage. It proposes an integrated approach in order to stay ahead of the crowd.

There are several terms that should be explained. First, it is important to define what communications are. Traditionally, with a marketing mix approach, one of the four 'Ps' is promotion. For many, the promotions mix and the communications mix are one and the same. The important distinction to be made, however, is that with the use of the word 'communications', a clearer understanding might be had of the targets that are involved. For example, market members are not the only targets, there are other audiences. For marketing to be successful it needs to target communications at a diverse range of stakeholders and audiences who are both internal and external to the organization.

There is also a distinction to be made between corporate communications and marketing communications. However, it can be agreed that, as most organizations may need to communicate with target audiences about non-marketing matters, all marketing communications are also corporate communications and that the communication of corporate image is an important aspect of marketing. Marketing communications are not, therefore, only concerned with the promotion of products and services (offerings). As the image of the organization will necessarily impact on the marketing of the offering, marketing communications are also concerned with the promotion of corporate image.

This text has a keen focus on one industry. It considers the dynamic, diverse and expanding events industry. However, the scope of this industry is great, with all levels of sports, arts, music and business activities for spectators and participants, clients and consumers, locally and globally. This is an industry that includes contests and tournaments, fetes, fairs and festivals, parties and receptions, performances, shows and displays, rallies and ceremonies, conferences and exhibitions. These are organized by a diverse range of players that includes governments, institutions, profit and non-profit organizations, as well as individuals. Consequently, a variety of examples are used to reflect this diversity and the international nature of the industry. A mixture of local and major events from the UK, mainland Europe, the USA, Australia and Asia, are used throughout the chapters and, in addition, key points are demonstrated via the use of case studies that include Liverpool, the European Capital City of Culture in 2008, the Guinness Witness festival, both the Tribeca and Sundance Film Festivals, the Tour de France, the Oakland A's, the ICA, the Barnes Exhibit, Singapore Chinese Orchestra, Gillette, Procter and Gamble and the UK Post Office.

The size of this industry as a whole is clearly substantial, but is difficult to quantify. The diversity is such that there are questions about what might be included in an overall measurement. For example, the increasing use of sponsorship across all sectors can be identified with market data on what is spent on acquiring rights, but not on the arguably larger amount that is spent on exploitation. As a consequence, data on the extent of spending on communications are mixed. While there is regular market reporting for business spending in sectors such as corporate hospitality, exhibitions and conferencing, there is little knowledge about how the vast numbers of sports, arts and music events up and down every country go about their communications. What this text can report on though, are specific examples of innovative activity.

The events industry is distinctive. It is unique in many ways and as a result there are important challenges and opportunities for both the marketing of events and the use of events as communications tools. While generic marketing communications practices and theory are all applicable in this industry, there are factors that require specific consideration. For example, events are transient in nature, those that attend an event are also a part of that event and as an event is produced it is simultaneously consumed or experienced. Participants clearly contribute to the product but spectators impact on each other too and are therefore contributing to each other's entertainment. The event, as an entertainment product, is also individually subjective and so in an audience of several thousands, each experience is unique with each individual's needs being satisfied or not. The job of communicating to these types of target markets is therefore complex and unique.

In further preparing the communications plan, it is also not unusual to find many players in the industry cooperating despite being competitors. Examples can be found across all of the industry's sectors too. For example, sports teams that are in the same leagues work together to administrate and further promote their sport. The same can be found between venues, arts and music organizations.

The above factors are considerations for the actual event product itself. There are also ancillary products that offer other opportunities, memories for example. While the event is transient, its legacy can be long term and marketers can harness that for enhanced communications for and through events. Event footage for the current event, used alongside the booking systems for the next event on year round websites, is one such mechanism. These are the types of opportunities that need to be built-in to the planning process and as such are considered throughout this text.

There were several choices to be made when the approach for this text was first considered. The decision to follow an integrated marketing communications (IMC) approach was an easy one to make. This position is discussed at length in Section One. The recommendation is that integrated communications strategies be designed to meet marketing objectives by communicating with a range of target audiences, not just customers, and including employees, and that this is best achieved by assessing the effectiveness and efficiency of all forms and combinations of contact and then by selecting the best of those options. This process can thus ensure that the selected forms of contact and message have synergy. IMC is a way of communicating coherently with target audiences for better results and so this is a common thread that runs throughout the text.

The choice of what to put in and what to leave when it comes to writing a text that is focused on the events industry is a difficult one to make. The decision in the end was to proceed with an approach that considers two key perspectives: how events communicate with their markets; and how events are used as corporate communication tools. The result is a text that considers both an innovative approach for event marketing communications and an innovative approach for the use of events for the marketing communications of other industries.

So what is innovation? Innovation in marketing communications is not necessarily about being first with new ways of doing things, it can also be about renewal or alteration. To innovate is to renew, alter, or introduce new methods (Webster's New World Dictionary, 2000). The extent to which change is required is only as much as it takes to achieve the objectives set. Therefore, new ideas, concepts, tools, techniques and strategies are not required every time and repeat strategies can still be considered innovative if they are successful again. In determining innovation then, this text looks to how effective communications strategies are and have to be to achieve the objectives set for them. If new communications strategies are needed, or existing ones renewed or altered and the objectives are achieved, then innovation has been applied.

The text is divided in to four sections. The first sets the scene and describes exactly why an integrated approach to marketing communications is effective. This is achieved by looking both at how events should approach their markets and how organizations should consider events as communications tools.

Section One starts with the marketing plan, with the first chapter providing an overview of the communications planning process and the importance of integration. Each of the key elements of the marketing plan is then covered in Chapters 2, 3 and 4, research and analysis, targeting and communication objectives, and strategy. The aim is to build an understanding of the planning process and the integration aspect of communications. The need to research the current organizational situation, competitor activity and customer groups is highlighted. The result of this is an identification of trends, challenges and opportunities in the marketplace. This is not a one-off exercise, however, as continual evaluation throughout the process is required as Chapter 2 prescribes. One of the initial areas of the marketing plan then is a clear identification and understanding of target audiences. Chapter 3 covers the identification of target segments and stakeholder groups, description of their characteristics and an understanding of their communication preferences. The chapter then goes on to discuss the need to have objectives for each event and each stakeholder group as well as broader communication objectives that fit within existing marketing and corporate aims. The importance of developing these levels of objectives based on the information gained from the initial pre-planning is stressed. Chapter 4 provides an overview of the strategic tools available to achieve communications objectives. It also highlights the need to fully integrate a variety of activities over the long term. The focus here is on the strategic combinations of those techniques that will have the most impact and be the most effective within the events industry.

Much of the innovation gets delivered via the individual tools that are utilized in communication programmes. Section Two presents each of the tools that are available for event marketing, chapter by chapter. Chapters 5, 6 and 9, for example, are concerned with tools that can deliver both to personal and non-personal targets. Public relations (PR) techniques (Chapter 5), are vital in the event manager's armoury. While successful PR comes at a price, it is often a cheaper, and therefore more popular, choice. The decision to use PR begins with the identification of all stakeholders, from customers to suppliers and from the local community to event participants. The chapter continues with the process for the strategic use of PR tools and techniques and also specifically considers two further areas – news media relations and the use of created media – and the importance of media partners for event promotions.

The chapter on E-marketing communications (Chapter 6) covers the importance of the use of the world wide web in order to market an event, not only to live but also virtual audiences. Websites can provide a transient event with longevity through the delivery of regular content and year round sales opportunities and are, therefore, loyalty-building tools. Additionally, they provide ticket sales mechanisms that can capture attention, provide live coverage of an event and provide another revenue stream from truly global markets. This chapter also covers the use of e-mail, SMS and other electronic forms of communication.

Chapter 7 looks at advertising and its delivery to non-personal markets. The event budget may not always extend to on-air advertising, but the recruitment of broadcast partners may provide pre-event promotional traffic. Radio partners can also offer valuable event entertainment content as well as in their broadcasting of an event. They can arrange or supply the high profile performing talent in the case of music events, for example. Similarly, promotional exchanges may prove just as valuable as paid-for advertising in the printed news media. The process for designing advertisements and how they can be used to reach non-personal audiences is discussed in detail.

Chapter 8 considers an approach for the development of event sponsorship programmes and how sponsors can be recruited in order to enhance the event communications platform. Cross-promotional agreements with sponsors can enable an event to reach otherwise inaccessible markets, but reach them at a sponsor's own expense. Such sponsors are highly sought after and so the process to recruit them becomes critical. This chapter considers the development of sponsorship programmes by focusing on the key aspects for building sponsor relations, signing and encouraging those sponsors that will undertake exploitation programmes and implementing sponsorship evaluation in order to improve the sponsor recruitment process.

Sales promotions (Chapter 9) can be utilized by event managers to 'push' key distributors, partners and sponsors into improved performance via incentive programmes. Equally, 'pull' strategies can be used directly with consumers. This chapter considers how events have built-in rewards for such purposes in the form of tickets, as well as the opportunities to work extensively with well-chosen commercial partners.

Chapter 10 considers the predominantly personal market reach of direct and relationship marketing. There is an increasing need to move towards personalized, individual communications with certain customer/stakeholder groups in order to achieve success. This has been made possible through the developments in database and communication technology and is desirable due to the increasing cynicism of today's consumer and the overuse of non-personal targeted methods. The focus in this chapter then, is on methods for communicating directly with customer groups and the use of one-to-one communications to develop long-term relationships.

Section Three is concerned with how events can be used by organizations as communications tools. There are three main ways in which organizations can engage with existing events or utilize custom-made purpose events. These three areas of promotions, sponsorship and corporate hospitality are covered in Chapters 11, 12 and 13. Chapter 11 considers how events are used as promotional vehicles by all kinds of different organizations, in launching, exhibiting and demonstrating products. The level of innovation required to capture market attention is high and this chapter closely scrutinizes the critical factors for practising organizations as well as highlighting aspects that managers of all other kinds of events would do well to consider.

The focus at the start of Chapter 12 is the question, 'why is event sponsorship such a popular form of communication?' Only thirty years ago this was not a justifiable decision and many sponsorships were philanthropically founded. Now, however, while sponsorship success is still difficult to measure, there is a process that can lead to a return on investment. Critical to this process is the need to establish sponsorship 'fit', the setting of measurable objectives, the need to exploit sponsorship rights with additional communications, and evaluation for improved performance. This chapter considers each of these factors in turn, in order to identify how sponsorship can now become an accountable and effective communications tool.

Chapter 13 considers how the traditional use of corporate hospitality and entertainment can be used to develop relationships with key customers, suppliers and employees. While the evidence for such is not yet founded well in research, the growth of corporate spend in this area suggests that host organizations assume it works. As assumption in business is never enough, the chapter promotes the call for more research and the setting of measurable objectives and their subsequent evaluation.

The final section (Section Four) is concerned with the not too insignificant issue of how to ensure future success. Having addressed the research and strategic needs for the marketing plan in Section One, the event communications tool chest in Section Two, the use of events by organizations as communications tools in Section Three, the final consideration focuses on implementation, evaluation and control and an identification of trends that will affect future decision making. In particular, Chapter 14 focuses on the management of the communications plan over the planning period. Ensuring the effectiveness of communication strategies is only possible if their impacts are measurable and so all aspects of the communications strategy need to be regularly evaluated against the objectives set. The ways in which this can be achieved are therefore important and are addressed through the consideration of measurement and the use of a variety of methods and data sources, including internal operational data, as well as scanning the external environment and using market research. Such findings are vital in ensuring the success of future communication plans as well as providing control data to allow for adaptations in the current plan. The process of setting and adhering to a budget is an integral part of marketing communications planning and is closely related to the issues of measurement and control. This chapter therefore concludes by outlining the techniques for negotiating and setting budget requirements through the costing of communications methods and media prior to the implementation of the plan. The emphasis is on the importance of continuous monitoring of the plan in line with the budget and the various methods that can be employed to achieve this.

The final chapter summarizes the continuous thread running through this entire text, the need for longer-term planning. Chapter 15 considers the current trends in marketing communications and the challenges and opportunities that are likely to arise in the future. In particular, it considers the impact of one-to-one enabling technology, the ever-increasing need for innovative media and the postmodern dedifferentiation occurring between audience, media and event.

Finally, there are several important texts that competently cover the area of integrated marketing communications (Shimp, 1997; Kitchen, 1999; Pickton and Broderick, 2001; Fill, 2002; Hill et al., 2003; Clow and Baack, 2004; Smith and Taylor, 2004), but there have been none, to date, that have specifically addressed event marketing communications or the events industry as a whole. While these generic texts are recommended, it is hoped that this text offers new aspects for practical and theoretical consideration and encourages further research and analysis of what is a vital industry.

References

Clow, K. and Baack, D. (2004) *Integrated Advertising, Promotion, and Marketing Communications*, 2nd edn. Pearson Prentice Hall.

Fill, C. (2002) *Marketing Communications: Contexts, Strategies and Applications*. Pearson Education.

Hill, E., O'Sullivan, C. and O'Sullivan, T. (2003) *Creative Arts Marketing*, 2nd edn. Butterworth-Heinemann.

Kitchen, P. (1999) *Marketing Communications: Principles and Practice*. International Thomson Business Press.

Pickton, D. and Broderick, A. (2001) *Integrated Marketing Communications*. Financial Times/Prentice Hall.

Shimp, T. (1997) *Advertising, Promotion and Supplemental Aspects of Integrated marketing Communications*, 4th edn. The Dryden Press.

Smith, P. and Taylor, J. (2004) *Marketing Communications: An Integrated Approach*, 4th edn. Kogan Page.

Webster's New World (2000) *College Dictionary*, 4th edn. IDG Books Worldwide.

Section One
Integrated Marketing Communications

Trafalgar Square, London. A month of free events, July 2004. 'Summer in the Square,' coordinated by the Greater London Authority, consisted of a series of events; Bollywood Steps (dance displays), a Children's Art day, Square perspectives (dancing on a transparent stage), Trafalgar shores (Caribbean dance, seaside puppetry), Masquerade (Nigerian drama), Love in the Square (music performances), the Magic Flute (street opera), and the Norwich Union London Sports Park (athletics displays and coaching). This represents a diverse set of events collectively brought together under one theme.

The four chapters in this section provide an overview of the communications planning process and the importance of an integrated approach. The aim is to build an understanding of the key stages of the process.

Chapter 1 considers the process as a whole and describes the integrated approach to marketing communications, putting into context its application in the events industry and providing a model of event communications planning.

The subsequent chapters consider the three key elements of the marketing plan: research and analysis throughout the process; the targeting process and setting objectives; and the formation of innovative strategies.

Marketing Communications Planning

Research and Analysis

Communication Objectives and Targeting

Communications Strategy

Chapter 1
Marketing Communications Planning

Objectives

- To introduce the concept of integrated marketing communications
- To discuss the need for a marketing communications planning process
- To evaluate the models of communication planning
- To provide an overview of the key stages in the communications planning process

Introduction

When considering marketing communications within the corporate and marketing strategies of an organization, it is necessary to emphasize the long-term and integrated nature of those communications. This requires the consideration of communication objectives which may not be achieved for several years, such as brand loyalty or attitude change, rather than a simple focus on the short term, such as sales figures for the next event. This chapter highlights the long-term nature of developing successful communications plans and stresses the need to utilize and integrate a wide variety of tools, techniques and media within the plan.

Integrated marketing communications

Communication is the process whereby thoughts are conveyed and meaning is shared between individuals or organizations. A general model of communication is given in Figure 1.1. This model recognizes the possibility of the receiver taking a different meaning from the communication than that intended by the sender due to the encoding/decoding process and the 'noise' associated with

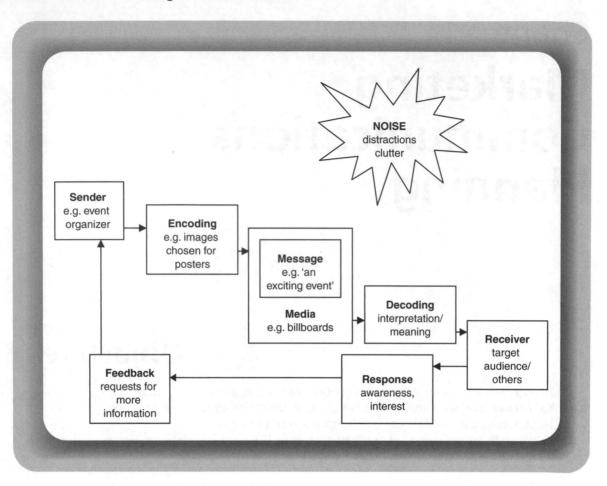

Figure 1.1 Major elements in the communication process.

the process. This emphasizes the need for careful planning and control of the communication process, as even highly controllable communication methods, such as personalized direct marketing, need to be carefully monitored to determine their effects on the receiver.

Marketing within events relies heavily on communication whether this be in directly informing potential customers of a product offering, in creating a brand image in the marketplace, or through customer feedback and market research. Marketing communications represent the collection of all elements in a brand's marketing mix that facilitate exchanges by establishing shared meanings with the brand's stakeholders. The brand can refer to an individual product (one event), a group of products (a programme of events) or a wider organizational brand (the event organizer, the location, the sponsor). The stakeholders will consist of a range of groups such as existing and potential customers, employees, sponsors and the local community.

When the audience of a marketing communications message decodes or translates the message they can do so on a number of levels. The Wirthlin Report (1999) describes these levels as a ladder from the communicator to the audience. The lowest level consists of rational components, the product's attributes (e.g. venue, performers, date) and the functional consequences of using the product (e.g. entertainment). The higher levels are the emotional components consisting of psychosocial consequences or personal emotional outcomes (e.g. 'made me forget my worries') and personal values or major goals and ideals (e.g. self-esteem, peace of mind, love). Communication that operates on all levels is likely to be more effective in building a longer-term change in attitude and behaviour.

A number of factors have led to a move away from the traditional promotions mix for marketing communications (personal selling, advertising, sales promotion and public relations) to the development of the concept of integrated marketing communications (IMC). Integrated marketing communications has been defined in a number of ways:

a concept of marketing communications planning that recognizes the added value of a comprehensive plan that evaluates the strategic roles of a variety of communications disciplines . . . and combines these to provide clarity, consistency and maximum communication impact (Duncan and Everett, 1993).

The coordination of all promotional activities to produce a unified, customer-focused promotional message (Pickton and Broderick, 2001).

The harmonization of customer-orientated promotional messages (Fill, 2002).

All consistent interactions a stakeholder has with an organization (Schultz, 1998).

An organization's unified, coordinated effort to promote a brand concept through the use of multiple communication tools that 'speak with one voice' (Shimp, 1997).

These definitions illustrate the continuing development of integrated marketing communications as a concept. Generally, it appears to be agreed that IMC came to the fore in the 1990s and evolved due to a number of reasons. First, a reduced faith in the effectiveness of the mass media and, consequently, the move towards highly targeted communication methods and, secondly, due to the greater demands being placed on marketing communication suppliers and the increased need to demonstrate return on investment. Thirdly, there is the need to coordinate and integrate the ever-widening array of communication tools and media available to the marketer (Table 1.1).

The complexity of the reality of IMC is clearly demonstrated in Hartley and Pickton's (1999) model of the 'mindscape of integrated marketing communications' and 'the wheel of integrated marketing communications' developed by Pickton and Broderick (2001). These models present the marketing communications techniques included within the traditional categories of advertising, sales promotion, public relations and personal selling, but illustrate the requirement for these to overlap and

Table 1.1 Comparison of traditional versus IMC perspectives

Traditional marketing communications	Integrated marketing communications
Separate functions: fragmentation	Integrated into one strategy: synergy
Starts with organization (goals, products)	Customer orientated
Specialist practitioners	Generalists
Fragmented communication programmes	Consistent communication programmes
Shorter-term objectives	Relationship/brand building objectives
Mass audiences	Targeted to stakeholder segments

to be used in a number of differing ways. The use of a combination of one-to-one communications and one-to-many communications for both image and brand management as well as customer contact management is a vital aspect of IMC. In recognizing the variety of techniques, the numerous potential objectives and differing target audiences plus the overlaps between these, the models illustrate both the potential benefits of IMC and some of the reasons for it not being adopted within many organizations. These barriers to IMC include the difficulties in managing the process and the choice of whether this is done in-house or through an agency. There are also problems in overcoming the mindset of the traditional segmentation of the promotion components and defining the scope of IMC (i.e. does it also include corporate and internal communications).

In order to overcome some of these issues, planning models have been developed by a number of authors and these will be considered in the next section.

The methods for managing IMC are of lesser importance than the acceptance of the concept that any communications plan needs to consider and use, where appropriate, a variety of communication tools and that in doing this it is necessary, and beneficial, to ensure consistency of the message (shared core meaning) and complementarity of the methods.

Importance of a planning process

In order to gain competitive advantage and to ensure added value for the customer, the communication process needs to be planned in a systematic and controlled manner. With an ever-increasing choice of communication methods and ways of combining these, it is vital that any decisions made are based on accurate, up-to-date and relevant information.

The planning of any process allows management to assess the risks and returns of any course of action before deciding upon it. If marketing communications are developed in an *ad hoc*, fragmented manner, then they will be difficult to monitor in terms of objectives, budget and return. The risks involved, therefore, in investing relatively large amounts of time, expertise and financial resources can be minimized by careful planning and their investment justified by the meeting of clearly defined objectives measured through carefully planned evaluation procedures. A further benefit is that a wrongly chosen communication strategy is more likely to be identified at an early stage if a planning process has been followed. This can then be modified or shelved before more serious damage is done. Similarly, the early identification of problems in implementation can be facilitated by the planning process.

An often overlooked benefit of planning is in its cyclical nature. Each new planning cycle benefits from the lessons learnt in the earlier plans, i.e. learning from previous mistakes and successes. This again requires systematic and objective evaluations of the outcomes and process of the previous communications plan. Using such past experiences in a more formalized manner can help to ensure increasing levels of efficiency and effectiveness in any future communications plans.

In order to ensure that communications operate at a strategic rather than tactical level within the organization, objectives need to be set for the longer term. The planning process can help ensure that these are set within the constraints of the organization's resources and the external environment and that they are set for the long, mid and short term.

The difficult task of integrating the various aspects of marketing communications and of ensuring a consistent core message to all stakeholder groups can only be achieved through a well-planned communications campaign. The integration, consistency and complementarity needed to gain synergy and hence increased customer value and competitive advantage will only happen if a systematic and well-defined process is followed.

There are, of course, some possible drawbacks to a formal communications process. Successful marketing communications, to a large extent, rely on creativity and innovation. An overly formalized or restrictive planning system could be in danger of stifling this creativity in favour of tried and tested methods. The need to pre-test, retest, monitor and evaluate can lengthen the development and implementation time for a campaign and may provide competitors with the information and lead-time to launch counter campaigns to reduce any impact. A planning process needs to be developed, therefore, which does not inhibit creativity and is not overly bureaucratic and formalized.

Marketing communications planning

Models of communications planning generally tend to be based on the planning framework of situation analysis, objective setting, strategy development, budgeting, implementation and control (Cooper, 1997; Smith et al., 1997; Tucker Knapp, 2001; Fill, 2002). Each model has its benefits and drawbacks. For example, Cooper (1997) clearly demonstrates the cyclical nature of planning and emphasizes the creativity needed within communications planning. However, this model is focused on advertising and therefore does not show the integration and coordination of other communications methods. Fill (2002) provides a useful overview of each of the areas that need to be considered, bringing in marketing research and agencies to the situation analysis and recognizing the levels of objectives (corporate, marketing and communication). This model usefully splits promotional strategies into pull (aimed at end customers), push (aimed at intermediaries) and profile (reaching a range of target groups). The key elements of Fill's (2002) marketing communications planning framework are:

- context analysis
- marketing objectives and positioning
- marketing communications strategy
- development of the promotional mix
- implementation
- evaluating and monitoring performance.

However, as Kitchen (1999) points out there are disadvantages to structured planning in that it can lead to 'me-too' strategies, it can encourage seeing customers as targets rather than partners and can give sometimes a dangerous illusion of control. Creativity and intuition need to be provided for within the planning process, as does the recognition that the earlier stages of the plan (formulation of objectives and strategies) are closely related to implementation and control and that the process is not necessarily sequential. The process for event planning (Masterman, 2004) shows the iterative nature of planning which needs to be adopted within the communications plans of event organizations.

A non-sequential yet structured process which encompasses all the elements of IMC (consistency, integration and complementarity) and allows for the creativity, intuition and innovativeness of the events industry is the ideal. These qualities may not be easy to combine in one model, but should still underpin the communications process for events organizations.

Overview of marketing communications planning

Situation analysis

The initial stages in any planning cycle are to gain an understanding of the current position and the context within which the plan will operate. This involves the gathering, analysis and interpretation of information from a wide range of sources.

The most important area to research is the organization's stakeholders with whom it will be communicating. An in-depth understanding is needed of each group's current attitudes to, opinions of and beliefs about the organization, its brands and its events. Knowledge of purchase behaviour and each group's views of competing products will also be needed. Specific information is required on their reactions to past and future communications campaigns, their media preferences etc.

Other areas that need to be researched are competitor activity, the views of intermediaries, suppliers and employees and the wider external environment. This includes legal and political changes relating to marketing communications, advances or innovations in communication technology and general social trends which may affect communication preferences.

Although often discussed as the first stage, information gathering needs to be ongoing and should inform each aspect of the communications plan. The research into communication specific issues should become part of the organization's overall marketing information system which will include competitor and market intelligence, environmental scanning and wider marketing research as well as data generated internally by the day-to-day operations of the organization. The research needs for events marketing communications are discussed in more depth in Chapter 2.

Objective setting

Once a thorough understanding of the stakeholders, external environment and the organizational context has been gained, it is then possible to set communications objectives for the campaign. These will often be the first part of a written marketing communications plan and will be used to steer the rest of the process. Communications objectives will be set within the framework of wider marketing objectives of the organization and these in turn will have been set to achieve the corporate objectives.

Communication objectives should not include overall sales value, profit margins or market share, but should encompass goals specific to the direct effects of communication, e.g. brand awareness, response rates, attitude change, offer take-up, personal recommendations etc.

The communications plan may include sub-objectives for each stakeholder or target audience and for periods of time within the planning cycle. Separate objectives for each communications method should not be set at this stage, as this presumes the strategic choices yet to be made and jeopardizes the integration of the overall communications strategy. The setting of communication objectives is covered in detail in Chapter 3.

Targeting

Deciding on the audiences, or recipients, of marketing communications needs to be done at an early stage in the planning process. It may be necessary for this to be done both before and after objective setting. As the communications plan is likely to be set within the context of a marketing plan, target groups may well have been identified as part of the overall marketing strategy. If this is the case then these 'predetermined audiences' need to be focused on in the research stage and described in detail in the situation analysis. Objectives can then be set for each group already identified. It is then necessary to apply a further breakdown of these groups once the communication objectives have been set. For example, an objective to increase awareness of the interactive aspects of Glastonbury Festival's website may require the targeting of distinct segments, i.e. past customers, existing customers (those with tickets) and would-be customers (those who could not get tickets), whereas initial targeting in the marketing strategy may have been 'eighteen to twenty-five-year olds who listen to live music'.

Targeting is an essential part of successful communications as it recognizes the preferences and needs of each different group, which can then be reflected in the chosen strategies. These preferences and needs will be widely different between some groups, e.g. sponsors, attendees, local community, but may also vary within groups. For example, the visitors to the Ideal Home Show will include couples, families and organizational buyers and these can be further split into those who live in the UK to those from overseas, or those who attend regularly and first time attendees etc.

Identifying target audiences, further segmenting each audience and then specifying their characteristics, preferences and behaviour allows communications methods to be tailored to their needs and therefore those methods are likely to be more successful in meeting the objectives. The additional cost involved in creating separate targeted communications campaigns is far outweighed by the benefits gained in terms of both efficiency and effectiveness.

Positioning and message strategies

In order to ensure the consistency and integration required, it is necessary to determine overarching strategies for positioning and for the communications message.

Positioning refers to the image in the mind of the audience of the organization, its brand, its events or its services relative to their image of competing products. The desired position will be developed based on the research undertaken in the situation analysis, the focus of the communication objectives and to some extent predetermined from the marketing plan objectives and strategy if these exist. As positioning reflects the perception of the brand by the target audiences, it is important to develop appropriate positioning strategies for each target group. For example, a corporate event organizer will recognize that being perceived as developing the most innovative and creative events may be important for some FMCG (fast-moving consumer goods) clients, whereas being seen as highly reliable with high levels of service may be key for financial sector clients. These specific positioning strategies need to fit within the overall image of the organization and its brand if consistency and synergy are to be achieved. Therefore, an overarching positioning statement is developed and adapted positioning strategies for each target market are fitted within this. Without the overarching strategy the audiences are likely to receive mixed, confusing or at worst conflicting messages.

The message strategy is developed from the positioning statement to provide a consistent and repeated image to the target audiences. Again this will be adapted in form and style for each target group, but the overall message will remain the same.

The strategic options available will be partly determined by the organization's competitive position (market leader, challenger, follower or nicher), the product or industry life cycle (introduction, growth, maturity or decline), the strengths and weaknesses of the organization and the external environment. However, the most important determining factor should always be the needs and preferences of stakeholders.

Method and media strategies

The adaptation of the overall message to meet the needs of each target audience is achieved through the manipulation of the wide variety of communication methods and media available to the marketer.

An initial decision to be made is whether or not the methods will involve push or pull strategies or a combination of both. Push strategies are targeted at marketing intermediaries (agents, distributors, brokers) and pull strategies at end customers.

Methods involve choices such as stressing the USP (unique selling proposition) of the brand or the brand's image, creating a resonance with the audience, using rational or emotional appeals. Other choices need to select methods on the scale of one-to-one versus one-to-many communications, interactive versus passive and information based versus image based.

The methods of marketing communications have been traditionally grouped into the four categories of advertising, sales promotion, personal selling and public relations. However, with the advent of integrated marketing communications and the development of new and innovative methods, these categories have become less useful as many methods overlap and fit into more than one category. Pickton and Broderick's (2001) 'Wheel of IMC' demonstrates this well and clearly shows the wide variety of methods now available.

The message and method chosen will, to a large extent, determine which media are appropriate as will the characteristics and preferences of the target audiences. Media choices range from the traditional use of newspapers, sales people, press releases and prize draws to highly interactive websites, product placement in computer games, the use of SMS (texting) or ever more attention grabbing promotional events. The important and increasing role of events as a communication method used by other industries is covered in Section Three.

Creative combinations of a number of methods and media delivering a consistent message will ensure the success of a communications campaign. The diversity of methods and media available mean that there are unlimited possibilities for creating the new and innovative communications campaigns that are necessary in an increasingly overcrowded marketplace. Consumers are becoming ever more cynical and selective in their interest and responses to marketing communications and novelty and subtlety are required to capture and maintain the interest of these audiences exposed to thousands of marketing messages every day. The diverse range of methods available for communicating with event stakeholders is covered in Section Two.

Communications budget

Any communication campaign will be set within certain organizational constraints. These constraints will include the managerial style of the organization in terms of risk-taking, innovativeness and creative freedom and of course the willingness to commit financial resources. The determination of the budget for an integrated marketing communications campaign can be contentious as a quantifiable financial return on investment can be difficult to prove in accountancy terms. This difficulty again emphasizes the importance of having measurable objectives, as the achievement of these objectives can justify the original resources invested and can also be used to secure future budgets.

The ideal form of budget setting is 'objective-and-task'. This logical process suggests that if objectives have been set that are desirable, realistic and achievable then the finances should be made available to enable those objectives to be achieved. The budget negotiation process therefore takes place once the communications plan has been determined, i.e. this is what we need to achieve, this is how it can be done and this is what it will cost. If the resources are not available to meet the needs of the proposed plan then the objectives must be revised, although this would, perhaps, suggest that the original objectives were not set within an understanding of the organization's strengths and resources.

Although, objective-and-task budget setting is preferred, it is rarely the method used with most organizations relying on more traditional financially based criteria. These are likely to be based on a set percentage of last year's sales or a percentage of the overall marketing budget. If the budget is allocated prior to the determination of objectives and strategies then the budget becomes part of the situational context within which the communications plan is developed and objectives should be set within this constraint.

An understanding of how and when the budget is negotiated and set is an important element of the marketing communications planning process and has implications for the implementation, control and monitoring of the plan once determined.

Implementation

This aspect of the communications planning process is often given less emphasis with the focus tending to be on the creative aspects of strategy development, however, the best strategies will fail if wrongly implemented.

The practicalities of implementing a fully integrated marketing communications plan need to be addressed through cross-functional teams within the organization often complemented by the use of agencies and other external specialists. The coordination and management of these roles and organizations requires detailed planning and a clear delineation of duties and responsibilities along with a shared understanding of what is to be achieved. The key to successful implementation is therefore effective internal communications, as all those involved must send a single positive message to stakeholder groups at all points of contact.

The main aspects of implementation have been defined by Smith et al. (1997) as the 3Ms; men, money and minutes. These include the roles and responsibilities for each element of the plan, the costs involved and the timing and flow of tasks.

The management of the communications plan involves process management, resource management, internal marketing and communications, scheduling and budgeting with an overarching focus on the integration and coordination of a variety of resources and expertise. These areas will be considered in Chapter 14.

Measurement, evaluation and control

In order to ensure the success of a marketing communications plan, it is necessary to measure certain aspects both during and after the campaign and to evaluate these measures against predetermined criteria. These criteria need to be based around the objectives of the campaign often broken down by time-scale, target group or campaign tactic. The evaluation against these criteria will then provide the necessary indicators to use for control purposes. Control is the action taken as a result of the evaluation and may involve the decision to maintain or amend the existing plan as well as being the basis for future plan development.

There are, therefore, two aspects to control. First, to ensure that the plan is being implemented as it should be and secondly, to check that the strategies being implemented are having the expected effect, i.e. the control of implementation and the control of outcome (or efficiency and effectiveness control).

For example, as a part of its communication campaign a music festival advertised a free ticket hot line in the local newspaper. Interim measurements found that only 50 per cent of the claimed tickets were likely to be used. An evaluation of the reasons for this disappointing take-up discovered that it was largely due to customer dissatisfaction with the attitude of the telesales staff handling the ad response and that their lack of knowledge had deterred respondents from attending the event. This evaluation, therefore, suggested an implementation problem rather than a problem with the strategy and it was possible to switch to a more specialized telesales agency for the remainder of the campaign.

The methods used to measure and evaluate communications strategies are varied and can range from large consumer surveys to *ad hoc* sales force feedback, from complex statistical data analysis to intuitive interpretation of anecdotal evidence. All can be valid and useful as long as they are undertaken and interpreted in an objective, timely and systematic way and use the campaign objectives as their main criteria for evaluation. Methods that can be used to research campaign effectiveness will be considered in the next chapter as well as in Chapter 14.

The written communication plan

The written plan is a vital document for internal communications and implementation and should as a minimum include:

- objectives
- goals
- audience/s
- timetable, tools and budget
- evaluation.

In order to help achieve the shared understanding and integration of purpose needed, the plan should summarize the main issues and details of marketing communications activities, showing relevant background information and marketing communications decisions (Pickton and Broderick, 2001).

An example of the communications planning process is shown in Case study 1.1. This case illustrates how a well-developed communications plan helped a small-scale festival gain nationwide recognition.

Case study 1.1

The DoubleTake Documentary Film Festival

Situation analysis

This documentary film festival based in North Carolina, USA was founded in 1998. The festival had a narrow fan base and, due to this and its regional image, was failing to attract sponsorship investment. The lack of sponsors meant that the organization had less money to invest in building its brand to attract the better directors that were needed to attract a broader fan base and so the cycle continued. The key problem, therefore, was in changing perception among stakeholders from being seen as a regional festival to being a major player in the entertainment industry.

Aim: Broaden the appeal of the film festival

Objectives

- Increase advanced sales of passes by 50 per cent
- Increase overall attendance (seats filled) by 15 per cent
- Increase sponsorship $
- Gain recognition as one of USA's leading film festivals.

Target audiences

- Main focus: Mainstream entertainment enthusiasts (new target audience)
- Peripheral: Existing loyal fans (not to be alienated by new campaign)
- Existing and potential sponsors
- Industry press and associations.

Creative strategy

- Positioning: Research found that off-centre stories with an edge were most appealing. Needed to provide a 'taste' of documentaries as entertainment and the feeling that this style of entertainment could only be experienced at the DoubleTake Festival.
- Message: 'True reality is more entertaining than TV boardroom created reality.'
- Method: Mini-documentaries showing absurd and provocative real-life vignettes.
- Media: A low budget for media was provided so low cost but well-targeted cable channels were used such as MTV, P, Comedy Central plus coverage on NBC. These television advertisements were complemented by print ads in local newspapers and alternative news weeklies in order to re-frame mainstream audience perception of documentaries.

Integrated communications

The main campaign was television based but was extended to all touchpoints via websites, direct mail, point-of-purchase and sponsorship sales kits. Posters were also provided as premiums for sponsors.
   Budget for media: $500k.

Evaluation

- Advanced sales of passes up 177 per cent
- Seats filled up 31 per cent
- Sponsorship up 26 per cent and lead sponsor gained for next year
- Gained number of prestigious national recognitions.

Source: based on Effie Awards: Brief of effectiveness (2003).

Summary

Integrated marketing communications has provided the basis for much of the continued interest in one-to-one marketing and customer relationship management and has the potential to bring together the concepts of integration, alignment, measurement and accountability in communications (Baker and Mitchell, 2000). The merging of these ideas into an approach that recognizes and takes advantage of the convergence of traditional and new interactive marketing approaches is undoubtedly the way forward in marketing communications.

An integrated marketing communications programme includes written, spoken and electronic interactions with stakeholder audiences. These interactions are used to create awareness, interest and involvement in the organization, its activities, programmes, people, service and products.

The integration of a variety of communications methods ensures that the message remains focused and therefore achieves a far greater impact than traditional fragmented promotional methods.

A successful communications plan will be based on an understanding of target audience needs and requires the organization to spend time analysing their market position and determining objectives. Through this analysis the planning process encourages consideration of new marketing tactics, methods and media. The requirement for cooperation and coordination helps to build teamwork, commitment and focus, both at intra- and inter-company level, improving all internal and external communication. A well-developed and implemented communications plan will facilitate continual improvement through measurement and evaluation and will ensure efficient progress towards longer-term communication objectives.

In order to ensure these benefits a process for integrated marketing communications planning is needed which should involve consideration of:

- situation analysis
- objective setting
- targeting
- positioning and message strategies
- method and media strategies
- communications budget
- implementation
- measurement, evaluation and control.

The communications planning process for event organizations needs to include a staged process where the current position is researched, objectives set, target markets ascertained and communication messages implemented through a variety of methods and media. The plan needs to be implemented, measured and controlled with the results feeding into the next planning cycle. The whole process should be informed by continual research and evaluation and must allow for the flexibility, creativity and innovation necessary to produce effective marketing communications. A model which incorporates these factors is shown in Figure 1.2.

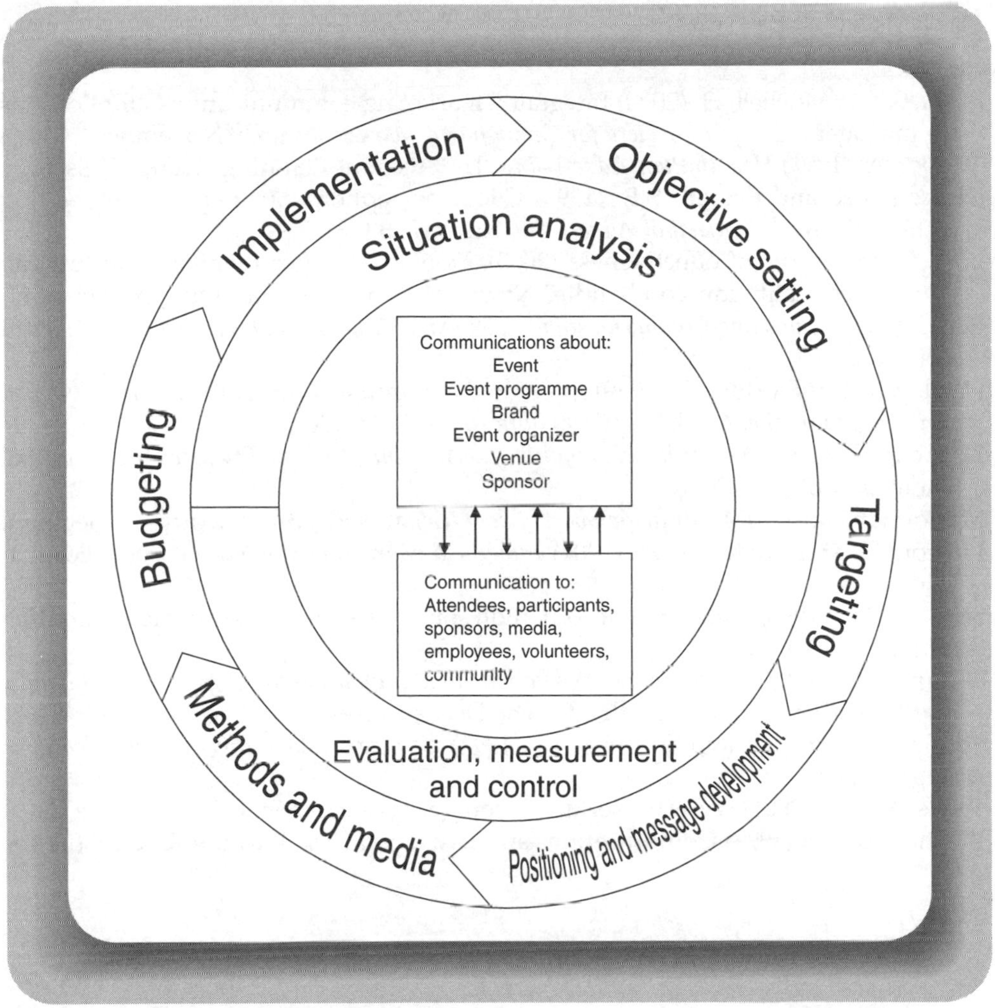

Figure 1.2 An integrated planning model for marketing communications.

Discussion points

1 With reference to Case study 1.1 and your own examples summarize the key elements of integrated marketing communications planning.
2 Identify and compare the benefits and drawbacks of applying a formalized marketing communications planning process in the following organizations:
   a) a large exhibition venue
   b) a community festival committee
   c) an international sporting tournament organization
   d) a wedding planner
   e) one more event organization of your choice.

References

Baker, S. and Mitchell, H. (2000) Integrated marketing communications: Implications for managers. *European Society for Opinion and Market Research*, November.

Cooper, A. (1997) *How to Plan Advertising*. The Account Planning Group. Cassell.

Duncan, T.R. and Everett, S.E. (1993) Client perceptions of integrated marketing communications. *Journal of Advertising Research*, 33 (3), 30–39.

Effie Awards: Brief of effectiveness (2003). DoubleTake documentary film festival: How much reality can you handle? New York American Marketing Association.

Fill, C. (2002) *Marketing Communications: Contexts, Strategies and Applications*. Pearson Education.

Hartley, B. and Pickton, D. (1999) Integrated communication requires a new way of thinking. *Journal of Marketing Communications*, 5, 97–106.

Kitchen, P.J. (1999) *Marketing Communications: Principles and Practice*. International Thomson Business Press.

Masterman, G.R. (2004) *Strategic Sports Event Management*. Butterworth-Heinemann.

Pickton, D. and Broderick, A. (2001) *Integrated Marketing Communications*. Pearson Education.

Schultz, D.E. (1998) Integrating information sources to develop strategies. *Marketing News*, 27 (24), 814.

Shimp, T.A. (1997) *Advertising, Promotion, and Supplemental Aspects of Integrated Marketing Communications*, 4th edn. The Dryden Press.

Smith, P., Perry, C. and Pulford, A. (1997) *Strategic Marketing Communications*. Kogan Page.

Tucker Knapp (2001) www.tuckerknapp.com (accessed October, 2004).

Wirthlin Report (1999) Comunications strategy toolkit. *The Wirthlin Report* 9 (6).

Chapter 2
Research and Analysis

Objectives

- To develop an understanding of the importance of research and analysis in developing effective event marketing communications
- To recognize the areas where research is needed in communications planning
- To evaluate and select appropriate information sources and primary methods for undertaking research
- To appreciate the need for ongoing research and marketing information management

Introduction

All strategic decisions need to be based on information drawn from a variety of sources. This chapter details why information is vital to the development of successful marketing communication strategies. Practical guidance is provided on sources of information and the techniques that can be used to generate relevant data. This information needs to be gathered before, during and after each event and at all stages in the communications planning process in order to create, monitor and improve marketing communication strategies.

Information for marketing communication decisions

In order to develop and sustain innovative communication strategies, event organizations need to gather, analyse and use information from a variety of sources. At the very least knowledge of the target audiences' needs and behaviour, market trends, competitors' offerings and the effectiveness of existing marketing communications is needed for future success. This information forms the basis of the situation analysis that is required at the start of the planning process, but also needed is a focused and continual gathering, analysis and use of information throughout the process. This in turn forms the basis by which the achievement of communication objectives can be measured.

Information is now more easily accessible than ever before with technology enabling the collection, storage, analysis and dissemination of information at the touch of a button. The problem for marketing communication planners is often not, therefore, accessing information, but more in selecting the most appropriate information for the decision in hand and in developing a system which will provide pertinent information to the decision maker as and when needed.

Understanding stakeholders

Understanding the various stakeholders of the organization is of the utmost importance as, according to the marketing concept, the organization exists to serve their needs while achieving organizational goals and should be customer focused in all its activities. These stakeholders will form the potential audiences or recipients of any marketing communications and therefore those communications need to be developed to meet their needs while achieving the organization's communication objectives. A knowledge of what the audience wants gives marketers an important advantage over the competition as this information facilitates rational decision making and helps reduce the risk of using finite resources inefficiently.

There are many types and levels of information required on stakeholder groups and this information should provide the central focus of a marketing database.

Identifying stakeholders

The first task is to identify all those groups that are the existing or potential audiences for any marketing communications. These audiences are likely to be made up of a number of differing stakeholder groups with varied needs, preferences and characteristics. There are then a number of steps that should be followed in gathering the information needed to understand the organization's stakeholders. First, key stakeholders have to be identified at the outset and on a regular basis as new groups emerge and existing groups may decline or increase in relative importance. Secondly, it is necessary to understand what each group and sub-group are looking for and to then map this against what the organization is looking for. It is then possible to evaluate if needs and expectations are being met and whether or not each of these relationships consists of customer and organizational goals that are in alignment (Mitchell, 2002). This process helps the organization to identify any previously overlooked stakeholder groups and also to recognize the differing needs of what at first appear to be very similar groups. For example, the communication needs of local sponsors will vary from those of national or international sponsoring organizations. The host community for a large music festival may contain those who support the festival and those who oppose it, each group, therefore, requires a different message strategy.

Reid and Arcodia (2002) define event stakeholders as 'groups or individuals who are affected or could be affected by an event's existence'. Primary stakeholders are those individuals or groups without whose support the event would cease to exist. These are the employees, volunteers, sponsors, suppliers, spectators, attendees and participants. Secondary stakeholders are those groups or individuals who, although not directly involved in the event, can seriously impede the event's success. For example, secondary stakeholders may include the host community, media, businesses, tourism organizations, government and the emergency services.

Table 2.1 Example of marketing communications stakeholder analysis

Conference organizer								
Stakeholder	*Present relationship*	*Desired future relationship*	*Needs of stakeholder*	*Importance of stakeholder*	*Communication from organization*		*Communication from stakeholder*	
					Message	*Media*	*Message*	*Media*
Speakers				V. high				
Delegates				V. high				
Sponsors				High				
Employees				Medium				
Professional bodies/ association				Medium				
Media				High				

When completed, this summary sheet presents an overview of the communication activity related to each of the stakeholders identified in the first column

The range of event stakeholders and the complexity of their interrelationships with the event organization and each other give an indication of the variety of opportunities for communication which exist. These stakeholder communication points need to be recognized and mapped in order to understand and, whenever possible, manage the communication effect.

The initial identification and summary of each stakeholder group serves as a starting point for further analysis of those groups of primary importance from a marketing communications perspective. Table 2.1 shows a structure for mapping stakeholders and their communication preferences for a conference organizer.

Describing stakeholder characteristics

Once stakeholder groups have been identified further analysis is needed. This could simply be the size and location of each group but, ideally, should also include some demographic information to give an overview of the potential communication issues. For example, are potential sponsors locally or nationally spread, can participants be reached through membership of an association or as individuals, what is the age and gender breakdown of attendees?

Stakeholder history

For those stakeholders with whom the organization has had past contact a historical analysis can be undertaken using past communications responses and evaluations. Most organizations will have a customer database which can be utilized for communications research and also have records of pertinent communication with past sponsors, the media and others. Although the customer database is likely to be transaction based, it can provide useful insights with the addition of relatively simple information, such as how did each customer book, how did they hear of the event, how many tickets did they purchase? If such a database does not currently exist it is vital to create and implement one as these 'stakeholder information files' should be central to marketing decision making and therefore to marketing communications planning.

Stakeholder opinions, beliefs, attitudes

As well as utilizing general marketing information, it is probable that more specific communications data will need to be generated. A detailed understanding of the audiences' psychographic background will help the development of meaningful messages that have resonance for that target group. An appreciation of each stakeholder group's lifestyles, interests, activities and opinions will facilitate a communication frame of reference, as well as allowing for more precise segmentation and targeting. Similarly, for organizational stakeholders (sponsoring companies, trade exhibitors, sporting bodies) an understanding is needed of the organization's mission, ethos and management style.

Stakeholder motivations, influences and behaviour

This involves investigating each stakeholder group's motivations for being interested or not in the product, the communication or the competitor's products. Motivations are inextricably linked with needs so, if the stakeholders' underlying motivations can be identified, then there is a better chance of defining and hence meeting their needs. Motivations may be linked to such things as achievement, belonging, status, love, esteem and are important indicators of communication message preferences. For example, a survey of conference delegates in the UK identified a number of different underlying motivations for attending which included interpersonal, educational and career needs (Tum and Wood, 2002). The communications message, therefore aimed at each group needs to reflect this motivation rather than assuming that all delegates attend a particular conference for very similar reasons.

In order to communicate effectively with the stakeholder, it is also necessary to understand their decision-making processes. The audience of any marketing communication has a number of decisions to make. First, whether or not to pay attention to the message. Secondly, whether or not to become involved with the message and to have an interest in what it is saying. Thirdly, whether or not to remember or internalize the information received and fourthly, whether or not to change their attitudes, beliefs, intentions or behaviour based on this information. This process relates the decision-making process model or 'PIECE' model of consumer behaviour to the advertising effects models. PIECE refers to the stages of the model, which are problem recognition, information search, evaluation of alternatives, choice and finally, evaluation post-purchase. In marketing communications we are not concerned primarily with a purchase decision but with the decision to engage at some level with the communications message. Table 2.2 illustrates how the decision-making process is related to engagement with marketing communications.

The stakeholder's ability and willingness to engage with a particular marketing communication message is influenced by a number of factors. These factors include the stage they are at in the buying-decision process, their information processing methods, their existing attitudes, values and beliefs and a range of internal and external influences. Internal influences are related to the individual and include

Table 2.2 Decision-making process for communication audiences

Recipient's decision-making process	Communication engagement examples
Problem-recognition	Need to be entertained; sounds interesting; that's unusual
Information search	What's it telling me? Am I interested ?
Evaluation of alternatives	Channel switching, page flicking, continue to read, listen, watch or not
Choice	Remember, ignore, misinterpret, tell others, search for more information, change attitude, beliefs, respond directly
Outcome	Awareness Interest Desire Attitude or behaviour change
Evaluation post-exposure	Compare with other communications, watch out for again, avoid

lifestyle, personality traits, personal resources, life-cycle stage, age and gender. External influences are related to society and include reference groups, social class, culture, economy. These influences affect the amount of attention to, interest in and retention of the marketing communication message. Therefore, an appreciation of these influences for each stakeholder group will help to ensure that effective communications are produced and will aid meaningful segmentation of potential target audiences.

As part of the decision-making process it is also important to gain information on who is involved in the 'decision-making unit'. The decision-making unit is the individual or group who are actively involved in the decision and this may be one individual, a couple, a group of friends, an organization, or a family. Consequently, marketing communicators need to recognize the different roles played by the various members of the decision-making unit and target their communications appropriately.

For example, Walt Disney World undertook marketing research in the Canadian market to ascertain why attendance by Canadians was declining. One of the findings indicated that parents believed Walt Disney World would be wonderful for kids, but stressful and expensive for them. Awareness was at 100 per cent and most Canadian families stated the intention to visit 'some day' and yet they still were not going. The qualitative research used focus groups with children in a separate room to their parents. The children were enthusiastic but the parents were negative and saw the experience as one with large crowds, queues and never ending merchandise. In summary 'this wasn't a holiday it was something you suffered for the kids'. Follow-up research with Canadian parents on site at the park found that, although they had initially come because of their children, they were surprised that they were enjoying it possibly just as much. The children also stated that they saw their parents transformed from their everyday selves into people who enjoyed the same things as them. The whole family were enjoying the same things, 'having fun together'. On the basis of this the communication campaign in Canada was changed from thirty second television advertisements showing rides, a parade, hotels, water parks, beaches, more rides and Mickey Mouse (creating the parent perception of exhaustion, expense and extra stress) to advertisements with the theme 'we are all the same inside', showing parents having a great time with their children and creating the parent perception of fun, holiday and sharing together (Thompson, 1997). In this case, both parents and children played a role in the decision-making process, with the children as major influencers but the parents as decision makers and purchasers. Although, this amounted to one decision-making unit, each unit member had differing needs and perceptions which were addressed through the marketing communications campaign.

Stakeholder communication preferences

More detailed information is needed on each stakeholder group's communication preferences. This information is unlikely to be routinely generated through the transaction systems or internal records and may not be part of the regular marketing research being undertaken. However, in order to ensure that communication messages are effective and successfully meet the objectives for each target group it is necessary to have an understanding of their style, format, frequency and audience media preferences. To do this stakeholder views need to be solicited, on past and current communications from the organization and its competitors. Media preferences can be fairly easily obtained through media readership and viewer breakdown figures, however, message style, content and format likes and dislikes are more difficult to ascertain and will often involve more qualitative research techniques such as discussion groups and in-depth interviews. These need to be undertaken at all stages in the communications campaign from concept testing prior to the development of the message through to post-campaign evaluation.

The importance of researching the target audience prior to developing the creative message is demonstrated in the successful advertising campaign used for Billy Graham's 1989 meetings in London. In 1988, the agency, Foote, Cone and Belding, was given the task of developing a communications campaign to attract a younger audience to the meetings of the Billy Graham Mission '89. Before developing the creative strategy, qualitative research was undertaken with groups of 21–34 year olds, with a total of four hundred being interviewed. This research ascertained that churches were viewed as places where only weddings, funerals and christenings took place and that religion was seen as 'boring and irrelevant to everyday life'. The research also showed that, although this group had little awareness of Billy Graham, they were more motivated to attend an event to hear a particular person speak than to hear about a particular subject. The research results were used to develop a campaign which avoided the use of the words 'god' and 'religion' and focused instead on the more neutral term of 'life'. A staged reveal teaser campaign (where information is left deliberately vague but intriguing to begin with) was used to generate interest in the event and in the personality of Billy Graham (Wolrich, 1990).

An example that demonstrates the necessity of pre-testing creative concepts is provided by the agency WCRS in its work for Mecca Bingo in the UK. The agency was approached by Mecca, soon after legal changes allowed for the advertising of bingo (the game of Lotto for cash prizes), to get women back to bingo and grow the business. Mecca's brief emphasized the 'serial opportunities to win' of bingo and the chance to make dreams come true. With a short time span limiting the amount of research that could be done, the agency chose to experience bingo first-hand using the qualitative research technique of participant observation, to gain further insights into the motivations of bingo players. This resulted in a change of emphasis from 'dreams coming true' to 'the delicious thrill of the recurring opportunity to be a winner' (a series of adrenaline highs). This theme was then discussed with a group of bingo players who agreed that it was the 'repeated buzz' which drew them to play the game, but further discussion also revealed other points of interest. The experience was highly ritualized with players having lucky pens, lucky earrings, always sitting in same seat and going through a ritual of preparation before going out to the bingo hall. The traditional language of bingo was no longer used and players were acutely aware of the negative image that others had of the game. The next stage of the research involved showing a number of fully developed ideas (shown as magazine advertisements) to a North London bingo group. The advertisements reflected a respectable image for bingo while maintaining some of the stereotyped traditions. It was at this point that the creative agency realized they were off the mark. The research respondents were 'disappointed' with the advertisements stating that this was 'how our husbands see it' and not how they experienced it. The advertisements were reinforcing some of the negative images that were forcing some of them to become almost 'closet' players. On further probing of their feelings it became clear that their husbands made fun of their enthusiasm for bingo, seeing it as an obsession and the rituals and preparation as a source of ridicule. It was only through these discussions that it became clear that the bingo players themselves compare their love of the game with their partners' obsession with football. This provided the insight needed finally to identify the real motivations of the bingo player. Going to bingo had many similarities with watching a game of football. It involved getting together with a single-gender group of friends, sharing a few drinks and experiencing highs and lows together. However, unlike many football fans the women could laugh at their rituals and had a good time whether they won or lost. Using this insight the campaign portrayed the experience of bingo using parodies of other sporting ads and through these analogies showed the game as the players saw it (Hutson, 1998). The Mecca Bingo campaign was highly successful but could easily have failed if pre-testing of the message and method concepts had not been undertaken.

Case study 2.1 gives a further example of the importance of research in developing effective and innovative campaigns.

Understanding competitors

Although the audiences of the communication campaign should undoubtedly be the focus of information gathering, research and analysis, there are other areas which also need to be researched. It will be difficult to predict and assess the impact of marketing communications without some understanding of competitor activity. Competitors need to be identified and monitored, in a similar way to stakeholders. A wider view of competitors is needed to include not only those directly competing with very similar product offerings, but to encompass those organizations that offer a product which serves the same customer needs. Identifying competitors from the customers' viewpoint of benefits provided allows the organization to recognize those competitors which operate in very different sectors which would, otherwise, have been overlooked. It also helps the company to understand that its competitors will change according to the customer group. For example, the National Exhibition

Case study 2.1

The ICA

The Institute of Contemporary Arts (ICA), based on The Mall in London, consists of a café/bar and exhibition space for arts events. The institution, supported by government arts funding, was considered an iconic establishment in the world of art and achieved other commercial revenues as a result. During the 1980s, 'up and coming' UK artists were only 'up and coming' if they associated themselves with this establishment, but by the late 1990s this mantle was already eroded. The impact of recession had also led to a dwindling stream of sponsorship and so, in 1997, the ICA decided on a new direction.

An advertising strategy was implemented primarily in order to recruit potential funding supporters but secondarily to help restore credibility and increase awareness.

Situation analysis

The threat of alternative galleries was already being realized with the Serpentine, Tate and Saatchi galleries all making an impact on both artists and audiences. In addition, the competition from the British Museum and National Gallery was ongoing.

There was, however, a point of differentiation to work with. The competition provided events for both living and dead artists, whereas the ICA only ever exhibited the works of living artists.

Targets

Potential funding supporters had to be identified. Hardcore artists themselves were already now using other galleries and, while they were of some importance, they were not considered as primary targets. One side of the solution was to target art savvy senior executives in media-related corporations, although the ICA knew that, in order to reach this target successfully, the communications would have to be innovative and stand out from the plethora of other pleas for money. The other side of the solution required research. In order to construct a target profile, current ICA members were interviewed. This revealed that the target markets would be trendy and hip London-dwelling art lovers, possibly working in fashion, possibly of the gay community. They had high disposable income and enjoyed private club memberships. The ICA defined them as 'cultural hipsters' and saw the links between the two sides in order to identify one target, a target with a sense of vitality and passion for life.

Focus

Links had to be forged between the ICA's policy of showing only living artists and this target. In order to achieve this, time was spent observing the ICA and other arts facilities. From the way the ICA was laid out and the way visitors reacted, it was noted that there was a spirit of an 'adult playground', a spirit that was interactive and spontaneous. For example, the bar was in among the art and the workshops the ICA provided encouraged debate. In contrast, other facilities created a more formal ambience. It was decided that the focus for the campaign would be 'Living Art'.

Communications

With such a focus, nothing other than living advertisements would suffice:

Direct male: a six-foot (1.8 m) man dressed in Lycra, platform boots and a gas mask. These 'messengers' would storm into targeted offices and hand-deliver ICA packages of facts and ten date-stamped free tickets. The tickets were to be given to friends. The targets were then contacted so that sponsorship opportunities could be discussed.

Press: a living press advertisement was positioned around London, at the ICA and outside competition facilities. He carried messages such as 'any questions' and 'see the art of the living'.

Outdoor: six uniformed people inside triangular panels moving together in synchronization. This 'living billboard' carried the message 'you should not have to die before you're discovered, ICA – Living Art', and appeared at London Fashion Week and Gay Pride.

Living icons: translucent body bags containing naked people but playing dead. These static advertisements were positioned around London's busiest streets and carried tags such as 'artist', 'songwriter' or 'sculptor'.

Cinema: free spots at key London cinemas were negotiated and an advertisement was shot containing scenes using the above tactics but with a focus on audience reaction.

The results

The results were acclaimed, by both the arts media and artists and the campaign was generally considered to have played a significant part in rekindling credibility, developing event audience and new sponsorship revenue that exceeded targets.

While innovation was evident, it was only enabled via effective research, targeting and planning.

Source: ICA (2004); Account Planning Group (1997).

Centre in Birmingham, UK, has a number of levels of customer, the events themselves (such as the Motor Show), the exhibitors at the show and the visitors to the show. If asked to name the alternatives each group would have a different perspective on who were the venue's competitors. For example, the Motor Show organizers may simply name other large UK venues, but the exhibitors would name other motor shows, other promotional methods and other ways of spending their marketing budget. The visitors would name other ways of spending time with their family on a Saturday, other ways of spending that amount of disposable income, or other ways of finding out about the cars on offer. Table 2.3 gives further examples of the levels of competition grouped in terms of brand competitors, product form competitors and customer need competitors. All levels need to be considered in any competitor analysis undertaken.

Once competitors have been identified it is important to continually monitor their actions and, in particular, their marketing communications. This type of market intelligence is relatively easy to obtain as, almost by definition, this information is in the public domain. Websites can be evaluated, media campaigns analysed and pubic relations monitored through the scanning of the press. Direct marketing campaigns may be more difficult to monitor but can be triggered through responses to sales promotions, direct response television, coupons and registering with websites. Once all communications material has been collected, analysis of it should provide insights into the competitor's communication objectives, target audiences and message and media strategy. This information can then be used to inform the development of future campaigns in terms of developing a unique position and offering, eliciting favourable comparisons, or in responding directly to competitor moves. The more often this type of competitor monitoring is undertaken the easier it is to predict their strategies and therefore anticipate them with pre-emptive rather than reactive campaigns.

Table 2.3 Levels of competition

Organization	Brand competitors	Form competitors	Need competitors
The US Open Tennis tournament	Other tennis tournaments	Other sports events	Other leisure pursuits
Edinburgh Festival	Other UK arts festivals	Other festivals	Theatres, garden shows, weekend breaks
The Moscow Ballet	Other Russian ballet companies	Other ballet companies	Other theatre performance groups
Birmingham National Exhibition Centre	Other UK large exhibition venues	All conference venues	Websites Trade directories

In further understanding competitors it is useful to analyse their past reaction patterns and, in particular, to evaluate if and how they have responded to an organization's marketing communication strategies. These reaction patterns will help the more accurate forecasting of the effects of an organization's own strategies as any negative effect as a result of competitor reaction can then be considered during the planning stages.

A competitor's ability to react will partly be determined by their strengths and weaknesses. These strengths and weaknesses will also suggest areas of competitor vulnerability and which areas to avoid when communicating the benefits of any product offering. For example, an awareness that a competing corporate events organizer has invested in a number of regional offices may affect whether or not your direct mail campaign is targeted at the regions not covered by that competitor or whether you deploy extra resources to your sales force based in those areas.

Other aspects of competitor behaviour will also influence the planning, development and effect of marketing communications. For example, an unanticipated launch of a new product, a cut in pricing or a move to extensive distribution by competitors may all negatively impact on current communications campaigns and, therefore, such activities also need to be monitored and where possible predicted.

Understanding the wider external environment

While customers and competitors are both outside of the control of the organization, they are closely related to it, as their actions will have an often direct effect on the success or failure of the organization. As well as these two key external forces, there are other variables in the external environment which need to be monitored. These factors are often denoted by the mnemonic PEST, which refers to the political, economic, social and technological forces affecting the performance of the organization.

The political/legal environment

The political environment's main influence on marketing communications is through legislation and taxation policies. Changes in government, whether national or local, often lead to revisions of policy, laws, directives and investment emphasis which may impact directly on the activities of the organization and its marketing communication choices. In the Mecca Bingo example detailed earlier, a relaxation in UK gambling legislation led to the reintroduction of media advertising for bingo and, in the Billy Graham's Mission '89 case, the choice of advertising message was restricted by legal constraints relating to the promotion of religion. Other areas of particular note for event communications are legislation relating to promoting to children, the promotion of and sponsorship by alcohol and tobacco products and the promotion of political and religious ideas and affiliations. These restrictions vary considerably in different countries and vary with changes in government or through social pressure. They, therefore, need to be monitored regularly and any likely political changes which will impact on future communications anticipated wherever possible.

The economic environment

The economic environment often has a direct impact on the financial resources and confidence levels of the organization, its competitors and its customers. An understanding of current economic climates, past economic patterns and future predictions will therefore help inform the development of appropriate communications plans. A market with high unemployment levels and low levels of disposable income will need to be communicated with differently from a market with full employment and increasing disposable income. Reminder, reassurance, 'back-to-basics' campaigns are more appropriate in the first scenario, whereas aspirational, brand image driven campaigns may be more appropriate in the second.

Economic factors also affect industry sectors differently and therefore it may be possible to take advantage of a downturn in parts of the economy to, for example, negotiate favourable rates for media space or for agency services. An economic downturn may, therefore, be a communications opportunity for some event organizers.

The social environment

The social environment includes general social trends, demographic, cultural and values changes. These changes may have a direct effect on the target audiences of the communication plan and are a vital part of future planning as they provide an indication of future communication preferences, purchase behaviour and target segments.

For example, research undertaken on behalf of Mintel (2002) suggests that older consumers suffer from information overload rather than decision overload. Older adults cope with the increasingly large amounts of information they are exposed to by sticking to known and trusted brands and recognized modes of behaviour in order to simplify their decision-making processes. The younger consumer, in contrast, tends to suffer decision, but not information, overload. They can cope with the amount of information and advice they are exposed to but find it harder to manage the number and range of decisions they have to make. Younger adults tend to be less brand-loyal and more willing to experiment with new products and brands. They tend not to limit their choices in order to simplify their decision-making processes. These findings indicate that marketing communications aimed at older target audiences should be selective and focused to reduce the negative impact of information overload, whereas communications aimed at the younger market need to support and simplify the decision-making process.

Increasing cynicism and scepticism of traditional marketing communication methods in older age groups and a willingness to accept marketing communications as part of youth culture in younger age groups has led to subtler forms of communication. An aspect of this move towards less obvious marketing communications is demonstrated by the blurring of the distinction between the communications method, the product and even the consumer. For example, the audience at a televised music event becomes part of the product, through their appearance and involvement, and if they are sporting the sponsors' brands they are also party to communicating that brand's image.

Ethical concerns also need to be monitored and predicted as they will need to be reflected in the communications if the message is to be accepted and effective. Concerns regarding the social responsibility of organizations have led to changes in emphasis with many organizations now communicating their corporate social responsibility programme to their main stakeholders. Similarly, worries about the use of personal data have led organizations to make their privacy policy a key part of their website homepage rather than consigning it to the small print. An understanding of changes in the ethical viewpoints of society will also help in pre-empting legal requirements. For example, growing social concerns regarding alcohol and tobacco consumption as well as data use have now been reflected in a variety of legal changes that have affected the performance of event organizations, for example, in the sponsorship of football, motor racing and snooker.

The social change that is easiest to monitor and predict is demographics. In many countries data are freely available from government sources on the demographic make up of that country and often include forecasts for future change. These data can provide information for selecting target groups, developing future campaigns and for predicting future spending and media preference patterns. For example, the population of most western countries is ageing and the younger population either declining in numbers or at least declining as a proportion of the whole population.

These predicted demographic changes can help communication planners to determine future changes in communication needs. For example, over the next twenty years, the UK population will shift towards the empty nesters/no-family and the post-family life stage and alongside this the number of single persons will rise. The general ageing of the population and the rise in single person households is likely to have contradictory effects leading to more fragmentation and segmentation of consumers (Mintel, 2000).

General trends in media preferences are needed to determine who is exposed to what, how often, when and with what impact. In recent years there has been a proliferation of specialist media catering to the needs of increasingly smaller target audiences, whether through lifestyle/hobby magazines, e-newsletters, digital TV channels or highly focused ambient media. This move away from mass media has obvious implications for marketing communications strategy and the communications planner needs to be continually aware of the variety of media available.

The technological environment

The impact of technology on marketing communications has been profound and will continue to be an important force to consider. Technological advances provide opportunities for innovation in communication methods and media as well as impacting on the behaviour of the target audiences. Developments in information technology, the Internet, telecommunications and digital television have allowed for the increasing personalization of communication messages through direct mail and e-mail, text-messaging and direct response television. The introduction of blue-tooth and wireless technology promises further innovations to come in interactive communications. For example, blue-tooth mobile phones can be used to receive further details of an event by simply pointing the phone at a billboard advertisement for the event and receiving information direct to the phone.

The international environment

It is no longer possible for an organization to view its area of operation as solely national. All events organizations exist in an international environment, whether or not they actively target international customers. A small event organizer servicing the corporate event needs of companies in their home town is now competing with international organizations and is visible to international prospects through the widespread use of the Internet. The Internet has broken down international barriers in terms of communication and distribution allowing both global firms and sole traders to compete on the same platform. Many smaller events organizations have taken advantage of this with a large proportion of them now using the Internet to promote their services (Wood et al., 2003). Thus, the international environment also needs to be monitored in terms of competitor activity, market and social trends and political, economic and legal changes.

Understanding the organization

The final area to be researched and understood is the organization itself. This involves an understanding of the organization's goals, ethos and management style as well as its capabilities and limitations, as these factors should provide the framework and resources for any communications plan. This internal analysis should include:

- an understanding of the ethos of the organization and the management style in terms of risk taking, creativity and tradition
- awareness of the organization's mission and its corporate and marketing objectives
- analysis of previous communication campaigns in terms of the results achieved and the reasons for those results
- an audit of the resources available: financial, time, experience and expertise
- evaluation of the skills and resources available through sub-contractors, outsourcing, networks, suppliers, distributors and any other partners.

The findings from these areas can be summarized under the headings of 'strengths', to help clearly identify distinctive competences that should be built on, emphasized and communicated, and 'weaknesses' in order to identify the constraints and limitations which should be recognized, minimized or overcome.

Secondary data

In order to provide much of the information listed in the previous sections, it is important to utilize a variety of types and sources of data. The cheapest and most easily accessible type of data is that which is generated by the day-to-day running of the organization. The usefulness of this type of data for marketing communications planning can be greatly enhanced by systematic and consistent report generation using database and query software. For example, an event booking system can easily incorporate information on which marketing communications generated the enquiry and media plans can be mapped against ticket sales and enquiry rates. These internal data are often the starting point for most research projects, however, caution is required as it is easy to become over reliant on internal data and to neglect vital external sources.

Quantitative internal data include information on ticket sales, accounts, customer records, media costings, merchandise sales and bar sales. Internally generated qualitative data might include sales staff reports, sponsorship bids/feedback, minutes of meetings, feedback from customer service staff, customer complaints and compliments.

The starting point for the collection of external data is to make use of information which already exists in some form. These secondary data can be quantitative, such as government statistics, on-line data, industry surveys, published market research reports, trade or association data, published financial data. They can also be qualitative in the form of news reports/articles, trade journals, other media, competitor sales literature, trade directories, CD-ROMs and websites. The continuous monitoring of identified key external sources creates longitudinal data, which can be used to anticipate customer trends, competitor reactions and media usage, and is vital for forecasting and hence long-term planning decisions.

Primary data

To complement these existing sources and to provide a richer picture of the organization's proximate macro-environment (customers, competitors, suppliers, publics), it is necessary to generate first hand data. As this process will be comparatively costly and time-consuming, it is important to have clear objectives for the research and to ensure that it can be carried out reliably (in-house or outsourced) within the given budget and time constraints. Again this primary information can be either quantitative or qualitative, or preferably, a combination of the two. Quantitative data can originate from larger scale surveys, resident panels, visitor profiles etc. and requires the application of correct sampling procedures to ensure validity and reliability. Qualitative data are normally smaller scale but give a greater depth of information and are useful for ascertaining opinions, feelings and attitudes and for identifying initial problem areas for further investigation. This richer information can be gathered using research techniques such as observation, focus groups, in-depth interviews with attendees, participants and sponsors and through recording staff and volunteer feedback and utilizing management notes and commentary.

A summary of the types of market research available to communications planning is given in Figure 2.1.

Secondary Research			Primary Research (external)		
Internal		External	Quantitative		Qualitative
(quantitative or qualitative)		(quantitative or qualitative)			
Box office sales		Government reports	Surveys		Interviews
Costings Accounts		Syndicated surveys	Test market		Focus groups
Prior reports Evaluations		Market research reports	Experiment		Case studies
		Trade press	Observation		Observation
		Websites			
		Media directories and ratings (BRAD, JICNARS)			

Figure 2.1 Marketing information sources.

While all of the areas above can be used to gain an overview of the market place and an in-depth understanding of customers and competitors in communications planning, there also needs to be a focus on message and media research. This specific type of communications research involves both pre-testing and post-testing of each element of the campaign and of the overall effect.

Pre-testing should be used at the various stages of communications plan development prior to the launch of the full communications campaign, whereby the plan develops and evolves because of these findings. Initial concepts and ideas, draft copy and images can all be researched as can media reach and effectiveness. Some of the methods available are shown in Table 2.4.

For example, a consumer jury test for an event flyer would require several potential versions of a flyer for the event and a number of possible headlines for each flyer. Each version could then be shown to a sample of respondents matching the target market characteristics.

Table 2.4 Pre-test methods

Method	
Concept tests	Expose consumers with target audience characteristics to main concept in words, pictures, symbols. Use focus groups, interviews or surveys
Rough tests	Test a number of 'roughs' (drafts of finished communication) by exposure to an audience who assess based on a number of criteria
Theatre tests	Measures brand preference before and after the screening of a broadcast advertisement (alongside others and within a programme)
Portfolio tests	Laboratory method using test and control communications to assess recall
Consumer juries	Potential audiences evaluate potential communications through ranking and pairing. Usually 50–100 participants
Physiological methods/ reaction tests	Skin response, pupil dilation, eye movement, brain waves measured to gauge reactions to various communication types
Readability tests	For written communications such as the Flesch measure of number of syllables per 100 words and SMOG sentence length and syllable counts
Comprehension tests	Measures accuracy of message transfer rather than preference or recall
Test market launches	Communication applied to a small test market area to assess effect on awareness, preference, sales
On-air tests	Broadcast in specific markets prior to full launch

The types of questions to be asked of the sample might include:

1 Which of these flyers would you most likely read if they came through your letterbox?
2 Which of these headlines would interest you most in reading the flyer further?
3 Which flyer convinces you most of the quality or superiority of the event?
4 Which layout do you think would be most effective in causing you to buy a ticket?
5 Which flyer did you like best?
6 Which flyer did you find most interesting?

Pre-tests show what is likely to work with a particular audience. A slogan which may seem persuasive to an adult may be confusing to a teenager and a poster which captures the attention of one group of teenagers may have no interest to another. Thus, careful pre-testing with different target audience types will highlight some of these issues before committing to a message and strategy.

Figure 2.2 provides examples of the types of questions asked of audiences viewing proposed communication messages.

Media research involves understanding the credibility, impact and reach of the types of media available. This can be undertaken through primary research with stakeholder audiences or through the use of secondary data available through various media tracking organizations.

1. Main idea communication and comprehension
   a) Which of these phrases best describes the message
   Easy to understand ___
   Hard to understand ___
   b) What was the main idea this message was trying to get across to you?

2. Likes/Dislikes
   a) Was there anything in particular worth remembering about the message?
   b) What did you particularly like about the message?
   c) What did you particularly dislike about the message?

3. Credibility
   a) Was there anything in the message that was hard to believe?
   b) Rate the message on the following scale
   Highly believable   Believable   Not very believable   Unbelievable

4. Personal relevance
   a) Was the message talking to:
   – someone like you
   – someone not like you
   b) Was the message talking to
   – all people
   – all people but especially young sports fans (the target audience)
   – only young sports fans (the target audience)
   c) Did you find the message
   Very interesting   Interesting   Not very interesting   Uninteresting
   Very informative   Informative   Not very informative   Uninformative

5. Reactions
   Too short   Too long
   Simple   Complex
   Entertaining   Boring
   Different   Same

Figure 2.2 Examples of standard theatre test questions.

Communications information system

From the discussion in this chapter it can be seen that in developing a communications plan, information needs to be gathered from a range of sources using a variety of methods. Some of this information needs to be gathered on an ongoing basis, whereas other areas will be collected on an *ad hoc* basis as necessary. Managing this to ensure that the communications decision maker can access the right kind of information, in the right form at the right time requires a system which can collate, store and disseminate in a manner appropriate to the organization. This system should utilize information technology, for the quantitative data in particular, but should also attempt to achieve integration between this and any qualitative data obtained in order to give better insights and inspire creative and innovative ideas. The resulting marketing information system should, therefore, ensure a continuous flow of pertinent information to the communications planner without restricting the creativity and freedom needed. An informal system is needed which takes into account the distinct nature of the events industry and the needs of integrated marketing communications.

Summary

The discussion within this chapter has highlighted the importance of research and analysis in developing effective marketing communications. Communications decisions based on accurate information have a much greater chance of being effective and of achieving more for the budget available. The information needed should focus on the target audiences, but an understanding is also needed of competitors, other external factors and the internal environment of the organization. The sources available to obtain useful information are many and varied and should include internal and externally generated data, primary and secondary sources and be of both a qualitative and quantitative nature. One of the greatest challenges in research and analysis for marketing communications planning is managing the ever-increasing amount of data available. These data are being collected on a daily basis and are being supplemented by one-off primary and secondary research projects. In order to avoid information overload some form of marketing information system is required which will ensure that decision makers get the information they need when they need it.

Discussion points

- Identify examples and discuss the use of internally generated data to support marketing communications planning for:
  - a conference venue
  - a sports organization
  - a community festival organizer.
- Use the Internet to identify sources of secondary data useful to the organizations listed above. Evaluate these sources for relevance, accuracy, timeliness and bias.
- Discuss alternative pre-testing methods for a regional radio advertising campaign.

References

Account Planning Group (1997) The ICA – From living art to living ads. www.warc.com (accessed October, 2004).

Hutson, A. (1998) Mecca Bingo: It's football Jim, but not as we know it. *Creative Planning Awards 1998*. Account Planning Group.

ICA (2004) www.ICA.org.uk (accessed October, 2004).

Mintel (2000) 2020 Vision: Tomorrow's Consumer – UK – March 2000.

Mintel (2002) Marketing to Tomorrow's Consumer – UK – April 2002.

Mitchell, A. (2002) Mapping stakeholders: In search of win-win relationships. *Market Leader*, 19, Winter, pp. 36–40.

Reid, S. and Arcodia, C. (2002) Understanding the role of the stakeholder in event management. *Event and Place making Conference*, 15–16 July 2002, Sydney, University of Technology Sydney.

Thompson, B. (1997) Walt Disney World: 'Not just a theme park'. *Canadian Advertising Success Stories 1997*. Canadian Congress of Advertising.

Tum, J. and Wood, E.H. (2002) Understanding motivation and maximising satisfaction of conference delegates. *UK Centre for Event Management Seminar* (September). Leeds Metropolitan University.

Wolrich, C. (1990) Bringing life to Billy Graham's Mission '89. Advertising Effectiveness Awards 1990. Institute of Practitioners in Advertising.

Wood, E.H., Blackwell, R., Bowdin, G. et al. (2003) *The national survey of small tourism and hospitality firms: Small firms in the events sector*. Leeds Metropolitan University.

Chapter 3

Communication Objectives and Targeting

Objectives

- To understand the process for establishing events communication objectives
- To identify target stakeholder audiences in line with these objectives
- To appreciate the importance of using consumer behaviour theory in understanding target audience preferences
- To demonstrate how sub-objectives for each target audience should be developed

Introduction

In developing a marketing communications plan it is vital to have clearly defined objectives. These objectives are the keystone of the plan as they will set the boundaries and direction for strategic decisions; determine the measurement and control procedures; and, to some extent, suggest budget requirements. Objectives are also necessary to communicate the plan to others in the organization and any external agencies involved in the communications process. In this way the objectives communicate the shared vision of the plan to all those who will have a part to play in its development and implementation.

The complexity of the event product means that for a large number of organizations there will be a number of levels of marketing communication objectives. These start broadly with communication objectives for the organization as a whole, often involving corporate image and parent brand. It may then be that objectives are needed for each programme of events within the organization's portfolio and then sub-objectives are required for each event within each programme. Once objectives at these levels have been determined, it is possible to identify target audiences and to develop separate objectives for each audience type.

This chapter will begin by illustrating the development of broad communication objectives within the framework of the marketing and corporate objectives using the information gained in the situation analysis and theories of communication effects. After developing sub-objectives at event level the process of targeting will be introduced. This involves identifying suitable market

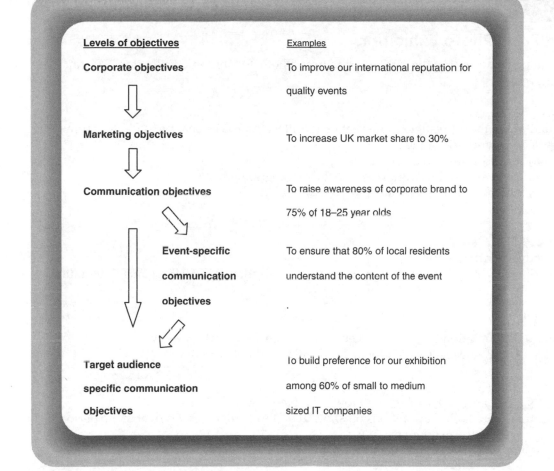

Figure 3.1 Hierarchy of objectives.

segments and gaining an understanding of their marketing communication preferences and behaviours. Based on this understanding objectives for each target group can be developed (Figure 3.1).

Setting communication objectives

Using the situation analysis

The research conducted in the situation analysis is used to determine suitable objectives by ensuring that opportunities and strengths are taken advantage of and that

Case study 3.1

World Press Photo Exhibition

The situation analysis for the 2002 World Press Photo Exhibition, Wellington NZ can be summarized as:

Strengths
- regarded as the most prestigious international contest in professional press photography
- represented a synthesis of life in 2001
- triggered powerful human emotions
- consisted of prize winning work from top 200 photographers
- never been held in New Zealand before
- free admission

Weaknesses
- new product for the location
- low media budget as brought by not-for-profit organization (NZ Netherlands Foundation)
- limited time as ran over 3 weeks only

Opportunities
- Wellington's reputation for local, indigenous and global cultural diversity
- local population who regularly attended museums and galleries

Threats
- venue (NZ academy of Fine Arts) had low awareness and familiarity
- competition. Three other exhibitions on show at well-regarded venues over same period
- low awareness of the exhibition
- timing. Quietest period for in-bound tourism

The communication objectives set for the exhibition needed to support the marketing objective of attracting 20 000 visitors in the 3 weeks of the exhibition (despite the fact that 10 000 was standard for the venue).

The communication objectives set by the appointed agency were:

1 Make the exhibition the most talked about exhibition in Wellington at that time
2 Create strong awareness of the exhibition over a short time period
3 Create greater value from NZ$13 000 dollar budget

Adapted from: The Communication Agencies Association of New Zealand, 2003. World Press Photo Exhibition (CAANZ, 2003).

threats and weaknesses are avoided or overcome. An illustration of this is given in Case study 3.1.

The objectives listed in Case study 3.1 took account of the challenges of low exhibition and venue awareness and limited budget and used the opportunities created by the unique aspects of the product and the potential target audience.

Fit with higher level objectives

Often one of the constraints for a communications plan is the corporate and/or marketing objectives which have already been set. As can be seen in the World Press Photo Exhibition example the marketing objectives and budget were challenging and needed to be considered alongside the situation analysis in setting realistic communication objectives. A further example is given in Case study 3.2.

At first the marketing objective and communication objective do not appear to be well aligned, but it can be seen that, by utilizing the situation analysis and undertaking further pre-campaign research, the communications agency isolated the key problem area and focused their efforts on this by moving the campaign to brand based (the millennium) rather than product based (the Dome). This overcame the problems of apathy and media cynicism.

Case study 3.2

The Millennium Experience

Strengths
- the innovative nature of the Millennium Dome
- once in a lifetime event
- government support

Weaknesses
- limited time
- high targets (12 million visitors)

Threats
- national apathy
- media cynicism
- misunderstanding of 'millennium'

Marketing objective

Attract 12 million visitors to the Dome (nation's top three visitor attractions yielded just over 8 million visits).

Communication objectives

Further research was used to determine that the uniqueness and magnitude of the millennium was not understood and therefore was a major cause of apathy and cynicism. The first objective was, therefore, to make the nation aware of what the millennium was and therefore create a desire to celebrate it in a unique way, i.e. by visiting the Millennium Dome. The main communication objective was summarized as:

to inspire people to consider the magnitude and significance of 1000 years.

Adapted from: McCann, B. (1999).

Objective setting tools

Strategic tools for general objective setting can be used and where necessary adapted for communication objectives. For example, objective gap analysis can be used to ensure that communication objectives are realistic and to help identify the changes needed in existing communication strategies to achieve them. The gap analysis technique involves plotting any previous communication achievements on a graph against time and extrapolating these to the future planning period. This then shows what can be achieved if current strategies are maintained. Any increase to the extrapolated figure identifies the strategies gap that needs to be filled by changes to existing communication strategies. An example is given in Figure 3.2.

Ansoff's matrix (Ansoff, 1989), traditionally used in setting marketing objectives, can also be adapted for use in determining communication objectives. This technique uses a four-quadrant matrix to identify areas for objectives to be set. The original matrix consists of new or existing products combined with new or existing markets. These combinations indicate the area in which objectives should be focused dependent on what has already been achieved, levels of market saturation, competition and organizational resources.

Market penetration (existing products/existing markets) carries the least risk and uses existing expertise. Extending existing products into new markets (market development) or developing new products for existing markets (product development) use capability in existing areas to expand in to new and the final option of developing new products for new markets (diversification) carries the most risk, but may be necessary if sufficient growth cannot be achieved through the other methods.

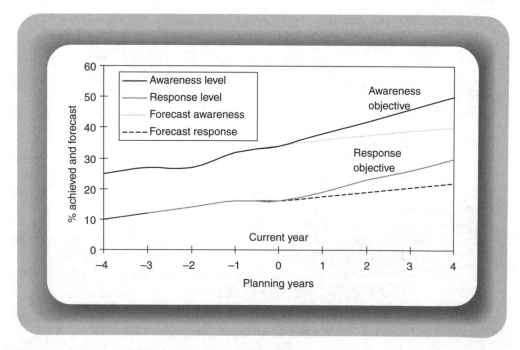

Figure 3.2 Communication objective gap analysis.

	Existing Communication Methods	New Communication Methods
Existing Audiences	Audience penetration	Communication development
New Audiences	Audience development	Communication diversification

Figure 3.3 The Ansoff matrix adapted for communications objectives.

The communications objectives matrix shown in Figure 3.3 suggests, for example, that if the marketing objectives are to attract new markets then the communication objectives need to focus on audience development and, if necessary, communication diversification. A knowledge of the target audiences preferences will determine whether or not new communication methods are needed. The matrix helps bring in to focus the alternatives for achieving growth and the risks associated with those various alternatives.

Gap analysis and Ansoff's matrix are both useful tools for determining realistic and achievable objectives as they illustrate the change required from present achievements and the risks involved, respectively. When writing objectives, it is essential to ensure that they meet a number of criteria. As already suggested they need to be achievable and realistic but also challenging. They need to be specific in terms of target audiences, product groups and timing and, perhaps, most importantly they need to be measurable. The objectives determine the control measures for the communications plan and, therefore, need to be detailed so that their achievement can be assessed during and after the plan has been put into place. The acronym SMART is often used to help planners word objectives appropriately. All objectives should be *s*pecific, *m*easurable, *a*ctionable, *r*ealistic and *t*ime specific.

For example, a SMART objective for achieving audience development might be:

To increase awareness of the event to 75 per cent of local residents by one week prior to the event commencing.

Communication theory and objective setting

A number of authors have attempted to identify and categorize the key areas of influence of communications. These are often referred to as communication effects and are closely related to the customer decision-making process. An awareness of the terminology and hierarchy of these effects is useful in determining communication objectives.

One of the most often used and oldest categorization of communication was developed by Strong in 1925 in relation to direct sales. The four stages identified are known as AIDA and refer to awareness, interest, desire and action. Similar but further developed models include Colley's (1961) DAGMAR stages, which are unawareness, awareness, comprehension, conviction and action and Lavidge and

Steiner's (1961) hierarchy of effects model (awareness, knowledge, liking, preference, conviction and purchase). These models all refer to the mental processes of the target audience and are very useful for focusing communication objectives on a desired outcome. Table 3.1 gives examples of communication objectives related to the communication effects models.

The range of communication objectives available can be summarized into a number of general categories. These are adaptations of those listed by Rossiter and Percy (1987) and Boone and Kurtz (2001).

- To provide information and through that create brand awareness.
- To enhance attitudes through changing perceptions of the organization, product or brand.
- To influence intentions by building product category wants and facilitating purchase.
- To increase or stabilize demand.

To summarize, the broader communication objectives need to be set within the constraints of the corporate and marketing objectives taking into account the critical success factors identified in the situation analysis and the range of communication

Table 3.1 Communication effects models and objectives

AIDA	DAGMAR	Lavidge & Steiner	Communication objective examples
Audience mental states			
	Unawareness		To create 50% awareness among 18–25 year olds within three months of festival
Awareness	Awareness	Awareness	To generate 20% increase in website hit rate within 2 months of festival
Interest	Comprehension	Knowledge	To achieve 10% request for festival brochure from local paper advertisements
		Liking	To be listed among top 3 national festivals by 60% of 18–25 year olds
Desire		Preference	To be positioned as the most entertaining festival of its type among all 18–25 year olds within 3 months
	Conviction	Conviction	To attain 10% of 18–25 year olds considering attending the festival at some time
Action	Action	Purchase	To encourage 75% of attendees to register as 'friends of the festival' within one month after the event

effects achievable. These objectives are the targets against which the success of the communications plan will be measured and therefore need to be communicated clearly to all those involved in the development and implementation of the plan.

Determining and describing target audiences

In order to meet the general communication objectives specific stakeholder groups will need to be identified and targeted. Once this has been done, the final level of objective setting can be undertaken where objectives are developed for each identified target group, as each group may have differing communication preferences.

Who they are

Before a target group can be selected it is necessary to identify all potential target audiences and to group these into meaningful segments. Markets must be segmented in order to differentiate the needs of different types of customer and hence better serve those needs. The segments identified in the marketing plan will be a useful starting point but may need to be further segmented to identify groups with differing communication needs.

Market segmentation can be applied at a very basic level using simple categories such as consumer/organizational markets or male/female segments or local/national/international markets. However, it is often more effective if a greater level of sophistication is applied in categorizing customers. This may involve psychographics using lifestyle, attitudes, opinions and interests to identify separate segments or can make use of consumer behaviour theory such as product involvement levels, key influences, or stages in the buying decision process.

Many events organizations will have a wide range of stakeholders and these will often involve individual customers as well as businesses and other organizations. The first stage in segmenting the market is to identify these potential stakeholders. Examples of these are given in Table 3.2 for an arts events organization, exhibition/conference organizer and for hockey event organizers.

Within each of the stakeholder groups identified in Table 3.2 there are a number of sub-groups. For example, the exhibitors (an organizational market) could be segmented geographically by national or international region, by company size, by previous exhibition attendance, by industry type or any combination of these criteria. For communications targeting it is important to segment the market to create groups who are likely to share communication preferences in terms of media, message and method. For example, this may involve segmenting by industry in order to create specific messages placed in trade magazines or by location in order to plan direct marketing campaigns and offers.

Whether the market is made up of organizations or individuals, it is always useful to segment existing/previous customers separately to new/potential customers. This allows for recognition of their past purchase behaviour, use of any information gathered and rewards for loyalty for past customers as well as introductory offers and more detailed information for new customers.

Table 3.2 Target audiences for events organizations

Arts events	Exhibitions/ conferences	Hockey events
Funding agencies	Visitors/delegates (actual and potential)	*Nationally*
Sponsors		Potential hockey players
Donors	Exhibitors (actual and potential)	People involved in hockey
Suppliers	Trade associations	People interested in hockey
Local/national government	Local, national and international media	Other sports related people
Management/board		Governmental organizations
Member ('friends')	Sponsors	Sponsors
Staff/volunteers	Staff	Former international hockey players
Customers (actual and potential)	Contractors	General public
Artists		Media
Schools, colleges		*Internationally*
Local community		Federation of International Hockey (FIH)
Local/national/international media		National governing bodies
		Participating national teams
		Embassies of participating teams
		International Olympic Committee
		International media

Arts events adapted from Hill et al. (2003); Hockey events adapted from Donia (2002).

Before selecting which groups to target, it is necessary to have some measure of their potential in terms of size, growth rate, frequency of attendance/use, spend, competitor activity and accessibility. This information can then be used to select the right group to meet marketing objectives and those selected groups can be researched further to identify their characteristics, preferences and behaviours.

An example of target audience identification is provided by the Tate Gallery. In 2000 the Tate opened a new gallery with the objective of doubling visitor numbers from 2 million to 4 million. Three existing markets were identified, tourists (20 per cent), 'art buffs' (the 30 per cent who had visited at least three times in the last 12 months) and 'cuspers' (the 50 per cent who had never visited before). It was determined that tourists would visit anyway as they followed guidebook advice and that the art buffs would not increase their frequency of visits due to any type of promotion. This left the 'cuspers' as the main segment to target in order to achieve the objective. This group was identified as large enough to provide the potential growth, as being interested in art but not knowledgeable, as being fairly up-market and willing to be influenced by the right type of promotion. These were people who would attend 'blockbuster' art exhibitions of famous painters and would visit well-known galleries when on holiday. Further research into this target group's preferences and behaviour enabled the development of a successful communications campaign for the new Tate Gallery (Alexander, 1999).

Their characteristics, preferences and behaviour

Once a target group has been selected, a detailed description or profile is needed of their characteristics, communication preferences and their behaviour. Many ticketed events have an ideal opportunity to gather information and research the preferences of target groups through their box office and ticketing systems, although, these data are rarely used to their full potential. For example, the box office is uniquely placed in that it provides the major intimate opportunity to capture information about actual customers, to find out who they are and how they found out about events. Someone in every group of people attending has to contact the box office, directly or indirectly via intermediaries, to purchase tickets (Tomlinson, 1992).

Segmenting target audiences

Target audience characteristics should include demographic, geographic and where possible psychographic information. This can be obtained through customer research or generalized from one of the many commercial segmentation systems available. Examples of well known pre-determined segments for consumer markets are ACORN and VALS (www.caci.co.uk and www.sric-bi.com/VALS). These have been developed using market research survey data to identify consumer segments with shared characteristics. ACORN uses geographic data combined with housing type, economic information and demographics to provide customer segments related to post code areas. VALS focuses on psychographic data to build up segments using consumer activities, interests and opinions. Many other marketing agencies can provide alternative segmentation systems or create segments from existing customer databases.

Although these pre-determined segments are useful, they tend to be of greater use for higher volume consumer products. The specialized nature of many events services requires segmentation methods which are tailored to the market. In many cases segmentation will not be required as the service offered is bespoke and each customer is communicated with in a personalized way.

Determining which characteristics are important for an organization's markets depends on the nature of the product and the markets it is communicating with. For example, a music event organization producing concerts throughout Europe will be interested in the musical tastes of its target audiences, location and travel behaviour, lifestyle and reference groups. Age, gender and economic situation may be of less importance. A corporate events organization would be likely to focus on past purchase behaviour, size of organization and available budget and may be less interested in the location and industry sector of its customers. The idea of 'consumer timestyles' has recently been put forward as a useful way to segment leisure services markets. Research suggests that the ways consumers perceive and use time has a significant effect on their choice of leisure activity and that identifying distinct 'timestyle' groups could provide a better understanding of leisure service customers (Cotte and Ratneshwar, 2003).

The characteristics of the target audience to some extent determine their communication preferences, although these will not always be clear from the market segmentation data and will often require further research. Information is needed on how they prefer to be approached, what influences them, the language and tone they respond to, how they access information and whom they listen to.

Consumer decision making

Several areas of consumer behaviour and communications theory are useful in determining what information is needed to help develop the right communications for each target audience. A comprehensive model of consumer decision making developed by Engel et al. (1995) is useful for identifying the areas that need to be understood if the audience is going to be communicated with effectively. Central to this model is the decision-making process.

The decision-making process

The decision-making process reflects many of the stages seen earlier in the communication effects models. The buying decision starts with the recognition of a need or problem to be solved and then moves on to information search. Once information has been gathered, either from existing knowledge or external sources, the consumer evaluates the alternatives they have available. Based on this evaluation a choice is made and after buying, using or experiencing the product the consumer evaluates that experience to confirm or adapt their opinions and attitudes. An understanding of these stages is useful for setting communication objectives as each stage can be informed or influenced by marketing communications but requires different communication methods.

Although the information search stage appears to be the focus for marketing communications, as this is when consumers are likely to be actively searching for information and will be most receptive, the other stages should not be overlooked. If the target audience is already aware of the event on offer then this information is already part of the consumer's internal search (memory, knowledge and experience). In this case the role of marketing communications is to ensure that the event being promoted is evaluated favourably against competing offers through emphasis of its unique features. The consumer group who have already attended the event and are in the post-purchase evaluation stage need to be reassured that they made the right choice and feel appreciated for their custom. This can be achieved through a variety of communication methods. For example, a personal courtesy call to determine how they felt the event went, a sales promotion offer for future events or a positive review of the event generated through public relations may be aimed at post-purchase customers. Marketing communications post-purchase and post-experience are particularly important in encouraging positive attitude changes which lead to future business and customer loyalty.

Decision types and consumer involvement

The decision-making process described suggests that purchase decisions are made rationally and logically with consumers gathering information on products which will solve their problems and evaluating these alternatives before making a decision. Not all decisions, of course, are made in this way. Often stages are skipped or the purchase is an 'impulse buy' requiring little or no rational thought. A useful way to categorize target audiences is through their decision-making behaviour. Certain people, or indeed organizations, may base their decision making on more emotional criteria, or will develop routine-response buying behaviour due to habit, lack of interest or loyalty. In these cases the 'information search' and 'evaluation of alternatives' stages are not followed and the customer moves directly from problem recognition to purchase. The type of decision making undertaken is linked to the perceived level of problem solving required for the purchase.

More extensive problem solving is required if the decision has a higher level of financial or personal risk, lower familiarity with the product class and a higher level of interest in the purchase. This will vary as different types of consumers purchase different product types. For example, a visit to watch the local football team play a home match may be routine for an ardent fan but may involve more extensive problem solving for a visitor to the town deciding on how to spend an evening.

Identifying customers' levels of involvement with the product can help target communications more effectively. Customers who are highly involved will be more receptive to detailed information from a variety of sources. Those with lower involvement will require more succinct, quick to assimilate information in order to make decision short cuts. Increasing customer involvement can be a communications objective as a customer who is more interested in the product group is more likely to develop brand loyalty. This can be achieved through encouraging an interest in the product itself such as the music genre, the sport, the venue, or through involvement with the communications through, for example, teaser ads, website features and trade and special interest magazines.

Organizational decision making

Although, the model described was developed for consumer decision making a similar process is often followed by organizations. The formality of the process will differ between organizational segments and, therefore, it is important to understand their buying behaviour before developing communications. Some organizations will purchase in a very rational manner with systems in place for gathering and evaluating alternative offerings, whereas others may rely more on an individual's personality, experience and preferences.

Decision-making unit

In understanding the stages of decision making, another important aspect for targeting is recognition of the decision-making unit and the roles within it. The decision-making unit is the individual or group of individuals who are going through the decision-making process. In consumer markets this may consist of one person, a couple, a group of friends or a family as discussed in the Walt Disney Resort example in Chapter 2.

In understanding the decision-making unit the organization can more clearly identify its customers and better focus its marketing communications. A company that focuses solely on the purchaser of their product may neglect to communicate with the user of the product. This may be true, for example, for purchases which are gifts or bought by adults for children, or bought by one member of the household for family use. The roles of purchaser and user in the decision-making unit may be supplemented by further roles.

The potential roles in a decision-making unit are the 'initiator', the person who first suggests a need or problem to be solved, the 'influencer' who has greater credibility in the information search and evaluation stages, the 'decider' who makes the final choice, the 'buyer' who performs the transaction and the 'user' who experiences the product. Individuals may play multiple roles and more than one individual may take part in each role.

For example, in the case of a couple considering how to spend the weekend, one partner may be the initiator in suggesting 'let's do something this weekend', both may be influencers as they discuss places and things to do, one partner may make the final decision and purchase the tickets and both will attend the chosen event. In a family decision, the children may be initiators, influencers and users with either or both parents as deciders and buyers. Indeed, the importance of children's influencing roles has been recognized by many marketers and is not limited to products targeted for children's use. For example, the 'pester power' of children in the supermarket has been used to promote washing powder by using promotions and packaging linked to popular cartoons. Car retailers are also recognizing the importance of children and in their communications are actively encouraging children to accompany prospective customers on showroom visits and test drives. Football, cricket and rugby teams have long targeted schools in their community programmes with the intent of developing young fans and in the knowledge that it is the parents who will buy the tickets and accompany their children to the game.

The decision making for many events products will involve a group of people, as many events are social occasions. Whether this is a group of friends attending a concert, a family watching a parade or a couple visiting an art exhibition, it is important to understand the roles each member plays in the decision and to communicate with them appropriately.

In organizational markets, the decision-making unit is often more formalized and is referred to as the buying centre. The roles within an organizational buying centre often include one or more gatekeeper, influencer, decider, buyer and user. As with consumer markets, it is important to understand that a number of individuals will be involved in making the decision and will need to be communicated with according to their roles. The gate-keeping role involves filtering information before it is evaluated by the influencers and deciders. Examples of gatekeepers might be a receptionist who screens sales calls or an assistant who determines non-junk mail from junk mail. At a different level this may be a sponsorship manager with no decision-making power gatekeeping for a marketing director. An understanding of these roles will help in developing marketing communication methods which will get through this screening process. The influencers in an organization will be determined to some extent by the management style and organizational structure. In some organizations this may involve working parties and committees, in others it may be middle management and in others the board of directors. Similarly, the role of decider may vary and involve more than one person. The buyer may be the person who can sign the cheques, the person in the formal role of purchasing manager or the finance director. The user may have very little involvement in the purchase decision but will be involved in post-purchase evaluation and feedback and is therefore important for future sales.

For example, the sales director of a small engineering firm decides that her sales force would benefit from a teambuilding event. She knows of a number of companies offering such services from direct mail promotions she has received. Her assistant (gatekeeper) passed on the ones addressed to her personally but threw out the other general flyers. A few of the salespeople (influencers) have attended such events when in previous jobs and share their opinions of good and bad experiences. The human resource manager (influencer) has also gained experience and a number of contacts for this type of service. After speaking to a number of events companies and discussing the alternatives with the managing director (influencer), the sales manager (decider) chooses an event management company to use. An order is raised and approved by the purchasing manager (buyer) and the event takes place attended by twenty-five sales people (users). In this case a number of people at different levels within the organization were involved in the decision. For each organizational customer it is imperative that the roles played by individuals are understood in order to effectively target the right audience at the right time with the right information.

Attitudes and beliefs

A common component of marketing communications objectives relates to the forming, changing or reinforcing of attitudes to brands, products and organizations. This is due to the understanding that attitudes form an important part of the decision-making process and that attitudes are often an indication of behavioural intent. Consumers have pre-formed attitudes to existing product groups, brands and organizations and once formed these attitudes are difficult to change. Attitudes are formed through a combination of learning, knowledge and experience and are made up of three components. These components are cognitive in that they refer to information and knowledge, affective referring to feelings and emotions, and behavioural, which refers to tendencies to act. Marketing communications objectives can be set to modify or build on any of these components. For example, the Millennium Experience example cited earlier (Case study 3.2) used information on the significance of the millennium to change people's attitudes to celebrating it and, in particular, they provided knowledge (cognitive component) which affected a change in feelings (affective component). The three components of attitude can be abbreviated to 'think', 'feel', 'do' and in some purchase situations this is the order in which the attitude will be formed. However, marketing communications can be used to encourage an initial purchase and based on this experience the consumer gains knowledge and develops feelings for the product – a 'do', 'think', 'feel' sequence. Sales promotions are often used in this way to encourage trial of the product in new customers. For example, special offer sports event tickets are made available through schools to encourage a younger audience and their families to experience the game. Impulse purchases often follow a 'do', 'feel', 'think' sequence and strong imagery and branding can encourage a 'feel', 'do', 'think' sequence. In this case, unusual and striking imagery on the posters and flyers for a theatre production can encourage attendance at the event without providing a detailed knowledge of the content.

A target market's existing attitudes towards an organization's products and its competitors' products is a useful way to segment the group further. Loyal customers with a positive attitude need their attitude reinforcing, whereas those with a more negative attitude need to be given reasons to rethink their opinions. New audiences need to be guided in forming positive attitudes through positive experiences and information.

Existing attitudes influence all stages of the decision-making process and through positive or negative bias will, to some extent, determine what information is sought and how it is evaluated. The marketing communications received along with the experience at the event will in turn influence attitude change.

In some respects, attitude change is one of the most difficult communication objectives to achieve as attitudes have a self-preserving nature. Once our attitudes are formed we have a tendency to filter information so that we assimilate more of that which confirms our existing attitudes and avoid or ignore that which contradicts them. We actively seek out others with similar opinions and attitudes through personal contacts or public media. Attitude change is often, therefore, a gradual and lengthy process and should never be set as a short-term marketing objective.

Influences on decision making

The attitudes and purchase decision-making processes of the target audience are influenced by a variety of factors. These interpersonal and personal influences are outside of the control of the marketer but need to be understood as they largely determine how an audience wishes to be communicated with. The interpersonal influences on the decision-making process stem from the consumer's culture and subculture, social situation and family (the influence of others). The personal influences are made up of individual motives and needs, learning and knowledge, self-concept, attitudes and perception as well as economic situation, personality, age and gender.

When communicating with a target audience it is necessary to understand that their receptiveness, understanding, retention and responses to the message will be largely determined by these interpersonal and personal influences. Because of this the influences on decision making also provide useful criteria for segmenting markets. Motives and needs are used in benefit segmentation to group audiences according to their reasons for using the product. Marketing communications can then be tailored to highlight the benefits sought by each sub-segment. For example, the audience enjoying La Boheme at the New York Opera may be there for a variety of reasons. Entertainment may be cited by many but also there will be those who wish to be educated, those who are there to socialize and those who are there to be seen (status needs). Similarly, the motivations of attendees at a conference may include educational benefits, business networking, socializing or having a break from daily routine.

The most useful influences to understand, from a marketing communication viewpoint, are those which involve other people such as family, friends, colleagues and peers. Recognizing how these influences affect a target audience allows communication messages to make use of role model figures and celebrity endorsements but, more importantly, to identify opinion leaders and generate word-of-mouth.

Reference groups and opinion leaders

Reference groups are groups whose values, standards and behaviour influence the behaviour of others. These may be groups that the consumer belongs to (actual reference group) or groups that they wish to belong to (aspirational reference group). A student away at university may belong to the reference groups of the student cohort, their friends back home, their family, their sports team and their colleagues at work. They also may aspire to belonging to the legal profession, the rich and famous or the hockey team. These reference groups, whether current or aspirational, will affect many of their purchase decisions. A desire to belong to the legal profession will influence educational choices but may also impact on clothing style and brand, car purchase and choice of leisure activities.

Reference group influence is closely linked with the motivating factor of belonging. In order to belong to a particular group it may be necessary to wear a certain style of clothes, listen to a particular type of music or go to see the right bands at the right venues. This type of influence is often stronger in children and young people and, indeed, the motivation not to belong can be just as strong. In order to fit with one group disassociation from another may be required. Marketing communications can make use of both aspirational group traits and disassociative group traits to create a positive image within a target market. This was done successfully by Ministry of Sound, the London-based music company, in their campaign to increase voting participation in young people. Advertisements were developed which portrayed characters from groups with whom the target market would not want to be associated. For example, one cinema advertisement execution showed a racist giving full voice to his opinions. The strap line at the end of each stated 'Use your vote, you know he'll use his' (Creative Planning Awards, 1997).

Reference group influences are particularly powerful for many consumer event products, particularly those that involve sports, arts or music. These areas have status, belonging, membership and aspiration inherent within them and role models are readily found among performers, sports people and celebrities. These role models can be used to communicate the personification of the aspirational reference group to a target audience. In this case the endorsement of an event by these 'significant others' can be a powerful communication tool.

Although, reference groups and role models are of great use in developing effective marketing communications, it is the opinion leaders within those groups who provide the greatest influence. Opinion leaders are those members who have power of influence based on their knowledge, experience and status related to a particular product group. They are seen as the experts or trendsetters in a field and are therefore observed, consulted and copied by other members or 'would-be' members of that reference group.

Due to their influence on others, opinion leaders are a vital target audience. They will often be innovators in that they try new products and experiences first and more often than not they will be evangelical in spreading the word of both good and bad experiences related to their area of interest and expertise.

If this group can be communicated with successfully they will greatly improve the reach and effectiveness of the message. Their opinions are seen as highly credible as they are independent of the organization and its promotional activities. This credibility is particularly valuable in markets where consumers are increasingly cynical and mistrusting of traditional promotional methods such as the youth segment. The findings from a study by White (2001) demonstrate that the youth market (15–24 year olds) is important to understand for a number of reasons:

- its complexity in number and strength of sub-segments
- changes rapidly in terms of short-lived trends and fashions yet some major trends are deep and pervasive
- seen as trendsetters for some key markets
- possible to market to this segment globally or regionally
- represents the future in terms of lifetime value.

Youth sub-segments are often described as tribes in which shared values cross national boundaries. These are often characterized by musical preferences and other attitudinal criteria.

In researching youth markets several techniques have been developed to identify opinion-formers and early adopters. The 'leading edge' is especially important and influential in this fashion-conscious and media alert market. However, these opinion leaders tend to be category specific rather than general (White, 2001).

Case study 3.3 provides an example of successful targeting of 18–24 year olds and demonstrates how important an understanding of the target audience is in developing effective communication methods.

Case study 3.3

Witnness

Witnness, a music festival created and owned by Guinness, ran for four years between 2000 and 2003. This two-day event featured top contemporary groups and artists at the Fairyhouse Racecourse, County Meath, in Ireland. In 2003 it featured 100 acts playing over five main stages.

The event was created with the key marketing objective of changing perceptions of the Guinness brand in its native land. In 1999, the brewer implemented research that identified that 60 per cent of 18–24 years olds rejected the Guinness brand. The task was to change that while not alienating existing consumers.

The strategy was to develop a sub-brand in the form of a music festival called Witnness. This sub-brand was to represent an almost underground street culture appeal that was to be directed at the identified target market and not beyond. The use of the name Witnness reflected the idea of being a witness to something mysterious and possibly dysfunctional, and utilized the 'nn' Guinness spelling. The year-long integrated communications plan consisted of three stages, each one with clearly defined objectives:

- *Stage one*: a teaser programme for eight months to create and build the brand name to specific awareness levels.
- *Stage two*: a clearer programme for four months for more direct communications utilizing a media launch event. The objectives were to drive ticket sales while still building the awareness via publicity. The links between Guinness and Witnness were made more open during this stage.
- *Stage three*: this involved the two-day festival itself with the objective of making the experience the best music event in Ireland via the quality of the acts. This included maximizing publicity and achieving 300 per cent return on media investment.

The targeting process was critical if Witnness was going to work. The comprehensive understanding of the target market enabled the communications plan to create a sophisticated event image. The plan, particularly in stages one and two, consisted of the innovative utilization of many PR techniques including the following:

- In order to accentuate the witness theme, police-styled accident/incident boards were designed and located roadside throughout Ireland. Cryptic messages were devised to drive readers to a dedicated Witnness website. The website contained clearer information concerning the festival, including acts and ticket-buying mechanisms. The boards were constantly moved from location to location for greater coverage and to keep the message fresh. Many were stolen as souvenirs.
- Graffiti sites were created in various locations.
- Video teasers in mock police evidence pouches were despatched surreptitiously to target news media.
- Female senior citizens were recruited and trained for a viral programme that was designed to create word-of-mouth. These representatives, nicknamed 'grannies', were utilized in bars where they gossiped ambiguously about a mysterious event. The mystery was maintained via deliberately ambiguous briefings to the 'grannies'.
- Contact reports pertaining to spurious meetings were deliberately placed and left in bars. These reports contained ambiguous links to the festival and both signed and unsigned acts that might or might not be appearing.

Source: Masterman (2004); Virtual Festivals (2004).

Inputs and information processing

The various influences described above can be understood and used by marketing communications planners but are outside of their direct control. The 'inputs', however, are determined by those individuals and organizations communicating with the consumer. From a marketing point of view the inputs to the decision-making process consists of all the information that the consumer is exposed to. This includes the promotional messages of the organization and its competitors as well as general media exposure. The volume of inputs that each member of a target audience is exposed to each day means that not all can be given attention. The input information is processed and much is ignored, dismissed or forgotten depending on the needs and characteristics of the recipient. The average British, Australian or American child is exposed to between 20 000 and 40 000 advertisements a year (Caulkin, 2003). The necessary filtering of information suggests that any marketing communications must have a resonance with their target audience and will need to stand out against the clutter and noise of other messages. The information processing aspect of consumer behaviour is discussed in greater depth in Chapter 4 in relation to message and media strategies.

Finalizing objectives

Once the target markets have been identified and understood, objectives can be refined to take account of:

- their level of involvement
- their purchase behaviour
- the stage in hierarchy of effects
- the levels of influence
- how information is processed.

The more specifically an objective can be determined the easier it will be to develop effective strategies to meet that objective. However, although this should be done for each event and each identified audience, it is not recommended for each medium. The objectives should remain 'media-neutral' as separating the campaign into methods and media detracts from the integration of each component and may result in a lack of synergy and effectiveness.

As the objectives become more specific, it can become more difficult to distinguish clearly between objectives and strategy. It is useful to remember that objectives are *what* will be achieved and strategy is *how* it will be achieved.

Some of the following terms are useful in phrasing event communication objectives: *to maintain, to build, to gain, to raise, to create, to establish, to reinforce, to improve, to convert, to achieve, to generate* etc.

Communication objectives and targeting examples

Following are a selection of examples taken from the marketing, communications or business plans from various events organizations.

Warwickshire and Worcerstershire Counties Bowling Association (WWCBA, 2003)
Objectives:

- to increase awareness of the Association's vision for the game of crown green bowls, its aims and objectives
- to project the WWCBA through media outlets seeking to comment on current issues and activities and generate feedback and to project the value of membership
- to improve the image of the Association as friendly, accessible to all and willing to listen.

Target audiences:

- people who live, play and support crown green bowls in the area
- people who can influence the WWCBA image (media, other associations, general public)
- potential major sponsors
- future client groups (e.g. school children, women).

US Tennis Open (US Open, 2000)
Objectives:

- to generate excitement for the US Open as an all-inclusive worldwide event
- to increase television viewership by at least 10 per cent
- to increase ticket sales in the New York tri-state area by at least 10 per cent.

Target audiences:

- traditional tennis fans
- broader sports enthusiasts.

Sydney Mardi Gras (2003)
Objectives:

- to maintain the profile of the Mardi Gras Season as a national and international celebration of gay, lesbian, transgender, bisexual and queer lives
- to establish and retain a diverse membership and volunteer base that is actively involved in the organization.

Target audiences:

- members and volunteers
- young people and women
- international markets with history of travelling to Mardi Gras
- international gay and lesbian media.

Maindee Festival, Wales (2002)
Objectives:

- to increase the number of participating groups and stallholders in the Festival
- to increase visitor attendance at the main 2003 event to 5000.
- to increase the number of (not public) funding organizations from two to four.

Target audiences:

- helpers, performers and stallholders
- community groups and street committees
- friends and family of the above.

It can be seen that these vary in terms of the specific nature and measurability of the objectives and the detail provided on target audiences, however, they all provide a valuable starting point for the development of marketing communications methods.

Summary

The communication objectives for event organizations need to be set within the context of the situation analysis and the higher level objectives of the organization. The communication objectives should be set broadly to begin with, encompassing corporate brand building but should then be made more specific to each event (or event programme) within the organization's portfolio and for each distinct target audience. In order to set specific objectives, it is necessary to segment stakeholder groups and to understand their characteristics, behaviours, influences and attitudes. This information can then be used to greater benefit in determining the most appropriate method, media and message to communicate with each group.

Discussion points

- **Identify the main target audiences for:**
  a) **the Beijing Olympics**
  b) **a historical event re-enactment society**
  c) **a national motor show.**
- **Critically evaluate the objectives and target audiences given for WWCBA, The US Tennis Open, the Sydney Mardi Gras and the Maindee Festival. Use SMART to structure your answers.**
- **Write four possible marketing communications objectives for an event of your choice.**

References

Alexander, R. (1999) *Changing the Perspective: Developing brand advertising for the Tate gallery.* Creative Planning Awards: Account Planning Group, London.

Ansoff, I. (1989) *Corporate Strategy.* Penguin.

Boone, L. and Kurtz, D.L. (2001) *Contemporary Marketing.* 10th edn. Southwestern.

CAANZ (2003) World press photo exhibition. The Communications Agencies Association of New Zealand. WARC.

Caulkin, S. (2003) A brand new kind of advert: Kids are king and schoolyards the new marketplace. *The Observer*, London. 6 April, p. 9.

Colley, R. (1961) *Defining Advertising Goals for Measured Advertising Results*. New York: Association of National Advertisers.

Cotte, J. and Ratneshwar, S. (2003) Choosing leisure services: the effects of consumer timestyle. *Journal of Services Marketing*, 17 (6), 558–572.

Creative Planning Awards (1997) The Ministry of Sound. Use your vote, or redefining the value of the vote. Account Planning Group.

Donia, L. (2002) Guidelines to develop a communications plan. Federation of International Hockey. September.

Engel, J.F., Blackwell, R.D. and Miniard, P.W. (1995) *Consumer Behaviour: International Edition*, 8th edn. The Dryden Press.

Hill, E., O'Sullivan, C. and O'Sullivan, T. (2003) *Creative Arts Marketing*, 2nd edn. Butterworth-Heinemann.

Lavidge, R.J. and Steiner, G.A. (1961) A model for predictive measurements of advertising effectiveness. *Journal of Marketing*, October.

Maindee Festival (2002) 2003 Marketing Plan. www.maindee.org (accessed September, 2004).

Masterman, G. (2004) A strategic approach for the use of sponsorship in the events industry: In search of a return on investment. In *Festivals and Events Management: An International Arts and Cultural Perspective*, Yeoman, I., Robertson, M., Ali-Kinight, J., McMahon-Beattie, U. and Drummond, S. (eds). Butterworth-Heinemann.

McCann, B. (1999) Turning a moment in time into a turning point in history. Account Planning Group. Creative Planning Awards.

Rossiter, J.R. and Percy, L. (1987) *Advertising and Promotion Management*. McGraw-Hill.

Strong, E. (1925) *The Psychology of Selling*. McGraw-Hill.

Sydney Mardi Gras (2003) New Mardi Gras 2003–2004 Business Plan. www.mardigras.org.au (accessed September, 2004).

Tomlinson, R. (1992) Finding out more from the box office. *Journal of the Market Research Society*, October. 34(4), 10–24.

US Open (2000) US Open Excitement. Effie Awards Brief of Effectiveness. NY Marketing Association.

Virtual Festivals (2004) www.virtualfestivals.com/fesivals/festival.cfm (accessed March, 2004).

White, R. (2001) Communicating with youth. Best Practice, World Advertising Research Center, November.

WWCBA (2003) Communications Plan 2002/3. Available from www.wwcba.com/communications_plan.htm (accessed September, 2004).

Chapter 4
Communications Strategy

Objectives

- To identify the range of tools used in determining event communication strategies and positioning statements
- To understand the information processing model and perception and their importance in developing effective communications
- To recognize the value of branding as a strategic marketing communications tool
- To understand the process and theories used in communications message development
- To appreciate the variety of communication methods and media available

Introduction

Effective communications require the integration and coordination of a number of elements in order to achieve the objectives set. This requires a clear strategic direction along with detailed sub-strategies addressing the different levels of objectives. The starting point for strategy development, once target markets have been determined, is the development of a positioning statement. From the positioning statement a number of strategic options may be available to achieve the desired position and outcomes. These need to be evaluated and the best option chosen and developed. This will lead to the campaign message, creative strategy or overarching theme. It is then necessary to select the most appropriate methods and media to put this message across to the selected target groups.

Communications strategy can, therefore, be defined as 'a pre-determined set of actions that differentiate your product from its competitors in terms that are positive and personally relevant to your key target audiences' (Wirthlin Report, 1999).

The theories of perception, information processing and branding provide a valuable underpinning in helping to develop effective communications strategies.

Strategy and positioning

For each communication objective set there will be a number of possible ways to achieve the desired outcome. These alternative strategies need to be generated through use of the information gathered in the situation analysis and the customer/target market analysis. This process involves the handling of information from a variety of sources including forecast scenarios and 'what if' situations. The complexity of this task has led to the development of several marketing tools, models and theories to aid the marketing planner in developing and selecting appropriate strategies. Although these models are undoubtedly useful, it is important to bear in mind that successful strategy generation and choice also requires creativity, insight and experience.

The strategic tools and models which can support communications planning decisions are discussed below.

Competitive position

Once the competitor analysis has been undertaken in determining the situational context of the communications plan, it is possible to identify and classify the organization's current market (or competitive) position. This process uses market share trends to determine whether the organization is a market leader, market challenger, market follower or market nicher. An organization that leads the market in terms of market share will have different strategic options to an organization focusing on a niche market or a smaller player in the field. The market leader is likely to follow strategies which maintain their current position and defend against attack from market challengers. These tend to be consolidation strategies and, from a communications viewpoint, the focus will be on brand strengthening, reassurance, loyalty and relationship building. A market challenger is vying for leadership and will therefore follow a more attack-led strategy in order to gain market share either from the leader or from the smaller followers and nichers. Communications are likely to stress what makes them distinctive from competitors and may use direct or indirect competitor comparisons. Marker nichers tend to be successful through following a strategy which avoids direct conflict with the larger players. This is achieved through the creation of a specialism in a particular area (product, service level, market). Their expertise in the chosen area protects them from attack and, if target markets are selected appropriately, provides enough room for growth. For example, many local sports teams could be described as market nichers. Their target market is limited geographically and therefore the direct competition is reduced. Competition still exists from other sports and other substitute leisure activities but their focus can be on developing a loyal local fan base. Growth, therefore, is not achieved through expanding the market but through market penetration (possibly via more frequent attendance) and product extensions (via merchandise and venue use for example). At the other extreme, market leaders, such as Manchester United Football Club, have been able to expand their market nationally and internationally though an emphasis on brand and image. Case study 4.1 illustrates how the Singapore Chinese Orchestra used marketing communications to move from being a niche marketer to achieving a larger international market share.

Case study 4.1

Singapore Chinese Orchestra

The Singapore Chinese Orchestra (SCO) was formed in 1996 out of what was formerly the People's Association Cultural Troupe, with a mission to form an orchestra of national standing. The orchestra has achieved that status and now looks ahead with the aim of strengthening its position as one of the leading professional orchestras in the Chinese orchestral world and beyond.

In the late 1990s the SCO readdressed its goals and strategies in order to strive towards this current position.

Situational analysis

The SCO was in some position of strength in that it was the only orchestra focused on Chinese music that was based in Singapore. This allowed the SCO to enjoy a niche audience as well as receive grants. As a young orchestra too, with young musicians, it was innovative in trying to meet audience expectations. Despite only a short history, it also managed itself with separate music and administrational functions in order to meet those expectations more effectively and efficiently.

The lack of any sort of threat from new orchestras forming and then entering the market was low and therefore helped strengthen this position.

In positioning itself in this niche market, however, the SCO was increasingly vulnerable. Appreciation of the arts, and in particular Chinese orchestral music, was traditionally low and the SCO was also relatively inactive in addressing that weakness. It was a young organization with little brand equity or awareness and was dependent upon grants and its own commercial revenues. As a non-profit organization it was also led by performance measures that were less tangible, such as quality of music and audience satisfaction, making it more difficult to evaluate and then improve. Economies of scale were also difficult to achieve because the SCO had no permanent venue for its concerts.

An analysis of the SCO's objectives and strategies reveals how it went about taking advantage of a number of opportunities.

Marketing objectives (2000–2004)

The SCO mission is to become an orchestra of international standing. In attempting to reach that goal it has had first strategically to develop a greater position of strength more locally in Singapore. Its short- to medium-term objectives are therefore:

- to increase awareness of the SCO and Chinese orchestra music to existing and new markets
- to reduce financial vulnerability
- to increase music provision via audience development.

Target audiences

In 2000, the SCO was able to identify that there were signs of an increase in the awareness of Chinese orchestra in schools, mainly in the form of emerging junior orchestras. At the same time it conducted an analysis of its own audiences and revealed their largest existing market was student orientated (60 per cent). The profile consisted of students of all ages, from schools to colleges, that were technically and Internet literate and mainly Chinese speaking.

In order both to increase awareness and music provision, the SCO therefore developed its strategies in order further to penetrate this student market. It also targeted smaller but new English-speaking markets of tourists and expatriates.

Venue

The SCO was able to move into a permanent home in 2001, the Singapore Conference Hall. This opportunity enabled the orchestra to plan more concerts and be more flexible in their planning, thus increasing the artistic provision while also increasing revenue and reducing financial vulnerability. It also helped to develop a firm base for the development of communications and develop a new image on which to base the development of awareness.

Grant funding

As a result of the focus on a student target audience, from 2000, the SCO was able to take advantage of new and increased funding opportunities and help to alleviate financial vulnerability. This included applying and getting grants from the Ministry of Information and the Arts and the National Arts Council (NAC) for assisting in the development of music education and developing local talent.

Communications

With greater financial resources the SCO was also able to undertake wider reaching communications.

It used non-personal media to develop awareness. Newspapers and arts magazines were successfully targeted and on radio station Passion 99.5FM it ran advertisements and coordinated interviews.

It created a number of 'Friends' and membership schemes in order to develop audience relations and numbers. These preferential treatment packages offered discounts, access to the talent, patron roll listings at the Hall, in print and on a newly created website.

The website was developed in both Chinese and English languages in order to reach existing and new markets. It was designed to feature the kind of technology that would appeal to the student targets, for example e-flyers, downloads and video clips.

A number of initiatives were undertaken in order to develop awareness to the student targets in particular. The initiatives were educationally based in order to increase knowledge of both the SCO and Chinese orchestra generally, and to ensure they received government funding. The 'Community Series', for example, consisted of outdoor concerts jointly organized with the National Parks Board that incorporated interactive and hands-on sessions for all those interested in learning about instruments. The 'School Series Community Concerts' were a direct provision into the NAC's Education Programme and consisted of popular song performance for appeal to that audience. Other schemes included 'Chinese Orchestra In-Focus' where students could visit the SCO in rehearsal.

The parks concerts were also a part of a wider 'Art Reach' programme that attracted expatriate English speaking audiences.

Source: Singapore Chinese Orchestra (2004); Cheng et al. (2001).

Product life cycle

Product life cycle theory is the recognition that products and services have a limited life span and that within this life they pass through a number of different stages. The stage at which the product is in the life cycle affects the types of strategy that are most appropriate. The four stages identified are 'introduction', 'growth', 'maturity' and 'decline' and are determined by plotting industry or product group sales (not individual brand sales) over time. The length of a product life cycle can vary with high fashion, fad products having a very short life cycle and other staple, essential products having a very long life cycle. The length of the cycle is often very difficult to predict and, although partly determined by marketing activities, it is also greatly affected by social, economic and technological trends. For example, the life cycles for different music genres vary greatly. Rock music has endured for over forty years, whereas punk was a major force for less than ten years. There are many criticisms of life cycle theory, one of which is the large number of products that do not appear to follow the standard curve or even go through all four stages. The plotting of sales is highly dependent on definitions of the industry or product group and the definitions of new product versus modified or extended product. The strategic usefulness of the product life cycle depends on recognizing when the product has moved from one stage to the next. This is far easier to see retrospectively than at the time of the change. Despite these criticisms, product life cycle theory has its uses in strategic marketing communications. The general stages help link the emphasis of communications to the current needs of the market place and a recognition that products decline suggests the need to be innovative in all areas of the marketing mix. For example, cricket events have seen a decline in attendance in the UK over recent years and, in order to respond to this, variations of the product have been introduced to extend the product life cycle. These include the introduction of one-day events and, more recently, cricket matches that are completed in one evening's play. This innovation is needed to extend the life cycle of existing products and in developing new products to replace those in decline. Some of the communications strategy implications of the product life cycle are summarized in Figure 4.1.

Portfolio analysis

Closely related to product life cycle theory is product portfolio analysis. These techniques plot the organization's product groups or strategic business units using a variety of criteria. The result is an overview of the positions of all aspects of the business and, when plotted over time, this gives an indication of trends for each product which in turn suggests the strategic actions to take.

The Boston Consulting Group (BCG) matrix uses the criteria of relative market share and market growth rates to categorize products into four groups. 'Cash cows' are those with high market share but low market growth, mature and successful products, 'stars' are the products with high market share and high growth, 'problem children' are those with low share but in a high growth market and finally, 'dogs' are the products where the company has a low market share and the market shows little growth. The Boston Consulting Group summarized the detailed alternative strategic directions for each as 'polish the stars, milk the cows, feed the problem children and shoot the dogs' (Hill et al., 2003). A variety of other portfolio matrices have been developed since this, for example, the GE/McKinsey matrix which uses the criteria of business strength and industry attractiveness. The aim of these portfolio models is to

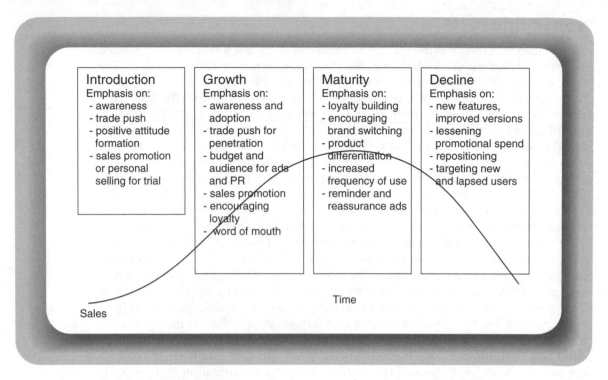

Figure 4.1 Marketing communications strategy and the product life cycle.

illustrate the dynamics at play within the product range. An understanding of how products support each other in terms of funding as well as complementarity aids decision making in terms of the whole product range. Although criticized for being overly prescriptive, when these matrices are looked at alongside the product life cycle they provide an understanding and forecast of each product's movement through the portfolio categories, emphasizing the need for portfolio management rather than simple brand management and highlighting the need to develop new product offerings.

For a smaller organization with fewer product groups, portfolio analysis may be of less practical use. However, the technique can be adapted to plot market segments or indeed individual clients to focus on market development rather than product development.

By adapting the matrices axis criteria further, models can be developed which have more relevance to particular industries. For example, Hill et al. (2003) suggest using 'likely audience appeal' and 'cost of production' to create a four quadrant matrix of use in planning a theatre's annual artistic programme.

To focus on marketing communications the products may be plotted using individual versus mass appeal and current market awareness level. Market segments can be plotted using their communication preferences, for example, rational versus emotional appeal and level of product involvement (Figure 4.2).

Adoption of innovations

Often communication objectives will be focused on building awareness among new customer groups and encouraging trials of new products. In developing strategies to achieve these objectives it is important to understand how new ideas, opinions,

	Low involvement	High involvement
Rational appeal	One-off attendees Buyers of tickets as gifts	Experts, Enthusiasts
Emotional appeal	Impulse purchasers	Fans, Supporters Members

Figure 4.2 A communications segment focused portfolio matrix.

attitudes and behaviours spread in the market and in society in general. Research conducted by Rogers (1962) concluded that markets can be divided into five distinct groups according to their propensity to adopt new products or ideas and that the adoption by each group is sequential in leading to a diffusion of innovation process. The distribution of the groups over time follows a normal curve with the percentage in each group calculated from normal distribution z scores (probability theory related to the measures of dispersion in data). The first group to adopt a new product or idea are known as 'innovators' and make up approximately two and half per cent of the total market that will adopt. This group tend to be younger, well educated and confident. They are excited by the unfamiliar and are willing to take more risks, although they are also image conscious with strong opinions. For any new event or existing event entering a new market it is important to identify and focus on the innovators in the initial marketing communications. A positive experience for an innovator will lead to the generation of word-of-mouth and provide a platform on which to build. This initial impetus will start to bring in the next group known as the 'early adopters'. Early adopters make up thirteen and a half per cent of the total audience and are essential to give momentum to the campaign. They are receptive to new ideas, albeit within a familiar area, they are well educated and have a high level of involvement with the product category. This is the group that contains the all important opinion leaders and will give the greatest boost to word-of-mouth referrals. The 'early majority' (thirty four per cent) and the 'late majority' (thirty four per cent) are less willing to take risks and will wait to be reassured by the experiences of the early adopters. Often older and more traditional in their values, they are initially suspicious of the new but will succumb once they see others doing so. Public relations, in terms of positive media coverage and reviews in non-specialist publications, helps to reassure these groups that the product is now mainstream enough for them to adopt. The final group to adopt a new product are known as 'laggards' and make up sixteen per cent of the total market. These are the people who may have never tried a similar product before so the experience is completely alien to them and therefore carries the highest level of perceived risk. While they are difficult to attract, they are often the first point of entry into a new market segment and can therefore provide growth in otherwise saturated markets.

Porter's generic strategies

The communications strategy needs to fit within the corporate and marketing strategies of the organization. In understanding this fit it is useful to consider the generic strategic direction that the organization is taking. Porter (1986) maintains that the only three strategic alternatives at this level are 'cost leadership', 'differentiation' or 'focus'. An organization trying to follow two or more of these is said to be 'stuck in the middle' and is unlikely to be as successful. A cost leadership strategy requires the organization to aim to lower its costs through economies of scale and standardization. The lower cost base can then be used to increase profits which can be ploughed back into product developments or as a platform for competing through lowered prices. A differentiation generic strategy suggests that the firm focuses on producing non-standardized offerings as each is differentiated for particular target markets. This allows the organization better to meet the needs of its target markets and to use this as its competitive advantage. A strategy of focus requires specialization in one area. This may be through focusing by product, by target market or by service level.

The three generic strategies have implications for marketing communications. A cost leadership strategy requires standardized communications and suggests an emphasis on mass communications. A differentiation strategy needs communication strategies tailored for each target market and a focus strategy may require more personalized communications.

Segmentation strategies

Porter's generic strategies have much in common with the strategic choices for market segmentation. Once the segmentation criteria have been determined and the segments formed and investigated, it is necessary to select those that will be targeted and the methods for marketing to them. If an organization chooses to offer a single marketing mix to all the targeted segments this is known as undifferentiated or mass marketing. Although this has obvious benefits for lowering production costs, it is a strategy that is highly vulnerable to any competitor choosing to satisfy better the distinct needs of the segments. Very few companies are able successfully to maintain an undifferentiated marketing approach. Even those offering global products, such as McDonald's or Coca-Cola, have adapted their product range, pricing structures, communications and distribution methods for different target groups. This strategy is only suitable where there are few competitors, in a market which is a monopoly or oligopoly.

Most event organizations will choose a differentiated or concentrated segmentation strategy. By serving multiple segments with different marketing mixes or concentrating on one market segment the organization can better meet the needs of its customers and defend itself against competitors. For example, a large regional theatre may ensure that its annual programme includes performances such as pantomimes that appeal to families, alongside popular musicals, traditional ballet and pre-school shows. These will be priced and promoted according to the needs of the target segments. Other smaller theatres may concentrate on a specific area such as ballet or opera or comedy productions.

A further segmentation strategy is one-to-one or micromarketing which involves adapting aspects of the marketing mix for each individual customer, i.e. market segments of one. This is often harder to achieve in consumer markets than organizational markets and is more appropriate when the product is of a higher value. A company that produces bespoke or customized products or services is following one-to-one marketing although the initial marketing communications may still involve mass media. For example, a corporate events organizer may build awareness through advertisements placed in industry magazines but will focus more on personal selling and account management once initial interest has been shown.

The TOWS matrix

The TOWS matrix (Weihrich, 1982) is a very useful tool for translating the situation analysis into a number of strategic options. The four-quadrant matrix is formed through the strengths, weaknesses, opportunities and threats determined in the SWOT analysis but uses combinations of these to create strategies (Figure 4.3).

Once all possible strategic combinations have been considered using the matrix, these can be evaluated using forecast outcomes and likely risk and against the objectives, strategic direction, management style etc.

Positioning

Positioning refers to the position that the product holds in the mind of the customer relative to competing products (Ries and Trout, 1982). It is how the customer

TOWS	Strength 1 Strength 2 Strength 3	Weakness 1 Weakness 2 Weakness 3
Opportunity 1 Opportunity 2 Opportunity 3	Max-max strategies For example, use strength 1 to take advantage of opportunity 2	Min-max strategies For example, overcome weakness 2 to take advantage of opportunity 1
Threat 1 Threat 2 Threat 3	Max-min strategies For example, use strength 3 to overcome threat 3	Min-min strategies For example, overcome weakness 2 to avoid threat 1

Figure 4.3 The TOWS matrix framework.

perceives the product offering in comparison to others. From a strategic viewpoint it is important to have determined the desired position for each target market. This desired position then drives the marketing mix for that target group. Marketing communications are often used strategically to change the existing position of a product or brand. This repositioning is undertaken to attract new target markets, gain market share, or revitalize products coming to the end of their life cycle. The communications role is to change existing attitudes to the product through the use of new imagery, information and comparisons.

A positioning strategy needs to be based on a good understanding of the current position held. This requires marketing research in each target market to assess how a product is perceived when compared with competitors. The result of such research can be summarized on a positioning map. This is a simple graph using any two positioning criteria and plotting each competing product on offer. A number of these will be needed as there are likely to be several criteria on which the products are evaluated. For example, a sports association may be positioned according to how progressive or conservative its image is perceived or according to the perceived value of membership benefits. A concert venue may be evaluated based on ease of access, atmosphere or performance. When researching the current position of a product it is important also to identify which criteria are most important to each target group. For example, smaller companies may view the costs of a conference organizer as the most important criterion, whereas a larger customer with more resources may select on levels of service. Examples of positioning maps are given in Figure 4.4.

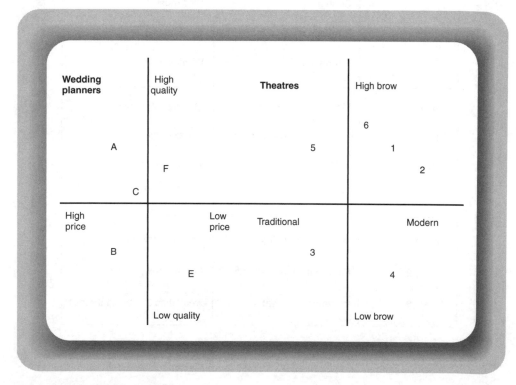

Figure 4.4 Positioning map examples.

In Figure 4.4 the major criteria for wedding planners have been identified as price and quality. The five existing competitors in the market have been plotted onto the graph to show their current positions. In this example company A holds the top end of the market and company E is seen as the 'budget' end. Company F is seen as good value and company B as relatively poor value. A company entering this market would need to choose how to position itself against the existing competition and according to the needs of the market. It could be that there is a gap in the average quality lower price area. If company C had undertaken the research, it would be apparent that they need to reposition themselves. They are competing directly with company F but are seen as higher priced and lower quality. They may choose to address this through a campaign to improve their quality image or may choose to differentiate themselves on other criteria such as innovative ideas or personal service.

The map for theatres uses the more intangible criteria of accessibility of the performances and image. In this example most of the theatres are perceived as catering for a high brow audience leaving the general populace, perhaps underserved. Theatre 1 may wish to reposition itself to differentiate its offering more clearly from theatres 2 and 6.

Positioning maps are a useful tool for evaluating the current competitor offerings and for suggesting future strategic action. If the maps are to be used in this way, however, it is vital that they are based on reliable customer research. This research first needs to identify the criteria used to evaluate competing offerings and then to gather the data on which to base a score for each competitor on those criteria.

An example of repositioning is provided by a study of Carmen the Opera in the UK (Currie and Hobart, 1994). This research identified the possibility of repositioning opera to make it accessible to a wider audience. Their recommendations for communication strategies to achieve this were to expose younger target markets to opera through educational establishment tours; to use the popular mass media to promote opera generally and to encourage the use of operatic pieces in advertisements and television programming; and to use the 'common man' approach to break down stereotypes and to provide a more accessible reference group. To attract these new target groups the opera needs to be positioned as spectacular entertainment and great value for money.

The process of segmentation, targeting and positioning is a crucial aspect of a marketing plan and often results in a positioning statement. This statement needs to be focused on within the marketing communications plan as communications are the main marketing mix influence on target audience perception.

The positioning statement creates 'clarity, consistency and continuity in the way the organization speaks to the market' (Kanzler, 2003). It clearly denotes how the organization (its product and brands) wishes to be perceived and is the core message to be delivered in every medium.

Perception and information processing

In order to follow the strategies formulated and then summarized in the positioning statement it will be necessary to understand and influence the target audiences' perception. Perception is the meaning attributed to the stimuli received via the five senses in conjunction with our past experiences, motivations and expectations. Perception is not therefore, merely determined by the inputs but also by the way the individual interprets these inputs. Most people are familiar with apparently simple images which are perceived differently by different viewers, for example, the face or vase picture often used in psychological studies of perception. The effects of factors other than the sensory stimuli on the target audiences perception suggests that understanding is needed of these other, individual factors (subjectivity, selectivity, past experience, categorization) and the ways in which a target audience processes information.

Information processing is how the incoming stimuli are converted, or not, into useful knowledge. The stages of information processing are exposure, attention, comprehension, acceptance and retention (McGuire, 1976). Exposure refers to ensuring that the target audience comes into contact with the message. This is obviously necessary and is an important part of communications strategy in terms of media selection, coverage and repetitions. However, exposure alone is not sufficient to ensure the effectiveness of the message, as most audiences will be exposed to a huge array of marketing and other stimuli every day. It is therefore impossible to pay attention to each one and the consumer must select the messages that are relevant or of interest in order to allocate their limited information-processing capacity. Consequently, marketing communicators must try to ensure that this attention selectivity works in their favour by targeting the right audience in the right way. A number of techniques can be used to break through the consumer's perceptual screen and the clutter of marketing communications stimuli. The two extremes of appeal are those that are based on hedonic (pleasure, emotional) needs and appeals that are based on cognitive (rational, logical) needs. These types of appeal form the basis of the consumer processing model (CPM) and the hedonic experiential model (HEM) of information processing (Kitchen, 1999). Much of the imagery in mass marketing communications attempts to gain audience attention through appealing to hedonic needs for example, sexual images, family occasions, love and enjoyment are all regularly used for a variety of products.

Cognitive appeals tend to require the use of words to convey the information that the prospective consumer requires. This type of rational appeal needs to be carefully targeted at those who have an involvement with the product and are more likely to be searching for information. Hedonic appeals can attract audiences through non-voluntary attention as can the use of novel or intense stimuli.

Attention, although desirable, is again not sufficient to ensure an effective communications campaign. An unusual, loud or annoying message may well gain the audience's initial attention but, unless the content is understood as it was intended, the message will not be successful. Comprehension of the message is most clearly linked with perception as it is at this stage in information processing where the target audience interprets and makes sense of the stimuli they have attended to. It is also at this stage that the individual's personality, experiences, existing attitudes and expectations are used to take meaning from the message. These individual factors will affect whether or not the message is viewed positively or negatively, which aspects are given the most attention and whether or not it is understood. If the message has been developed with the target audiences' specific characteristics in mind then it will use a frame of reference which they can relate to and will be understood and interpreted as intended. For example, a flyer promoting a music club night and aimed at a youth audience may not be understood by an older target market. The details of the venue, disc jockey name, music type and event name would be indistinguishable to those not 'in the know', in other words, without the correct frame of reference and prior experience.

Selective perception can occur when the message is subconsciously but deliberately misinterpreted. This happens when the message is made sense of through an inappropriate frame of reference as the audience perceives the message in such a way as to make it fit with their own experience and understanding. For example, a light smoker viewing a government advertisement on the dangers of smoking tobacco may choose to interpret the message as relating only to heavy smokers and not themselves.

Comprehension of the message will be followed by acceptance of the content if the message has been executed correctly. This stage in information processing involves the audience agreeing with what they have understood from the message. Acceptance is related to the credibility of the message source and media and the appeal of the images and words used. The same message delivered by two different sales people can achieve different levels of acceptance depending on the likeability, trustworthiness and professionalism of the person delivering the message. A glowing description of a new dance production on the dance company's website will gain less acceptance than the same copy presented as a review in a quality newspaper.

As long as the message has been appropriately interpreted then acceptance should lead to a positive attitude change. This means that the audience is now positively predisposed to the product. However, this is still not sufficient to ensure that the product is considered among the alternatives when the consumer is deciding on a purchase. For this to happen the knowledge gained through exposure, attention, comprehension and acceptance of the message must be retained in the consumer's memory. This final stage in the information processing model determines whether or not the information gained is used in the search stage of the decision-making process. In order to make the message memorable, and therefore make the information in it easily retrievable when needed in decision making, a number of techniques can be used. Concretization involves making the intangible more tangible, for example, the use of characters (the Esso tiger) or celebrities to reflect the characteristics of the product. Easily memorized strap lines or catch phrases such as 'beanz, meanz, Heinz' can be used as an aide-memoire as can catchy songs and jingles. Repetitions of the same message can increase retention but only up to a certain point. Too many repetitions can lead to the consumer mentally switching off or a negative feeling about the message. Far more preferable is reinforcement of the message through a variety of media to build retention through an integrated and consistent message without the boredom of enumerable repetitions. Another highly effective way to increase retention of the message is through the use of branding. The brand name, logo, colours and associated imagery can be used in a variety of media and message formats and provide the consumer with a heuristic (mental short cut) to use in selective retention and information retrieval. One of the first actions taken by bidding host cities for the Olympics is the development of a logo and related imagery.

Persuasion

The aim of moving the target audience through the information processing stages of exposure, attention, comprehension, acceptance and retention is, ultimately, to influence the consumer's attitudes and behaviour in some way. This influence by marketing communications is termed persuasion and refers to the guiding of an audience to the acceptance of a belief, attitude or behaviour through rational and emotional appeals. The act of persuasion is not necessarily manipulative but the techniques used can be. In order to persuade an audience, marketing communications have been known to use exaggeration, unsubstantiated claims or lies. For example, telesales callers may lead the recipient to believe they are undertaking market research and sales promotion offers may encourage purchases without fulfilling the promised reward. However, these unethical practices are in the minority and will have a negative impact in the longer term.

Six tools of influence used in marketing communication and other types of persuasion have been identified by Cialdini (1988). These are reciprocation, commitment and consistency, social proof, liking, authority and scarcity. Reciprocation refers to the returning of a favour. The consumer feels they owe the organization their custom because the organization has done something for them. Corporate hospitality is often used in this way with the organization 'treating' its clients and potential clients in some way in the hope of gaining their custom in return. Of course, reciprocation is not automatic and will depend on the audience's perception of the sincerity of the offer.

Commitment and consistency as a tool of influence use our inclination to see a decision through. Once some sort of commitment has been made there is a tendency to alter attitudes and behaviour in order to remain consistent with that decision. Increasing the level of involvement with a product is one way to increase that commitment.

Social proof refers to our desire to follow appropriate acceptable behaviour. If we are unsure of how to act we will look to others and follow their lead. This influence is used in new product adoption through the recruitment of opinion leaders.

Liking and authority are used to build rapport and respect between the communicator and the audience. Marketing communications use attractive voices and characters and similarities with the target audience in order to promote liking of the character and hence liking for the product. Similarly figures either real or fictional who are perceived as having authority within the target audience and for that product are used to build credibility.

If a product appears to be in short supply and demand appears great this perceived scarcity can increase the appeal to the target audience. For example, demand for tickets for an event tends to increase if the market believes the tickets will sell out. This appeal is more likely to make people purchase sooner but will not necessarily achieve more purchases and can backfire if the perceived difficulty in obtaining a ticket goes on to deter other consumers from trying to purchase.

Branding

Branding is important in marketing communications as it is inextricably linked with image, perception and attitude. The brand is not simply the name and logo but is made up of the consumer's perception of all the tangible and intangible aspects of the product.

Brands can be viewed as consisting of the four interrelated dimensions of functions (what it can do), personality (how people feel about it), differences (how it is better) and source (where it comes from, parent company, pedigree) (Randall, 1999). The brand image transmitted to the market place will be most effective if all four aspects work together to give brand consistency. Because brands have both emotional and rational appeal, they are vital in bringing about long-term attitude and behavioural change and are therefore an important aspect of any marketing communication strategy aimed at building loyalty.

For example, in 1986, The London Philharmonic Orchestra recognized that it was struggling to differentiate itself from the other three London orchestras and was relying on the performance of 'star' conductors and soloists to draw the crowds. The agency, Saatchi and Saatchi, was appointed to improve their fortunes and soon realized that a strong and valid brand identity had to be created. This would give the orchestra personality and added value and would position it above the indistinguishable pack. This was achieved through ensuring that the orchestra was consistently referred to as 'the London Philharmonic' and through a communications campaign encapsulating the idea that 'we put a lot in so you get a lot out'. This ensured an emotional commitment from the orchestra to the audience and vice versa. The personalities within the orchestra were then developed and used within a variety of advertising campaigns (Moss and Nunneley, 1990). The success of the campaign was undoubtedly due to the creation of a consistent brand image which included the four brand dimensions.

Message development

The development of the communication message begins with the objectives and the positioning statement. The overall theme of the campaign needs to be encapsulated succinctly and then built upon to create specific messages for each communication method and medium to be used. Examples of overall creative themes are:

We put a lot in so you get a lot out – The London Philharmonic

Make sense of life – Billy Graham

Goin' to work. Every night – Detroit Pistons

Game for all. Game for anything – Belfast Giants

Help us grow the game we all love – USTA

Telling the story of the train – National Railway Museum

Although creativity is an important aspect of successful marketing communications, it is not enough to ensure effectiveness on its own. Effective communications must be based on a well-developed marketing strategy, on a detailed understanding of the target audience and on well-defined objectives. The communications must be persuasive and must gain the audience's attention. They must also be honest and credible and, as Shimp (1997) states, must avoid 'the creative idea from overwhelming the strategy'.

Frazer (1983) suggests that there are seven main alternative message strategies. A 'generic strategy' describes the product or benefits with no indication that it is better than alternatives. This is a suitable strategy for a market leader and can be used to encourage use of the organization's brand as the generic term for the product, for example, Hoover (for vacuum cleaners), Coke (for cola drinks), Xerox (for photocopiers) and Tippex (for correction fluid). In sport, the London tennis championships are commonly referred to as the 'Stella' due to title sponsorship by Stella Artois.

A market challenger in a previously market leader dominated market may use a 'pre-emptive message strategy' to make a generic claim as a basis for superiority. What they claim here is, perhaps, no different from competitive offerings but, because they claim it first, competitor response options are therefore limited. The Gillette razor message 'the best a man can get' is an example of a pre-emptive generic claim as it makes no particular benefit comparisons but assumes a position of superiority.

A message which emphasizes a unique product benefit to differentiate itself from the competition is known as a 'unique selling proposition' (USP) strategy and a message which uses psychological rather than physical differentiation is a 'brand-image strategy'. For example, The Ideal Home Exhibition Scotland uses the message 'It's right up your street' to emphasize the unique benefit of a convenient location to its target market, whereas the Glastonbury music festival has developed a strong brand-image strategy using the emotional ties that previous festival goers have developed, along with their shared experiences and press coverage.

A message strategy focused on 'positioning' must make the most of competitive advantage by stressing what they do best and is an important aspect of many of the other strategic alternatives. The National Exhibition Centre in Birmingham refers to itself as 'the busiest exhibition centre in Europe' and therefore by implication positions itself as the most popular. The Notting Hill Carnival positions itself against the many other street/community and national festivals by emphasizing that it is 'Europe's biggest street party' and therefore the one to attend.

A 'resonance strategy' uses messages which have a high degree of shared meaning with the target audience. The audience can relate to what is being depicted and therefore feel closer to the product on offer. In the repositioning of opera for a wider target market a resonance strategy using 'ordinary' people would be appropriate to overcome the existing perceptions that opera is for older, wealthier, upper class audiences.

The final strategy identified by Frazer is an 'emotional strategy'. Many leisure products such as consumer event attendance are purchased for emotional rather than rational reasons. An emotional appeal is often therefore more suitable. Emotional appeals can use negative as well as positive messages and make use of a range of human emotions, for example, love, nostalgia, excitement, fear and guilt. The Ministry of Sound campaign to encourage young people to vote used a negative emotional appeal to induce fear and guilt in its depiction of bigots and thugs using their vote and the strapline 'Use your vote. You know they will'. Positive emotional appeals are often used in promoting sports events using nationalism, pride, excitement to involve the target audience. 'Football is coming home' was used at UEFA's Euro '96 in the UK to portray an image of the sport returning to its point of origin as well as the hope that England might win a tournament again.

Emotional appeals are particularly effective for products which are used to satisfy the higher levels of motivation or need. Many event products tend to be purchased or attended to satisfy the needs of self-esteem (the place to be seen, networking, social climbing at conferences, ballet and exhibitions), belonging (being with peers, fitting in to a reference group at concerts and football matches), self-actualization (gaining knowledge, widening horizons, cultural improvement at arts events, educational events and cultural festivals).

Semiotics and signs

In developing the message there is likely to be a combination of images, words (written and spoken), sounds and other stimuli (smell and feel) depending on the media to be used. The message is therefore transmitted by a variety of stimuli which must be translated (encoded) into signs by the message creator and then interpreted (decoded) by the target audience. The term sign refers to 'anything that stands for something (its object) to somebody (its interpreter) in some respect (its context)' (Peirce, 1995). The study of signs and how they are interpreted is called semiotics and is a useful tool in the creation, pre-testing and evaluation of marketing communications. An important area of semiotics is the difference between denotative and connotative meaning. Denotative meaning is shared in that the sign has the same meaning for everyone, whereas connotative meaning varies between individuals according to their experiences, knowledge and situation. In developing communications messages it is important not to assume that the meanings of that message will be shared as different target audiences and individuals within those groups may associate different connotative meanings to them. An in-depth understanding of the message recipients is required to ensure that the message will be interpreted as it was intended and that the signs do not have unforeseen negative connotations. These differences are most apparent across cultures but also occur within national, sub-culture and even family groups. For example, the smiley face symbol, ☺, may fairly universally denote happiness but in some sub-cultures also represents the drug ecstasy. The colour black is associated with mourning in western cultures but can also denote smartness (in business attire), being cool (in youth culture) and membership of the goth sub-culture (hair, makeup and clothing).

Communications messages often use syntactic techniques to help put across a complex message in a few words or symbols. The use of simile to compare the product to some other object with desirable characteristics is one such method. For example, 'as good as it gets', 'the most fun you can have . . .', 'as smooth as silk'. Metaphors achieve this through a less obvious association with a desired image and allegory extends the metaphor to images outside of the message itself in that the associations are made in the consumer's mind. The Athens 2004 Olympics used both metaphor and allegory to build the association between the modern games and the rich history and mythology associated with the original games and with Greece.

Likeability, attractiveness and credibility

It may appear obvious but the likeability of a marketing communications message and method is one of the factors most closely related to sales increases (Pickton and Broderick, 2001). The interesting point here is that it is the likeability of the advertisement not necessarily the product which has more of an effect on sales. However, it is also suggested that we are more likely to like an advertisement if at that time we find the product relevant and of interest.

Of course there are occasions where the target audience may find an advertisement entertaining while maintaining little or no interest in the product. Many people enjoyed the long running humorous campaign for Hamlet cigars without ever having any intention to purchase or smoke a cigar. The sophistication and artistry in many forms of marketing communications makes them entertaining in their own right and therefore more attention getting and more memorable.

Communications that use humour and warmth or are seen as clever or unusual are not only remembered but are also talked about and then generate further coverage and interest.

Other techniques used to increase the likeability or attractiveness of a message include the use of music, sex and celebrities. Music can improve the mood of the audience making them more receptive and can convey some of the characteristics of the product. However, the use of silence can also be effective in gaining attention in noise cluttered media. Sex appeals are used in many media to communicate about a wide range of products, however, they are most effective if linked directly to the product's features or benefits rather than used gratuitously. Celebrities may be used to enhance the credibility of the message through their expertise. They can be used to make the product more attractive by associating it with their own characteristics and they can be used to develop trust through the feeling that someone you know, albeit only through mass media, uses this product. Events clearly have their own built in mechanism here as they can encourage participants to also be part of the events promotion.

Other appeals may focus on the negative aspects of not using the product using fear as the motivator. For example, Specsavers the opticians, ran advertisements showing wearers of spectacles being ridiculed for their choice of eyewear style with the slogan 'he should have gone to Specsavers'.

Pre-testing

All aspects of message development need to be tested before moving on to the final stages. The message concept, images and words can be tested using a variety of techniques including focus groups, interviews, experiments and observation. Concept boards depicting the main elements of alternative messages can be used to stimulate discussion among selected target audience members, either individually or in groups. This should indicate how the audience perceive the messages, how they interpret meaning and what associations the words and images create. The likeability of the possible messages can be assessed through a sample of consumers ranking their preferences and/or discussions on what they like and dislike about each message. Levels of persuasion and attitude change are more difficult to gauge but can be assessed to some degree using similar methods and focusing the discussion on how the messages make them feel about the product. Experiments and observation can be used to measure the level of attention and interest displayed when viewing or listening to a number of potential messages.

Pre-testing is essential in refining the message and ensuring the effectiveness of the creative concept. Once this has been undertaken the next strategic choices are how best to execute the message in terms of communication methods and media choices.

Method and media choice

The effectiveness of a well-developed creative message will remain largely dependent upon the choice of methods and media used to execute it. Creativity is also important at this stage in determining new and innovative methods and media in order to gain maximum coverage, impact and effect. In an integrated marketing communications campaign a variety of methods and media is employed to convey a consistent message. The campaign is said to be 'media-neutral' in that the message concept is developed without a specific medium in mind ensuring that the message is the same no matter how and where it is placed (Wigram, 2004).

The methods and media used will be dependent upon a number of factors including the target audiences, their communication preferences, media access and stage in the decision-making process. Product characteristics will also affect the choice. For example, a complex, expensive product such as an overseas conference will require different methods of communicating with its target audience than a weekly comedy night in a local club. Other factors that also need to be considered are the product life-cycle stage, the current and desired brand image and the organization's resources and expertise.

Communication methods

There is a wide variety of methods available for communicating the desired message. These methods include any one or combination of the traditional promotional mix of personal selling, advertising, sales promotion and public relations but also extend beyond this into word-of-mouth, corporate identity, sponsorship and corporate hospitality, e-marketing, exhibitions and events and merchandising.

In order to create brand synergy it is necessary to utilize many methods and media. Such an integrated campaign will deliver 'messages and experiences which are relevant to different audiences; which are sensitive to alternative channels and environment; and which collectively deliver the brand vision' (Wigram, 2004).

The main method types are summarized in Table 4.1 and discussed in depth in Section Two.

Table 4.1 Communications methods

Method	Definition
Public relations	Communications from the organization to any of its stakeholders such as local community, employees, suppliers
Publicity	Generating news to be covered by the media. Non-paid for media space
Corporate identity	Developing a consistent image for the organization as a whole, using stationery, livery, uniforms, logo and in-house publications
Lobbying	Communicating with influential bodies to influence their actions such as government, regulatory bodies, sports associations
Internal marketing	Intra-company communications to develop loyalty, commitment, shared vision
Corporate events	A form of internal marketing used for reward, information provision, motivation, and training
Direct sales	Contact between the producer and the purchaser using no intermediaries
Telemarketing	One-to-one communication using the telephone
Personal selling	One-to-one communication using face-to-face contact
Customer service	Additional (to sales) care offered to the customer before during and after purchase and use

Continued

Table 4.1 (*Continued*)

Method	Definition
Word-of-mouth	Encouraging one-to-one communication between target market members
Exhibitions	Opportunity to display products in an environment which brings buyers and sellers together
Promotional events	Events which communicate with a selected group of people about the organization and its products (such as product launches, product trials, opening ceremonies)
Corporate hospitality	Entertaining current and potential customers
Merchandising/ point-of-sale	In-store displays used in retail environments to encourage point-of-sale purchases
Promotional merchandise	Products linked to the core product but with a promotional focus (for example, theatre programmes, souvenirs, T-shirts, photos)
Sales promotions	Communicated offers which add short-term value to the product (such as prize draws, two for ones, free gifts, competitions)
Advertising	Mass media communication where space is bought. Can be corporate, brand or product based
Direct response advertising	The audience can respond immediately to the advertisement via the transmitting medium
Product placement	Arranging for the organization's products, venues to be seen or referred to in the media
Celebrity endorsement	Communicating the products benefits and characteristics through connections with a celebrity or authoritative person
Testimonials	Using existing customers opinions within the message such as satisfied customer quotes, excerpts from reviews. Can be combined with celebrity endorsement
Sponsorship	Contribution (financial or in-kind) to an activity (often a sport, music or arts event) by an organization usually in exchange for name, brand or product exposure
Direct mail/e-mail	Mass communication in written form. Can be personalized to the recipient

The grouping of the methods in Table 4.1 attempts to give some indication of similarities between methods, however, there is some overlap between the methods. For example, celebrity endorsement can be used in many of the other methods. There is also an overlap between the methods and the media used, for example, telesales defines both the method (personal selling) and the medium (the telephone). Although the groupings in the table indicate similarities, there are other links which have not been shown, take for instance, the link between sponsorship and promotional events or between promotional events and publicity. Electronic and Internet marketing has not been listed as these techniques fit more easily into media types.

Media choices

The choice of medium for conveying the message is many and varied and is closely related to and limited by the communication methods. Therefore, method and media choices should be made in conjunction with each other in order to ensure that the most appropriate combinations are selected. Table 4.2 details the media available and their uses.

Table 4.2 Media choices

Medium	Description	Used for
Television Local, regional, national, international	High impact medium with potential to reach large audiences. Digital television allows for direct response and proliferation of channels has led to more precise targeting	Advertising Publicity/public relations Sales promotion Sponsorship Product placement
Cinema	Very high impact due to focused attention of audience. Targeting through location and film selection	Advertising Product placement Sales promotion Sponsorship
Radio Local, regional, national, international	Low impact low cost medium. Quick to produce and air so can be topical. Targeting by region and listener profiles	Advertising Sales promotion Public relations Sponsorship
Printed media Newspapers, magazines, trade journals, directories	Low impact and cost Precise targeting can be achieved. Some have long life (directories and quality magazines)	Advertising Publicity/public relations Sales promotion
Posters Outdoor media boards, transport Indoor transport, shopping centres etc.	Low cost and short exposure time but good repeats and geographic targeting. Requires strong visual message or short written to gain attention	Advertising
Ambient media	Unusual external media used to gain impact and publicity. Can be dramatic (40 foot high football) or understated (tattoos, traffic lights)	Publicity Promotional events Advertising

Continued

Table 4.2 (*Continued*)

Medium	Description	Used for
SMS Text/picture messaging Blue tooth broadcasts	Non-personalized message received personally as text message. High attention level but can be intrusive. Direct response possible	Direct marketing Sales promotion Customer service
Telephone Personal calls, recorded message calls, call hold ads	Personalized one-to-one medium, although can be mass through recorded messages. Can put across complex information and gain a direct response	Advertising Personal selling Customer service
Mail Flyers, letters, e-mails	Can be highly personalized if database technology employed. High impact if well designed. Highly targeted with direct response. Can be seen as junk mail	Advertising Direct marketing Sales promotion
Web page Own web page, other organizations' web pages, search engines Banner ads, pop-ups, search engine listings, website referrals, click-throughs	Can get across complex information to an international audience at low cost. Targeting difficult to achieve and monitor. Gives direct response and interactivity	Advertising Public relations Direct sales Sales promotion Customer service Internal marketing
Person to person	Very high impact but high cost. Complex information can be explained. Direct response and interactivity guaranteed	Personal selling Customer service Word-of-mouth
Exhibitions and events Trade fairs, consumer exhibitions, corporate events, product launches, press conferences Other events (sports, music, arts)	Highly targeted and high impact. Multi functional in generating sales, publicity and relationship building	Direct marketing Publicity Internal marketing Sponsorship Product placement Sales promotion Customer service

In selecting appropriate media it is necessary to consider the characteristics of each main medium type and then to evaluate the specific options within each type. For example, it may be that television advertising has been selected as one of the main thrusts early on in the campaign due to its coverage and impact. As television has been chosen as the medium the next choice is to select the television channels and times.

Choosing the most appropriate media mix should begin with a focus on the already identified target audiences. The choice is therefore initially limited by the reach of the medium only including those media which target the required audiences. The next criterion will be the appropriateness of the media for the message to be conveyed. It is necessary to assess which will give the greatest impact, exposure and credibility, which will allow for feedback and which will enhance the image and create associations with desirable values.

A secondary consideration will be the cost, although, if the best media and methods have been chosen to meet the objectives set, then the budget should be made available. If the budget is insufficient then the objectives may need to be revised. This is the ideal objective and task budgeting, however, in many cases the budget will be determined irrespective of likely outcomes and will therefore be a limiting factor to media choice.

The World Press Photo exhibition provides a good example of the use of a variety of media to get across a single message. The target audience for the campaign was primarily residents of Wellington, New Zealand (where the exhibition was being held) and secondarily frequent visitors, business travellers and those who lived in a three mile radius. The message concept was summarized as 'see the world through the eyes of the best press photographers'. The media strategy ran over a short period of three weeks and integrated five different elements. These were:

1 Television to create broad awareness using a sense of bigness and a strong emotional appeal. Regions and channels were chosen to match the target audiences' geographic and demographic characteristics. Television advertisements ran from three days before the exhibition to the end.
2 Local press was used to support the television advertisements in building awareness and to build curiosity. These full page advertisements used 1000 words to describe the photos based on a reversal of 'a picture paints a thousand words'. Smaller advertisements were used as reminders towards the end of the exhibition.
3 Outdoor advertisements were placed in bus shelters and on retail posters to build curiosity and ensure a strong visual presence that would entice people to attend.
4 Ambient media were used by placing exhibition snapshots (with a message on the back) in customers' photo wallets and by placing clear mock camera lens advertisements in taxi windows. This encouraged curiosity, word-of-mouth and additional publicity.
5 The camera lens concept was also used in a pop-up advertisement online. The mouse moved a mock camera lens which became a click-through banner advertisement once the mouse was clicked.

This integrated multi-media campaign ensured a combination of high reaching and high exposure activity focused on the key local audience as well as using ambient media tactics to surround and surprise the target group. Over 32 000 people attended the exhibition, 22 400 more than the standard for the venue and 12 400 over the campaign objective (CAANZ, 2003).

Once appropriate methods and media have been chosen pre-testing is again required to ensure that the message is reaching the desired audience and is having the expected effect. This can be achieved through piloting aspects of the campaign in limited areas or again through the use of focus groups, interviews, observation and experiments.

Summary

The communications strategy must be based soundly on the situation analysis, customer research and the objectives of the organization. There are a number of issues to consider in developing appropriate strategies which require an understanding of the importance of developing a clear positioning statement and putting this across to the target audience. This communications process involves the development and testing of a creative concept, message, methods and media to ensure that the campaign will appeal to the audience's needs and will move them through the information processing stages.

The Wirthlin Report (1999) suggests that in determining whether or not the communication strategy is appropriate it should be judged against the following criteria:

1 Communication messages must harmonize with and leverage the product's most favourable position in relation to competing messages and products.
2 A communications strategy must build on the positive elements of the product's history.
3 The strategic frame of reference and the strategic positioning of the product must be able to endure over a long period of time and under a variety of circumstances.
4 The communications strategy must have credibility within the organization before it can gain credibility outside.
5 The organization should be committed to reinforcing and meeting the perceptions and expectations conveyed by the communications message.
6 The communications strategy must not be easily countered by media or opponents and should reflect anticipated shifts in the positioning of competitors.

Discussion points

- Select appropriate positioning criteria for the following events sectors:
  a) conference planning
  b) exhibition organizers
  c) sporting venues
  d) community festival organizers.
- Find four examples of marketing communication messages for events products (flyers, posters, advertisements, websites, direct mail). Critically analyse each one in terms of:
  a) who the target audience appears to be
  b) the creative concept
  c) the objectives of the message in terms of decision-making stage and information processing level
  d) the message appeal (rational, emotional)
  e) the impact, credibility and longevity of the medium used.

References

CAANZ (2003) World press photo exhibition. The Communications Agencies Association of New Zealand. WARC.

Cheng, L., Lam, K., Kim, M., Sim, N. and Ching, T. (2001) Case study: Singapore Chinese Orchestra. www.asiacase.com/sco_text4.htm (accessed April, 2004).

Cialdini, R.B. (1988) *Influence: Science and Practice*, 2nd edn. Scott Foresman.

Currie, G. and Hobart, C. (1994) Can opera be brought to the masses. A case study of Carmen the opera. *Marketing Intelligence and Planning*, 12 (2), 13–18.

Frazer, C.F. (1983) Creative strategy: A management perspective. *Journal of Advertising*, 12 (4), 40.

Hill, E., O'Sullivan, C. and O'Sullivan, T. (2003) *Creative Arts Marketing*, 2nd edn. Butterworth-Heinemann.

Kanzler, F. (2003) The positioning statement: Why to have one before you start communicating. www.marketingprofs.com (accessed 2004).

Kitchen, P.J. (1999) *Marketing Communications: Principles and Practice*. International Thomson Business Press.

McGuire, W.J. (1976) Some internal psychological factors influencing consumer choice. *Journal of Consumer Research*, 2, 302–319.

Moss, S. and Nunneley, C. (1990) The London Philharmonic – A great performance. Advertising effectiveness awards. Institute of Practitioners in Advertising.

Peirce, C.S. (1995) Some consequences of four incapabilities. *Journal of Speculative Philosophy*, 2, 140–151.

Pickton, D. and Broderick, A. (2001) *Integrated Marketing Communications*. Pearson.

Porter, M.E. (1986) *Competition in Global Industries*. Harvard Business School Press.

Randall, G. (1999) *Branding: A Practical Guide to Planning Your Strategy*, 2nd edn. Kogan Page.

Ries, A. and Trout, J. (1982) *Positioning: The Battle for Your Mind*. McGraw-Hill.

Rogers, E.M. (1962) *Diffusion of Innovations*. Free Press.

Shimp, T. (1997) *Advertising, Promotion, and Supplemental Aspects of Integrated Marketing Communications*, 4th edn. The Dryden Press.

Singapore Chinese Orchestra (2004) www.sco.com.sg/english (accessed October, 2004).

Weihrich, H. (1982) The TOWS matrix: A tool for situational planning. *Long Range Planning*, 15 (2), 54–66.

Wigram, J. (2004) Media-neutral planning – what is it? Account Planning Group. www.apa.org.uk/content/articles (accessed February, 2004).

Wirthlin Report (1999) Communications strategy toolkit. *Current Trends in Public Opinion*, Wirthlin Worldwide, August, 9 (6).

Section Two
Communications Toolkit

Happy Halloween. Thirty-one on the 31st! The 2004 and 31st New York Village Halloween Parade provided entertainment literally for the masses. The event consisted of 50 000 costumed marchers parading 6th Avenue in lower Manhattan in front of an estimated two million spectators of all ages. The Village Halloween Parade Inc advisory board consists of 60 community leaders and politicians that ensure that this event is not only socially and culturally beneficial but that it also impacts economically. The event is estimated to bring $60 million into New York City. One of the event's key communications tools is its website through which it reaches participants, spectators and sponsors all year round (www.halloween-nyc.com).

This section provides an evaluation of the personal and non-personal communications tools that can be used for event communications. It considers current and best practice and also an innovative approach for managers of events.

Each chapter considers a different communication tool by reviewing theoretical frameworks and research and comparing and contrasting those with industry practice.

The essence of an integrated approach to marketing communications is that the tools are selected in combinations that will achieve marketing objectives. While the tools are considered on a chapter by chapter basis, they are done so in an integrated context in order to demonstrate how public relations, E-marketing, advertising, sponsorship, sales promotion and direct and relationship marketing can be used coherently and harmoniously to achieve those objectives.

Public Relations

E-Marketing Communications

Advertising

Event Sponsorship Programmes

Sales Promotion

Direct and Relationship Marketing

Chapter 5
Public Relations

Objectives

■ Understand the role and value of public relations in the events industry
■ Understand the function of public relations in integrated marketing communications
■ Identify the planning process and the requirements for a public relations plan
■ Identify ways in which public relations techniques and tools can be innovative

Introduction

In an industry where traditional mass media and methods are often too expensive an option, the value of public relations for mass and personal media communications is high. This chapter aims to build up a conceptual framework for the development, planning and implementation of event public relations (PR) by focusing on first, role and function and then on the building of a PR plan that is comprised of a set of techniques and tools that are fully integrated into the overall communications mix.

While event communications are often dominated by PR activity because it offers relatively inexpensive alternatives, such activity can also carry the highest level of credibility. Consequently PR is arguably a critical component of event communications.

What is PR?

Black (1993) maintains that PR is planned in an effort to create goodwill and mutual understanding between an organization and its publics. Jefkins and Yadin (1998) discuss the creation of understanding via knowledge. Thus PR can be described as a two-way process. Organizations can impart knowledge but they also require a response for PR to be successful.

If organizations are on one side of this relationship, who or what is on the other? An organization should be aware of parties, individuals or groups that may bear influence on their performance. These are the event's stakeholders and those that can be identified as priority targets can be referred to as target publics. The communication with each of these publics needs to be carefully tailored in order to affect a change in the opinion of that public. A traditional objective is not only to change perception from poor to good, but also from good to better. For example, even when perception is considered to be good it needs to be sustained and possibly enhanced. However, it is difficult to determine exactly what a more favourable opinion is as the perception of such is personally derived. It is also difficult to perceive favourably of certain situations, take for example those situations concerned with human suffering. A more reliable role for PR is therefore concerned with affecting changes of opinion through the dissemination of knowledge for better understanding (Jefkins and Yadin, 1998).

Another common view of PR is that it is only concerned with press relations. PR is also a corporate, financial, marketing, community and an internal activity. The primary role for event PR is to change the opinions of those parties that can bear influence on the success of the event and that can therefore include a range of different publics and the company.

PR is therefore focused on credibility and reputation and consequently with external perceptions. It is not concerned with how an organization perceives itself, but how its target publics perceive it. An organization must therefore identify how it is perceived in order to change opinion, further highlighting why PR is a two-way process.

While PR has this strength it cannot operate alone. It needs to be a part of an integrated strategy for communications that has common and cohesive themes that extend across all forms of communications. PR can support and be supported in this sense by advertising, direct marketing, sales promotions and personal selling (Yeshin, 1998; Pickton and Broderick, 2001; Fill, 2002). This is not always an easy process in practice as Clow and Baack (2004) consider, as in many organizations, the PR role concerns more than just marketing communications, there are separate PR and marketing departments. For many small event organizations this is not an issue. For example, it is common for several roles to be played by the same people, although this does not necessarily mean that integrated marketing communications (IMC) are being practiced.

PR has two key roles. On the one hand it supports marketing activity in the form of promotions and is indeed a key promotional tool for the event marketing mix and the creation of an environment in which it is easier to conduct marketing (Jobber, 1998). On the other, it is also the tool that disseminates non-promotional information to other target publics that are important to the organization (Jefkins and Yadin, 1998). For events, PR has a much wider role to play than just in its support of the marketing push. It extends to managing communications with all those organizations, groups and individuals that are considered an important factor in the successful implementation of the event (Yeshin, 1998; Pickton and Broderick, 2001; Fill, 2002). Piercy (2000) refers to PR as the creation and then maintenance of images that are relevant to different publics. These might involve communications concerned with the changing of opinion or provision of information that are targeted at local

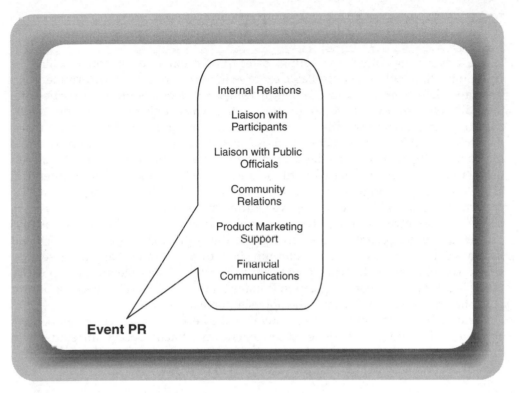

Internal Relations

Liaison with
Participants

Liaison with Public
Officials

Community
Relations

Product Marketing
Support

Financial
Communications

Event PR

Figure 5.1 The role of public relations (Masterman, 2004).

pressure groups, community leaders, financial institutions and event participants
(Figure 5.1).

Publics

PR is not optional (Jefkins and Yadin, 1998) as stakeholder groups will form their
own perceptions of an event however active that event is in generating PR. Therefore
the objective should be to improve understanding and knowledge via the active
development of PR. If stakeholders will form their own perceptions, then organizations have little choice but to try to influence those perceptions and there are two
basic approaches an organization can take. On the one hand they can be proactive in
taking the lead in disseminating knowledge to target publics. On the other, they can
be reactive and respond to target publics' requirements and needs with new knowledge. Either way, they will ultimately have little control over how their publics will
perceive them. For example, target audiences can be informed that an event will be
all the better for a change of venue next time around but no matter how well planned
and vigorous that PR activity was, the outcome cannot be managed. The organization has no final editorial control and so the best that can be achieved is an attempt
to influence that final perception and improve understanding. It is therefore important that PR, whether proactive or reactive, is a two-way process and an understanding of the levels of perception are assessed prior to any PR plans being made.

The benefits of PR

Using advertising, direct marketing, sales promotion and personal selling as communication tools is a controllable exercise in that an event can determine, compose and deliver exactly what content it wants. PR depends on third parties and their discretion over what is disseminated. In this way events rely on various media to act as catalysts and conduits to impart key PR communications to target publics. Furthermore, this process relies on those media accepting and imparting those messages in the same positive light as they are received from the event. An advertisement is designed and placed with the media exactly as the originator intended. This is because the originator is paying for that privilege in choosing to purchase advertising space. While PR incurs expenditure and is seldom totally without cost, it does not involve any bought media space. PR is designed, but is not always accepted, or indeed is not always portrayed as the originator intended and recipient media will use their discretion to determine how they will impart any of those messages. The objective is to achieve as positive a result as possible and, if a positive result is achieved, the communication is made all the more credible because a third party has endorsed it. Of course, the opposite can also be true.

The credibility that comes with positive results becomes a source of competitive advantage. The use of PR to develop customers, investment, bargaining status with buyers and suppliers, staff relations and new business can result in competitive advantage and an event that exceeds customer expectations.

The uses of PR

The uses of PR can be categorized as follows:

- *Customer retention*: using PR activity such as events, launches and media liaison to support marketing push to retain customers, grow sales and market share.
- *Investment*: using PR activities such as corporate hospitality to encourage new and further investment via the development of investor relations.
- *Bargaining status*: using PR to build brands in order to achieve better relationships with suppliers and customers.
- *Staff relations*: using PR to portray a healthy organization in order to attract and maintain a desired quality of staff.
- *Business development*: initiating and building new business through PR activity such as events, corporate hospitality and business-to-business communications in order to develop business from new or existing customers.

Functions of PR

In order to achieve the above, there are a number of functions that can be performed by PR and these can be categorized as shown below.

Opinion forming

Any one person usually has settled opinions on most aspects of life. These opinions can of course be radical, even dysfunctional, but many will be socially conforming and widely accepted by many. Any of these may be self-deduced but may also be influenced by other significant opinion formers. These opinion formers can include family, peers, colleagues, dignitaries and role models. We also know from research that opinions can also be influenced by marketing communications, including PR (Wirthlin Report, 1999). Opinions are held at various degrees of acceptance. In particular a person can hold strong opinions and these are difficult to influence and affect. PR techniques are used to attempt to influence opinion and because they can have more credibility than other forms of communications, they may have more capacity to tackle the higher barriers that are presented by firmly held and existing beliefs when communications become distorted or even dismissed.

Some media will be perceived as being more credible than others and so the skill in managing PR is in selecting appropriate messages, techniques and tools for the right target publics. Strong opinions will not be changed quickly and so the sustained effort of PR, as part of an IMC effort, is often required. For example, the task of convincing UK football target publics in the 1990s that football stadia and matches were viable entertainment customer options presented many barriers. The disasters at the 1985 European Cup Final in the Heysel Stadium, Brussels and the FA Cup semi-final at the Hillsborough Stadium in Sheffield in 1989, created widespread distrust of the safety in football stadia. In addition, there were issues of hooliganism throughout the 1970s and 1980s. Consequently, various bodies and organizations collectively realized that they needed to take action. The product of football as an entertainment was developed with the introduction of all-seater stadia, family enclosures and greater policing and stewarding, but over a long period. This development had to be communicated at several levels and over long periods. For football clubs and their own target publics in particular, this included the use of media to convey messages that demonstrated that more children and women were attending matches in an effort to show that the game was safer.

Research has demonstrated that editorial content is more credible than advertising. Earned media such as consumer reports, recommendations by peers, news articles and magazine articles for example, are generally more believable than paid media such as a television commercial, a salesperson, a direct mail leaflet (Wirthlin Report, 1999). The task of changing opinion and particularly firmly held beliefs, therefore requires the use of such PR techniques.

Internal relations

PR techniques are also important within organizations. Management needs to communicate to staff and use internal communications techniques to create better harmony in and between employees and with management itself. First, the idea that management might desire to communicate with staff at all does itself go some way to achieving this. Then the use of activities like company events, such as parties, seminars and conferences, need to be employed to develop a sharing of organizationally desired values for performance. Policies, management guidelines and controls are also disseminated internally via launches, meetings, newsletters, budgets, memoranda and reports.

Employees also want to know about job security and how their employers will meet their personal and professional expectations. Communications that inform staff of market share, new investments, new products and increased sales can achieve this. When there are negative times ahead, information concerning how the organization will trade is also important.

Internal relations are not only concerned with top down communications. Counselling management is also an important aspect and clearly communications play a key role in disputes, proposing new projects and reporting on performance.

The importance of employees for successful integrated marketing communications also highlights the importance of the development of internal relations and thus the role internal PR needs to play.

Participants

The participants of an event are target publics. The artists in a sculpture exhibition, the entrants in a triathlon, the members of an orchestra and the disc jockeys for a club night all require particular communications. They want to know the profile of the event, which other participants are taking part, which media and sponsors are involved. They also want to know whether the event is participant or spectator led (where one or the other provides the greater numbers). These types of information are important if the participants are to be satisfied in their choice of event this time and also in making a future choice next time. PR can also aid the recruitment of the elite participants that are important for spectator-led events.

Public official liaison

PR is not only concerned with mass communication. Individuals can be equally important target publics. Public officials who control municipal decision making are important for events that require any form of licence, for example, licences in connection with alcohol consumption, music and performance. Local safety, fire, police, medical and disability organizations, and their officers, are also key relationship groups that may need to be developed.

These communications will need to be sustainable over the longer term too if the events are to be repeated and even become permanent fixtures. On-going relationships with municipal officers and publicly elected representatives will be needed. For the physical construction of new venues, key publics will be planning, building control and disability officers and for events that involve a bidding process, councillors and members of parliament may also be important, and of course those governing body officials that vote.

Other important publics include any governing bodies or associations that are key to the event. For example, arts bodies awarding grants, and the supply of other resources or membership support, and national and international governing bodies of sport for sanctions, resources, supply of officials, and as the coordinators of event bidding processes.

Community relations

The local community, or that community in which an organization operates, represents another set of target publics. Principally, this is because that community is likely to be the major provider of employees. In addition, there are local pressure groups that may need to be communicated with. Examples of this type of PR activity commonly occur in the form of local sponsorships (Irwin et al., 2002).

The sponsorship of local sports teams, arts and social projects are used to develop closer links with the community and events organizations themselves can use this technique quite effectively. The Wilmington Blue Rocks minor baseball club, in the state of Delaware in the USA, sponsors local schools baseball teams and actively sends its players to local schools for coaching and community driven projects (Wilmington Blue Rocks, 2004).

Product support

This function concerns the role PR plays in the communications mix (the promotions elements of the marketing mix). Essentially, this function is the development of customer relations where communications are product related and concern the building of brand quality and reliability. Through an integrated effort, whereby PR is used to communicate the same messages that are imparted in advertising, personal selling, direct marketing activities, PR can lend support that helps the push for market position and differential. Furthermore, editorial coverage that gives details about an event, where and when it will happen, how tickets can be attained, but in addition provides positive comment, can communicate a depth of credibility that other communications cannot. It is also important to let customers know how responsive an organization is to their publics' needs and how socially responsible it is. Post-event coverage via reports and reviews can also create reassurance and develop loyalty.

Communications for product support also need to consider relations with event participants and their associated family, managers. There are also partners or associates that are important as suppliers of key resources. These include venues, sub-contractors, promoters, producers, marketing and ticketing agencies and their connections with the mix of product, price, distribution and promotion.

Financial relations

All organizations require investment in one form or another and event organizations can acquire funding from banks, governments, sponsors and shareholders. Current investors need to be informed, in some cases by law, of performance in order to keep track of their investment and its return. While PR techniques are used to disseminate this information concerning past performance, the event organization is also interested in attracting further investment, either from existing or new investors. The focus then needs to change to future strategies with the communication of positive messages when performance is buoyant as well as when times are more difficult in order to demonstrate that the organization is a stable and proactive prospect.

Crisis management

The ability of the organization to be proactive and responsive in order to manage itself through crises also relies heavily on PR communication with investors, financial media and shareholders in portraying how secure the organization is and will be. A pre-emptive approach can also be used in order to prevent crises. The Glastonbury Festival consistently uses the media to disseminate information about its security arrangements, for example. Its creation of a 'super fence' in 2002 in order to stop gatecrashers has been a newsworthy item ever since and is utilized pre-event in order to deter festival goers without tickets (Resident Advisor, 2004).

Press, television and radio relations

Last, but not least, is the responsibility of developing positive relations with the press, television and radio, the news media. These media are the vehicles that will assist in reaching other target publics. This illustrates that PR is not optional, as reports will be made when and how editors think fit. They will report to their target publics any items they deem to be newsworthy and therefore maintaining liaison with those media in order to influence what is published can be a critical exercise.

In an integrated approach to marketing communications, the whole organization is in harmony so that messages have synergy. It is therefore important to understand that whatever the message, and whichever the target public, there is always a marketing function. The functions above may or may not be directly related to product support and more concerned with corporate communication objectives but, ultimately, they are all concerned with the development of the organization so that it can perform successfully to provide its offerings to its target markets.

PR process

Whatever the nature of the communication and the function to be performed, the targets need to be identified. This is achieved via a process of target analysis, the first stage of the process of planning PR communications. The analysis extends to the identification of all of the event's stakeholders and publics and the form of communication they should receive. At this stage of planning it is important that these messages are an intrinsic part of the overall communications plan and certainly not in conflict with it. The result is a list of who should receive what communication.

The identification of key publics begins by disregarding the general public in order to ensure that more specific groups are identified. The process is then essentially a straightforward break down of broad publics stage by stage, an identification of those 'gatekeepers' that may be involved, and where publics may overlap so that consistency can be maintained in the nature of the communications. Gatekeepers are those individuals, parties or organizations that sit between an organization and it accessing its publics directly and as a result they are targets themselves. The full targeting process, adapted from Black (1993), can be seen in Figure 5.2. As an example, it is impractical for an art event to reach the whole or general public and so reachable targets are identified. Broad groups would include arts lovers, government and arts governing bodies. More definable publics would be corporate ticket buyers, the regional arts council and local arts groups. Further breakdown might produce targets of corporate ticket buyers that have previously purchased, the marketing department at the local office of the arts council and local arts group members, respectively. Gatekeepers might be identified as being an agency with a database of corporate names, the personal assistant for the director of marketing, or the secretary of one of the local arts groups, respectively. The overlapping might occur in those persons that appear in one or more of the groups. It can be seen

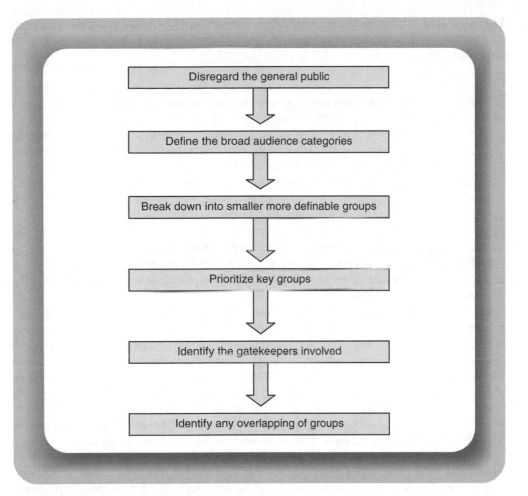

Figure 5.2 Identification of publics (adapted from Black, 1993).

that this process allows event communications to be targeted more efficiently and effectively.

An event organization's publics might consist of media, customers, employees, stockholders, suppliers, government agencies and the members and various groups of the local community in which it operates (Boone and Kurtz, 2002) as discussed earlier. Therefore, if the right message is to be disseminated to the right recipient, the way in which each organization identifies its target publics becomes a very individual and unique task. In early 2004, Leeds United plc was put into administration. Its appointed administrators, Ernst and Young, managed to sell some of the assets of the plc (including Leeds United Football Club and its stadium, Elland Road) on to new owners. A letter was sent to all shareholders informing them of the outcome of the administration. The letter incorporated a copy of a press release that gave further details of the situation including the securing of the financial security of the football club (Ernst and Young, 2004). This example of the use of two simple PR tools, a letter and a press release, shows how publics can be targeted and also how they can overlap. First, the letter was targeted only at shareholders. Secondly, the press release was also sent to media targets who, in turn, ensured that key information was targeted at significant other publics including club fans, the city, creditors, governing bodies such as the FA, the Premier League, club sponsors and suppliers.

For economic and efficiency reasons it may not be possible to reach all of the desired targets and so the analysis should also include scheduling, costing and prioritizing. Communication message content can then be developed for each target public. The result is a PR plan that is integrated into the event communications plan. Jefkins and Yadin (1998) follow a six-point process consisting of situational analysis, definition of objectives, identification of publics, selection of media and techniques, budget planning and evaluation. However, for a greater appreciation of an IMC context this process needs to be adapted. For example, while Jefkins and Yadin emphasize the importance of identifying corporate objectives and aligning the PR activity accordingly, their process would do better to begin with the identification of organizational objectives. For integrated planning it is essential that the first activity of any planning process model be the identification of an organization's overall objectives so that any specific objectives for PR can be aligned accordingly. If there are event management agencies involved then the plan has to be aligned with the owning body/client's objectives.

Another important consideration for a planning process model and an IMC approach is that PR is not planned in isolation. The selection of communications, whether they include the use of advertising, sponsorship, sales promotion, personal selling tools or PR, needs to be made so that the final combination of communications meets the objectives of the overall marketing plan. If PR tools are to help provide an effective as well as efficient integrated solution, then their planning needs to be derived out of a process that evaluates all communications options together. The proposed planning process in Figure 5.3 therefore begins with the identification of organizational objectives and follows an IMC approach.

In order to determine if PR can provide communications solutions it needs to be evaluated against all other options. This is a cost versus benefit exercise and therefore options need to be generated early in the process and then weighed up so that the best combination can be determined. In order to evaluate PR in this mix there are a number of key steps. First, internal and external publics need to be identified. This is followed by the selection of appropriate messages for each public and the tools and methods by which these messages will be disseminated, including the choice of appropriate mass, personal or interactive media with prescribed measurement criteria. Other information required at this stage includes the identification of the editorial tone, style and policies of any intended print, Internet, radio or television news media vehicles, including publishing and broadcast details such as content deadlines, frequency of publication, circulation or audience size, and target reader/listener/viewer profiles. Research into these areas will provide valuable information that will aid the selections that have to be made. The costs of implementing the PR solution can then be ascertained in order to evaluate effectiveness.

If PR tools and techniques do provide effective and efficient solutions for the overall communications plan then the specific PR objectives and strategy are re-confirmed and executed. This implementation of the PR plan involves the logistical scheduling of the selected tools and vehicles to be used, the setting of any completion deadlines and the designation of responsibilities for those personnel that are required to implement it.

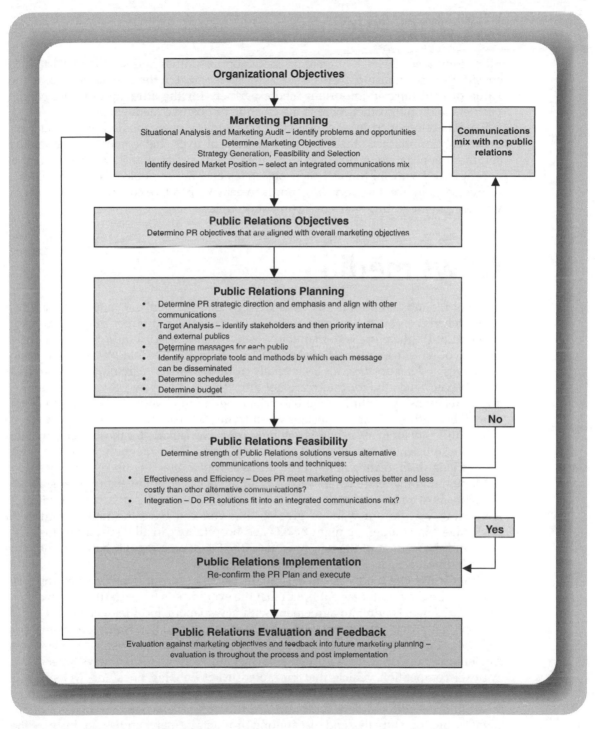

Figure 5.3 Public relations planning process. Process for the planning of public relations in integrated event marketing communications.

PR and events

PR encompasses the task of creating media opportunities and so it is important to consider the relationship events have with the media. On the one hand there is the value of recruiting all-important media partners for the attraction of commercial partners and on the other there is the creation of positive media exposure.

Events are reported in or commented on by many news media but, as has been previously established, the event has no control over that content. Whether the comment is negative or positive, some media will air or publish what they feel is appropriate for them, to meet their objectives and not the objectives of the event. Conversely, an event's overriding aim is to achieve positive coverage for the event without paying for the space or airtime it occupies.

News media

Some of the most important PR tools are provided by media such as publications, radio, television and the Internet in order to reach desired target publics. A major function of PR therefore is to maintain positive relations with these media in order that favourable communications might be achieved. Reaching mass marketing objectives and supporting sales, especially prior to the event, are not always so easily achieved when the messages are not attractive and newsworthy. Consequently, strong relationships with key media and a range of innovative techniques in order to evoke an attraction are important when trying to create the desired exposure.

The difficulty for many events is getting started, particularly for those events that do not have sufficient power to attract almost any news media attention. For new events the challenge is in creating newsworthy items as well as building up key relationships.

Maintaining the relationship once it is forged is easier but needs to be sustained. As with most relationships it often takes compromise and perhaps the giving of something you do not want to give so that you can have the favour returned. Backstage passes, opening night tickets and hospitality can all be used for this purpose and the feeding of the news media with stories on a regular basis can help to build individual as well as organizational relationships.

The recruiting of media partners is another way of forming media relationships. In this sense they are target publics in that the event needs to reach them with a particular message. Having an agreement with newspapers, local television and radio stations can provide the event with a package of promotional traffic pre-event. For example, the Vivienne Westwood fashion exhibition at the Victoria and Albert Museum in London in 2004 formed a partnership with *The Times* newspaper (UK). A ticket competition vehicle that promoted ticket booking lines and website was utilized in a quarter page space with a photograph of one of the exhibition exhibits. In addition, media partners could also contribute to the event with free entertainment by broadcasting live and distributing products or merchandise. In this way the event could gain some control over the media output by agreeing activities in a contract. However, there is a note of caution here. The larger the event, the greater the risk of alienating the media with whom there are no agreements. Therefore an event must assess the likelihood of this occurring prior to any agreement that requires exclusivity on the media partner's side.

A further consideration is the extending of a media relationship into a sponsorship. Again the word of caution is that other media interest may become depleted as a result.

One of the traditional ways in which the news media are kept informed is via the media or press release. More enhanced information packs might contain plans, schedules, photographs, video footage and data discs as appropriate. While this sort of information is despatched en-masse, it is still important to target news media that will then reach other intended target publics. For closer media relations, this information may also be supplied via individual personal contact.

There are a number of ways in which the news media can then be used to disseminate event communications. These techniques can be broadly categorized as follows (Jefkins, 1994).

Advertorials

Advertorials are paid for space but are designed to read like editorial. As a result they are not necessarily a PR technique. However, the skills of PR copywriting are valuable in creating them, thus demonstrating the importance of not creating divisions between the work of advertising and PR and adopting an integrated approach. The Athens 2004 Olympics used advertorials in order to alleviate issues that were arising out of damaging media coverage. This coverage pertained to delays in the construction of several venues for the event (Mewshaw, 2004; *The New York Times*, 2004; *The Observer*, 2004) and so advertorials were produced that extolled the benefits of visiting Greece generally and the Olympics specifically. These advertorials appeared as sections in *The Observer* (UK) and *The New York Times* (USA) in 2004 and contained reports on the beauty of the Games' facilities.

Feature articles

These are one-off contributions or regular columns that can be by-lined by a representative of the event or by a journalist who has been carefully briefed. They allow a depth and a quality of information, as they can be lengthy if required.

Advance articles

An advance notification of the event using pictures, information and competitions can provide briefer information. The New Orleans Jazz and Heritage Festival, for example, uses press releases to update key news media with line-up changes in order that they then report through to target audience ticket buyers. For the 2004 Festival, details were issued concerning the final inclusion of the group Santana and changes to dates for Lenny Kravitz and Steve Winwood (New Orleans Jazz and Heritage Festival, 2004).

Spokespeople and expertise

The use of event managers who have created a reputation for strong opinion can be popular with news media. They will be readily called when the media want a reaction to a story and therefore need to be available at any time. Targeted media, therefore, need to be kept aware of how to contact them quickly in order that this opportunity for additional exposure is taken advantage of.

Results servicing

For major sports events there are mechanisms in place that will distribute scores, reports and league standings. These results services are of general interest to news media at all levels.

Listings

There are also news media that provide entertainment guides with listings of daily, weekly or monthly events that their readers may be interested in. Keeping such media informed on a regular basis is important and may involve providing full event descriptions. However, while the likes of *Time Out* provide valuable details to target audiences, they also provide reviews and can therefore be just as negative as they can be positive in the exposure they give to an event.

Reader offers and competitions

One of the mechanisms that have continued to be popular in the events industry is the use of event tickets and hospitality for use in reader offers and/or competitions. Sales promotions techniques such as competitions can include details of the event and ticket hotlines thus aiding pre-event ticket sales. The arrangement will be mutually beneficial as media are interested in being seen to be providing extra value and services to their own publics.

Created news

When there are no opportunities to use the traditional techniques above there may be a case for creating newsworthy items. These 'hooks' will require research and the innovative use of aspects of the event in order to attract media attention.

Research in itself is of interest to the news media. Event related research can get coverage and can communicate important event messages at the same time. All PR communications need to be targeted and so the choice of media and the research topic have to be a good fit. For example, market-related research findings might be targeted at trade-related media. For example, survey results find that a significant percentage of exhibitors at an event require greater user-friendly technology. This information will be of interest in that industry and might therefore serve as a hook for appropriate media.

Creating links with other events is another hook. Pre-event PR can link into other events by acknowledging them in their communications even though there are no formal partnerships or associations. A local event may adopt a theme or simply take advantage of the popularity of a higher profile event in order to create a hook. For example, a village fete creating tag-lines that utilize associations with Henley Rowing Regatta, horse racing at Royal Ascot or tennis at Wimbledon may achieve local media coverage. For Liverpool Capital of Culture 2008 there were associations that were strategically created with events such as the Aintree Grand National, the Liverpool International Tennis Tournament, World Book Day and Noel Coward written plays, all of which were pre-event and as early as 2004 (see Case study 5.1 for further examples).

The 'millionth' customer hook is a created technique that is used quite widely. Again, Liverpool Capital of Culture 2008 provides an example where it utilized its

Case study 5.1

Liverpool: European Capital of Culture 2008

Liverpool, one of the UK's major cities, won the right to host 2008 European Capital of Culture. Its bid defeated a number of other UK cities for this privilege and, since the award on 4 June, 2003, the event has provided an impetus for city regeneration including airport expansion, a new light tram system, arena and conference centre. The city is using the event as a focus for cultural events and projects and a new organization, Liverpool Culture Company (LCC), was formed to drive the event.

LCC's communications strategies include the following:

- The title of European Capital of Culture 2008 is being used as a central theme across a number of other events of all types and scales.
- The six-year lead-in to the event is being developed with yearly Capital of Culture themes. The second year, 2004, incorporated a series of integrated events that were designed to celebrate Liverpool's multi-cultures and religious faiths. The 'Friend Ship', a model float, was constantly on the move around the city promoting the theme. The year closed with 'Reminiscence', a festival of light involving the illumination of some of Liverpool's most famous buildings. The ship visited every Liverpool school and engaged with 40 000 children. The themed years demonstrate a utilization of Liverpool's PR equity:
  - 2003 Celebrating learning: marking the centenary of Liverpool University and including challenging 150 000 people to learn a new skill
  - 2004 Faith in one city: including the Anglican Cathedral foundation stone centenary
  - 2005 Sea Liverpool: including a Mersey River Festival
  - 2006 Year of performance: Liverpool's 3rd biennial and the return of international golf to the Royal Liverpool course
  - 2007 Heritage: the city's 800th birthday with a new published history.
- A dedicated website is in operation with bid history, regeneration objectives explained, project event details and commendations of support, all designed to drive participation.
- An e-newsletter, 'Culturewise', is also targeted for event awareness and to drive participation. A database of targets was created initially via a sign-up and support mechanism instigated during the event bidding process – 150 000 names have been collected via the website and the following mechanism:
  - 'Bottle your Culture.' Celebrity participants were used to encourage all kinds of Liverpool residents to put a message in a bottle. The idea was to get people to write down what they thought of Liverpool. The ideas were used to kindle a local ownership of the bid.
  - Educational links have been integrated into the 'Friend Ship' project not just through school visits but also lesson plan materials that can be downloaded from the website.
  - Partnerships have been forged and municipal agencies integrated into the event, including Liverpool Museum, Maritime Museum, Liverpool Libraries, Everyman Playhouse, Royal Liverpool Philharmonic Orchestra, Sport Linx and the Tate art gallery so that they can utilize themes in their own activities and thus enhance the event. Other supporting organizations include the North-West Tourist Board, Everton Football Club, British Telecom, Virgin Trains and media partner the *Liverpool Echo*.

Source: Liverpoolculture.com (2004a–d)

connections with National Museums Liverpool and the latter's 1.5 millionth visitor in March 2004. This approach can utilize any number of 'records' and the news media regularly pick up on record consumption numbers for strawberries, champagne and salmon sold at English summer sporting events such as the previously mentioned Henley Regatta, Ascot and Wimbledon. The London Boat Show supplied news media with a photo of a 50-foot yacht travelling by road to Earls Court prior to the event in December 2002. The event organizers had information they wanted to communicate via the media to mass audiences that included show dates, current venue and the change of venue for the 2004 show, which it achieved via the issue of this unusual photo and a press release. Again, usable hooks also included show data such as the consumption of 50 000 pints of Guinness.

Other created techniques include the exploitation of any goodwill the event can be associated with. Links with charities and community projects can be beneficial in this way for example. By creating an award and then honouring someone of repute or at least of media interest is another form of goodwill. The goodwill is used to appeal to target audiences and is therefore considered newsworthy. In July 2004, Coca-Cola launched a '£1 million Goal Chase' in connection with the announcement of its sponsorship of The Football League in England. If the 72 teams in the league could collectively score a record 4500 goals or more in the 2004/2005 season then the £1 million would be used to fund a young, up and coming apprentice footballer at each of the clubs for one season (The Football League, 2004). This mechanism used a record as a target and goodwill in order to appeal to both the teams and their fans and as a result was able to attract media coverage across television, radio and newspapers. *The Times* (2004) even saw its way to create a pertinent heading for its article on the story, 'Goals are the real thing for sponsor'. However, to also demonstrate that media coverage cannot be controlled, later on in the year, *The Guardian* (2004) reported on the first day of the football season, that while the launch of limited edition Coca-Cola cans in the colours of each of the clubs in the Championship division of The Football League was a good idea, the soft drinks giant had seemed to have forgotten that cans cannot be taken into football grounds.

Event PR tools

In addition to the press, television and radio, PR uses media such as events, sponsorship, websites and the various methods of making contact in person. As with most tools there are advantages and disadvantages depending on their point of use.

Events

As indicated earlier, events are PR tools in themselves and a common form of communication. They require targeted invitees and provide opportunities for social interaction that can be useful in reinforcing communications. They can be expensive in both time and costs. Media launches, exhibitions, conferences, seminars and public consultations are all events that can be used effectively to communicate to target publics. When the Football League, in England, broke the news that Coca-Cola was to be its title sponsor in July 2004, it did so via a media launch in Piccadilly Circus, London. This location provided opportunities for press photographers and camera crews to feature the representatives from the respective organizations in front of the colourful backdrop of the Coca-Cola giant advertising screen that is located high on the buildings there. The screen was used to display the newly incorporated title of the newly launched competition.

Sponsorship

While sponsorship is a key provider of event revenue, it can also be used as an event PR tool. Generally, there are elements of PR in sponsorships as they generate goodwill (Jefkins and Yadin, 1998). In what often appears to be a strange combination, a fairly common example of this is large nationally significant organizations sponsoring local sports teams. The objective is to reach out to the local community that provides the organization with its employees. However large the organization is, its immediate operating environment represents a number of key local stakeholders and sponsorship can help to reach out to those groups.

Websites

Events of all kinds offer information for interested publics via other organization's websites that also offer further links to other sources of information. Clubs, teams, societies, governing bodies and rights owners, festival and concert promoters and film producers all use the Internet in this way. They are utilized as marketing communication tools to disseminate booking information as well as direct opportunities for tickets sales. However, they are also used to impart historical information, results, performance details and interactive mechanisms such as competitions for fans. Event websites are also used by the media to access press releases, by businesses for contact information and by shareholders for performance results. Some operate secure access for dedicated media contacts.

Personal contact

Personal contact can be in the form of meetings, conversations and even interventions in that they can be a cold call or involve an intercept in the street. They can be face to face, by telephone, video link and electronically by e-mail or message. The spoken word is now considered a very valuable tool as it can attain a very personal communication where there are opportunities to be persuasive and counteract any objections. There are also opportunities for relationship building because of the one-to-one medium they offer.

This opportunity regularly to communicate with publics is made easier when appropriate data are collected in order to enable better targeting. This might be through the collection of names and addresses from competition mechanisms or from previous ticket purchases.

The use of word of mouth as a tool is a planned PR activity. Commonly it is referred to as something that happens rather than it being an engineered medium. However, viral marketing is growing and the planned use of individual representatives to create word of mouth can be one of the most powerful of communication tools. For example, the planned visiting of bars by trained representatives in the Witness event communications programme was used in creating an underground feel for the event and used teaser mechanisms to provoke the passing on of key but ambiguous messages. Importantly, it was only one of several tools used in an integrated communications effort (see Case study 3.3).

PR innovation

The key stage of the PR planning process is the situational analysis. It is there that the events assets are evaluated and, as each event is unique, it is there where an advantage may be identified in the attracting of target public attention. This is where the innovation is to be gained.

Event managers have to identify what is uniquely newsworthy and of interest for the event, this amounts to the PR equity in the event (Masterman, 2004). Figure 5.4 identifies where PR equity might be gained via the categories of participants, products, programme and partners.

For there to be any equity there need to be newsworthy items that can be used to maximize target public interest. An innovative approach to PR is gained in its planning. The identification of any PR equity is critical in order for communications to be competitively successful, but the targeting of the right publics with the right communications with the right tools is just as important.

The unique and various points of interest that form the events PR equity provide the focus for these communications. Each target public should receive a tailored communication utilizing whichever points of equity evoke most interest.

The worldwide launch of Microsoft's MSN8 in October 2002 attracted worldwide media coverage (*The Guardian*, 2002a). The product was much anticipated but in order that media would carry pictures, Microsoft did not have to do too much more than utilize its own Bill Gates on stage at a New York media launch event. The stage itself was a very simple affair with nothing more than a large screen on which to demonstrate the product. It was the host that provided a hook and the equity. Celebrity Rob Lowe, who was a popular television star at the time, was also used.

Formula 1 motor racing regularly uses media launch events to attract media attention. In addition to key driver personalities and owners, the revealing of new race cars and their latest technology, attracts interest in the extra sought after pictures. For example, Ferrari, Jaguar and Renault achieved significant press coverage with pictures across a number of newspapers and magazines in 2002 with this kind of PR approach (Event, 2002; *The Mirror*, 2002a).

An unusual record was used as a hook for the Flora London Marathon in 2002. A number of newspapers picked up on the events runner who came in last. Lloyd Scott, a cancer victim himself and raising funds for Leukaemia research, finished the race five days after it had started and did so wearing a deep-sea diving suit complete with helmet. The event organizers created a photo opportunity with a spurious finish, complete with sponsorship signage for Flora and Timex. The story and pictures made the front covers as well as the sports page of several UK newspapers (*The Guardian*, 2002b; *The Mirror*, 2002b).

Evaluation of PR

Traditional PR evaluation involves measuring frequency and size of the media coverage. A general list can be seen in Figure 5.5. Specific approaches will count up the numbers of opportunities to see increasing or decreasing complaints and enquiries. Gains/losses in market share are also commonly used but at best can only be indirectly linked to any PR activity. Assessing impact value is another method

PR Equity
Participants
The artists, groups, ensembles, teams and players, either individually or collectively, are unique to any one event at that particular time. Their celebrity, prowess, expertise or other achievements and personality.
Examples:
Taking one or numbers of artists and using them as figure head(s) or spokespersons in the marketing communications plan. Specific activities might include interview features in the media, appearances at special events.
Products
The numbers, nature and availability of tickets, corporate hospitality, merchandise, whether free or priced.
Examples:
Use of sold out, sold in record time, record number of sales, exclusive merchandise, limited free merchandise on purchase or attendance/participation.
Programme
Current perspective: The nature and prospect of the competition and entertainment on offer at the next event, its content, duration, rules used, technology used, calendar position, prices, competition with other offerings (direct and indirect competition), dignitaries and celebrity attending.
Examples:
Records that might get broken, intriguing combinations for key participants in prospect. Latest technology and new rules on trial, new dates, timings and ticket prices, head to head competition and reasons for competitive advantage.
Historical perspective: Previous event programmes, competition and entertainment provided, records and achievements accomplished, data, facts and figures concerned with competition and event operations.
Examples:
Records broken, archived outstanding performances, record numbers of champagne and strawberries served, largest number of stewards to ensure safety.
Partners
The sponsors, funding and supporting shareholders and stakeholders.
Examples:
Credible sponsors make news when they are recruited and in their activities. Supporting partners may include local or national dignitaries, media, officials or celebrity. Responding to local pressure groups or the competition with comment.

Figure 5.4 PR equity (adapted from Masterman, 2004).

Attendance data	Measuring event attendance, numbers and/or quality of sponsors and participants – linking previous results if possible in order to produce indirect links to PR activity Any improvements in numbers etc. can only be indirectly linked to changes in PR at best
Equivalent advertising costs (EAC) or Equivalent media value (EMV)	Can look impressive and therefore widely used. Advertising and PR perform different functions and so they cannot be compared on an equal basis
Shift in awareness and quality of awareness	Opinion polls can reveal that awareness has increased/decreased and additional research may reveal that the depth of knowledge has increased/decreased
Media impact value	Involves applying a value to media and then multiplying that by the frequency of report. This allows higher values to be allocated to those media that are most important to the event and then comparisons across all media on that basis. The subjective nature in the application of arbitrary values for each medium concerned discredits this method
Enquiries/complaints received	Reports that generate enquiries can be directly related to PR activity. Complaints received can be indicative of how publics are receiving and perceiving event communications
Frequency of media reports	Measuring how many times an event is reported is an indication of some value when assessing which media are most likely to report
Sightings and opportunities to see	An article that appears in more than one type of medium can be multiplied by the numbers of readers, listeners, and viewers those media have in order to measure the volume of coverage. At best these are only possible sightings and the quality or depth of any understanding is not measured
Market share data	Market share may improve during PR activity but only indirect links may reasonably be inferred
Tracking – time taken to improve	A more credible approach to any of the above methods is to record and then compare results over time

Figure 5.5 Methods of evaluation for PR.

but the allocation of an arbitrary level of importance to each medium is very subjective and therefore a dubious decision.

There are also issues with the use of one of the most commonly used methods of evaluation, that of quantifying the value of the space/time achieved as if it were advertising. This consists of measuring the PR space achieved in publications, on television and radio and so on, in column inches/centimetres and minutes and calculating how much it would have cost to purchase the same as if it were bought space. There are two problems with this method. There are no actual negotiations taking place and so only rate card costs may be applied. However, rate card prices are seldom paid in the industry. The second problem is that advertising involves paying for space while PR does not and so there is incomparable credibility. However, the use of this method, Equivalent Advertising Costs (EAC), might be successfully used to evaluate the frequency and quantity of PR over time. By tracking EAC it is at least possible to see by how much PR activity has increased or not.

In an industry that is increasingly looking for return on investment, the surest methods of evaluation are by market research. The use of survey and interview methods is required in order to get usable evaluation of PR success. For example, surveying by how much target publics have been affected by PR activity is a more confidence inspiring method by which to evaluate PR. The fact that research can be expensive does go some of the way to explain why it is not a common practice in the industry. However, PR is considered an important tool and arguably the most important an event has for communication purposes and so any feedback on its effectiveness should be important. The case for conducting thorough research therefore needs to be made.

Summary

In a competitive industry an innovative approach towards communications is essential. The innovative use of PR can provide a critical level of credibility that is not obtainable via other types of communication and is therefore arguably the most important form of communication an event has at its disposal.

The role of PR extends beyond that of the other forms of communication that are ostensibly concerned with the support of products and sales. While PR is a very important function of the promotions mix, it also plays a wider role in delivering other communications to publics that have a bearing on the event's success. An event's target publics can therefore include investors, pressure groups, employees and partners and communications with them can involve more than just the promotion of products.

Innovative communications can be developed from the unique attributes of the event. This is a form of equity and provides the basis for the style, tone and content of each communication. In turn there are various tools by which these communications can be disseminated. PR tools can access both mass and personal media and therefore offer a broad range of opportunities to communicate the event. Alongside the traditional methods lie the innovative applications that are offered by developing technology. The Internet and the future promise of wireless communications offer additional and welcome opportunities. For PR to be successful, however, there need to be strategic choices. The communications that are developed in order to change target public opinion are clearly critical, but their success is dependent upon strategically selecting the right communication, for the right target public via the right range of tools.

Discussion points

- Identify one piece of event breaking news in any one form of medium:
  - ○ consider who initiated the news and for what purpose
  - ○ identify the type of techniques implemented to create the news
  - ○ analyse the editorial stance and determine to what extent the piece is to the event's advantage.
- Identify all the target publics for Liverpool 2008, European Capital of Culture and determine what communication content will be of most interest to each.
- You are the public relations manager of a large international exhibition and conference venue management group. Your organization has just taken over a locally owned, long established, but ailing medium-sized venue that is based in another part of the country. There are no plans to change the business significantly but you do intend to invest in refurbishment and hopefully expand the business. In the short term, however, there will be some job losses as your organization seeks to increase efficiency and make the business more competitive:
  - ○ identify your key target publics
  - ○ what messages would you wish to communicate?
  - ○ how would you deal with the issue of the job losses?
  - ○ what techniques might you use, both in the short and long term?
- You are a public relations consultant to a large provincial city involved in making a bid to stage the World Athletic Championships. The city has a long-term strategy for sport and bidding for major sports events. Since losing out in the bid for the same event 8 years ago there have been improvements to the city's infrastructure and facilities:
  - ○ what key factors will you need to consider?
  - ○ what research will you require?
  - ○ what techniques and messages with which target publics will you use?

References

Black, S. (1993) *The Essentials of Public Relations*. Kogan Page.

Boone, L. and Kurtz, D. (2002) *Contemporary Marketing 2002*. Thomson Learning.

Clow, K. and Baack, D. (2004) *Integrated Advertising, Promotion, and Marketing Communications*, 2nd edn. Pearson Prentice Hall.

Ernst and Young (2004) Letter to all shareholders of Leeds United plc, 19 March, 2004.

Event (2002) 100% Renault. March.

Fill, C. (2002) *Integrated Marketing Communications*. Butterworth-Heinemann.

Football League, The (2004) Breaking News/League News www.football-league.premiumtv.co.uk (accessed 30 July, 2004).

Guardian, The (2002a) MSN8 Launch. 2 November.

Guardian, The (2002b) Flora London marathon. 20 April.

Guardian, The (2004) The soft drinks giant Coca-Cola, to help celebrate their sponsorship. . . 7 August.

Irwin, R., Sutton, W. and McCarthy, L. (2002) *Sport Promotion and Sales Management.* Human Kinetics.

Jefkins, F. (1994) *Public Relations Techniques*, 2nd edn. Butterworth-Heinemann.

Jefkins, F. and Yadin, D. (1998) *Public Relations*, 5th edn. FT/Prentice Hall. Ch 5.

Jobber, D. (1998) *Principles and Practice of Marketing*, 2nd edn. McGraw-Hill.

Liverpoolculture.com (2004a) www.liverpoolculture.com/newsletter/2004/index.html (accessed 31 March, 2004).

Liverpoolculture.com (2004b) www.liverpoolculture.com/get-news-and-events/faith-in-one-city.htm (accessed 31 March, 2004).

Liverpoolculture.com (2004c) www.liverpoolculture.com/get-news-and-events/friendship.htm (accessed 31 March, 2004).

Liverpoolculture.com (2004d) www.liverpoolculture.com/get-the-lowdown/byc.htm (accessed 31 March, 2004).

Masterman, G. (2004) *Strategic Sports Event Management: An International Approach.* Butterworth-Heinemann.

Mewshaw, M. (2004) Olympian orphosis. *The New York Times Magazine.* 7 March.

Mirror, The (2002a) Irvine's axe threat. 5 January.

Mirror, The (2002b) Worth the weight. 20 April.

New Orleans Jazz and Heritage Festival (2004) www.nojazzfest.com/pr (accessed 8 April, 2004).

New York Times, The (2004) Greece advertising supplement. 7 March.

Observer, The (2004) Greece: Going for Olympic Gold. 29 February.

Pickton, D. and Broderick, A. (2001) *Integrated Marketing Communications.* Pearson Education.

Piercy, N. (2000) *Market-led strategic Change: Transforming the Process of Going to Market.* Butterworth-Heinemann.

Resident Advisor (2004) www.residentadvisor.net/news.asp?ID=5432 (accessed 18 November, 2004).

Times, The (2004) Goals are the real thing for sponsor. 29 July.

Wilmington Blue Rocks (2004) Marketing partnership opportunities. www.bluerocks.com/MKTG%20Brochure%202004.pdf (accessed 18 November, 2004).

Wirthlin Report (1999) Current trends in public opinion from Wirthlin Worldwide. March, 9 (3).

Yeshin, T. (1998) *Integrated Marketing Communications.* Butterworth-Heinemann.

Chapter 6
E-Marketing Communications

Objectives

- To consider the variety of event communication opportunities offered by new electronic media
- To recognize the importance of the Internet as a medium for mass and personal communication
- To understand the uses and limitations of new media and methods

Introduction

Although much of e-marketing communications fits into the categories of traditional communication methods, for example, the Internet provides another medium for mass advertising and e-mail provides a cheaper method than post for direct marketing, the exponential growth in the use of electronic tools and media and their increasing sophistication warrant the need for a separate and specific discussion.

This chapter will consider how e-marketing communications create the opportunity to market the event to not only live but also virtual customers. Websites can add longevity to an event with film footage and year round sales opportunities and so build customer loyalty. Additionally, they provide ticket sales mechanisms that can also capture attention. They can provide live coverage of the event and another revenue stream from a new virtual market that can be on the other side of the world. The Internet, therefore, can create a blurring of the boundaries between product, promotion and distribution and the opportunity for highly creative and innovative event marketing strategies.

It is the interactivity and precise targeting capabilities of electronic media coupled with, in many cases, its relatively lower cost that has driven its growth against traditional media. However, the greatest benefits are to be gained when e-communication tools are used alongside traditional methods to give additional contact points and a reinforced consistent message. The value of each separate tool is leveraged in this way to create a greater synergy and effectiveness.

The e-marketing tools that are most appropriate for events products are described below along with a discussion of their uses, advantages and disadvantages.

Websites and 'brochureware'

An event organization's website can serve many functions for many different target groups. It can be a source of information for employees, investors, sponsors and researchers as well as for current and prospective customers. The website can communicate about the organization and its product offerings in an interactive way allowing the Internet user to select the type of information they wish to access and creating a dialogue between the organization and the user when needed. At its most simple the website can be merely an online version of a printed brochure. However, to make use of the unique properties of the Internet, websites should be far more sophisticated using regularly updated information of interest to the various target groups and displaying this using multimedia images, text and sound. Interactivity can be used to gather data from visitors, respond to requests and to take orders. Effective websites generate loyal visitors who return on a regular basis to access new information. This does not necessarily mean that they are loyal to the company or its products but it does mean that a relationship has been created that can be leveraged in the future.

The Internet as a marketing communication tool is particularly important in the information search and evaluation stages of the decision-making process. An Internet user is actively searching for information on a type of product or service and will gather that information easily from a number of websites in order to compare and make a decision. There is often, therefore, a clearer link between this form of communication and purchase behaviour than with other methods.

Uses for events

Organizations involved in the creation of events are likely to showcase their services using a brochureware website. The website will include much of what would be in a printed brochure in terms of services offered, contact details but can also demonstrate expertise by showing previous events through photographs, video clips and testimonials along with client lists and links to client websites. Brochureware content is enough to drive people to the site if they are already searching for this type of service but, in order to gain the attention of others, richer content is needed. This may be advice offered and updated regularly on issues related to the events. For example, an organization specializing in team-building and motivational events would do well to include content which demonstrates the importance of these activities. This may include regularly updated articles from the press and academia on workforce motivation along with examples of what can be achieved following such events. This type of additional value content should retain a higher level of objectivity and distance from the organization than promotional literature in order to give it credibility and hence value. For example, the website of LVS Events includes details of the services they offer enhanced by some sample case studies of past clients and an online enquiry form. They also offer advice on event organization through a page offering 'ten easy steps for organizing events'. Kinetic Event Solutions offer a 'VIP area' for existing customers which, upon registration, provides additional value through live delegate registration tracking, downloadable presentations and photos, post-event feedback and a number of other services.

Exhibition organizers and venues have used the idea of 'virtual' exhibitions to show case their product to exhibitors and attendees. Here the exhibition is recreated in an online format and used as a taster for the real thing. There is also some growth in e-exhibitions as a replacement for the actual exhibition and this aspect of promotional events will be covered in Chapter 11.

The websites of event venues need to cater for a number of distinct stakeholder groups. This will include past and potential attendees, exhibitors, sponsors, promoters, performers and the media. The attendees will need easily accessible information on 'what's on'. The promoters and performers will require some information on past and current events but will also need details on the capacity of the venue, facilities and location. The media will need to be able to access up-to-date press releases and potential sponsors will require information on target audiences, sponsorship packages and benefits. The home page of any venue website, therefore, needs to direct visitors to the appropriate areas for their needs and ensure that links into the website take each group to the appropriate information. Within the attendees visiting the website there is likely to be a core group of users who return regularly to view updated event programmes. This will be an important target market for theatres, concert venues and exhibition centres and is often made up of those about to make a purchase. The key aspects of the website for these users will be the ease of searching via dates, event type etc. and the content of the information provided on the events in the programme. This could include a description, reviews, interviews with performers and participants. A key facility for this group will also be the opportunity to purchase tickets online. A study of the performance segment of the sports industry, however, reports that very little emphasis is placed on interactive Internet marketing. Sports organizations lag behind the rest of the entertainment industry in terms of online consumer/seller relationships and in particular online ticket sales (Brown, 2003).

The links from and to a website are vital aspects of their usability and interest. These links may not directly encourage purchase but they do encourage repeat visits and liking for the site. For example, a theatre website may include links to the sites of the theatre groups who are performing, links to art associations or even links to other venues in the area. Although these links may create traffic for the competition, a reciprocal arrangement ensures that the total market grows and in effect makes competitors into partners. Supporting the consumer in their search and evaluation of alternative offerings can be an important factor in developing loyalty and liking for the website and the organization.

Many events will be accessible online via a number of websites. For example, the European tour of a successful music group will be listed on the event organizer's/promoter's website, the venues' websites and the performers' website. This is not necessarily created through links but merely through the inclusion of similar content. One aspect of Internet marketing communications is therefore to ensure that all relevant websites are provided with accurate information on the event in a usable and consistent format.

The characteristics of a good business website can be summarized as (Hart, 2003):

1 Clear strategic objectives for the site which fit with other communication methods
2 Customer led rather than product driven content providing different areas for different customer groups

3 Value added content updated regularly and customized for different user groups
4 Content management ensuring a dynamic rather than static site
5 Data quality management
6 Professional design and usability projecting a consistent corporate image
7 High interactivity and functionality allowing customers to contact key personnel in the organization and each other
8 Easy to navigate and quick to download with regular usability testing
9 E-communications strategy to complement the website
10 Effective marketing of the website.

Advantages

Websites for event organizations provide a relatively inexpensive medium for reaching a wide target audience. The number of people online is growing rapidly and now includes a wide range of demographic groupings as well as many international markets. The web has been one of the major factors in the increase in event tourism as sports fans, festival goers and conference delegates can now easily access information on events worldwide alongside online travel companies.

Websites are also popular due to the apparent ease of measuring their effect. Software can be used not only to count the number of visits to a site but to build up a picture of the visitor through the way they use the site, which site they came from and which site they moved to. 'Cookies' can be used to customize the site to each visitor ensuring that the information they require appears when they access the site. The website can also be used to gather customer data to be used in other communications methods through online competitions, information request forms and site registration requirements. Non-ticketed events that often find difficulty in maintaining contact with attendees have used photos posted on the website to encourage attendees to visit the site and to provide contact information in order to download their photo.

The flexibility offered by websites is also an advantage over other traditional media where lead times for content changes may be months. A website can be updated or amended almost instantaneously and can therefore reflect topical issues, provide real time images and react to user inputs and requests.

The opportunity for interactivity offered by websites can be capitalized on within the events industry through, for example, e-commerce facilities, reservations and ticket sales, Internet communities and chat rooms, question and answer sessions and live broadcasts. Users can choose to interact anonymously or can opt in to a personalized service through online data collection.

A website will only be successful if it is integrated with the rest of the marketing communications methods. For example, other online and offline methods need to be used to encourage visits to the site through banner advertisements, web links, advertising campaigns and merchandise including the web address. The site can be used to create more involvement with advertising campaigns and sales promotions through related content, downloads, games and competitions. Customer data gathered via the website can, with the user's permission, be used in direct marketing campaigns and content posted on the website can serve public relations objectives. For example, the Tulip Festival in Wynyard, Tasmania used a number of techniques to create interest on its website and to link this to other aspects of the campaign. A web cam was used to encourage return visitors to the site by showing the daily progress of a growing tulip. Involvement was encouraged by the facility to purchase a tulip bulb online to be planted in 'the avenue of tulips'. This also raised funds from a worldwide target market including many who would not attend the festival. An online competition was included to gain interest, attract visitors to the site and to obtain visitor data. The website content was further integrated with a teaser television campaign, town signage, television, radio and press features as well as more unusual activities such as distributing tulips at the airport. All of the activities and the website were integrated under the umbrella of the rebranded festival 'Bloomin Tulips' (Wynyard Tulip Festival, 2004).

The opportunity to integrate with and leverage additional value from other communication methods is an important advantage of website marketing.

A well-constructed and accessible website can move a prospective customer through all the stages of the decision-making process from need recognition to actual purchase and on through to post-purchase reassurance and loyalty. For example, the Edinburgh International Festival website provides the visitor with information likely to create the need to be entertained through taster video clips and offers alternatives in the range of events involved in the festival. These can be selected through searches relating to dates, times, art form and content. The tickets can be booked online and post-purchase attendees are encouraged to post their comments, reviews, read the reviews of others and browse the photos of the festival. This multi-functional nature of websites makes them a unique communications method and a very powerful marketing tool.

Disadvantages

Although websites have many advantages there are some drawbacks which also need to be considered. A website, no matter how state of the art it is, should not be used to replace other methods of marketing communications or even as a reason to cut down on the use of other types of media. This is partly due to the staunch media and shopping habits of consumers (Reedy et al., 2000), but also due to the fact that a successful website relies on users accessing it. The website, therefore, needs to be promoted using other online and offline media. This may in fact increase the overall communications budget, at least in the short term. Therefore, although the website itself can be created inexpensively the additional costs of attracting visitors to it can be considerable.

Websites need to be regularly maintained with updated and changing content and features. Out-of-date information or content that rarely changes may negatively impact on the image of the organization. Therefore, if the resources are not available to maintain the site it may be better to opt not to have one until they are. It is also important to delete web pages when necessary as information relating to last year's events can confuse this year's prospective clients. Many local authority event websites, among others, create new pages each year for their festivals but neglect to delete the old ones. These are readily found by prospective customers via Internet searches creating misunderstandings over dates and content and leading to an unprofessional image.

Websites are in the public domain and therefore any information posted on them (unless protected through user registration) is accessible to anyone. This has led to a generally more open business philosophy and positive implications for consumers and employees but does also mean that competitors will regularly scan websites for information that can be used strategically. It is important therefore to provide open and honest information to those who need it while, at the same time, using caution in posting sensitive material. A quick overview of event organizer websites where the main customers are business clients suggests that pricing information is often seen as sensitive. These same sites, however, are happy to make public their event ideas and even their business plans and future strategies which could be used by competitors to gain advantage. On the whole, strategic intent should not be specifically detailed but tactical aspects such as price and product information are needed by the client and is of little use to competitors. Even when the product is bespoke, an idea of price levels can be given through previous examples of events undertaken and general rates. Event companies whose main audience are consumers will generally list prices on their website and in doing so facilitate bookings online. However, this is not appropriate for all event products. For example, sponsorship package details with pro forma 'sign up and pay' type approaches used on event websites do detract away from the tailored opportunity event sponsorship should be offering.

As well as the threat from competitors using the website as a source of intelligence, a further disadvantage of the Internet is that it showcases the organization's products against a large number of competing products. The alternatives available to the searching customer are easily accessed and compared. For many of the early Internet companies this led to price wars and the subsequent failure of many initially successful companies. However, this only emphasizes the need to develop and communicate a sustainable competitive advantage through factors other than price. Competitive advantage based on niche marketing, specialization, innovation, quality or service levels, for example, is far easier to sustain and will stand up against other offerings.

The sheer volume of information on the Internet can detract from the impact of website content, however, Internet clutter is less of a problem than in the traditional media as the users themselves are selecting what they access. Despite this the Internet user is fickle and will not spend valuable time on a site which is not attention grabbing, fast at downloading and easy to navigate. The design of the homepage is vital in drawing the user in and persuading them to access further information from the site.

Although the Internet has the advantage of reaching a wide international market, this can lead to problems in targeting the required audience. This can be overcome through careful use of search term listings, links with other websites and the use of web directories. These are covered later in this chapter.

A final word of warning relates to the non-governed nature of the Internet. There are no overseeing bodies or associations ensuring the truthfulness, acceptability and ethics of website content as there are with other media. This has greater implications for Internet public relations and word of mouth but also affects website content. Content which is, perhaps inadvertently, offensive or misleading may be negatively affecting site visitors without being brought to the attention of the website owner. This may be true of sites which have adult content, as this is the target audience for their events, but can be accessed by younger Internet users. For example, the websites for some music events may reproduce explicit lyrics or use sexual or violent imagery in line with the performers image. As with the event itself the website may need to carry warnings of its content and suitability.

Other Internet tools

As well as the use of websites, the Internet offers other communication opportunities. These are generally forms of advertising using the Internet and the websites of others as the host. Internet advertising uses a variety of techniques including banner advertisements, pop-ups and click-throughs. It also encompasses the use of search engine listings and directories to encourage visitors to the website. A further aspect of the Internet is the opportunity for partnership marketing through joint or consortium websites, referral sites and online agencies or e-tailers.

Uses for events

The main objective of Internet advertising is to generate traffic to the website. Strategic Internet advertising can ensure that appropriate audiences are targeted by the careful selection of carrier websites and directories. These advertisements, whether pop-ups, banner advertisements or links, will encompass a direct response feature in that the user can immediately click through to the website. Although offline promotion may also encourage visitors to the website, it rarely has the benefit of allowing immediate access. However, direct response digital television does have this facility.

Events organizations can use a variety of other sites to advertise their products. These range from the websites of other business organizations such as venues, caterers and ticket agencies to local, national and international tourism websites, trade associations and government agencies. For example, Ticketmaster.com carries banner advertisements for a variety of events including, at one point, a syndicated advertisement for museum exhibitions. Ticketmaster.co.uk has feature advertisements and publicity for specific shows and packages alongside advertisements for travel companies and credit cards.

These sites are useful for events with a wide appeal, but banner advertisements and pop-ups can be expensive and are often ignored. A more useful online promotional method for many event organizations is to use directories and search engines to encourage visitors to the website. These will be generally cheaper than advertising on a popular site and are more focused in their targeting. Directories range in form and scope and include local business directories, travel guides and international trade directories specific to the industry. For example, Medicalconferences.com provides a specialist website for this type of conference worldwide and provides free publicity for any conference organizer willing to register their event. Another directory example is given in Figure 6.1.

Search engines also offer paid-for advertising in the form of 'featured sites' which appear more prominently in search result listings when particular 'adwords' are used in the search term. These are relatively expensive but are often necessary when first launching a new website. One benefit of these bought search terms is that usually they are only paid for by click through rate (user sees the listing and clicks to enter the website) rather than by the number of times they are viewed. Search engine marketing (SEM), therefore, requires an understanding of the users' search behaviour and has accordingly moved from the realm of web designer to marketer (Smith and Taylor, 2004).

The art of obtaining natural listings on search engines or search engine optimization (SEO) has become a business in its own right with agencies specializing in website design that makes use of the various ways search engines search and generate results lists. Search engine providers constantly refine their systems in order to overcome some of the unethical practices used to get a website to the top of the list. For example, one of the more important factors looked for when ranking searched for websites is the number of relevant sites linking into the website. The practice of link farms and link exchange programmes which create vast numbers of links regardless

Costs

Page	Size	x1 ($)	x3 ($)	x12 ($)
Home	300 x 60		1350	4000
Organizer	300 x 60		1100	3250
Service provider	300 x 60		825	2475
Newsletter sponsor		500	1400	4500
Newsletter listing		350	950	3150

Note: Above dimensions are in pixels and are width x height. Frequency is by month. Prices are quoted in US dollars.
Advertiser's Special Bonus: Link to advertiser home page (online advertisements only), free listing on exhibitions-world.com

Readership Analysis		Geographical Analysis	
Trade & industry decision maker	32%	Europe	33%
Marketing director	25%	N. America	29%
Manufacturer	19%	Pan-Asia	26%
Exhibition organizer	9%	China	10%
Trade & industry association	7%	Other	2%
Information centre	4%		
Foreign commercial office	2%		
Product manager	2%		

Figure 6.1 International online directory example.
Exhibitions Round the World is a search directory of over 6000 exhibitions taking place in 100 countries – available in both print and online editions. It is a reference tool for trade show visitors and exhibitors and provides a promotion platform for organizers, venue and exhibition service providers. *Source:* www.exhibitions-world.com.

of relevance is frowned upon by search engine providers and can lead to websites being banned from the search listings. However, encouraging relevant and useful sites to link to the organization's website should be part of the continual website management process. Most websites will provide web links for free if the link adds value to their own site visitors and if the link is reciprocated. The other side to this process is to discourage non-relevant sites from linking to a site. This is hard to enforce, although larger organizations have managed to do so through the legal system. For example, Universal Studios have successfully prevented other websites from linking directly to movie clips and images on their site, although they have not been able to prevent sites from linking to their homepages.

To check the number and type of websites with links to your own site you can simply type 'link:' followed by the website URL into the search engine. All linking websites will then be listed. For example, link:www.mardigras.org.au results in 121 linking sites to the Sydney Mardi Gras website and these include travel companies, gay and lesbian sites and accommodation. The Edinburgh International Festival has 540 links through google search and includes, travel guides, media, hotels and special interest music and arts sites.

Although there are a number of factors which can be incorporated into website design to increase its chances of a good search engine listing, most search engines are wise to any tricks and scams and will penalize for them. The best rule of thumb is that 'content is king' and if the content is right then the search engine listing will follow (Grant and McBride, 2000).

A related alternative to web links and advertising is the use of referral websites. A website is chosen that clearly targets a desirable market for the event and a referral link is negotiated. The link is paid for on a piece rate each time a user clicks through to the event organization's website. Payment can be made simply on click through or on purchase made. This type of referral agreement encourages the linking website to give more prominence to the link and therefore encourages more visitors and limits costs by only being paid for when it is used. For example, a referral link to an events website may be negotiated with an accommodation or travel provider, a special interest group or the websites of other events.

Smaller events organizations may choose not to have their own website but to join a web marketing consortium of similar or related organizations or to make greater use of online directories and agencies. These options reduce the costs to the organization and can increase value to the visitor through the ease of accessing a range of information in one place. There are many online agencies for consumer event ticket sales which also provide promotional opportunities and information. These agencies will either charge for the service through a price premium paid for by the customer or through a percentage of the ticket price or both. In business-to-business events the many trade associations can provide an Internet platform for their members.

Advantages

The benefits of using the Internet as an advertising medium are that it can very precisely target relevant customer groups through the selection of the carrying websites. This overcomes the disadvantage of the untargeted nature of the Internet generally in that through online advertising, web links and referrals the visitors to the website can to some extent be controlled and monitored.

The effectiveness of online advertising can be easily monitored through various web metric programmes giving an indication of online customer behaviour as well as simple counts.

Media cynical consumers have a greater trust in the integrity of search engine listings and links from credible websites than in traditional media messages, as these appear as more objective information rather than promotion.

The often more effective method of web links, referrals and shared sites can cost relatively little and can also help the organization to form valuable partnerships.

A final benefit is the opportunity offered to recoup some of the costs of website design and maintenance through selling advertising space and links on the organization's own website.

Disadvantages

One of the main drawbacks in online advertising is that, in a medium which is based on user choice and selection, unsolicited advertisements can be viewed as intrusive and annoying. This is certainly the case for pop-up advertisements, the use of which now appears to be in decline. Pop-up advertisements can delay the visitor's access to a website and can be difficult to close and therefore block other information.

The visitor loses patience not necessarily with the advertiser but with the hosting website. Many websites are therefore no longer allowing this type of Internet advertising and have limited advertisers to banner and feature advertisements which are more suitably integrated into the website content. This loses the attention getting benefits of pop-ups but is likely to result in more genuine interest click-throughs.

The annoyance factor of Internet advertisements has led to a proliferation of advertisement blocking software available at little or no cost to the Internet user (O'Connor and Galvin, 2001). This software can block pop-ups and can detect advertisement content in banner advertisements and prevent it from being displayed. This is a benefit to the Internet user wasting download time on graphic advertisements but is bad news for the web-based advertisement agencies and those organizations spending a growing proportion of their communications budget on Internet advertisements that may never be seen.

Internet public relations

As well as an advertising medium, the Internet should also be incorporated into the communications plan as a valuable platform for public relations.

Uses for events

Features, reviews and news generated around the event and the organization should be regularly fed to other websites in the same way as it would be issued to the print, television and radio media. These websites will add the information to their content creating additional exposure, interest and credibility. News should also be a permanent feature of the organizations' website and should include all current media releases plus relevant news from further afield providing a source of information and therefore extra value for the visitor.

A list of Internet media needs to be developed and maintained to ensure that the relevant publics are kept informed and to maximize exposure and impact. These will not necessarily be merely the online versions of traditional media (newspapers, television channels etc.) but will be wider reaching, encompassing the websites of other event related organizations. These may include the websites of arts and sports associations, city guides, educational institutions, venues, fan clubs and clients. News about the company's successes, employee activities and the events themselves need to be shared as widely as possible and these can be generated internally or gathered by scanning existing media. For example, a favourable review printed in a local newspaper can achieve global exposure if circulated via the Internet. The Internet media releases should be produced following the same guidelines as for public relations generally but can encompass multimedia content as appropriate.

Advantages

As with the traditional media, website authors are constantly looking for content to add value and currency to their sites. Therefore, well-targeted media releases are often welcomed and once a relationship has been established are actively sought out.

One of the main benefits of Internet PR is that information can be uploaded and accessed almost immediately by a global audience. There is no production time lag and therefore new and updated information is available as it happens and at no extra cost (Ihator, 2001). This can be very useful in pre-empting or counteracting negative publicity.

Any media releases can include a web link for further information and can therefore be used to generate website traffic. This can encourage new target markets and again increase exposure and interest.

Disadvantages

One of the disadvantages of publicity generally is the lack of control that the organization has over content. Information may be provided to relevant websites in a ready to use format but is likely to be edited and added to by many in order to present an objective viewpoint. This enhances the credibility of the website as a source of information but also means that negative publicity may also be included. This problem is no different from the traditional media but is exacerbated by the ungoverned, unfiltered nature of much of the Internet. Monitoring and controlling what is published on the Internet about the organization and its events is very difficult. It is impossible to prevent publication of what could be untrue rumours and stories so it is doubly important to monitor and respond to these, where necessary, as quickly as possible through websites with accepted credibility for each targeted public.

E-mail marketing

Contacting and being contacted by potential and existing customers by e-mail has seen exponential growth as a communications medium. Very few event companies worldwide are now without e-mail capability and the majority of individuals in a large number of countries around the world can be contacted via work or home e-mail addresses. E-mail marketing is often linked to Internet marketing in that access to and interaction with a website creates the initial e-mail contact by registering with the site, information requests, queries or online ordering. However, target market e-mail addresses can be requested at any point of contact, for example, through sales promotion participation and are routinely included in organization contact details.

E-mail marketing is therefore the use of an electronic medium for direct marketing as it entails personalized contact with a target audience.

Uses for events

E-mail marketing is used by many event marketers to contact previous event attendees with offers, information and to gain feedback. In order to do this the event organizer needs to be able to capture e-mail addresses and gain the addressees' permission to contact them. This can be done relatively easily for online ticket purchasers, organizational clients and events where registration is required, but is more difficult when tickets are purchased in person or by phone or indeed for non-ticketed events. In these situations other means of gathering e-mail addresses can be used. For example, digital photos can be taken at the event and in return for the attendee's e-mail address the photo can be accessed online and sales promotions can be used in the form of competitions and prize draws which require the winner to be notified via e-mail. The collected e-mail addresses can then only be used for marketing purposes if the recipient has given the organization permission to contact them in this way. This now needs to be done through 'opt-in' rather than 'opt-out' choices and the opportunity for opted in addressees to opt out needs to be repeated regularly. This is not only a legal requirement in most countries but also makes good sense from a customer relationship point of view. Unsolicited e-mail or spam can alienate potential customers and even those who have opted in may have forgotten they have done so. A post-event evaluation e-mail can be a useful way of obtaining permission to contact the attendee with further information. The attendee providing the organization with their e-mail address is not in itself permission to use it for sending unsolicited information.

Successful e-mail marketing uses carefully targeted messages to ensure that recipients only receive offers and information of interest. These can include graphics and audio to gain attention but these should be used carefully due to file size and company filters of attachments. Requests via e-mail for information, advice, quotations, tickets etc. need to be responded to quickly and in a personalized manner. E-mail is viewed by many as an alternative to the telephone rather than the postal system and therefore an almost immediate response is expected.

Advantages

E-mail communications can be tailored to the needs of individual customers and can be effective at all stages of the decision-making process. However, the response to e-mailed information is improved if the recipient is already aware of the organization or the event. This may be as a past customer or through visiting the website or through being exposed to advertising and sales promotions. E-mails should therefore be integrated with the rest of the communications campaign and maintain a consistent overall message and image.

E-mail is one of the cheapest and quickest methods for reaching a large number of recipients with a personalized message and also provides the opportunity for direct response.

Disadvantages

The problems with using e-mail stem largely from its overuse and misuse. Inbox clutter and e-mail spam (unsolicited e-mails) create target audiences who are quick to press the delete button. In order to cut through this clutter the sender needs to be recognized by the recipient through previous contacts and the sender needs to recognize that they have given permission for their e-mail address to be used in this way. The headline of the e-mail needs to get the reader's attention and the body text should be short and relevant to the reader with links to the website in order to gain further information or take advantage of the offer. E-mails should always include a signature, name and contact details rather than being sent anonymously from the company and should always offer the opportunity to unsubscribe or opt out.

The database used for e-mailings requires constant updating and cleaning to ensure the legality of the contacts being made and the effectiveness of correct targeting. Repeated opt-out and permission renewal requests can help in filtering out the less likely prospects.

A disadvantage of direct e-mail over direct postal mail is its intangibility and transience. Although images can be sent via e-mail, samples and free gifts cannot. The text or image can be viewed and deleted in a matter of seconds whereas as letters, brochures, programmes, merchandise sent by post may remain 'on display' in the home or office for days or weeks.

Event companies that use e-mail to replace other personal selling methods may be saving money but will lose out on the relationship building and persuasive benefits of telephone or face-to-face contact. This is particularly true in business-to-business communications where e-mail has its uses but can never achieve the results that phone calls and personal visits can.

A final word of caution is also needed in launching a large-scale e-mail campaign without estimating the resources needed to respond. The speed of design and implementation and the low cost of this method mean that large-scale campaigns can be instigated by relatively small companies. If successful this can lead to an audience response that cannot be dealt with and subsequently may result in bad publicity, negative word-of-mouth and a detrimental company image.

E-viral marketing

Closely related to the use of direct e-mail is the use of e-mail as the conduit for word-of-mouth (or word-of-mouse) campaigns. This type of creation or encouragement of word-of-mouth is known as viral marketing. The premise behind viral marketing is that the market itself will spread information if it is presented in the right way. In order to do this, the organization needs to use or create an idea linked to the event or organization and then communicate that idea to a small but carefully selected target audience (opinion leaders in the form of individuals, groups or websites). The idea for an e-viral campaign can be text, a graphic, audio or video clip or website link, but it needs to be attention getting. This can be achieved through the use of humour, shock, enlightenment, information, special offers, or interaction. The targeted audience (or seeds) finds something of interest in the idea and therefore passes on the information to others, these others then pass it on and so on, the virus spreads. Although, not limited to e-mail this method is one of the fastest for spreading word-of-mouth as each recipient can forward on the information quickly, at no cost and to many contacts.

Uses for events

E-viral marketing can be a very effective way of generating interest in an event and is particularly successful in youth markets where the 'inside' word on events and performers is far more persuasive than any overt marketing communications. For example, campaigns can be seeded at music and entertainment specialist websites where opinion leaders in those markets can access the idea and pass it on. The idea can be in the form of a humorous photo taken at an event, a teaser clip linked to an advertising campaign or simply a topical joke. For the campaign to work the forwarded e-mail should make some connection with the event. For example, the Commonwealth Games website provides visitors with the opportunity to use its interactive e-postcards to send messages to friends with a photo from the previous Games (Commonwealth Games Federation, 2004). This works better if the connection is subtle and underplayed through the simple addition of a website link, although more overt encouragement, using competitions and games and the promise of more of the same, can be used to gain more information through contact details. A viral marketing clip of the Budweiser advertisement first shown during the 2003 US SuperBowl was reaching the inboxes of thousands of Europeans within days of it being released on the Superbowl and Budweiser websites.

An example of business-to-business viral marketing is provided by a campaign developed by e-traction for Conference Calls Unlimited and later for Convoq, a web-conferencing product provider. The campaign used an online graphic called '@work' which displayed animated office characters at work in an office (Anderson, 2004). To add more workers to the office the viewer needed to click 'add staff' and tell a friend about the site. The graphic was seeded by e-mail to 97 000 of e-tractions opted-in recipients meeting certain demographic criteria. The results within a few weeks were 23 000 visitors to the @work site, 8000 referees, 28 000 referrals 14 000 of which visited the @work site and most importantly 6500 click-throughs to the host company's website (Anderson, 2004).

There are also many sites which gather viral marketing examples (www. viralbank.com and www.viralmeister.com) and therefore extend the life and exposure of these campaigns.

Advantages

E-mails received from friends and colleagues are far more likely to get through the inbox clutter and gain the recipient's attention. The credibility of the forwarder source adds to the credibility of the sponsoring organization and at the same time endorses the brand. This voluntary spreading of a message creates exponential and self-perpetuating exposure for very little cost with the possibility of reaching a large global audience within weeks of seeding. There are approximately 891 million electronic mail boxes around the world (Perry and Whitaker, 2002) and this figure is set to rise as more and more people around the world gain access to this technology.

Disadvantages

Although this technique entails insubstantial media costs, there are other costs in the initial set up of e-viral campaigns. One of these costs is in the research needed to identify suitable 'seeds' or opinion leaders, to understand their preferences and contacts and to gain their permission to send them the 'idea' e-mails. The second cost is in the creative development of a suitable 'idea'. In developing the idea there needs to be a clear focus on the characteristics of the targeted opinion leaders in order to create something innovative and of value.

Care needs to be taken to avoid the creativity of the campaign from obscuring the product being offered. A successful creative idea may lead to exponential spreading of the message and interest, involvement and loyalty to that message without achieving attitudinal or behavioural changes towards the brand, product or organization. This can happen if the idea is memorable and likeable but is not explicitly associated with the product.

A possible disadvantage of e-viral campaigns is that the message can get lost among inbox clutter and worse be perceived as spam, chain e-mail or one of the many e-mail scams. One way to overcome this is to use a pull-seeding mechanism using the websites dedicated to virals (The Lycos Viral Chart, Viralbank and punchbaby.com) which attract an audience willing to send them on (Howell, 2003).

The Adidas International 'Beat Rugby' campaign demonstrates the importance of integrating e-viral activities with the rest of the online communications. Adidas International used partnerships with the sport of rugby and the All Blacks New Zealand team to produce an online campaign allowing them to reconnect with a core global audience of sports fans aged between twelve and twenty. The campaign was based around an interactive game accessible via the Internet and an accompanying media campaign to encourage fans to visit the Beat Rugby website.

The components of the campaign included:

- the development of the game itself
- paid online advertising on dedicated rugby sites worldwide
- comprehensive online viral marketing
- use of Adidas affiliates as promotional channels
- use of the All Blacks to promote the game URL address.

This successful integration of online components related to the brand resulted in 43 000 rugby fans from over 20 countries downloading the game, becoming members of a global rugby community and having an interactive experience with the Adidas brand (CAANZ, 2001).

Internet communities

A more sophisticated and value-laden focused use of the Internet than the organization website is the creation of Internet communities. An Internet community replicates social behaviour in hyperspace (Hoey, 1998) allowing individuals with shared interests to interact, gather information and learn from each other. An Internet community can provide a 'one stop shopping mall', providing, on regular visitation, access to everything that they need or want to know about a particular topic, brand or event (Wills, 1997). Such Internet communities can be encouraged via use of part of one organization's website or can be created by a group of organizations with shared target audiences.

Uses for events

Internet communities offer many opportunities for event organizations as the shared interest that brings an audience together at an event can be used to create the forum or community on the web. The Adidas International example cited earlier uses the shared interest of rugby and online gaming to create a globally interconnected community. Similar examples include the use of fan or supporter websites to connect audiences with interests in sports, music and film. Conference organizers can enhance the value of their offering through online discussion groups and forums focused on conference themes, encouraging a greater virtual participation than is possible at the physical event. This creates further interest and understanding of the event and its content and encourages wider attendance in future years.

As more and more people gain access to the Internet, the use of Internet communities in support of community festivals will be needed. These may be initiated by community groups or local government and will encourage the sharing of knowledge and experience on a wider scale. This will not only benefit attendees in terms of schedules, reviews and insider knowledge, but will be a valuable method for recruiting participants, volunteers and sponsors. Such forums will also help develop the skills and knowledge of those involved in their organization through learning from the experience of others around the world.

Glastonbury Music Festival (www.glastonburyfestivals.co.uk) has managed to create a sense of community within their website through the inclusion of message boards, information openness and web casts. The message boards allow communication between those who have already attended the festival, first-timers and those who were unable to get tickets and covers a number of subject areas. These include 'general banter', 'tips and advice', 'let's meet-up', 'lift-share', 'your experiences' and 'ask infoman'. These message boards also provide the opportunity for Glastonbury Festival Ltd to get information across to a wide audience in an effective manner. The boards were also used to discourage non-ticket holders from attending following problems in previous years and the message was able to be reinforced by contributions from the charities benefiting from ticket purchases. Web casts allow those who cannot attend to feel included in the Glastonbury experience and were used to great effect in 2001 when the festival had to be cancelled.

Other online festival communities can be found at www.virtualfestivals.com and www.efestivals.co.uk which provide a generic rather than brand based content plus links to the web communities of the major festivals.

Advantages

The use of Internet communities provides a forum for word-of-mouth information to be spread but with some degree of control and the ability to monitor what is being said. Also, the monitoring of discussion boards and forums is now a recognized and useful new addition to marketing research tools (Poria and Harmen, 2002) and provides the additional benefit of the opportunity to respond immediately to users' comments.

When created sensitively these virtual communities are seen as a useful resource by the user and therefore create extra value to the brand of participating organizations. The information provided in such forums is generally viewed by users as being objective and credible as it is not issued directly from the organization and is therefore more effective.

Disadvantages

In order to prevent misuse of the forums and possible offence to users the content needs to be regularly monitored and policed. The censoring of posted messages, however, has a negative impact on the credibility of the content and therefore needs to be handled openly with clear guidelines published for users. Most message boards require registration to ensure the users with anonymity and security and in registering the user agrees to abide by the forum's rules. For example an excerpt from the terms and conditions for the efestivals' forums includes an agreement not to 'post any material which is knowingly false and/or defamatory, inaccurate, abusive, vulgar, hateful, harassing, obscene, profane, sexually oriented, threatening, invasive of a person's privacy, or otherwise violative of the law' (efestivals, 2004). These types of forum will often use an independent moderating team who monitor content for any breach of the published terms.

As with Internet public relations, it is not possible to have complete control over this form of communication and posted messages and chat room comments may include negative comments. However, the opportunity to respond to these in a public environment is likely to be beneficial to the corporate image and will help to create a long-term positive image of the openness and responsiveness of the organization.

Database marketing

Description

Although this topic is dealt with more comprehensively in Chapter 10, it is useful at this stage to understand some of the technological advances which have led to the increased use and effectiveness of direct marketing. Database marketing is an extension of the direct marketing methods of personal selling, direct mail and telesales, but this is made more effective through the collection, analysis and use of computerized customer records. Through the constant gathering of customer data from transactional systems, marketing research, promotional responses, queries and complaints a fuller understanding can be achieved of the market place. This should lead to more and better targeted campaigns allowing marketing communications to be tailored to each member of the target audience's needs. Database direct marketing is not, therefore, a one-off leaflet drop, cold calling or the casual distribution of flyers, but a long-term commitment that allows for the development of two-way communication and a lasting relationship with each customer and prospective customer.

Uses for events

Most event organizations will routinely collect data from their customers at point-of-purchase, at the event and post-event. This may be via their own booking systems and box offices or those of agencies. It may be through personal contacts, through account management and complaint analysis or through marketing research and evaluations. A wealth of customer data is, therefore, readily available and can, through analysis, be used to improve the organization's direct marketing effectiveness. Box office systems are used to target direct mail to those customers who have attended previous events. These can be used to promote events with a similar content or be combined with sales promotion to move a new target audience to an, as yet, untried event type. Exhibitors making use of the same exhibition each year can be offered a pre-prepared package based on their past usage and conference delegates can be kept informed of other conferences and conventions in related fields. The recognition of past contacts in marketing communications is often the starting point for developing a relationship with the customer which can in turn lead to increased loyalty. A delegate returning to the same conference a year later who is greeted by 'welcome back Mr Smith' and an offer of the same newspaper, special menu and transport service that he received last year will know that his previous custom was remembered and appreciated. This can be achieved by simply linking previous purchase history to registration software and ensuring that communications with each customer are recorded in a usable way. These resulting customer information files should then be central to the organization's marketing information system and used to inform all future communications with that customer (Wood, 2004).

Advantages

The use of a well-managed and maintained database can cut down on the amount of direct marketing undertaken as each communication can be carefully targeted to the recipient's needs. This reduces the possibility of the negative impact resulting from unwanted or irrelevant contacts and junk mail.

The database allows for the development of a one-to-one relationship with a large target market and is therefore particularly useful to organizations with a large customer base and for events where there may otherwise be little personal contact.

The database itself has a value and is now often included as an asset in balance sheet valuations. The information contained on the database can also be rented or sold to other organizations and can therefore become an additional source of revenue for the organization. However, this can only happen if permission to do so is gained from each listed customer.

Disadvantages

It can sometimes be difficult to gather the information to begin database marketing if there is very little 'formal' contact with customers. This may be the case for non-ticketed, free or open access events. For these types of events customer data need to be gathered in a more purposeful way, rather than relying on existing systems. Methods used to capture customer data could include the use of promotional campaigns such as contests, photo downloads, free gifts and prize draws requiring some form of contact in order to participate. Event evaluation research questionnaires can include the option to join mailing lists and attendees can be encouraged to visit and register at the event's website.

One of the main difficulties in database marketing is not gathering the information but putting it to good use. This is an argument for keeping the system simple to begin with and allowing it to grow in complexity as the organization's skill in using it grows. Badly targeted direct marketing as a result of poor database use can have a highly detrimental effect on the company's image. This is often a result of databases which are not 'cleaned' regularly to update contacts and to delete those who no longer have an interest in the company and its products.

The legalities of database use have been tightened up in many countries over the last few years with stricter data protection and privacy acts. Although these vary depending on the data use and the country, the best course of action, from both a legal and marketing point of view, is always to ensure that you have the customer's permission and that this permission is renewed on a regular basis.

A final disadvantage is that the overuse of an electronic database and automated personal communications can undermine the use of personal knowledge and contacts. These will always remain vital in smaller businesses, those operating in niche markets and more often than not in the business or organizational events sector.

Mobile telecommunications

The use of mobile or cell phones as a marketing medium is increasing alongside the improvements in technology. As more and more of the billions of mobile phones worldwide are able to send and receive text, graphics and video, connect to the web through WAP and blue tooth technology, the more opportunities there are for these to be used for highly targeted and high impact one-to-one marketing communications.

Uses for events

Text messaging (SMS) can be used in variety of ways by event organizations, particularly those whose audiences are younger consumers. Sports marketers have been using this technology for a number of years to provide extra value to fans. In exchange for opt-in permissions and contact information, registered users can receive texted team news, real time match scores, promotional offers and 'at match' deals on merchandise and catering.

Mobile phone marketing is also used to good effect in conjunction with telecommunications sponsors of events. The Orange network sponsorship of music festivals, sports events and cinemas has created many opportunities to provide extra services for attendees via their mobile phones, while creating a direct and practical link between the event and the sponsoring brand in the consumer's mind.

The location-based marketing benefits of mobile phones also offer a number of possibilities. Mobile phone technology means that the location of users can be pinpointed accurately when they use their phones and they can therefore be sent location relevant messages. For example, Guinness has used this information to guide customers to pubs holding Guinness promotions. Exhibition organizers are beginning to use this technology to provide personalized routes around exhibitions and to transmit focused messages as the attendee passes particular stands.

Mobile phones therefore provide a personal level of interactivity with the event itself and with other forms of promotion. For example, text response numbers can be used to elicit requests for further information or to buy tickets in response to television, radio, outdoor advertisements or to take part in sales promotions.

Mobile phone partnership marketing is a growing area where network operators form partnerships with other organizations to create a branded phone service. Existing examples of this include *The Financial Times* newspaper in the UK, Mtelevision in Sweden and Hesburger restaurant chain in Finland. Performers are already beginning to take advantage of this additional branding tool with the highly successful Hong Kong based music duo, Twins, recently launching a branded phone service. The Twins SIM card provides access to Twins news, concert details, ringtones, e-cards and a loyalty scheme (Moore and Ahonen, 2004). Other performers, music and sports event organizers and associations are sure to follow this trend.

Advantages

The main advantage of mobile phone marketing communications is directly linked to the importance of this communication device to the consumer. The mobile phone is highly personal, more so than the fixed line phone which is often a shared resource (family, friends, office) or e mail. Most users keep their phone within arm's reach day and night and respond quickly to voice, text and multimedia messages. Although SMS and MMS messaging are currently used largely by the youth market, penetration into other demographic groups is rapidly increasing, helped on by popular television shows which ask for text message interaction and voting.

Messages sent to mobile phones can be very precisely targeted and timed for maximum impact. Timing becomes an important aspect of message delivery as unlike direct mail and e-mail the message is likely to be viewed or listened to as soon as it is transmitted.

The interconnectedness of mobile phones makes them ideal as conduits for viral campaigns. The increasing convergence of technology means that the mobile phone is now also used as a browser and camera allowing for the development of more innovative ways to communicate with each individual user.

Disadvantages

The personal nature of the mobile phone, although increasing the impact and responsiveness of this medium, can also be a disadvantage. Unwanted messages will be seen as highly intrusive and can have a very negative affect on the recipients' attitudes to the brand. Ill-targeted messages and those where explicit permission has not been sought are most likely to be viewed negatively. It is therefore, important to tailor any messages to the precise needs of each target group, to renew permissions regularly and to provide easy opt-outs.

The newness of the technology in mobile telephony has created barriers to use in some target groups and a mistrust of making purchases and sending personal details via this method. This can be overcome with assurances of security and privacy and through the gradual adoption of the newer aspects of the technology.

Digital television and radio

Description

Digital television and radio allow for higher quality transmissions, more channel and programming choices and a higher degree of interaction than analogue systems. The move to this technology therefore increases the uses and effectiveness of these media for marketing communications. Interactivity is provided in a similar way to the Internet, with the viewer or listener being able to click for additional information, to respond to surveys, to enter competitions and to make purchases.

Uses for events

The proliferation of channels on digital television means that event organizations who may have discounted television media due to its relative cost are now able to target interested groups in an affordable way through advertising, programme sponsorship and even their own channels. For example, Manchester United Football Club have a digital channel, MUtv, that reaches fans worldwide and due to its interactivity creates a community in a similar way to a website.

Radio has traditionally been used to advertise both local and national events and, with the advent of digital radio, this is likely to increase. The global reach of specialist digital radio channels allows for the development of 'communities of interest' based around musical tastes, interests and lifestyles and regardless of geographic location. The screen display allows for further information to be accessed and purchases to be made in response to the programme content or advertising message being broadcast. This facility has led to the medium being described as 'radio with a buy button' (Smith and Taylor, 2004). For example, a listener who hears a music track which they particularly like will be able to interact and discover the band's concert dates and locations and book tickets.

An example of the successful use of direct response television was its use by the United States Tennis Association during the 1999 US Open. Their goal was to acquire 10 000 new members during the two weeks of the event focusing on the 97 per cent of US tennis enthusiasts who were not already members. The campaign used two television advertisements, one providing an emotional link to the game and the other focusing on the rational benefits of joining and providing a direct response link. The results were almost 17 000 new members with twenty-four airings of the advertisements (an average of 700 people joined as each advertisement ran) (Effie Awards, 2000). The success of this campaign was largely due to the careful targeting and timing of the advertisements. The link to the US Open event provided a clear target audience and an emotional backdrop for the advertisements adding credibility and excitement to the campaign. The ease of making an immediate response made use of the emotion and excitement generated at the time of viewing. Although, this campaign simply used a toll-free telephone number to illicit immediate responses it demonstrates the power of television interactivity which has now been enhanced by the adoption of digital technology.

Advantages

Direct response television combines the emotional impact of television with the interactivity of the Internet. Digital radio offers globally available specialist channels with instant interaction. Both are capable of building communities through communication between users as well as communication between the advertiser and the users.

The proliferation of channels in both these media creates the possibility of highly focused targeting and therefore less media spend wastage.

Disadvantages

Although the switch to digital television is happening fairly rapidly in many countries, the adoption of digital radio is far slower and at present this limits its effectiveness for marketing communication.

The interactivity of digital television can be frustrating for those used to the Internet as interaction times can be slower. It is also worth remembering that television is viewed from a distance, unlike websites displayed on personal computer screens and therefore the message content cannot be put across in the same way. Different skills are needed for developing digital television content than for designing websites and content should not simply be duplicated or transferred from one medium to the other.

Summary

The possibilities for event e-marketing communications are constantly expanding with the introduction of new technologies, the convergence of established technology and the discovery of new and creative ways of using these technologies. The Internet has had a major impact on marketing communication emphasis through the use of websites and e-mail. This medium has empowered consumers through information and choice and has led to opportunities for communicating in a more open, objective and therefore credible manner. This communication is more effective when event customers and other interested parties contribute to the communications message. This can be done through the passing on of messages of interest (e-viral) or through contributing to forums

Case study 6.1

Website Development

The key to successful website development is finding the correct balance between content and revenue generation. An increasing requirement is also that any revenue generation content be directly linked with editorial content for better results.

The development of event-led websites is widespread, but best practice is being considered continuously to a point where site owners are often revamping their sites. Self-managed sites are clearly more controllable, but linking with others can offer more economic solutions. Many events around the world, for example, would be worse off without the reach of Ticketmaster sites. In 2003, Ticketmaster sold 100 million tickets valued at US£4.9 billion for 8000 event-related clients.

Essentially, it is the desire for information that drives customers to event or distributor sites and so for revenue generation to work, the editorial content has to work well.

49ers.com, the San Francisco 49ers (NFL) site, was readdressed in 2003. It has always had a record of innovative revenue generation, but its owners are still very much aware even now that they have previously pursued a line where their content was insufficient and that it was not attracting money-spending fans. In the past it has adopted editorial policy that has prevented 49ers fans getting 49ers news from this site first. In 2002, for example, the team released a key team coach, but the website made no reference to this breaking news. Fans found out from other sources. Site designers recognized the issue and warned that continued use of such policies would drive fans away let alone get them to spend money.

The 49ers use their site to develop and extend the 49ers brand and now managers evaluate it as more lucrative than stadium, radio or publishing activities. They do not use banners, pop-ups or under advertising. The use of their red and gold colours, is predominant to a point where advertisers messages are redesigned using these colours. There are limits on the number of sponsors and only those that meet minimum levels of investment and are targeting nationally are recruited. However, while their control of their commercial content in these ways is tight, it is only half the job. They also have to produce up to the minute news and editorial content that is exciting.

For example, 49ers marketplace auctions one-of-a-kind merchandise items such as the pom-poms that were used in a player's touchdown celebration. A player's car has even been auctioned. Fans can also pre-select alerts in their My 49ers ENews for breaking stories and ticket information updates, but just happen to receive messages from 12 sponsors when they do. Over 100 000 fans receive ENews.

The 49ers at one time had their site managed by an agency but decided that they needed to control all input. Their approach is that no organization is as close to 49ers fans as the 49ers organization.

Fulham FC, of the English Premiership, had the same approach when it revamped its provision early in 2004. They, too, found the integration of editorial and commercial content a challenge. They created a 'Friends of Fulham' vehicle where any fan, season ticket holder or not, could sign up to receive regular updated information via text and e-mail. The site now features an official message board for fans, chat forums and its own fantasy football management game and league. This focus on fans has been extended with ground breaking post-match in-depth player interviews and coverage of post-match press conferences. As a result the club reports one of the highest visitor stay durations of all official Premiership club sites, thus helping boost commercial return opportunities.

Chat forums feature successfully on intermediary sites in the music industry too. Sites such as these are important distributors of event tickets and they successfully encourage both visits and stay durations via these forums. The customer focus is strong with message boards for particular events in key site positions that enable nostalgia to run riot.

The common theme throughout these cases is that strong editorial content is the key for commercial website success.

Source: Berridge (2003); Efestivals (2004); Fulham FC (2004); Sport and Technology (2004); Ticketmaster (2004); Virtual Festivals (2004).

and discussions (Internet communities). Case study 6.1 provides a variety of examples of how events organizations are successfully applying these e-marketing communications techniques.

Database technology used in conjunction with e-mail provides organizations with the opportunity to communicate personally with a carefully targeted group of potential customers, focusing the message on their specific needs. Mobile communications can be used in a similar way with the added benefits of location and time targeting and added impact and response rates.

The traditional media of television and radio can also now be used interactively creating new opportunities for events organizations to use media which may not have been previously considered.

Other tools of e-marketing communication are also likely to increase in usage for example, i-kiosks (interactive screens) which can be placed in a variety of highly targeted locations and can offer information, gather feedback and provide booking and ticket sales. These can be used during events to add value to the experience and gather feedback or can be used in other locations to sell or distribute tickets. For example, i-kiosks placed in bus and train stations have been used to issue theatre tickets.

Although e-marketing tools will become an increasingly important part of the marketing communication mix, it is unlikely that they will replace the more established methods and media. Their usage should enhance the effectiveness of traditional methods by providing more points of contact, greater interactivity and easier to achieve integration.

Discussion points

1 Compare the websites of four event organizations from a marketing communications perspective.
   For each one consider:
   o level and type of interactivity
   o added value to the visitor
   o links and partnerships
   o differentiation for each target audience
   o relevance and currency of content.
2 Discuss the uses and usefulness of mobile phone marketing as part of the communications plan for:
   o a local community event
   o a major sports tournament
   o an industrial product exhibition.

References

Anderson, H. (2004) Fun @work: Viral marketing for the office. E-tractions. www.e-tractions.com/convoq/run/atwork and www.e-tractions.com

Berridge, K. (2003) Marketing and enabling technology: Beyond content, turning a website into a profit center. A paper delivered by the Senior Manager of Corporate Partnerships, San Francisco 49ers, at Sport and Technology 2003. November 13–14, New York Marriot Eastside, New York. Street and Smith.

Brown, M.T. (2003) An analysis of online marketing in the sport industry: User activity, communication objectives, and perceived benefits. *Sport Marketing Quarterly*, 12 (1), 48–55.

CAANZ (2001) Adidas International Beat Rugby. The Communication Agencies Association of New Zealand.

Commonwealth Games Federation (2004) www.thecgf.com/interactive/ecard.asp (accessed October, 2004).

Edinburgh International Festival (2004) www.eif.co.uk (accessed June, 2004).

Efestivals (2004) www.efestivals.co.uk/forums (accessed October, 2004).

Effie Awards (2000) Direct response television. New York Marketing Association.

Exhibitions around the world (2004) www.exhibitions-world.com (accessed September, 2004).

Fulham FC (2004) www.fulhamfc.com (accessed October, 2004).

Glastonbury Festival (2004) www.glastonburyfestival.co.uk (accessed July, 2004).

Grant, D. and McBride, P. (2000) *Guide to the Internet: Getting Your Business Online*. Butterworth-Heinemann.

Hart, S. (2003) *Marketing Changes*. Thomson.

Hoey, C. (1998) Maximising the effectiveness of web-based marketing communications. *Marketing Intelligence and Planning*, 16 (1), 31–37.

Howell, N. (2003) Catching the bug. *New Media Age*, 10th April, 31–32.

Ihator, A.S. (2001) Communication style in the information age. *Corporate Communications: An International Journal*, 6 (4), 199–204.

Kinetic Event Solutions (2004) www.kineticeventsolutions.co.uk/vip.htm (accessed September, 2004).

LVS Events (2004) www.lvsevents.co.uk (accessed September, 2004).

Medical Conferences (2004) www.medicalconferences.com (accessed September, 2004).

Moore, A. and Ahonen, T. (2004) Mobile marketing: How to succeed in a connected age. *Market Leader*, 24, Spring.

O'Connor, J. and Galvin, E. (2001) *Marketing in the Digital Age*, 2nd edn. Prentice Hall.

Perry, R. and Whitaker, A. (2002) *Understanding Vital Marketing in a Week*. Hodder Arnold H&S.

Poria, Y. and Harmen, O. (2002) Exploring possible uses of multi-user domains in tourism research. *Tourism Today*, 15–33.

Reedy, J., Schullo, S. and Zimmerman, K. (2000) *Electronic Marketing*. Dryden Press.

Smith, P.R. and Taylor, J. (2004) *Marketing Communications: An Integrated Approach*, 4th edn. Kogan Page.

Sport and Technology (2004) www.sportandtechnology.com (accessed October, 2004).

Ticketmaster (2004) Ticketmaster.com

Virtual Festivals (2004) www.virtualfestivals.com (accessed October, 2004).

Wills, G. (1997) E-postcards from the other side. E-postcard 8, http://imc.org.uk/imc/news/occpaper/postcards/

Wood, E.H. (2004) Marketing information for impact analysis and evaluation. In *Festival and Events Management: An International Arts and Cultural Perspective*, Yeoman, I., Robertson, M., Ali-McKnight, J., McMahon-Beattie, U. and Drummond, S. (eds). Butterworth-Heinemann.

Wynyard Tulip Festival (2004) www.bloomintulips.co.au (accessed June, 2004).

Chapter 7
Advertising

Objectives

- Evaluate the role and value of advertising in the events industry
- Understand the appeal of advertising and how it works
- Understand the process by which effective and innovative advertising communications are designed and scheduled
- Identify the options and critical factors for advertising campaign management in integrated event marketing communications
- Identify the different classes of advertising media and types of vehicles available for event marketing communications

Introduction

There is no doubting the extensive use of advertising. According to Clow and Baack (2004), as individuals we are, on average, subjected to at least 600 advertisements per day. This is a figure that has increased quickly as a result of an ever-expanding variety of media. Television, radio and printed media are still commonly used in advertising today, but now they compete with the exciting opportunities that have emerged via the Internet, as discussed in Chapter 6. As a result advertising does not have to be expensive. While some classes of media such as television and some wide reaching vehicles such as national printed media can be beyond event budgets, there can be alternatives that can not only be more affordable but also more effective because they are more finely targeted. The use of media such as transportation, printed materials, billboards, the telephone and the Internet offer event managers a wealth of advertising options for integrated marketing communications (IMC) decisions. The value brought by commercial partners and the opportunities for joint advertising programmes also assists this process. In addition, the fragmentation of media means that television advertising is more widely affordable with highly specialized and targeted digital channels. It should be clear that with such a varied and extensive range of advertising media on offer, it is no longer too expensive an option for event managers of even the smallest event.

This chapter is divided into eight sections in order to demonstrate the value of advertising as a communications tool. First, its role in event communications is discussed and this is followed by the consideration of what it can achieve and the identification of advertising objectives. The next two sections then go hand in hand. First, the factors that affect management decision making are identified and, in particular, the decision to implement campaigns in or out-of-house. Then the process of managing campaigns is considered.

The next sections turn to the design and production of advertisements and media planning and buying. A review of the various media that are available for event organizations follows and finally evaluation is discussed. The case study in this chapter examines the advertising process by considering an advertising campaign associated with the Tour de France. The focus throughout is on advertising that utilizes non-personal media.

Role of advertising

The first point to make is that advertising is just one component of an event's integrated marketing communications. It is simply one of the promotional tools available. Unfortunately, advertising is a word that is all too frequently misunderstood in that it is used to represent all promotional activity and, in order to understand its role as a communications choice, this is an important distinction to learn.

There can be confusion for example between advertising and publicity (Pickton and Broderick, 2001). There were distinctions made in Chapter 5 on how publicity is subject to editorial alteration and therefore not guaranteed to be delivered at all or in an unmodified form. On the one hand, publicity occupies space or time that is not paid for, whereas on the other, an advertisement is guaranteed delivered, with an unmodified message, at an agreed rate for the space or time slot used. It is required that advertising be clearly identifiable as such too. Advertisements that are deliberately designed to look like publicity, for example, are required to carry statements acknowledging that they are advertising (see Advertorials in Chapter 5).

Distinctions are also required between advertising and sales promotions on occasion. The distinction is still required despite the use of both to form effective integrated communications. An advertisement that carries a money-off offer, a competition or a voucher for premium merchandise is using a sales promotion technique. It is important to make these distinctions when discussing these disciplines in an academic sense, but the distinction is also important in industry. When talking about combinations of communications devices or preparing plans such as separate campaigns for advertising or public relations, for example, being able to make the distinction will ensure that no confusion arises (Pickton and Broderick, 2001).

Having made these distinctions, it is perhaps easier for many event organizations to understand that an IMC programme is more than just a collection of communications and advertising strategies. It involves clear messages, both internally as well as externally, among staff as well as suppliers and customers (Clow and Baack, 2004). This can be so because many such organizations are small with no separate departments for different aspects of communication and individual event marketers have to undertake many marketing roles. Advertising too has seldom been an option for many events in the past with the choices of television, radio and national press in particular, often being too expensive. While in other industries advertising often accounts for the majority of promotional spend, for the events industry the seeking out of other forms of communications has often been a necessity.

The increased and varied advertising options of today are alleviating that dilemma. For some events advertising is the central focus where other communications points of contact are used to support those advertising messages. For example, in a consumer focused IMC plan, where advertisements are designed to deliver an event message and drive ticket buyers to website addresses, and where ticket offers are delivered on-pack via commercial partners and in competitions via publicity. Advertising can also be used as a support mechanism in business-to-business focused plans where, for example, trade advertising is designed to support the recruitment of event sponsors and by preceding direct marketing methods such as personal follow-up calling. The role of advertising, as a valuable part of an IMC approach, is clearly one that can be used to reach both consumer and business markets.

Pickton and Broderick (2001) propose that the key benefits of advertising are that it can reach mass audiences, increasingly now on a selective targeted basis, and that it does so at relatively low costs. They maintain that it is therefore both efficient and effective in reaching the right targets. They also maintain that it is effective for brand maintenance and arguably brand development in that it can reach high numbers for awareness and demonstrate brand differentiation. Shimp (1997) agrees and also maintains that advertising is critical to the successful introduction of new brands and the defence of established ones. Getz (1997), in agreeing that advertising can create and increase awareness for an event, also indicates that it can convert demand into sales. Pickton and Broderick (2001) note that while advertising has not been traditionally recognized as being that effective in encouraging customers to such action, suggest that this is misconstrued and highlight how classified advertising is perceived by many users as being particularly strong in inspiring sales. This perception would appear to be the case in the events industry where classified advertising is widely used as a relatively inexpensive option for the delivery of event content and sales information. The rear halves of UK newspapers are testament to this with advertisements, sometimes ten to a page, for music concerts from a variety of organizers and promoters. For example, in June 2004, *The Sunday Times Magazine* featured advertisements for a Classical Spectacular at the Royal Albert Hall, Circus Oz at the Royal Festival Hall, Tom Jones outdoors at Castle Howard, Opera North in Leeds, Simon and Garfunkel in Hyde Park and various tour dates and venues for Brian Wilson, Madonna and Elton John (*The Sunday Times*, 2004a). The content of each was simple; who is on, where and when are they on and most importantly for this choice of advertisement, telephone and website details that aid the ticket purchase process. The use of advertising that drives customers to websites, where further and greater amounts of information can be delivered, is also perceived as being an effective and efficient way to spend an event advertising budget.

The questions need to be asked – does advertising work, and can it really be directly and unquestionably linked to sales? Pickton and Broderick (2001) maintain that results show that it can positively affect awareness, attention, interest, perception, opinion, attitudes and sales, and that the fact that so much resource is put behind this form of communication is testament to the perception that advertising does work. Crosier (1999) agrees that the size of the advertising business, on a global scale, implies that advertisements can communicate, at least often enough, with target markets and persuade them to revise their beliefs more positively and then act accordingly.

The positive effect of advertising is also more than likely not in question in the eyes of those practitioners that use it. However, little is known about how it works, despite extensive research, there is no one dominant theory (Jobber, 1998; Crosier, 1999; Pickton and Broderick, 2001; Clow and Baack, 2004). The problem is that there are so many tasks for advertising to perform that any one single theory cannot be sufficient (Jobber, 1998). Consider the objectives for product advertising and the non-personal promotion of event ticket sales and how they differ from the objectives of an organization, combinations of organizations, or a government and their promotion of the idea of staging an event. While advertising is considered an effective tool for affecting sales and other product-related objectives, it is also a valuable way of promoting institutional objectives that may be concerned with a concept, philosophy or goodwill (Boone and Kurtz, 2002).

One approach for an understanding on how advertising works is to view it as a strong or a weak force. For example, on the one hand advertising is considered strong enough to increase knowledge, change attitude and then persuade to buy, in other words, a conversion theory. Those supporting this view would argue that sales increase as a result of advertising that creates strong differentiated brands (Jones, 1995). This view has its base in the USA and was developed nearly 80 years ago. A textbook framework for the effective delivery of sales was developed where an individual passes through stages of awareness, interest, desire and action, commonly referred to as 'AIDA' (Strong, 1925). Lavidge and Steiner (1961) developed this into the 'hierarchy of effects' model that is still used today as a predictive measure of advertising effectiveness.

This approach has been consistently opposed, however (Crosier, 1999). Opponents maintain that advertising does not convert but rather reinforces values, maintains brands and defends market share (Ehrenberg et al., 2000). Thus advertising has the effect of not recruiting new buyers but bearing influence on existing buyers so as to retain them and possibly get them to buy more. Ehrenberg (1988) offered an alternative model, where the stages an individual goes through are awareness, trial and reinforcement or 'ATR'. Advertising is, therefore, seen as having a weaker effect.

One of the major weaknesses that opponents of the 'hierarchy of effects' model put forward, is that it is entirely descriptive and does not offer any explanation as to how advertising works. The hierarchy model portrays what happens, in a range of circumstances, but not why individuals respond to advertisements, as they are perceived to do (Crosier, 1999). Despite the objections to the 'hierarchy of effects', its use as a basis for advertising decision making is still prevalent today. Crosier (1999) maintains that 'AIDA' is still providing the underpinning of much contemporary advertising strategy and goes further to suggest that while there is discrepancy, it is preferable while there is no common and agreed theory that all practitioners can happily comprehend and implement.

The argument between the two views is about where the sales come from rather than advertising having no effect on sales. There are two points to make here. One is that it does accentuate the importance of targeting the right audiences. For example, where should advertising be aimed, new potential markets or existing markets? Secondly, the questions that exist concerning how advertising works clearly impact on the decision making that is required when determining advertising objectives. What objectives can be achieved with advertising?

Advertising objectives

The ultimate aim for advertising is to stimulate sales and increase profits (Jobber, 1998). More holistically, Boone and Kurtz (2002) recommend that marketers use advertising to accomplish three objectives: to inform, to persuade and to remind. From an operational perspective and in order to plan advertising campaigns, there are a number of communications objectives that have more strategic meaning. IMC goals and objectives have been discussed previously in Section One and advertising goals are only developed in accordance with those that are collectively determined for the overall IMC plan. Therefore, advertising can assist with objectives such as the development of market position. However, integrated but separate advertising goals are still required in order to produce strategic advertising campaigns and there are several objectives that advertising can thus achieve.

Building brand image

It is generally agreed that the primary role of advertising is longer-term brand building (Crosier, 1999). Equity has to be built into the brand so that it consists of a set of characteristics, values and benefits that make it more desirable. Advertising can play an important role in building brand equity when it is used in combination with a product that can credibly live up to the billing and can then be used to develop market position and ultimately competitive advantage.

By using advertising copy and visuals to develop, or reinforce, an image or a set of brand associations, an event can be positioned in the market and therefore in customers' minds. The same can also apply when a repositioning of the event is required. Correcting misconceptions that are held by customers can be a critical strategy for an ailing event for example. One of the tasks would be to persuade customers that a particular brand is superior to others (Clow and Baack, 2004). This is not always an easy task when a change of mind is required. Getz (1997), for example, lists persuasion as an advertising objective for events whereby a need is generated for the event. This might involve showing the negative consequences of not attending an event by advertising details of any improvements that have been made. Missing out on new and better performers and performances, for example. Alternatively, if the offering is already of good quality, demonstrating a missed experience by including testimonials from those that have previously attended may also work.

Creating awareness

Part of the brand-building task is the development of brand awareness and market position and advertising is an effective tool for this job. Brand awareness can help customers recognize and recall an event when they are considering purchase options. The task is to create top-of-mind awareness; the status achieved when customers recall a particular brand more than others.

Awareness is also a pre-condition of purchase and again advertising can be used to create this necessary condition. The content of such advertising is therefore clearly informative in nature. Simple forms can inform audiences of the artists, venues and dates. More sophisticated messages can involve details of an improved event such as one with more artists, stages and better levels of service. The creation of awareness is clearly important for new events and also for the development of audiences for established events.

A secondary but not insignificant objective for events may be to create awareness for partners such as sponsors and charities/causes. With the right sponsors and charities the exercise would serve a dual purpose in that the benefit of the association would help develop the event brand. A common, though not necessarily effective or aesthetic practice, is to include sponsors' logos on event advertisements for example. Fortunately, there is less use now of these sponsors' 'flash banners' that have no synergy with the content of the advertisements to which they are attached.

Stimulating action

Advertisements can be used to encourage action. Direct response advertisements, for example, can instigate a response that can also provide a direct measurement of sales. Advertising in this form can therefore be proven to result in purchase action. Other forms of action can include instigating calls and hits to advertised telephone numbers and also websites, which may or may not eventually lead to sales, but can also at least be measured. Other advertisement content might also be used to stimulate trial. Jobber (1998), for example, suggests that the sale of some products suffer because of a lack of trial. Incorporating sales promotions into advertising can work here with price and merchandise strategies in particular (see Chapter 9 for more on sales promotions). The nature of the content of the advertisement can be designed to stimulate trial by adopting a certain style. For example, 'you'll never know until you try' may inspire trial. Advertising for the Millennium Dome in the UK suggested that anyone who did not visit the event was merely a 'sheep' following media opinion. They were highlighting that it had to be tried before it could be judged.

Awareness reinforcement

Once brand equity and a clear market position have been achieved, it is important to reinforce that awareness. Advertising can help to remind customers of an event and reinforce its particular image. This becomes a critical exercise when annual or infrequent events are up coming. Reinforcement with regular customers is also often a necessity. Price changes or changes in purchase mechanisms may be required and, for infrequent events, a simple reminder of how to purchase tickets may be needed. Finally, even for those brands with strong equity, there is an argument for regular advertising in order to defend market position and maintain top-of-mind awareness, although this may be more applicable for frequently run events.

There are other objectives that are often applied to advertising. Advertising in order to support the efforts of sales staff for example (Jobber, 1998), or in support of other marketing efforts (Clow and Baack, 2004), or to drive traffic to websites or encourage interest in sales promotions. By seeing these as attributes of advertising helps to confirm that as a tool, advertising sits alongside other communications tools to achieve overall IMC objectives and message delivery.

Advertising management

In an IMC approach, advertising decisions are taken at the same time as those for all the other forms of communication. The planning process therefore follows a necessarily similar systematic progression as that for PR (discussed in Chapter 5). Figure 7.1 depicts the advertising planning process for an IMC approach.

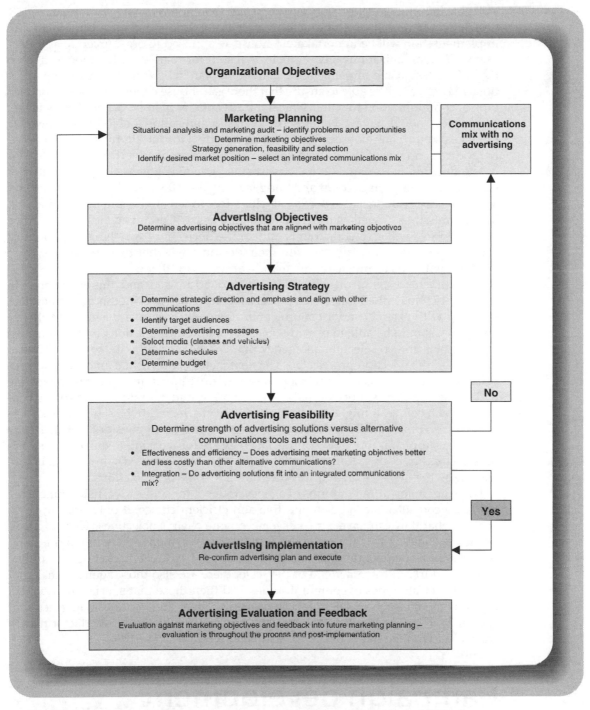

Figure 7.1 Advertising planning process. Process for the planning of advertising in integrated event marketing communications.

When it comes to the management of advertising, there are a number of key decisions. The first is deciding on how much of the advertising development and implementation will be undertaken in-house as opposed to outsourced to agencies. Many event organizations rely on their own staff for marketing function and often they plan, design and implement the marketing plan in its entirety. Larger organizations may of course be able to ensure that there is in-house expertise in place for each type of communication function. One of the advantages of in-house marketing is that employees should have a better sense of the organization's objectives. However, there is also the choice of seeking specialist expertise for certain functions via external sources and one of those choices is the appointment of advertising agencies.

The decision to use an external advertising agency is governed by a number of factors. The size of the account and budget available is the first. Agencies are clearly a cost and so the budget also needs to include fees for creative input and media buying commissions as well as the costs for media space. Certain agencies may not be interested in smaller sized accounts and so the decision of which agency to select can often be a two-way process with them deciding whether they are interested in working with you as much as you are in working with them.

How much to spend on advertising is next addressed and this is covered in Chapter 14. This is then followed by a decision on which agency can do the best job. Working with external service suppliers brings objectivity to a business. In theory an agency should be able to provide objective marketing solutions that circumvent internal bias and so selecting an agency that can be worked with comfortably is a key part of the selection process too. The next factor concerns the amount of appropriate creativity an agency can bring. In-house operations may get stale over time and so the appointment of external creative work can invigorate an advertising programme. Of course, it might also be the case that staying with the same external service can become equally redundant. The selection has to consider not just how creative a supplier is, but how appropriate they are for working in the relevant business sector. For events, it may be that those who have worked with events before and know the industry are more appropriate for some organizations.

There are many different forms of agency. Indeed, for some advertising functions, freelance consultants can be an effective and efficient choice, if only from the perspective that they can have a greater focus on one client's objectives. There are full-service agencies that will not only provide a creative, media planning and buying service, but also integrate sales and trade promotions, direct marketing and public relations work. At the other end of the scale, there are also those agencies that specialize in certain types of communications and then those that specialize in certain types of media, such as television advertising. There are also those agencies that specialize in certain business and industry sectors. The final selection factor then is concerned with the depth of service that is required.

Campaign development

Having decided how advertising is going to be managed, an event organization can then focus on the development of a specific programme of advertising. Developing an event advertising campaign involves the preparation and integration of the programme into the overall IMC plan. This entails the adoption of the overall IMC objectives (see Figure 7.1).

The first step involves an analysis of the event's communication market. This analysis considers the opportunity available for advertising in terms of the level and nature of competitor activity, the identification of key target audiences and review of previous communications and of current market position. The key to this analysis is the identification of the media usage behaviour of target markets and the media utilized by the competition (Clow and Baack, 2004).

The next step is to establish advertising objectives that are aligned with the overall IMC objectives. By considering IMC objectives alongside the opportunities and constraints that arose out of the communication market analysis, the objectives for the advertising programme can be made.

Before a budget can be finally set a draft schedule is required. This involves identifying and then selecting the most effective and efficient media classes, vehicles and time periods in order to meet the objectives set. It is critical that this schedule is appropriate and matches the desired messages. The advertisements can then be produced.

Advertising design and production

At the heart of an advertisement is the 'advertising platform'. This is the basic selling proposition and so it has to be important to the target market and also communicate competitive advantage (Jobber, 1998). Hence the importance of an understanding of the target market's media choices and behaviour. An advertising platform is developed in order to achieve advertising objectives and is therefore inextricably linked with IMC objectives. Platforms are then translated into advertising messages, in the form of visuals, words, sounds and symbols, so that they will hopefully appeal to their intended target audiences.

The creation of advertisements begins with the preparation of a creative brief. The brief consists of several elements including an objective, defined target market, the message and theme, any supporting material that can substantiate the message, such as research or testimonial and any constraints that there may be on the process, such as legalities. The Oakland A's baseball organization, for example, briefed advertising agency McCann Erickson San Francisco, to create a television campaign for early 2004 (Adforum, 2004). The organization's marketing objectives were to develop incremental revenue from a sales base that was ostensibly one that consisted of walk-up ticket purchase on the day of the game. They wanted to get the one or two time ticket buyer to buy four or five times, the four and five timers to buy seven or eight times and those that came to eight games (third of a season) to become season ticket holders. In addition to other marketing communications, it was decided that television advertising would also work. The advertising objectives were the development of awareness and fan loyalty and the targets were the existing fans. In a local campaign entitled 'A different brand of baseball', the agency created a theme that was designed to demonstrate how different the 'A's' were from the rest of the major league. An advertisement, labelled 'Bazooka', was then produced, based on the selling of the 'A's' baseball experience using the players and unique Oakland attributes depicted in past game footage. This is a simple example of a brief where the agency was provided with marketing objectives, clear targets supported by sales data and a base for a message that was focused on the development of loyalty.

Several theoretical frameworks can be used in order to provide a development framework in the design process. For example, the previously discussed hierarchy of effects model, means-ends theory and a visual versus verbal model are commonly discussed in advertising theory. The first two frameworks can be used to develop leverage points that can move a consumer through a process of first understanding the product and then linking that with their own personal values. Thus an advertisement can be designed by following the sequential steps of AIDA in order to instigate attention, interest, desire and then action. Using the means-ends theory as a framework involves trying to move target audiences through a chain reaction and to a belief that the product will achieve their personal values. The aim is to link a product's attributes to the benefits they can bring. By using leverage points, the idea is that audiences can then perceive links between those benefits and their personal values (Clow and Baack, 2004). In a magazine advertisement for the 2004 Nantucket Iron Teams Relay, two simple images are featured (Figure 7.2). The picture of a pair of running shoes with the date of the race printed underneath and a second picture of a pair of 'flip-flop' beach shoes with the date of the day after the event printed underneath alongside the copy provide leverage points. The copy is targeted at 'iron man' racers for their run, bike, paddle and swim race around the beaches, harbours and roads of Nantucket in the USA. The racers get to party after

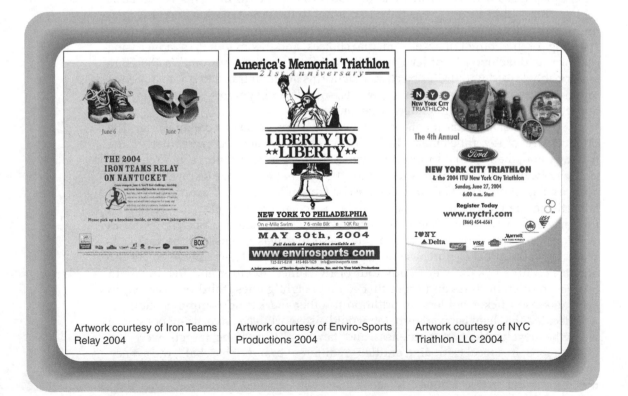

Figure 7.2 Advertising execution frameworks.

the race at a local venue too. The combination of pictures and copy are designed to promise that there is not just a great experience to be had at the race, but also immediately after it and the next day via more leisurely activities. The full-page spot colour advertisement was placed in *Metrosports New York* (2004) magazine and was competing with several other racing advertisements (America's Memorial Triathlon and the New York City Triathlon). The means-end chain consisted of the attributes of three different experiences over two days. The pictures and copy leverage these into benefits of energy expenditure and competition, fun and relaxation that a target audience may then transform into personal values such as excitement, accomplishment and happiness. Figure 7.3 features another event and a series of three advertisements in order to illustrate the means-end chain concept.

The third framework lets the advertisement designer decide on the extent to which the content will be verbal as opposed to visual. This decision is clearly made by considering the nature of the message.

Whichever framework is used, the first step in advertising design is to determine message strategy. This is the tactic that is used to deliver the message theme as prescribed in the creative brief. There are four types of strategy used: cognitive, affective, conative and brand (Clow and Baack, 2004).

Cognitive message strategies

These are informational or carry rationalized arguments. They could incorporate a unique selling point or carry direct and straightforward generic information about a product. They could also be 'firsts' in that they pre-empt the competition in making a particular statement of superiority. They could also carry direct comparisons with the competition.

Affective message strategies

These strategies are designed to inspire emotion in order to affect target audience reason and then link them to the product, possibly by helping audiences to recall experiences or by eliciting powerful emotional feelings.

Conative message strategies

These strategies are intended to inspire action. The actions may be to return a coupon, hit a website or visit a store for an exclusive offer and clearly have the capacity to be used alongside other forms of communications.

Brand message strategies

Unlike the other types of message strategies, brand focused strategies are intended to build brand image and brand user image. Image building advertisements will focus on the brand and its personality. Alternatively, user focused advertisements will focus on the type of person who uses the brand. Events have a ready made and effective way of doing this via the use of celebrities, star performers and talent and their endorsement of the event.

An advertisement requires an execution framework, a production style that again involves the consideration of the nature of the message. There are some common

Figure 7.3 Means-end chain theory. Artwork courtesy of ICEP Portugal 2004 (**See Appendix on pages 309–311 for larger images and more legible text**).

forms that are used and these include animation, a slice-of-life for a touch of realism, dramatization, testimonial, authoritative, demonstration, fantasy and informative. Many of these speak for themselves. Figure 7.2, for example, features the '2004 Iron Teams Relay' and two other event advertisements featured in the *Metrosports New York* (2004) magazine. These advertisements can be compared and contrasted in order to demonstrate the use of frameworks. All three advertisements are informative in nature. The 'Iron Teams Relay' and the 'New York City Triathlon' events use still photography to demonstrate the activities involved. The former is clearly a more abstract message using pictures of footwear. The 'Liberty to Liberty' Triathlon uses a single drawing to create imagery to inform.

An advertisement also needs appeal and over the years there have been examples of any number of themes used. Clow and Baack (2004) provide seven major types of advertising appeal that are considered to be successful in developing advertisements: fear, humour, sex, music, rationality, emotion and scarcity. There is an element of fear created in the advertisements in Figure 7.2, for example; a fear of not being able to meet the challenge set by the events and this can transform into a personal value of accomplishment. Pickton and Broderick (2001), on the other hand, offer thirty-five ways to gain attention in advertisements and include the use of testimonials, use of personalities and spokespeople. This kind of appeal is an effective appeal for events because event participants are not only the core product they are also often available for use in advertising. This can be the case whatever the profile of the participants involved. Clearly, the use of imagery and the endorsement by high profile sports star and cyclist Lance Armstrong was important for the Tour de France and their 2004 television advertising campaign (see Case study 7.1). Similarly, the use of pop-star Madonna in costume, by her promoters Clearchannel, Solo and Caliente Entertainment, in a print campaign was no less important. Concert advertising can often be purely informative with no use of imagery. For Madonna's 2004 World Tour entitled 'Re-invention', however, it was deemed important for a print advertising campaign that depicted her evocatively dressed in period costume (*Sunday Times*, 2004b).

Finally, the design process involves one further decision – which sources and spokespeople to use? Up to 20 per cent of all advertisements have a celebrity spokesperson (Clow and Baack, 2004) and again events have that ready-made resource there if they wish to tap it.

Figure 7.3 Means-end chain theory. Artwork courtesy of ICEP Portugal 2004 (**See Appendix on pages 309–311**).
These three advertisements were used by the Portuguese Trade and Tourism Office, ICEP Portugal, in conjunction with Portugal UEFA Euro 2004. The objective was to leverage the attributes of a major event and the country as a tourist destination. To illustrate the 'means-end chain' concept, first consider the product on offer, 'Portugal as a holiday destination'. The attributes are a range of flexible activities and facilities that are classic through to modern, attractive and world-class. The benefits are focused on a football championship and a full and varied holiday experience that can be gained 24 hours a day. The leverage points use abstract images that interrelate tourism (beach, castles, sunshine and clear skies) and football (modern stadia and green pitches). In addition, the copy relates to the event as well as to non-match time and how it can be spent. These leverage points help the reader to transform the benefits into any number of personal values such as excitement, fun, happiness, pleasure, sense of belonging and accomplishment.

Case study 7.1

Tour de France 'Cyclysm'

The US television channel Outdoor Life Network (OLN), in collaboration with the Tour de France, developed a series of advertisements with the focus on a new word. They created a campaign entitled 'Cyclysm' that ran in the spring/summer of 2004 in the USA. The event

organizer's objective was to create further awareness of the race in the USA, in particular to non-cycling fans and OLN had been appointed media broadcast partners accordingly.

The media vehicles used included Comcast owned television networks, including OLN, and cable operators. Print media included newspapers, such as *USA Today*, and magazines, such as *Sports Illustrated* and *ESPN*. Outdoor posters were also used. The total value of the advertising space booked was approximately $US20 million.

The television creative was focused on the US born Tour de France five-time champion, Lance Armstrong. This was an appropriate choice of spokesperson considering the high status and profile Armstrong had at that time in his home country. The themes used were his quest for a sixth win, his rivals and the historical nature of the race. The appeal was one of drama that had a 'mythological' look and gave Armstrong an iconic persona. The creation of a new word was in order to show that no word existed that would aptly describe the nature of the relationship between Armstrong and the race. The advertisement, seen opposite, uses a single shot of Armstrong against shafts of light. The network name and race dates are also shown and together with the title 'The Cyclysm is upon us' are intended to provide an informative yet dramatic execution framework. The lack of a bicycle and pictures that demonstrate the race or the sport of cycling is to be noted, as the intention is to focus on the appeal of Armstrong to wider audiences.

Source: Bernstein (2004). Artwork courtesy of © 2004 Outdoor Life Network, OLNTV.com.

Advertising planning

It was indicated earlier that it is important that the media used match the advertisement and its design. This media selection is conducted in two stages. The first stage considers the types of media classes that are appropriate. The major media classes have traditionally been television, radio, press, cinema and outdoor sites (Crosier, 1999), but to these there are now added a number of other media. These are introduced later in this chapter. The second stage is then to select individual vehicles from each class. Only then can there be any accurate assessment of the potential value of an advertising campaign or indeed its cost. The production of an advertising schedule is therefore clearly based on research into which media classes and then which vehicles will be appropriate selections. This research can be guided by a number of criteria (as covered in Chapter 14):

- *Reach*: this refers to the number of people, households or businesses that a media vehicle is exposed to in a certain time period.
- *Frequency*: this is the average number of times the advertisement is exposed in a certain time period.
- *Gross ratings points*: this is a measure of the impact or the intensity of the media schedule and is calculated by multiplying a media vehicle's rating by the frequency/number of insertions of the advertisement.
- *Cost*: the total cost of the advertising programme offers a comparative measure when determining the value of the advertising programme. A calculation of cost-per-thousand is also a common cost criteria; the cost in reaching 1000 of the media vehicle's audience.

- *Impressions*: this represents the total number of potential exposures of an advertisement to an audience. In other words, it is the total number of people, households or businesses in the market regardless of whether they have seen the advertisement or not.
- *Continuity*: this criterion is concerned with the pattern of the exposure. The pattern can be continuous, pulsating with a minimal level of advertising that increases at periodic intervals or discontinuous with advertisements at intervals only. The transient nature of events makes it difficult to apply some of the accepted recommendations from marketing texts. Shimp (1997), for example, suggests that advertising be strategically exercised consistently. In contrast, events can advertise too early and year-round advertising activity for an annual event may well be inefficient and ineffective. For one-off events the advertising is more often than not going to be in a discontinuous schedule. For those event organizers with year round programmes, the advertising that is implemented for specific performances is still going to be discontinuous in nature, but there maybe opportunities to produce corporate messages for whole event portfolios which could effectively follow a pulsating or continuous schedule.

Advertising media selection

Selecting which media class is appropriate is governed by four criteria – via the determination of the cost per opportunity, deciding on whether to compete where the competition is active, whether the budget is appropriate and whether there is an appropriate match for the requirements of the message (Jobber, 1998). Ultimately, the decision of which media to choose is based on which can provide the most effective and efficient solution for the achievement of objectives. The media classes available are discussed below.

Television

The advantage of television is that an advertisement can be produced in action thus enabling products to be practically demonstrated. Visual appeal of colour and movement can be combined with sound, unlike the one-dimensional opportunities that are delivered in press, radio and poster advertising. This allows the creative to build atmosphere effectively in order to build brand image. Events can be visually and audibly vibrant and so television can be an important selection. The 2003 World Athletics Championships in Paris used television effectively to build an image for the event by showing athletics sporting action as if it were being staged in the streets of the city.

Television schedules also provide opportunities for repeat showings that can be frequent and over short time periods. Television advertising is, however, transient in nature and unless it is recorded it cannot be referred to once it has been broadcast. Repeat scheduling therefore becomes more of a necessity than an added benefit. It can be a disadvantage too if they are shown frequently, whereby television advertisements lose the capacity to appeal and attract interest. Advertisers then have the problem of having to produce further advertisements at further cost. It is not necessarily the advertising rate that is an obstacle for event advertisers, but the costs of production of effective advertisements, which can be relatively high.

Another advantage/disadvantage of television advertising is its capacity to intrude. This is where an advertisement intrudes on a viewer without their voluntary attention. Intrusion though, is exactly that and can work either way. Scheduling for slots around the right programme is therefore important if the advertisement is going to grab attention and appeal. Advertising clutter is another issue and with some channels commercial breaks can be too frequent and overly long. Paying to get in at the beginning and end of breaks has therefore become more important.

The advent of digital television has increased the number of channels available around the world and that in turn has helped to lower advertising rates. With the creation of specialist channels, advertisers also have the opportunity of targeting more effectively. The networks in the USA and other countries offer similar advertising opportunities through local channels.

Pan-European advertising is possible via specialist channels such as MTV, Cartoon Network, NBC Europe, TNT and Eurosport. MTV has increased opportunities for further targeting by regional advertisers with the provision of four European services – UK, Northern, Southern and Central Europe. For example, the Heineken sponsored 'Jammin Festival', part of the 2004 Olympic Cultural Olympiad programme of events was advertised on MTV throughout the Mediterranean. Locals and holidaymakers alike were being reached with the ultimate objective of selling tickets and gaining exposure for the sponsor.

Infomercials are another type of television advertisement. Similar to in-print advertorials, they allow more information to be delivered in a format that appears more editorial than commercial. Widely used in the USA and listed as 'Paid Programming' in television listings, they may be of limited use for advertising for many events but for certain event types they could be effective. Shopping channels of course specialize in such broadcasting and offer immediate purchase opportunities. Sports products and memorabilia, art and music are all advertised and sold via this method and so it is not implausible that the use of slots to sell event-related products may simultaneously achieve advertising objectives for event awareness and image building.

Of all the media classes, television offers the highest potential for reach. While this is represented in the relatively higher rates paid, the cost-per-contact is relatively low. Therefore, as with all media selection, targeting is crucial.

Newspapers

Newspapers have high degrees of credibility. They are relied on to provide fact and story and as a result can be effective advertising selections. A clear advantage of in-print advertising is that readers can take time to take them in if they so wish. They may even revisit when they wish at later times or pass the paper on to another reader, although in general newspapers have a short life. Newspapers also offer targeting flexibility as advertisements can vary from locality to locality via regional and local editions.

One key advantage of newspapers for event organizers is that they offer community prestige (Boone and Kurtz, 2002). The local newspaper can have a deep impact on a local community and local advertisers can therefore become involved in that. As well as intensive coverage and reach into the majority of local homes, certain newspapers can be used for integrated communications that can see advertisements, advertorials, editorial and sales promotions all in the same edition. The use of media partners in this way is examined later in the chapter.

With newspapers comes the advantage of being able to create a number of impressions relatively inexpensively. For example, the Cleveland Indians (US Major League Baseball) used a series of print advertisements in newspapers, in the city, for sales objectives. Three advertisements were created and all used pictures of tickets with titles that offered an alternative to watching a live game. The alternatives were obviously less attractive options. The depicted jobs of cleaning the gutters, mowing the lawn and doing the laundry were typical weekend tasks that either men or women could be doing instead of seeing the Indians.

There is also flexibility in terms of size and colours, but reproduction can be poor. Other disadvantages are that advertisements compete with editorial for a reader's attention. Targeting can also be difficult to achieve with specific markets, although there are usually sections to a newspaper that at least enable some flexibility – sports, entertainment, arts and television sections for example.

Magazines

There are two forms of magazine and both are of interest to event organizers. Consumer magazines and business/trade magazines offer subdivided classes and flexibility in reaching sports, arts and music readers of all kinds with specialist periodicals. Further flexibility is offered with each via various distribution schedules and pagination opportunities. Flexibility in size and colour is on offer too as are integrated communication opportunities as with newspapers. All of this enables selective and precise targeting to accompany the advantages of long life and normally good production quality.

Business-to-business magazines offer opportunities for those events that are seeking partners. These may even be suppliers. The Libya 2010 bid team, for example, took a rather rare step in placing an advertisement on the back cover of *Sport Business International* (2004). Libya was one of six countries that submitted bids to stage the 2010 FIFA World Cup and used an advertising vehicle that was distributed to sports business professionals of all kinds, including those in the sports stadia construction sector. The advertising copy was concerned with attracting tenders for the building of the facilities the country needed for the hosting of the World Cup and so the use of this particular media vehicle was well targeted. What is of concern is the timing of the placement. The advertisement requested that expressions of interest be submitted by the end of March 2004 and yet FIFA declared the winning bid (South Africa) less than three months later leaving little time for tenders to be produced and then processed.

Sponsors can also be sought using business-to business advertising as the Central Intercollegiate Athletic Association Schools (CIAA) demonstrated in spring 2004. The association was celebrating its sixtieth anniversary and used the *Sport Business Journal* (2004) for a full-page colour print advertisement that showed how its television audiences had grown over the years. A contact name, number and website were also included in the copy.

Consumer magazines are also highly segmented offering sophisticated targeting opportunities. There are specialist magazines that can offer reach to readers of different genres of music that can deliver advertising solutions for pop, rock, classical, opera and club event promoters and the opportunities for sports and arts events are no less attractive through both trade and consumer titles. A good example of the diverse opportunities that are available was shown by the 2004 Olympics and an advertisement for an event that was as much for cultural activity as it was for sport.

In collaboration with the Greek Tourist Authority, the organizers placed an advertisement in the June issue of the British Airways in-flight magazine. The objective was to attract tourists to Greece because of and in spite of the Olympics.

The disadvantages of magazines in general are that they can often have long lead times and that can be unfortunate for event advertisers if there are changes to the event programme in the mean time. There can be wastage too with a current issue displaying an event advertisement that has already been staged because of its long issue period. Costs can also be high and for many magazines, advertising clutter is a major problem. Some magazines can carry up to 20 consecutive pages of advertisements in their front halves for example. However, because magazines can be passed on and shared they do have a longer lifespan than many other media.

Radio

Obviously radio is creatively limited to sound, but that can also be considered its attraction. Even though it is a mass medium, radio has a remarkable propensity for creating one-to-one relationships and intimacy (Clow and Baack, 2004). They can be targeted relationships too. Breakfast, morning, afternoon, drive-time, evening and weekend programming can all deliver different audiences. The format can also offer flexibility in that there are not just music, news, sport and talk stations but with music there are different genres on offer – golden oldies, pop, rock, jazz, classical and country to name a few. As a result lifestyles can be used to target very specific audiences. Add to that the flexibility of local, regional and national opportunities and not only can this be an effective targeting process it can also be an efficient one. Web-cast radio has also increased the sizes of these audiences not just into new territories such as offices, but also on an international basis and special factors such as the portability of radios and reach into cars and other transit make radio a very useful selection. The development of commercial free digital radio services may, however, limit the opportunities.

The beauty of local radio for event organizers is its place in the community. Local stations work hard to provide service to their communities not just in programming but also events and promotions. They actually get out into the community and listeners are integrated into programmes. Events want to reach the same audience and radio advertising can therefore be an effective medium, especially when used in conjunction with PR to generate further publicity via this medium.

While radio offers short lead times for relatively inexpensively produced advertisements, they do have short lives and listeners are often engaged in other activities at the same time making their attention more difficult to grab. National coverage will also not be an attractive selection for all event organizers as there are difficulties in having to contact multiple stations in order to achieve it. In addition, the placing of too much information into radio advertisements can mean less recall and the giving out of telephone numbers for ticket sales is often a challenge that some advertisers believe is best solved by annoying repetition. Repetition in this way is not necessarily an innovative solution.

Outdoor

The term 'outdoor' traditionally refers to billboards, posters, transportation, illuminations, artworks and street furniture. This form of advertising has a long life and is considered a low-cost option because it has broad reach. Targeting is generally therefore not that specific, although billboard rotation systems and relocation packages can be purchased in order to reach new territories. Billboards, in particular, can be large, spectacular and some can become iconic sights. Sites on the Marylebone Road in London have become sought after by advertisers because of the amount of traffic on one of the busiest roads in Europe. The Stella Artois Tennis Tournament has used billboards effectively there in the past, particularly in animations of the rivalries between players such as Edberg, McEnroe and Connors. Other advertisers have created one-off three-dimensional sites with running water, live models and full-size cars. Billboards are therefore not necessarily limited in their creativity as some might have it. Short exposure time is a problem though. Drivers pass billboards quickly even if they pass them frequently and so messages need to remain uncomplicated. In that sense they are limited in their depth of delivery.

Targeting is not altogether a lost cause with all outdoor media. The organizers of the 2004 Tribeca Film Festival in New York were able to billboard and locate fly-posters in the Tribeca area before and during the time of their event, for example. Advertising on street furniture such as seating, public notice boards, illuminations on the sides of buildings and in displays can all be located for geo-demographic segmentation, although exposure will also be to non-target audiences. Advertising on the street itself via lampposts was a method used by the 2002 Commonwealth Games in the host city of Manchester. They also produced a giant sized poster of Jonah Lomu, the New Zealand rugby union player and placed it on the side of a building, a move that, unfortunately for them, backfired as the player did not actually end up participating in the event, thus demonstrating the issues of lead times and the use of endorsement.

Transportation offers a number of opportunities. Trains were a popular choice in Athens for 2004 Olympic Games sponsors where Cosmote, Hyundai and Samsung decorated the rail cars. In addition to the common use of trains, buses and taxis there are also blimps (balloons) and aeroplane banners. There are clear differences in the exposure times for these forms of advertising and their advantages and disadvantage is their mobility and therefore their targeting limitations.

Fly-posting has become a popular medium, particularly for music and club promoters. They are pasted up in specific locations and have the added audience appeal of contravening local laws in many of those locations. This is something that has been addressed by some municipal authorities with the provision of boards and freestanding structures specifically for fly-posting. Interestingly, the appeal is not the same and many promoters ignore these and continue as they used to.

There is also the use of less traditional methods to consider, those advertising activities that involve people, for example. Case study 2.1 in Chapter 2 shows how the ICA Gallery in London went about increasing awareness of its philosophy of only exhibiting the works of living artists by literally using people as live advertisements.

It is also worth including the example of Nike's use of giant footballs in its ambushing of UEFA Euro 2004 as an example here. In various European cities the manufacturer placed giant replica footballs, high on the sides of buildings. They were a different approach that caught attention. They managed to secure more attention when a ball fell on the top of a BMW car in Bangkok (*The Financial Times*, 2004). An *in-situ* ball in Prague can be seen in the photograph at the start of Section Four. This was an innovative and integrated use of advertising by the perennial ambushing sports manufacturer and is clearly an indication of the level to which event advertising must aspire. Such use of ambient media is generally more akin to publicity stunts to generate PR and word-of-mouth than mass media advertising.

Cinema

This can be both in the form of film trailers at theatres as well as on videos and DVD for home rental. They have the same advantages of movement, colour and sound as television with the added benefit of a captive audience watching a large presentation. Repetition cannot be achieved with too many viewers as few are regular enough, but local theatres can offer further targeted opportunities for local advertisers even though the costs are relatively high per exposure. Film festival organizers unsurprisingly use this medium because of the targeting potential it offers. Examples include the 'Instinct' titled campaign for the Vancouver International Film Festival, 'Hunters' and the Atlanta Festival and 'Director' for the London Film Festival.

Indoor

Posters, displays and signage can be used indoors as well as outdoors. Municipal authorities often have the opportunity to use their own buildings for this purpose. Clearly the targeting can be quite specific but the exposure limited both in numbers and time. Airports offer opportunities for event organizers that want to reach tourists and returning locals. The Tuscan Challenge motor racing series has a low profile in the UK and uses advertising above luggage collection points at Manchester airport in its marketing strategy. The medium uses plasma screens and advertisements in rotation enabling the attributes of the event to be seen in action, although not in sound.

'Ambient' media opportunities include another useful point of contact in male lavatories. The placement of advertisements above individual urinals has proven effective for certain advertisers attempting to reach males in clubs, pubs and bars, for example.

Internet

The Internet has provided a whole new world of opportunities for events in particular. Event organizers have been able inexpensively to set up websites that offer year round advertising potential. Like newspapers and magazines the draw is to the factual and editorial information but, in addition, websites offer interactivity. Internet users usually go to websites that attract them and so related advertising can actually be of interest.

The major benefit of the Internet is the relative ease with which creativity can be achieved and in short lead times. Targeting can also be specific with the use of engage technologies that record site-to-site traffic movement. This can be used to create data and customer profiles that can be matched to database profiles so that advertisements can then be sent on to appropriate targets. Events can also target business prospects as well as consumers via the Internet.

As this medium becomes more sophisticated and overused it will raise more issues. It is the fastest growing medium in history, apparently taking only five years to reach fifty million users, while television and radio took thirteen and thirty-eight years respectively to reach the same threshold (Clow and Baack, 2004). It is no wonder that there is now an issue of clutter. Already the use of banner advertisements is becoming obsolete with the advent of banner stops. Clutter is therefore a problem that users are taking action against.

Event organizers like US major league teams have managed to use the technology to collect profile data and then advertise with direct e-mail. You only need to buy one ticket for one major league baseball game at the Yankee Stadium in New York and you will receive weekly, if not more frequent, e-mails with offers from the Yankees. Make the purchase via Ticketmaster, their ticket agents, and you will receive direct e-mail from Major League Baseball (MLB) too.

Internet advertisements do not have the intrusion value of television as they can be removed. Advertisers tried to retain them with video and other animated presentations but that is now considered obsolete. Advertisers are using interstitial advertising techniques whereby an advertisement interrupts without warning but almost as quickly software has been produced that prevents such pop-ups if desired. Thus demonstrating how quickly this medium requires innovation for successful advertising.

Tele-marketing

Advertisements can be placed into on-hold systems for captive but relatively small audiences. While this results in one-to-one contact, it is derived from a non-personal approach. The advertiser is not personally making the call. It is just maximizing a random opportunity. The costs are low though and for events this can be worthwhile. Those events that manage their own telesales can easily use on-hold systems to advertise further opportunities at the same and other events. Events that appoint ticket and hospitality agents should also ensure that their event is included in their agents' on-hold systems and also that it receives maximum billing over any competition. This is not always that easily achieved of course as the agents control that medium.

Printed materials

The use of printed materials includes leaflets, brochures and shopping bags. 'Leafleting' is used by many event organizers and to some effect. Regular newsletters were used by the New York 2012 Olympic bid team, for example, in order to foster community support. One such issue focused on the city's hosting of the 2003 Fencing World Cup and the leaflet was able to promote one event through the other (NYC 2012, 2004). NYC 2012 had also forged links with the Tribeca Film Festival of that year too and so the leaflet was able to feature the launch of 'Fencing month in New York City' that had previously taken place.

Leafleting can be effectively targeted if materials are distributed 'live' outside another event venue and a leafleting team will also not want to miss the opportunity of carrying self-liquidating promotions in the form of event dates and details on their own and freely distributed clothing. Distribution can also be implemented via high street locations such as retailers and or places that have a common interest. Sheffield's 'Art Market' used art galleries throughout Yorkshire in the UK as self-service distribution points for its 2004 event for example, whereas the '2004 Durham Summer Festival' organizers were a little less discriminate and used as many retail points in their city as possible. Printed materials can also be dual purpose. In Rome, Italy, the organizers of the '2004 Romaeuropa Festival' used a folded fifty by thirty-eight millimetre sheet as a leaflet which, because of its larger size, could also be utilized as a poster.

Media partners

The importance of media partners for successful PR and the development of sponsorship programmes are covered in Chapters 5 and 8, respectively. An important aspect of media partnerships for events is ensuring that there are advertising components in any agreements with newspapers, television, radio and Internet partners. Whatever the extent of the agreement, an event should try to secure advertising space with their media partners. The deal can be efficient if it is agreed as an in-kind relationship (no money exchanged) and effective for both parties as it demonstrates the closeness of the relationship. Each medium will want to drive the mutual audience involved to more usage and so it is in their interests to have event advertisements in place. The partnership between Glastonbury 2004 and *The Guardian* national newspaper in the UK, for example, was forged in order that both could attract and sustain a new target audience. The 2004 Rochester Jazz Festival in Canada formed an agreement with a local newspaper, *The Democrat and Chronicle*. The event wanted to achieve two objectives. First, they wanted to attract sponsors and so they secured an agreement with the media owners Gannett to provide a range of advertising opportunities that could then be passed on to sponsors as and when they were signed. Secondly, they wanted to secure direct advertising for the event and so space was agreed for festival advertising in various Gannett owned special publications as well as the newspaper and its website. Gannett also produced a 200 000 run of the festival programme. In return the media group received introductions to festival sponsors so that they could sell advertising across all the dedicated festival printed media vehicles, on-site kiosks and corporate hospitality packages (IEG, 2004). If the agreement is in-kind in this way, it is advisable for the event to try to secure the partners' assistance in production, particularly for television and radio, because production can be expensive and therefore a prohibitive factor.

Events need not limit themselves to the normal selection of media partners of television, radio and newspaper. Other media can be very effective. The organizers of the Pepsi Extravaganza, a two-week long lifestyle event staged in London, agreed an in-kind partnership with London Underground. Trackside posters were designed to advertise the event, the re-opening of the event's nearest underground station, Angel Islington, and also that joint tickets could be purchased for the event and journey at all London Transport Authority stations.

Advertising evaluation

The selection criteria used in order to choose media vehicles from the above designated classes can be creative but traditionally come down to a cost-per-thousand calculation (Jobber, 1998). Research is therefore required into each potential vehicle and particularly data concerning their audience ratings. Reliable data are researched and produced by a number of independent organizations. For example, in the USA, Nielson Media Research collects television viewer data via various methods, including diaries, in order to calculate ratings and audience share of programme watching. These kinds of data are used to help space sellers determine advertising rates and advertisers identify whether advertisements have reached their target audiences. Other organizations in the USA include Starch INRA Hooper, Mediamark Research and Burke Marketing Research. For national radio networks data in the

USA, there is Radio All-Dimension Audience Research (RADAR). In the UK, research for radio is provided by Radio Joint Audience Research (RAJAR), with UK television data provided by the Broadcasters' Audience Research Board (BARB). The latter produces weekly reports based on information from 3000 households with metered television equipment. Researched data for outdoor media and poster sites is collated by Outdoor Site Classification and Audience Research (OSCAR) and cinema ratings are provided by Cinema and Video Industry Audience Research (CAVIAR).

The purpose of evaluating advertising is to measure whether it has achieved the objectives that were set for it. Therefore, the precise nature of what is researched depends on the nature of the objectives. If objectives are concerned with sales or market share, then research will be focused on sales and share movement, whereas if they are image related then research will be focused on consumer or business awareness and attitude.

Jobber (1998) points out a common problem in the advertising industry in his warning that the key to evaluating advertising is not in winning industry awards but on consultation with the target audiences. For successful advertising and feedback into that creative and logistical process, evaluation needs to take place before, during and after advertising has been executed. Pre-testing is part of the design and production process and is used to test if it is creatively achieving objectives before execution. Once an advertisement has run it should also be post-tested to see if has achieved the whole job. The most used forms of evaluation measure image and attitude change, sales change and usage rates and change. A number of research techniques are used, including pre-test focus groups, customer surveys for recall and statistical analysis of actual sales data.

This returns us full circle to the discussion earlier of there being no real understanding of why advertising works. A dichotomy arises when the objectives that are set cannot be measured because the process by which they might or might not be achieved is not understood. Crosier (1999) maintains that there are issues with current evaluation techniques and indeed the whole approach to evaluation. He suggests that there are difficulties at the start of the process when objectives are not designed to be measurable and that this is all too common across all industries. Without measurable criteria, advertisers have to rely on the standard technology of social research and, in particular, attitude and opinion scales and these, he maintains, do not provide proven causal links with behavioural change. He, like many, await the development of tests that truly measure the effectiveness of advertising and its ability to take target audiences from increased awareness through to action. Jobber (1998) agrees and acknowledges that advertisers do in practice set actual sales figures as measures and, despite difficulties in relating cause and effect, they believe they have to continue to use sales changes until there are better methods.

Summary

While there is a lack of understanding in why advertising works and there are questions over evaluation techniques, advertising will remain an enigma. Yet, despite these anomalies, advertising is clearly a very popular tool and is, at the very least, perceived to be an effective method of marketing communication. The extensive amount of usage on an international scale is testament to this.

However, many forms of advertising have previously not been used to market events. Advertising has often been perceived as expensive and out of reach for many event budgets. This has changed with the multitude of advertising opportunities that now exist and now events have all forms of advertising at their disposal. The traditional staple media of television, newspapers, radio, outdoor and cinema are now more diversified via regionalization, digitalization and other technological developments and, as such, offer affordable event advertising solutions. Add to these the opportunities that come via the Internet and many more events can now innovatively access a full range of advertising media for IMC.

Discussion points

- Select three events of your choice from the arts, music and sports sectors and:
  - compare and contrast the advertising objectives for each event
  - evaluate how these objectives fit, or otherwise, into overall IMC plans
  - compare and contrast the advertising targeting for each event
  - comment on the success of each advertising campaign by referring to the evaluation implemented.
- Select an advertising campaign for another event of your choice. Identify the selections of media classes, vehicles and schedules involved in order to analyse the objectives and target audience.
- Using the same campaign select one advertisement and analyse the creative and the intended message by identifying the means-end chain involved.

References

Adforum (2004) www.adforum.com/adfolio (accessed 16 June, 2004).

Bernstein, A. (2004) No word could describe the Tour de France, so OLN made one up. *Sport Business Journal*, May 31–June 6. Street and Smith.

Boone, L. and Kurtz, D. (2002) *Contemporary Marketing 2002*. Thomson Learning.

Clow, K. and Baack, D. (2004) *Integrated Advertising, Promotion, and Marketing Communications*, 2nd edn. Pearson Prentice Hall.

Crosier, K. (1999) Advertising. In *Marketing Communications: Principles and Practice*, Kitchen, P. (ed.). International Thomson Business Press.

Ehrenberg, A. (1988) *Repeat Buying: Facts, Theory and Applications*, 2nd edn. Charles Griffin.

Ehrenberg, A., Scriven, J. and Bernard, N. (2000) Advertising established brands: An international dimension. In *The Handbook of International Marketing Communications*, Moyne, S. (ed.). Blackwell.

Financial Times, The (2004) Thais look at a car crushed by a giant football promoting the Euro 2004 soccer tournament that fell from a billboard above a shop in Bangkok. 1 June.

Getz, D. (1997) *Event Management and Event Tourism*. Cognizant.

ICEP Portugal (2004) Portuguese Trade and Tourism Office. New York.

IEG (2004) Anatomy of a local event/newspaper sponsorship. *IEG Sponsorship Report*. Sample Issue. IEG.

Jobber, D. (1998) *Principles and Practice of Marketing*, 2nd edn. McGraw-Hill.

Jones, J. (1995) *When Ads Work: New Proof that Advertising Triggers Sales*. Simon and Schuster.

Lavidge, R. and Steiner, G. (1961) A model for the predictive measurements of advertising effectiveness. *Journal of Advertising Marketing*, 25 October, 59–62.

Metrosports New York (2004) The 2004 Iron Teams Relay on Nantucket. Advertisement. April.

NYC 2012 (2004) Informational leaflet. Spring 2003. NYC 2012.

Pickton, D. and Broderick, A. (2001) *Integrated Marketing Communications*. Financial Times/Prentice Hall.

Shimp, T. (1997) *Advertising, Promotion, and Supplemental Aspects of Integrated Marketing Communications*, 4th edn. The Dryden Press.

Sport Business International (2004) Libya 2010 advertisement. Issue 89, March.

Sports Business Journal (2004) CIAA 60th Anniversary. May 31–June 6, 2004.

Strong, E. (1925) *The psychology of selling*. McGraw-Hill.

Sunday Times, The (2004a) Advertising. Magazine section, 20 June.

Sunday Times, The (2004b) Madonna concert advertisement. Magazine section, 16 May.

Chapter 8
Event Sponsorship Programmes

Objectives

- Develop an understanding of the advantages of a strategic approach to the recruitment of sponsors for innovative event communications
- Identify the process involved in targeting appropriate sponsors and developing sponsor relations in order to achieve communications objectives
- Identify the role played by sponsorship in event communications in order to achieve competitive advantage

Introduction

The task of developing new sponsorships with revenue objectives in mind is difficult enough without also introducing criteria that focus on the role sponsors might play in enhancing event communications. However, this chapter proposes that a strategic approach to the development of sponsorship programmes in this way can not only lead to enhanced communications reach at no extra cost to the event, but also lead to sponsor renewal. Event sponsors that exploit their event rights by integrating them into their own communications programmes are doing so at their cost and, in addition, are complementing the events communications effort. In so doing, sponsors are more likely to be successful in achieving their sponsorship objectives and react positively to renewing and developing the relationship.

This chapter identifies the process by which this is achieved. In particular, the importance of aspects such as researched targeting, provision of tailored rights and continuous development of sponsor relations are discussed. The focus in Chapter 12 is concerned with how sponsors utilize event sponsorship to achieve their communications objectives, whereas the focus here is entirely from the event organizer's perspective.

Targeting

Bargaining power and the capacity to attract desired sponsors at desired levels of sponsorship are all the more easily achieved by those events with pedigree. Pedigree in that they are sought after properties that offer alternative communications solutions, effectively reach target markets and do so more efficiently than other forms of communications. As an alternative to advertising, sponsorship has, for example, scored well in offering more value for money. However, not all events, particularly new events, are able to demonstrate such a level of pedigree and so the attraction of those sponsors that make the most successful communications partners is not always that simple. Ineffective targeting can make this practically impossible.

The only way of credibly demonstrating pedigree is to present existing or new potential sponsors with research data that identify how their sponsorship objectives have been or can be achieved. For the recruitment of new sponsors, research also forms the basis by which appropriate targets are identified. This process involves two key steps (Masterman, 2004a,b).

Step one: event target markets

Research data are required in order to determine the event's target markets. A profile can be achieved via demographic, psychographic and behavioural research of all the audiences. It is also important to identify the size of each market reached. Event audiences that actually attend are important, but so are the markets that are more widely reached via any communications tools that are to be utilized, for example, mailing lists and news media coverage. Any data on product preferences and buying behaviour can also be of critical importance.

Observation research methods can be used, but surveys and focus groups may be used more reliably. The issue for event managers is that this can be an expensive exercise and this in turn explains why this is not a common practice throughout the industry. However, if further justification for research is required, then the information and data that research provides do serve other marketing purposes and in particular in aiding decision making in the event planning process for customer targeting. In addition, targeting is an exercise in effectiveness and efficiency. The more comprehensive the data and analysis the more clearly defined the targets will be and therefore the more effective the communication. Equally, more effective targeting will lead to less waste in resources and greater efficiency.

Step two: matching organizational target markets

Sponsorship is a mutual agreement for an exchange of benefits (Sleight, 1989; Meenaghan, 1998). Event target markets therefore need to match up with a sponsor's target markets and it is incumbent upon the event to ensure that it can demonstrate this in any approaches it makes to potential sponsors.

Various research methods can be applied in order to collect data and much can be sourced in the public domain. Financial accounts, trading and industry figures, market trends and forecasts, government reports, trade news media and marketing news media are all useful sources of information. Other event and sponsorship activity in the industry can be indicative of current trends, but there are limitations to their use. For example, many sponsorship agreements are negotiated a year and more in advance and, as most organizations work ahead on their annual budgets, it is future trends that are of more concern. Potential sponsors themselves are obviously a key source of information and critically pertinent information will be forthcoming at investigative meetings with them. A comprehensive collection of information would include marketing and sponsorship objectives, a profile of all their target markets/publics for pertinent brands and/or corporate communications and an audit of all their marketing activity, results and plans. There is still the initial approach to be made, however, and it is important that in making that first contact there is an understanding of the organization's target markets. There are two reasons for this. First, a lot of the event organization's time and resources can be wasted if the approach does not have a firm grasp of the needs of the potential sponsor. The second is one of credibility. It is critical that the approach is credible in the eyes of the sponsor and that is achieved via thorough research and knowledge.

The more research methods that are used, the better, in order to build a comprehensive picture. However, this is not a one-off exercise. Individual sponsors' marketing requirements, activities and results are constantly in flux and so event organizations must continuously collect such data.

The phrase, 'sponsorship fit' is used generally to describe the mutual appropriateness of entering into a sponsorship. It represents more than just a matching of target markets. It concerns the whole set of rights and how they meet specific requirements and will ultimately meet objectives for both the sponsor and the event. Mullin et al. (2000) maintain that the relationship must function as a partnership where both sponsor and event receive benefits that can be exploited in order to meet objectives. However, it also concerns the issues of credibility and reputation with stakeholders and the ethos of each partner. Even if target markets match and objectives can be met, there may still be an inappropriate 'fit'. The fit between health-related sports events and alcohol and tobacco have presented issues in the past as have music and arts-related events where artistic integrity has been in question in the seeking of sponsorship funding (Masterman, 2004b). Audi, the car manufacturer, sponsored evenings at the Royal Opera House (ROH) in London during 2002 and 2003 and their rights included an illuminated logo on the outside of the ROH grade one listed building, as well as cars on display on the adjoining Covent Garden pavements. It is clear that the opportunities to reach target consumer markets made this an attractive prospect for Audi, but the benefit to ROH appears to have been little more than revenue. All events run the risk of over-commodification and, as a result, the risk of alienating their customers. On the other hand, the provision of a fleet of Rover cars for the Manchester 2002 Commonwealth Games provided that event with a saving in expenditure, the sponsor with the opportunity of increasing awareness for a new model and participants and officials with much needed courtesy transportation.

Fit can also be concerned with the relationships between individuals. The capacity to work with particular people has played a part in many long-running sponsorships and highlights the importance of building individual relationships in the sponsorship industry. The nature of matching characteristics and image between event and sponsor and the need for such for successful sponsorships is covered in greater detail in Chapter 12.

Relationship building

The work to establish a relationship begins with the targeting process. It is reasonable to assume that the greater the preparation, the more likely there will be a welcome reception from a potential sponsor. Even having received an initial negative response an event can, with careful handling, develop a relationship over a longer period in order eventually to nurture a sponsorship. For credibility, any approach must be tailored and bespoke.

Many events describe opportunities for sponsors and even partners and yet they make contact with potential organizations with offers of pre-determined sets of sponsorship rights. This off-the-shelf approach portends to supply a package of benefits that has been designed with no specific sponsors in mind and as a result is unlikely to meet any individual requirements. There is clearly no bespoke tailoring in this approach. Conversely, a tailored service begins with research into the precise marketing needs and objectives of specific and potential sponsors and the subsequent presentation of event sponsorships that are presented as marketing solutions. This can establish footholds for sponsor/event relations but the process does not start and finish there. It is important that this approach is applied throughout the life cycle of the sponsorship and then even beyond that. For example, new sponsorships can be grown and past sponsors can become sponsors again thus demonstrating that the relationship should be continuous. If events want to be successful, then it is incumbent upon them to ensure that this happens.

The types of objectives that sponsors seek to achieve are discussed at greater length in Chapter 12, but it is objectives such as the driving of sales, increasing brand awareness, increasing corporate awareness, developing internal relations and achieving competitive advantage that sponsorships need to be aligned to. An event sponsorship needs to consider their potential sponsors' objectives at an early stage and in order to develop the relationship, continuous reassessment and alignment throughout the life cycle are required. This includes ensuring that the sponsorship is evaluated against these objectives and that the results are then used to develop a greater or realigned solution. The process consists of four steps (Masterman, 2004a):

- *Step 1*: determine the requirements of the sponsorship
- *Step 2*: develop measures for evaluation
- *Step 3*: provide a sponsorship solution with a set of event rights that meets the objectives of both the sponsor and the event
- *Step 4*: agree payments and/or provision of products/services to be made by the sponsor in return for the determined event rights.

This four-step process is an on-going requirement. Existing as well as new sponsors can be developed throughout this cycle. The value of relationships is that they can be more easily developed and have the potential to be less costly than recruiting new sponsors. Lachowetz et al. (2003) have conducted research that demonstrates that those events that focus on developing closer ties early in the sales process go on to earn more loyalty when it comes to sponsorship renewal. This may also mean that maintaining and developing existing sponsor relations is a more effective and efficient sponsorship approach. The closer a partner is, the easier it is going to be to realign to changing needs and objectives over time and so renewing sponsorships is becoming a priority (Lachowetz et al., 2003).

How are relationships nurtured in this way? Relationship marketing literature has demonstrated the importance of trust and commitment (Baker and Sinkula, 1999; Mavondo, 2000) and communication (Mohr et al., 1996). Relationship marketing can only be maintained over long periods when there is trust between the parties involved and this is achieved via effective communication between event and sponsor. Meenaghan (1998) and Hoek (1998) both maintain that partnership and cooperation are key to sustainable communications. Effective communication will involve developing the relationship jointly and from an event's perspective this could mean allowing a sponsor to input into key event decisions. The trust can then come from a confidence in the other party knowing that they are focused on mutually beneficial objectives and that promises will be honoured. Trust is therefore an outcome of previously successful interaction (Farelly et al., 2003) and consequently something that is built over time. Trust, can also come from the knowledge that there is a degree of flexibility on both sides for change. A degree of flexibility, even when it comes to honouring promises and adhering to contracts, will be needed as the relationship grows because the need for change can occur at any time.

Farelly et al. (2003) reported results from their studies that indicated that the more effective the communication process, the greater the commitment to the relationship. They found that this was due to greater communication allowing partners to know where they stand and representing an indication of commitment to keep the relationship going, both of which can be reason to plan for the long term. More significantly though, they identified that strong market orientation has a positive association on the key factors of communication, commitment and trust. Sponsors with high levels of market orientation are therefore more likely to display greater commitment to a relationship. The most attractive sponsors are therefore those that implement market research in order to devise and integrate sponsorships into their marketing communication strategies.

It is critical for event organizations to be market orientated too. It was indicated earlier that it is important to acquire the kind of knowledge about appropriate sponsors that will assist in presenting them with sponsorship solutions, as opposed to going to them at the outset with a pre-determined sponsorship package. However, this is not to say that the event management team should not have prior knowledge of all the rights opportunities that are available. It is important that an event audit is completed, an inventory of all the assets that could be given over or bundled into rights. The assets can be categorized into eight general areas as displayed in Figure 8.1, the seventh of which, function, is key to ensuring that each sponsorship is bespoke. While any of the event assets may be bundled together to form a tailored set of sponsorship rights, it is the inclusion of rights that are intrinsically functional to the sponsor that will make a sponsorship unique. This is not a magic ingredient, it is the sponsor, its image or its brand being a functional part of the event. It is not always possible for this to be a basic function, but the sponsorship should be a shop window for a sponsor's products or services. This is the window that is seen by mutual target markets and so not only are objectives addressed, the relationship grows too. As convoluted as it may appear, Lanson Champagne provides a function at the Wimbledon Tennis Championships. The 'official champagne' is served throughout the event to corporate guests and is also available for purchase in the event's bars.

Samsung are another sponsor that enjoys functional showcases at events. At the 2004 Olympic Games in Athens they were the provider of 'Wireless Olympic Works' (WOW), a package of information services delivered to handheld devices provided

Event audits

An audit of an event consists of an evaluation of all possible assets in order to create an inventory of possible sponsorship rights that can be combined to provide sponsors with tailored marketing solutions.The audit areas may be categorized as follows:

Physical

> The division of the event into physical and geographical assets such as sites, zones, locations, venues, levels, indoor or outdoor.

Territory

> The division of the event into local, regional, national catchment areas. This can include division by round of competition.

Time

> The division of the event into timeframes, including by session, day, or again by round of competition.

Programme

> The division of the event into its various running order components. This might include pre-event, mid-event and post-event ceremonies, entertainments and other functions.

Supply

> The identification of ways in which expenditure can be reduced and/or the event enhanced via supply of key services, people or product by sponsors.

Status

> The placement of one or more sponsors into a successful sponsorship programme structure. (See Figures 8.2 and 8.3.)

Function

> Creating new rights opportunities that are tailored for individual sponsors whereby a function within the event provides a showcase for product and/or services and enhanced communications with target markets.

In addition, the identification of ways in which sponsors may assist in event communications is attractive for both event and sponsor:

Communications

> Media partners can provide enhanced event communication potential. In addition, all sponsors offer the event new target markets and publics. Each of the event's sponsor's employees, suppliers and customers may offer new opportunities, for example.
>
> Furthermore, all sponsors that are active in exploiting their rights offer the event supplementary communications potential that with negotiation can also include input into the running of the event.

Figure 8.1 Event auditing for sponsorship programme building (adapted from Masterman, 2004a).

to event officials, staff and media (*The Sunday Times*, 2004). The service helped improve communication systems and provided a key information service for the event. At the same Olympics, Swatch, the IOC's 'official timekeeper', not only provided timing for the sports competitions, but also a new 'On Venue Results' (OVR) service. At previous Games this service of providing accurate measurement and scores throughout the event was performed by a number of sponsors and suppliers. Swatch was able to bring new technology to Athens that enabled immediate competition results at 35 different venues simultaneously (*The Sunday Times*, 2004). In all three examples, as well as providing important function, each of these sponsors was able to showcase products for key communications of their own.

The 2004 Moore Heritage Festival of the Arts and Humanities in Florida, USA, provides an example of how an audit of the events assets can work. Its mission was created in order to promote an awareness, appreciation and celebration of the lives of civil rights campaigners Harry and Harriette Moore. The event created a series of educational seminars around a four-day concert weekend. It also identified that, in addition to centre stage title sponsorship and programme advertising, a reception, giveaway tote bag, ribbon-cutting ceremony, Gala silent auction and an awards dinner could all be sponsored.

There is another category of asset that is important. Bundled rights might also include aspects of an event's communications programme, because there is an opportunity for the event to partner with those sponsors that can either pay for communications that might also not have been possible, and/or provide such communications as media partners.

Event sponsorship rights

Event sponsorship rights, when bundled together, include an acknowledgement of the status the sponsor acquires through the relationship. This usually involves a name of some description and over the last thirty years or so that event sponsorship has been developing there has been a range of vocabulary and terminology used. They can be referred to simply as sponsor, but in recent years, and perhaps as a result of closer relationship building, there are now partners and partnerships. Of course, an event can use whatever names it wants. For example, the International Olympic Committee (IOC) refers to its key sponsors as partners in its 'TOP' programme. The English Football Association (FA) has FA partners and refers to them as pillars. Other acknowledgements across the industry include hosts, friends, supporters and corporate champions and the variance only demonstrates that events can acknowledge their sponsors as they and their sponsors mutually see fit. Generally, there are five levels at which to associate with an event and acquire sponsorship rights and these are shown in Figure 8.2. These levels can consist of any agreed set of rights and name acknowledgement.

When developing a number of sponsorships into a series or programme, the key is to design each one so that it can complement and sit comfortably alongside the others. This requires an approach that reviews the programme as a whole and balances the sets of rights so that there is sector exclusivity and no unnecessary duplication that will lead to over-commodification at the event. Sector exclusivity was once seen as a benefit and right in itself but is now expected by most sponsors. It is possible for the event to segment sectors and still achieve exclusivity, however, and those

Title rights

These rights include the sponsor in the title of the event so that all references pertaining to the title of the event include the sponsor's corporate, product or brand names as agreed. These rights usually extend to the graphics that are produced for the event, including any event logos. The event has to manage the use of the event title by others, including media, so that these rights are maximized. Communications partners can also be successful title sponsors but to maximize the opportunities with all media and get other broadcasters and publishers to acknowledge the title in full requires careful management.

Presentership rights

These rights allow an acknowledgement of the sponsor alongside the title of the event rather than being incorporated into it as above. These rights may or may not extend to the event graphics. Typically a sponsor's corporate, product or brand name will feature prior to, or immediately after the event title. Again the event has to manage the use of the title and accompaniments carefully as it is easier for media in particular to omit a presenting sponsor acknowledgement.

Naming rights

These rights are associated with physical structures such as arenas, stadia, halls and galleries. They are usually long-term agreements whereby a sponsor's corporate, product or brand name will be associated with a renaming of the building concerned.

Category rights

Sponsors with category rights have exclusive representation from their trading sector of the market. Once seen as a negotiable right and benefit, sector exclusivity is now more contemporarily seen as a prerequisite. An event should allow for all sponsors to enjoy sector exclusivity so that they can fit comfortably and work together in a sponsorship programme. Communications partners can be successfully incorporated into a sponsorship programme and also enjoy sector exclusivity.

Supplier rights

Supplier rights can, and wherever possible should be, enjoyed by all sponsors. In some way the event should incorporate all its sponsors, their products or brands, as functions of the event. The agreement to supply services, people and product can be in the form of sponsorship-in-kind or be in addition to sponsorship fees.

Figure 8.2 Sponsorship status levels (adapted from Masterman, 2004a).

events with sufficient negotiating power can achieve a greater number of sponsors as a result. The 2004 Wimbledon Tennis Championships, for example, had six official suppliers from the drinks sector as sponsors. This was made possible by differentiating their sets of rights as well as acknowledging their exclusivity by segmenting the drinks sector. Buxton supplied the official mineral water, Jacob's Creek the official Australian wine, Lanson the official champagne, Nescafe the official coffee, Robinson's the official still soft drink and Coca-Cola the official carbonated soft drink.

The temptation for many events may be to attempt to recruit as many sponsors as possible, but not all events manage their programmes as well as Wimbledon and avoid the clutter of the commercial message. Few sponsors are seen around Wimbledon Championship tennis courts for example. This is not the case at the French Open, however, where they adopt a different approach and have all sponsor logos depicted in a uniform green and black colour-way in an attempt to manage clutter. For most events the dangers of over-commodification and the ensuing clutter are that sponsors messages become diluted.

The opportunity to achieve greater revenue streams from sponsorship is an important aspect of event management and the inclusion of levels of status in programmes is another way of differentiating sponsors in order that they may work alongside each other.

Event sponsorship programme structures

There are three basic ways to build an event sponsorship programme (Masterman, 2004a). If there is one sponsor the structure is simple and can be referred to as solus sponsorship. If there is more than one sponsor the event sponsorship programme can be structured in one of two ways. The first of these allows the event to have different levels of acknowledged sponsorship status in a tiered hierarchical structure. The second allows for sponsors that are acknowledged at the same status whether they have identical sets of rights or not. Its nature is therefore flat because there is no hierarchy involved. Figure 8.3 describes these more fully.

With flat and tiered structures it is possible to build programmes consisting of sponsors that can sit comfortably together and be implemented at an event so that they can achieve their objectives, thereby enabling the event manager to address revenue maximization.

In 2003, the Toronto Pride event managed to combine twenty-five sponsors into its programme. In a tiered sponsorship structure it had two top-tier sponsors, Labbatt Blue beer and the Government of Canada. The next level down saw two more sponsors in Via Rail Canada and Delta Chelsea Hotel. In all there were six levels of sponsorship, diamond, platinum, gold, silver, bronze, supporting organizations, and three media partners, the *Toronto Star*, CityTV and *Now* magazine (Toronto Pride, 2004).

Sponsorship is not always used to generate revenue. In order to reduce expenditure and/or add value to the product, sponsorship-in-kind is sought. Sometimes referred to as contra deals or trade-outs, sponsorship-in-kind still involves mutual benefit but with no money changing hands. It is not a new form of sponsorship but it is a growing one (Mintel, 2000). The benefit to the event comes in the form of product or services that are of importance to the delivery and management of the event. In return, a sponsor providing resources such as people, equipment, product, decorations, printed materials and communications mechanisms, can be provided with sponsorship rights to the equivalent value. The saving of event expenditure is a prime driver in wanting to attract organizations in this way, but a longer-term view

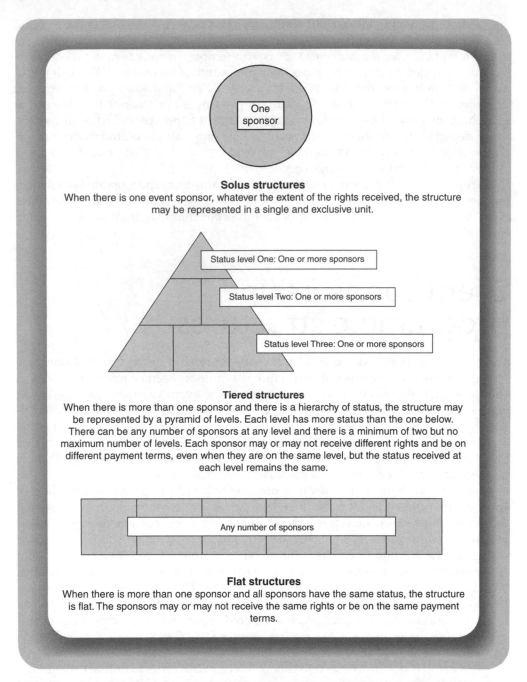

Figure 8.3 Sponsorship programme structures (adapted from Masterman, 2004a).

is also to consider those organizations that can augment the event entertainment product, even when expenditure for this was not part of the original budget. Greater renewal rates may be achieved as a result. The same view can be taken with communications. If a media partner can supply communications mechanisms that were not originally budgeted, the effect can be wider reach for the immediate event as well as those in the future. Some sponsorship agreements enjoy a combination of both fees and sponsorship-in kind, such as Asda and its sponsorship of the 2002 Commonwealth Games in Manchester. The supermarket chain provided staff and volunteer uniforms for the event together with a relatively smaller fee that represented 10 per cent of the overall agreement.

Sponsorship evaluation

The traditional view of evaluation is for it to be implemented, if at all, at the end of the event. It is important to reflect on the fact that many events are reluctant to evaluate at all let alone assess the impacts of its sponsorship programme. The reluctance is borne out of the need to move on to the next revenue driven project rather than devote any resources to an exercise that does not directly generate revenue. There may also be reluctance due to a belief that it is incumbent upon the sponsor to engage in such research. However, that is not necessarily a widespread undertaking either. An IEG/Performance Research (2004) survey of corporate sponsorship decision makers for example, revealed that 86 per cent of respondents typically spent less than the equivalent of 1 per cent of the amount of their total sponsorship spend on evaluation. Nearly half of those spent a zero amount and the most common form of evaluation used by the sponsors surveyed was via internal feedback. Only 27 per cent of respondents used customer focused research. Pope and Voges (1994) conducted research that found that there was a link between those sponsors that experienced shorter sponsorships, of three years or less, and those who failed to set objectives and then evaluated them. Sponsorship evaluation can lead to indirect revenue generation, however, and a longer-term and more enlightened perspective is that research has the capacity to demonstrate how an event can help sponsors achieve their marketing objectives. Post-event research is therefore a critical factor in the recruitment of sponsors (Thompson and Quester, 2000).

Continuous evaluation of the sponsorship is necessary as opposed to only post-event assessment. As identified earlier, in order to build sponsor relations there is a need to accommodate change when necessary and the longer a relationship has been going the greater the chance there is that this kind of flexibility will be required. There are various methods to evaluate sponsorship and they are concerned with three basic questions: how clear was the sponsorship visibly; who took notice; and did it achieve the objectives set for it (Masterman, 2004a)? If an event was to have helped drive sales and sales were made possible via the event, then sales figures will be a reliable evaluation. Shifts in market share as a result of sponsorship are a more subjective assessment, however. Traditional evaluation approaches also involve the calculation of media value. Applying subjective impact values, counting frequencies of reports and measuring opportunities to see or hear in the form of determining circulation coverage are popular choices of evaluation in the sponsorship industry, particularly in sport. They are probably so popular because they can provide such impressive results. For example, Joyce Julius and Associates in the USA provide sponsorship related research services and work for both sponsors and events. In 2004 they conducted research for a mid-west US university and the task was to determine media value for a proposed sponsorship package that included title rights for a single match plus season long scoreboards and other signage. The results indicated that 66 per cent of the exposure any sponsor would receive would stem from the scoreboards signage and 39.3 per cent of that would be attributable to the stadium's main scoreboard. They also indicated that any sponsor would draw US$720 000 of media value over the season (Joyce Julius and Associates, 2004). Nielson Media Research, the leading US media tracking research organization, launched a new sports service in July 2004. Its 'Sponsorship Scorecard' is designed to count how many times event television audiences see sponsors' advertisements and for how long. In what it calls an assessment of the value of a sponsorship, it reports on how often a logo, for example, is seen in one broadcast, by how many people and for how long. This results in what it then calls 'impressions' (*Sports Business Daily*, 2004). While these methods may be of use in assisting with an overall picture, measuring reach and exposure, unfortunately, they are not a reliable evaluation of the quality of awareness levels or shifts of such over time. Nielson's results in this instance are more numbers of sightings than they are a measurement of target market impressions. Research into whether a sponsorship has achieved its intended communications objectives can be more reliably assessed using target market and attitudinal surveys, focus groups and interviews (Sleight, 1989). Data showing increased awareness of a particular sponsor's brand are not of much use if the level of perception is not measured. For example, numbers of sightings of logos and advertisements does not inform on perception of brand values, benefits, pricing and availability, whereas questioning intended targets can. A more comprehensive approach to evaluation will also utilize research data that are collected at different time intervals in order to track movement and shift.

Sponsorship and communications

The purpose of this chapter is to discuss ways in which sponsorship and sponsors can be an important part of the event communications mix. The focus for the chapter so far has been to identify how sponsorships are relationships that need to be carefully targeted and then built in order for them to be successful. This has been necessary in order to establish the base from which sponsorships can be geared as supplementary communications. Sponsors that are willing to exploit their acquired sponsorship rights to the full are the sponsors that can provide considerable further event communications and so the focus now turns to how that is made possible.

Rights exploitation

Event sponsorship rights are clearly a critical aspect of the sponsorship relationship. However, it is not in the interest of either the event or the sponsor for the latter to rely solely on its negotiated rights if it is fully to achieve all that is possible from the relationship. In order that the sponsorship is maximized to its fullest potential it is necessary for the sponsor to exploit or leverage those rights. By supporting a sponsorship with resources that are over and above the costs of the rights, a sponsor is more likely to reach its target markets to a greater extent. This is achieved by integrating the sponsorship into a wider programme of communications activities and, because there are clear associations with the event, the event itself receives wider exposure. The added benefit to the event is that this extra exposure is over and above its own communications activities and at the sponsor's expense.

There are some references to leveraging guidelines in some texts where, for example, the rule of thumb should be to spend so many more times the amount spent on the rights themselves. Graham et al. (2001), for example, suggest 3:1, (three times the amount of the sponsorship rights fees involved). In 1996, however, Coca-Cola spent over ten times the amount their sponsorship rights cost them for the 1996 Olympics in Atlanta (Kolah, 1999; Shank, 1999). Thompson and Quester (2000) concluded that there is little empirical evidence to show how much exploitation is enough and their own research did not identify an optimal level. However, their findings did indicate that the effectiveness of sponsorship is directly related to the degree to which sponsors are willing to exploit their rights. A survey of corporate sponsorship decision makers revealed that collectively they spent an average of 1.3 to 1 (IEG/Performance Research, 2004). This ratio was higher in 2003 at 1.7 to 1. These are average ratios of course and were not intended as anything other than analysis data. There can be no generic guidelines for sponsorship exploitation as it involves an assessment of what is required to achieve a job that is entirely unique and individual. For Coca-Cola the job entailed spending at that level in order to maximize their opportunity in their home town. The key consideration for any sponsor is the nature and extent of the communications that the sponsorship is to be integrated in to. In particular, how strong the strategy has to be to reach target markets, with what messages and under what kind of market conditions. Even those sponsors that have little other communications activity will need to support their rights with further resources to reach their target markets effectively.

If an event's communications effectiveness can benefit from exploitation, it makes good management sense for events to seek out those sponsors that will undertake such leveraging. To enable this, the sponsorship recruitment process should include an assessment of how sponsors can potentially combine their communications efforts directly with those of the event. In this way, the event at least will be able to attempt to steer all communications towards its objectives. The unique selling point being that the exploitation is likely to be more effective for the sponsor if they are more closely related to the event.

In the longer term, the advantages are that both an event and a sponsor are more likely to be more successful with their communications, the relationship will be that much closer and as a result a sponsor is more likely to want to renew. For the event this is also less expensive than the alternative of finding a replacement. Sponsor relations are enhanced still further when several sponsors can be encouraged to partake in co-promotions.

In an example of co-promotions and sponsors providing valuable function at an event, Accenture and Compaq, sponsors at the 2004 World Economic Forum in New York, joined forces to provide wireless technology that enabled delegates to download event information while they were attending the event. The 2004 Sundance Film Festival in Park City, Utah, USA, provided a similar service to its delegates as can be seen in Case study 8.1. The example demonstrates how the development of function and co-promotions between the event and its technology sponsors is a way of growing relationships with sponsors for mutual benefit.

Another example of how sponsor exploitation can benefit both event and sponsor is provided by the 2002 London Film Festival and its sponsor Morgan Stanley. In order to exploit their rights and maximize the sponsorship for its product, the Morgan Stanley credit card, the bank linked with the website 'This is London' and

Case study 8.1

Sundance Film Festival

Prior to the 2004 event, delegates at the Sundance Film Festival had always been used to not only carrying around a phone-book-sized catalogue, but also repeatedly searching through its many pages for information on exhibits, film screenings, film-makers' data and maps.

For the 2004 event, Hewlett Packard (HP) teamed up with Symbol Technologies and FluxNetwork Inc. to provide all that information and more via wireless solutions. HP provided 500 Jornada Pocket PCs that the event distributed to key delegates, producers and journalists. The provision of the FluxNetwork software alone was valued at $100 000. A 'hotspot' network was set up whereby these PCs could be updated with daily downloadable information, including useful easy to use daily schedulers, at convenient places around the town. The event wanted to get participants digitally communicating and in new ways that made their experience more efficient and effective. The 'hotspots' were located in film venues, the event headquarters and at its Digital Centre where other sponsors were exhibiting. HP and its partners benefited from the showcase opportunity for their latest technology and, in particular, the opportunity to enable the media to sample and review new capabilities and use it as a focus for advertising and website promotions.

The development was successful, with suitably impressed media and delegates and the event is developing the relationship with its partners so that more participants can benefit at future events. They also envisage that the service will have the capacity to view on-line films so that reviewers can discuss them with immediate dialogue wherever they are.

The case study demonstrates that through the exploitation of rights via the provision of functional event services, sponsors are more likely to achieve their sponsorship objectives. Those sponsors who approach their rights in this way are therefore more likely to renew their agreements, thus making the event's job in developing its sponsorship programme a lot easier. It also shows that the further leveraging of a showcase via sponsor-led communications also goes further to extend the promotion of the event.

Source: Wi-Fi Planet (2004)

the regional newspaper the *Evening Standard*, two Associated New Media products. In so doing, the bank was able to provide a one-stop shop for all festival news and coverage and develop brand awareness through new and traditional media (Associated New Media, 2004).

Accenture provides further examples of how it has worked with events as a media partner and then grown into a sponsor. In 2003, they worked with the Metropolitan Museum of Art in New York, USA, to produce a virtual Manet/Velazquez Spanish painting exhibition via the sponsor's provision of the Museum's website. In another sponsorship, of The Louvre in Paris, Accenture has not only provided a valuable function for all the museum's events via the creation of a website, in addition it has provided target market research data that have helped to recruit two further sponsors in the bank Credit Lyonnais and Blue Martini Software. In a three-year arrangement, from 2000 to 2003, Accenture has provided sponsorship-in-kind in the form of expertise to the value of one million euros and helped to ensure The Louvre's new Internet strategy was entirely commercially funded (Accenture, 2004). The growth of media partners into event sponsors in this way can lead to a closer relationship. On the one hand, a media sponsor is a broadcast partner and, on the other, it can enjoy sponsorship rights too. The dangers of other media shunning the event as a result, however, is a critical consideration in deciding whether or not to go this route.

Gaining competitive advantage, goodwill and credibility

There are further advantages for an event when sponsors leverage their rights. In enhancing the communications effort that generally assists the event and its target market reach, an event can gain competitive advantage over both its direct and substitute competitors.

Further or more valuable sponsors may also be attracted. Potential sponsors may covet the opportunities that exist with an event because they have either observed or been shown the communications results achieved by existing sponsors. The event is able to give added value in this way.

The event can not only enhance its appeal and service to its sponsors it can also add value to the event product and its appeal to its audience and participant target markets. By attracting sponsors that are willing to develop new ways of communicating with mutual target markets, the latter can benefit from a greater event experience. The provision of intervals that are entertaining, concourses that have extra attractions, competitions and free or more product that is readily available can all help to exceed the expectations of spectators and participants.

In addition, appropriate sponsors can bring an amount of credibility to an event that can be an important factor in the development of brand equity and the appeal to customers. The adding of a specific sponsor may add to the appeal of the event and therefore communications effectiveness simply because that sponsor adds to the value of the event brand and also because that can also then mean wider communications reach. For example, a sponsor with charitable connections can not only add to the appeal of the event because of the goodwill it might impart, but also through the links with news media and associated celebrities that then extend the capacity of communications. Coca-Cola sees the importance of its international sponsorship profile as an important factor in achieving successful communications at much more local levels. It has a key sponsorship objective of maintaining its profile as a national sponsor but, through local initiatives and through global sponsorship, on an international level (Business2000, 2004). In achieving this it clearly has some globally significant associations, for example, it is associated with the world's two largest events, the Olympics and the FIFA World Cup. The Coca-Cola Form and Fusion Awards are targeted elsewhere, however. This latter event was created in 2000 in Ireland and was targeted at schools to educate and promote art and fashion. In its second year the event doubled its number of participants to 2400 students and held its final in Cork in front of a 2500 audience. Coca-Cola Ireland exploited the event to achieve nationwide media coverage in order to meet its own communications objectives and help the event gain greater reach as well.

Summary

The strategic development of sponsorship programmes is a way in which events can be more efficiently managed. Sponsors that are achieving their objectives, for example, are more likely to renew their association with an event and renewal is a less expensive option than replacement. A strategic approach that is founded on targeted recruitment is also a way in which events can be more effectively managed. Those sponsors that are able and willing to exploit their association, for example, provide enhanced event communications.

To be efficient and effective in this way, events need to recruit the right sponsors and this involves finding those that fit. Sponsorship 'fit' is first concerned with mutual target markets. It is also concerned with the capacity of one sponsor to sit comfortably in the same sponsorship programme as others. Finally, it is concerned with relationship building and the on-going development of an association that is to an event's and sponsor's mutual advantage. Ostensibly this requires a targeting process that involves research in order to identify potential sponsors, the development of event rights that meet needs and are tailored for bespoke relationships and continuous evaluation that allows realignment and feedback for improved relations.

The process does not end on the signing of a suitable sponsor. The development of that relationship is important so that increasing expectations on both sides can be met. This is aided by the exploitation of sponsorship rights. If a sponsor exploits or leverages its rights with integrated marketing communications, it not only does so for its own gain, it also provides a level of communications that can complement and exceed the communications the event planned and budgeted for itself. The resulting mutual benefit is a sponsor that is more likely to achieve its sponsorship needs and an event that experiences more efficient and effective communications.

Discussion points

- Consider HP's provision of wireless Pocket PCs in Case study 8.1 and propose ways in which the services to delegates at the 2005 Sundance Film Festival can be developed for mutual benefit.
- Select an event and critically analyse the sponsorship programme by:
  - identifying the sponsorship programme structure
  - identifying and categorizing the sponsorship rights for all sponsors
  - identifying whether and how sponsors needs are being met via the development of tailored and bespoke relationships
  - commenting on ways in which the sponsorships can be developed for the next staging of the event.
- Select an event and consider how it could use research and evaluation in order to develop its sponsorship programme.
- Select an event that has sponsors that have enhanced event communications. Analyse how this has been achieved and make recommendations for future development.

References

Accenture (2004) www.accenture.com (accessed 26 April, 2004).

Associated New Media (2004) www.anm.co.uk/caseStudiesD (accessed 26 April, 2004).

Baker, W. and Sinkula, J. (1999) The synergistic effect of market orientation and learning orientation. *Journal of the Academy of Marketing Science*, 27 (4), 257–269.

Business2000 (2004) Case study: The Coca-Cola brand and sponsorship. www.business2000.ie/cases/cases/case6 (accessed 26 April, 2004).

Farelly, F., Quester, P. and Mavondo, F. (2003) Collaborative communication in sponsor relations. *Corporate Communications: An International Journal*, 8 (2), 128–138.

Graham, S., Neirotti, L. and Goldblatt, J. (2001) *The Ultimate Guide to Sports Marketing*, 2nd edn. McGraw-Hill.

Hoek, J. (1998) Sponsorship: An evaluation of management assumptions and practices. *Marketing Bulletin*, 10, 1–10.

IEG/Performance Research (2004) 4th Annual Sponsorship Decision-Makers Survey. *IEG Sponsorship Report*. Sample Issue. IEG.

Joyce Julius and Associates (2004) www.joycejulius.com (accessed 6 February, 2004).

Kolah, A. (1999) *Maximizing the Value of Sports Sponsorship*. Financial Times Media.

Lachowetz, T., McDonald, M., Sutton, W. and Hedrick, D. (2003) Corporate sales activities and the retention of sponsors in the NBA. *Sport Marketing Quarterly*, 12 (1), 18–26.

Masterman, G. (2004a) *Strategic Sports Event Management: An International Approach*. Butterworth-Heinemann.

Masterman, G. (2004b) A strategic approach for the use of sponsorship in the events industry: A search of a return on investment. In *Festival and Events Management: An International Arts and Cultural Perspective*, Yeoman, I., Robertson, M., Ali-Knight, J., McMahon-Beattie, U. and Drummond, S. (eds). Butterworth-Heinemann.

Mavondo, F. (2000) Measuring market orientation: Are there differences between business marketers and consumer marketers? *Australian Journal of Management*, 25 (2), 223–245.

Meenaghan, T. (1998) Current developments and future directions in sponsorship. *International Journal of Advertising*, 17 (1), 3–28.

Mintel (2000) *Sponsorship Report*. Mintel.

Mohr, J., Fisher, R. and Nevin, J. (1996) Collaborative communication in inter-firm relationships: Moderating effects of integration and control. *Journal of Marketing*, 60 (3), 103–117.

Mullin, B., Hardy, S. and Sutton, W. (2000) *Sport Marketing*, 2nd edn. Human Kinetics.

Pope, N. and Voges, K. (1994) Sponsorship evaluation: Does it match the motive and the mechanism? *Sport Marketing Quarterly*, December, 3 (4), 38–45.

Shank, M. (1999) *Sports Marketing: A Strategic Perspective*, Prentice Hall International.

Sleight, S. (1989) *Sponsorship*. McGraw-Hill.

Sports Business Daily (2004) Nielson unveils service measuring sports sponsorship. www.sportsbusinessdaily.com X (48), 23 April (accessed 23 April, 2004).

Sunday Times (2004) Section: Engineering in sport. 4 July.

Thompson, B. and Quester, P. (2000) Conference paper. Evaluating sponsorship effectiveness: The Adelaide Festival of the Arts. *Australian and New Zealand Marketing Academy Conference*, November–December, 2000. Visionary marketing for the 21st Century: Facing the challenge.

Toronto Pride (2004) www.pridetoronto.com/sponsors (accessed 26 April, 2004).

Wi-Fi Planet (2004) www.wi-fiplanet.com/columns/article.php/973441 (accessed 29 April, 2004).

Chapter 9
Sales Promotion

Objectives

- Evaluate the role and value of sales promotion in the events industry
- Understand the process by which effective and innovative sales promotion communications are designed and scheduled
- Identify the options and critical factors for sales promotion in integrated event marketing communications

Introduction

Sales promotion has grown into a significant element of the integrated marketing communications (IMC) portfolio of tools. For example, in the last two decades it has succeeded advertising as first choice for many organizations. This chapter will therefore examine the role of this important communications tool by considering how and why it has grown and what exactly it is capable and not capable of achieving. The key message throughout is that while sales promotion can make a significant contribution to an event marketing campaign, it serves that purpose only through working as part of an integrated set of communications. Its ultimate role is to affect end-user sales and all three ways of achieving this are explored by considering it as an external tool for direct appeal to end-user customers and for indirect appeal via intermediaries, as well as an internal tool for use with sales staff or other employees. The planning of sales promotions is also reviewed and is supported by an examination of the various sales promotion tools that are available to event managers and how they can be best used in an IMC approach.

Role of sales promotion

Sales promotion as a communications tool occupies a complementary position in IMC and provides a range of activities that can be used alongside and incorporated into other forms of communication. Boone and Kurtz (2002) define it as a range of marketing activities that are not personal selling, advertising or publicity, but perform a similar role; that of enhancing consumer purchasing and distributor effectiveness. Thus sales promotion can be an external activity with end-users and intermediaries but also an internal activity with an organization's own sales force (Smith and Taylor, 2004). Shimp (1997) describes sales promotion activities as communications that encourage either purchase or other action by changing the perceived value or price of products. Pickton and Broderick (2001) support that and further emphasize that while the significant proportion of sales promotion might be in the form of incentives such as money off, free premiums and prizes, they also have the role of motivating non-purchase behaviour such as encouraging requests for information and attendance at an event. In one definition, Shimp (1997) maintains that sales promotions are actions that only temporarily change perceived value or price, but Laspadakis (1999) makes a strong case that they are not necessarily short term. He maintains that, while they may take place over a short period of time, this does not mean that the effects have a short-term impact. Sales promotion therefore has a communication role to play in enhancing a brand's long-term interests. This may well be borne out in the events industry. Getz (1997), for example, proposes that sales promotion seeks to add value to a purchase or attendance and can therefore stimulate first or repeat event visits. A one-off promotion to attend an event can therefore attract attendance and in combination with a satisfactory event experience may then be able to enhance the brand and lead to repeat attendance.

Sales promotion is by no means a minor communications tool. Advertising was a more common choice of communication activity but, in the last 20 years or so, the shift from above the line to below the line activity has been emphatic. While Laspadakis (1999) suggests this shift has been due to economic changes, such as a change of power from retailers to manufacturers and demographic changes, with more women in employment, according to Smith and Taylor (2004), it is also due to a greater marketing emphasis on the development of relationships, the growth of direct mail, increasing customer expectations and the relatively high costs of other communications tools, in particular television advertising. There is now more spending on sales promotional activities than there is on advertising, although this does not diminish the effectiveness of advertising and its role as the most important tool for image building (Laspadakis, 1999; Smith and Taylor, 2004).

There are three categories of sales promotion. They can be direct to the customer, via trade intermediaries or distributors and internally through the sales force. All three approaches can be used in both consumer and business-to-business markets to good effect. Whatever the approach, the ultimate target for any sales promotions are end-users.

Customer sales promotion

Sales promotions that are directly focused on end-users are designed to provide a final reason why customers should select a particular brand over another. This could be in the form of a premium or a prize where the promotion acts as a trigger to affect new or increased usage. While advertising can increase the awareness, interest and desire for an event, sales promotion can inspire customers into action. Thus an integrated approach like this can enable events effectively to market to consumers and businesses. Discounts, gifts, premiums and prize promotions can not only be directed at previous single ticket buyers but also corporate hospitality clients for example.

Trade sales promotion

Intermediaries in the sales chain include retailers and distributors. In the events industry this could be an appointed agency for ticket, corporate hospitality, advertising or sponsorship sales where the aim is to inspire the intermediary to effect better end-user usage. The promotions can be received for the intermediary's own benefit or they can be received and then passed on to the end-user in order to achieve this. These may be in the form of special payment terms so that the agency can maximize profit, for example and, in so doing, the agency may in turn pass some of that benefit on to those end-users that buy in bulk. This approach might be used with promotions that are directed at consumer or business targets and their purchase of single tickets or hospitality packages. On the other hand, a sponsorship agency that is given special terms for the more sponsors they bring into an event would retain the full benefit of the promotion for themselves.

Internal sales promotion

Similar to trade sales promotion, the use of internal promotions is used to motivate or encourage those employees that sell to end-users. In offering incentive and motivation schemes that encourage the achievement of sales targets, an organization can again attempt to effect greater end-user usage.

Sales promotion objectives

The short-term value and tactical use of sales promotion is often misconceived as being its only virtue. Reactive response to poor sales performance can be effective in the short term, but there are calls for sales promotion to be recognized as a strategic as well as tactical tool. Clearly those that are involved in the sales promotion industry would encourage such calls but the argument does receive some support from theory. Laspadakis (1999) sees sales promotion as a tool that can enhance a brand's long-term interests. He maintains that sales promotion is strategic if activities are built in sequence so that each builds on the previous. In this way they can be used to develop the long-term interests of brands. Smith and Taylor (2004) agree and propose that these short-term tactics are bound together in an overall strategic framework for sales promotion that sits quite comfortably in a long-term IMC approach. Pickton and Broderick (2001) note that such activity might be just as easily described as being the forward planning of a series of short-term activities that is tactical rather than strategic in nature but do not doubt the value of sales promotion as a proactive element of a larger pre-planned integrated communication effort.

Thus sales promotion, in an integrated communication effort, can not only achieve the marketing objectives of increasing awareness and interest, it can also achieve the increasing of sales volume (through repeat purchase, greater usage frequency, discouragement of brand switching and widening and extending of use), development of sales leads, encouragement of trial, movement of excess stock, preempting or counteracting of competitive promotions, deflection from or emphasis of price, generation of publicity and development of intermediary relations. An event organization can therefore set a range of objectives for customer, trade and internal sales promotions.

Customer sales promotion objectives

Where the offers are of tickets, corporate hospitality, advertising, sponsorship, merchandise and licences direct to end-users in consumer and business markets, the following objectives apply:

- Develop repeat sales of existing offers to current customers by developing loyalty and discouraging switching to competitor offers
- Develop sales of existing offers to new customers
- Develop trial of existing products by new customers
- Introduce new offers to current and new customers
- Develop trial of new offers to current and new customers
- Pre-empt and counteract promotions for new and existing, direct, indirect and substitute competitor offers
- Develop sales leads and create database information for existing and new offers.

Trade sales promotion objectives

Where the supply is of numbers of tickets, corporate hospitality, advertising, sponsorship, merchandise and licences to intermediaries for their distribution to end-users, the following objectives apply:

- Increase existing supply to current intermediaries
- Introduce existing supply to new intermediaries
- Introduce new supply to current intermediaries
- Encourage current intermediaries to improve shelf, display or presentational space/time at their locations – for stands, posters, point of sale, merchandise, verbal acknowledgements (call-waiting, in-store public announcements and personal demonstration) and audio-visual equipment . . .
- . . . and to encourage them to provide increased exposure over their other competing offers
- Encourage intermediaries to develop their distribution penetration of both existing and new markets via the motivation of intermediary sales force and/or . . .
- . . . the passing on of the promotional benefit to those markets
- Move on stock-piles of tickets, corporate hospitality, advertising, merchandising and possibly sponsorship and licences, particularly when there are short lead times remaining
- Develop relationships with intermediaries via improved payment terms, exclusive agreements, database information collection and offer supply support mechanisms (point of sale, posters, technical advice, personnel, help lines and account management).

Internal sales promotion objectives

Where the offers are of tickets, corporate hospitality, and merchandise internally the following objectives apply:

- Stimulate sales personnel in order to introduce and sell new and current offers, and . . .
- . . . to meet sales targets, and . . .
- . . . to generate sales leads
- Provide direct support for sales personnel (point of sale, technical information, appropriate equipment and training)
- Provide improved payment terms of business market customers
- Encourage non-sales personnel to perform sales and generate leads, and . . .
- . . . develop improved customer relations.

In pointing out the objectives that can be achieved above, it is also worth highlighting the misconceptions about what sales promotion can achieve. The key is that sales promotion is not sufficient on its own and must be used as an integrated tool (Shimp, 1997). It cannot be a substitute for poorly trained sales or other staff. It will also not work if the promotion itself is not communicated. While the long-term value of sales promotion is highlighted in this chapter, it is also important to recognize that it does not, on its own, offer any reason for repeat purchase from either the trade or consumers. A brand requires integrated communications in order to achieve this. It is easy to understand, for example, that a money-off voucher or even a free gift promotion that leads to attendance at an event for the first time, is not going to encourage repeat visits. For repeat visits it is critical that the event experience and the nature of the event product itself meet or exceed customer expectation. Equally, if customer expectations are not met, sales promotion will not save a failing event product.

Sales promotion planning

The development of relationship marketing, growth of direct mail and increased customer expectation are why sales promotion has grown into the tool that it is today and this further illustrates the capacity for sales promotion to work with and across the whole range of marketing communications. It also emphasizes the importance of sales promotion in an IMC approach. Promotions can be used to increase loyalty and usage and can therefore be used to develop customer relationships by enhancing and getting better results from direct mailing and thus help fulfil customer needs for example.

The importance of sponsors in this process cannot be underestimated. For example, sales promotions activities that are created by sponsors or those that are created by the event and are participated in by sponsors can provide less expensive yet effective event communications tools (Getz, 1997). Further discussion on how sponsors should be encouraged by their events to exploit their rights via sales promotion and by leveraging jointly with other sponsors is covered in Chapters 8 and 12.

There are two ways in which end-users can be encouraged to action. The first approach uses a 'push' strategy that provides intermediaries such as retailers, wholesalers and agencies with incentives in order to increase their performance and achieve increased end-user action. An event 'push' strategy, for example, would focus on reaching intermediaries via trade advertising, personal selling and trade sales promotions and supply rewards such as event tickets or hospitality to those intermediary staff that have performed best. Alternatively, the incentives can be given to the intermediaries but then passed on directly by them to their end-users in order to achieve the same improved performance. The second approach uses a 'pull' strategy to reach and provide end-users directly with incentives in order to inspire action. In both cases, it can be seen that vehicles such as advertising, public relations or personal selling are required in order to communicate the details of the promotion, thus highlighting the dependency sales promotion has on other forms of contact.

The planning of sales promotion follows a staged process as do all other forms of communication and this process is itself an element of the overall process that is used to determine the IMC approach. Both Laspadakis (1999) and Smith and Taylor (2004) maintain that systematic planning is required before sales promotion decisions are made and propose similar frameworks that involve a staged process. The sequence of stages begins with an analysis of the environment to identify problems and opportunities for the brand, in order to determine the possibilities for the use of sales promotion. Stage two, they maintain, involves the setting of objectives for the problems and opportunities identified in that analysis. For an integrated approach to this process, however, it is critical that managers understand the importance of the relationship these initial stages need to have with the overall marketing plan. In particular, there are three factors to build in to the process. First, an analysis is needed in order to evaluate the value of any sales promotion options versus those solutions available via other forms of communication. Secondly, and in order to set a budget for sales promotion, an identification of the costs that might be involved is required as a part of this analysis. The evaluation and subsequent arrival at the best combination and integration of communications needs to be founded in an analysis that not only assesses promotional effectiveness but also cost efficiency. Thirdly, the final choice of sales promotion strategy needs to be an intrinsic part of the overall marketing strategy and so continual alignment with that plan is required.

Smith and Taylor (2004) offer some important general guidelines that provide some good advice for the promotion of events in their approach. They maintain that research is required at most stages of the planning process, including the use of focus groups to determine the effectiveness of sales promotional tools and then testing in limited areas to reveal any problems or opportunities before launching. Again the stage of the process at which this is undertaken is critical. Any problems and opportunities need to be identified and considered at the same time as those options that are available via other communications. Based on these factors, an IMC approach to the sales promotion planning process is therefore necessarily similar to that for public relations and advertising (in Chapters 5 and 7, respectively). A model is offered in Figure 9.1.

Problems with sales planning occur when there is a poor brand strategy and appropriate logistics for fulfilment are not put in place. The use of discounts or money-off may well be inappropriate for last-minute sales of an event's most expensive corporate hospitality boxes when the net price works out at less than the next price level down for example. Also, if sales promotion can be effectively used to

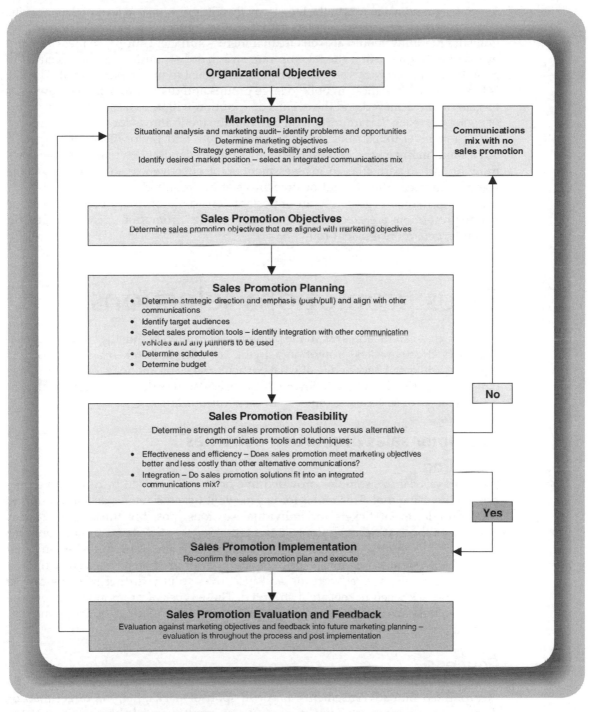

Figure 9.1 Sales promotion planning process. Process for the planning of sales promotion in integrated event marketing communications.

develop a brand's interests in the long term, then its poor use can lead to the opposite. There is therefore a need to plan activities that reflect the nature of the brand. Logistics planning should also ensure that there is sufficient supply to meet demand by accurately forecasting the take-up rate and that distribution can be executed in good time. This is always an issue when there are last minute tickets to sell. The key is to sell as much of these in bulk to large groups and distributors so that new sales targets can be achieved and the event's distribution will be easier with fewer points of contact to reach. It is important though that the tactic allows for sufficient time for the end-receiver to distribute large numbers. Smith and Taylor (2004) offer specific advice and maintain the importance of attention to detail when planning sales promotions and, in particular, to an assessment of the effectiveness and efficiency in the use of resources. The amount of time and staffing required in order to fulfil sales promotion demands is clearly an important consideration that needs to be made before promotions are executed. Outsourcing to sales promotion agencies might, for example, be a more efficient route.

Sales promotions selections

It is clear that careful and systematic planning is required before the selection of feasible and effective sales promotion activities can be undertaken and part of this planning will entail knowledge of what particular sales promotions tools are capable of achieving. To this end the following list consists of the sales promotions tools that are available for selection together with their various attributes.

Customer sales promotion activities

Sampling

Standard or trial size samples provided free or at a discounted price with the purpose of inspiring trial. This tool is for use in event ticket or retail sales programmes. For example, event tickets for individual sessions, possibly those that are less popular or those at off-peak times, provided alongside tickets for a more popular session in discounted packages. Event merchandise and catering sales may be boosted with similar 'two for the price of one' type promotions. They can be offered by direct mail or mass advertising and incentives to buy further sessions can be offered in-pack when tickets are distributed. These types of promotions can also be offered to business end-users as well as consumers with offerings of tickets in bulk, corporate hospitality or advertising sales.

Coupons

These are billets that offer contests to win prizes or price discounts. They can be incorporated into advertisements, on or in sponsor packaging, via direct mail or displayed at intermediary point of sale and, as a result, are probably more applicable for consumer directed promotions.

Premiums

These are items of merchandise or free services. They can be in the form of extra product in 'buy one get one free' promotions. They can also be self-liquidating if the costs of the premium are covered in the overall price or for example, if they are supplied by sponsors. This is the consumer directed tool that is used by the Oakland 'A's' in Case study 9.1.

Money-off

Money-off promotions are the most common sales promotion tool, but need to be carefully applied as they can have an impact on sales value and profits. 'Sales', of course, are the traditional seasonal application of the tool, but they can also be used for immediate reductions, for repeat purchase and for discounts on other products via direct mail, mass advertising and in and on-pack. It is a tool that can be used for consumer and business user alike but there are long-term issues that need to be addressed in order to protect the brand. A cheaper set of corporate hospitality facilities now may have a detrimental effect on future sales, particularly if the discounts are applied randomly. Clow and Baack (2004) refer to this as erosion of the brand.

Bonus and banded packs

This is where product is offered at the original price but with more of the product included or offered multi-pack. They have the effect of a reduction in price but without reducing pack-price. They can be used for event retail sales of all kinds including ticketing.

Contests

Contests can involve elements of skill or not and results can be revealed immediately or over time. Organizers can control the number of prizes and they are commonly used with media partners for awareness objectives. They can be en-masse with long exposure periods as well as for one immediate prize. Event organizers can use their media partners, for example, to give information about the event alongside a contest in their newspaper, or on their television or radio programme. This is publicity rather than advertising and therefore takes on the appearance of being supported by that media vehicle.

Cause related

The value of tying-in charitable contributions or donations to promotions is recognized by the event industry. First, associating with well-chosen causes can inspire perceived brand enhancement qualities. Secondly, the event also benefits from further defined targeting opportunities in the form of the cause's own supporters, possibly the gift of a database and the desired hook that is required to inspire end-user purchase. The dangers are that it is such an over-used tool and can appear a very tired mechanism. Often the charitable cause is a supplier of celebrities to the event and they in turn become the hook if they are features of the event itself. Golf and tennis tournaments that are in aid of charity are often pro-celebrity in nature where professionals and the stars of the entertainment world are attracted because of the charity and one another. The Harrods Pro-Celebrity Tennis Tournament, in aid of Muscular Dystrophy and held at the Royal Albert Hall in London, for example, was always able to attract its entertainment and tennis stars because of the mutual respect they had for each other. Tennis stars such as Stefan Edberg and Jim Courier were keen to appear with rock stars such as Rick Wakeman and Dave Stewart and vice versa. The risk with this approach is that the same faces each year can be a deterrent to an audience as can the lack of 'A' or even 'B' list professionals and celebrities.

Merchandising/point of sale

Any form of display, presentation and point of sale can work if it is placed at other events. This can be used to reach both consumer and business end-users. Such promotions can also work when undertaken in collaboration with sponsors in order to reach consumer end-users in particular. Demonstration of the event itself is critical and can be achieved via deploying attending personnel as well as audio-visual techniques. Information may be distributed, sales-leads collected and immediate sales effected prior to an event to increase awareness and sales revenue via use of this tool.

Information

The distribution of information is considered to be a public relations exercise or direct marketing, but when leaflets, brochures and catalogues contain money-off, contests and coupons they can utilize sales promotion tools as well. They can be distributed as printed materials as well as electronically to both consumer and business end-users.

Loyalty schemes

The extent of loyalty inspired by 'loyalty schemes' is debatable (Pickton and Broderick, 2001), but they are a popular tool that may be used by events. Season tickets for art, music and sports institutions, associations and clubs have long been common practice, but the development of technology has meant that event organizers can now track consumer behaviour by monitoring buying patterns and then utilizing that information for better targeting. The impact has, of course, been diluted by the fact that customers have the liberty to belong to multiple loyalty schemes. The argument against loyalty mechanisms is that the loyalty is extended to the scheme and not necessarily to the brand.

Refunds and rebates

For use in particular with consumer end-users, a refund can be used as a reverse form of applying money-off. The mailing-in of a voucher or receipt in order to activate a rebate is in effect a retrospective reward to a customer for making the purchase. Database building objectives can also be fulfilled via the use of this tool.

Joint and tie-in promotions

This involves the use of any of the above tools by the event in collaboration with sponsors and offered via direct mail, mass advertising, media partners and by sponsors on-pack to consumer end-users.

The Oakland 'A's' use promotional giveaways like so many other major league sports teams in the USA to encourage game attendance (see Case study 9.1). This form of sales promotion is uncommon in the UK, however. While it has been tested as a tool by some football clubs, it has not produced increased audiences.

Case study 9.1

Oakland Athletics: 2004 Promotional Schedule

The Oakland Athletics (A's), a Major League Baseball (MLB) team, is a confirmed user of match premium giveaways. This is a popular sales promotion tool used by the majority of MLB teams and one that is perceived in the USA to be a successful mechanism in achieving increased match attendance.

The promotions are advertised in order to make target audiences aware of the particular giveaway at each match. This is achieved with the use of prior newspaper and match advertising via the stadium plasma screen. The New York Mets also display their promotional schedule on giant outdoor posters at their stadium and on their giveaway fixture cards. Again, this is common practice throughout the MLB and the other US major league teams. The understanding is that giveaways can be ranked in order of attraction and according to the quantity made available by the supplier. They can then be allocated to matches that require the greater promotional pull. Suppliers have been recruited from existing and new sponsors and noticeably the premiums are not necessarily their obvious product. Typically, the suppliers brand each giveaway with their insignia. Other sales promotion includes fireworks and other entertainments, supplied by sponsors as general entertainment for the whole match crowd.

The 2004 schedule was as follows:

Date	Promotion/giveaway	Supplier	Quantity
5 April	A's rally towel	Prilosec OTC	40 000
10 April	A's calendar	Arrowhead Mountain Spring Water	15 000
11 April	A's umbrella	San Jose News	10 000
24 April	A's fleece scarf	Caesars Tahoe	10 000
25 April	A's bat bag	Majestic Athletics	10 000 kids
8 May	A's bucket hat	Macy's	7 500 women
9 May	A's stadium bag	Arrowhead	10 000
21 May	Fireworks display	Contra Costa	All fans
22 May	Player figurine	Wells Fargo	15 000
23 May	Player bobblehead doll	Cache Creek Casino	15 000
5 June	A's wobblers	Comcast	10 000
6 June	A's kids cap	Discover Financial	10 000 kids
11 June	Spider-man hand	Film Producers	20 000 kids
12 June	A's cap beer fest	Union 76	10 000
13 June	Player bobblehead doll	Mechanics Bank Bay Alarm	15 000
26 June	1989 Championship reunion celebrations	Crown Royal	All fans
27 June	Longs drugs/film	Longs/FujiFilm	
16 July	Fireworks display	Oakland Tribune	All fans
17 July	1974 'Swingin' A's cap	Blue Diamond Almonds	10 000

Date	Promotion/giveaway	Supplier	Quantity
18 July	Player bobblehead doll	5A Rent-A-Space	15 000
24 July	1989 World Series ring	A's	15 000
25 July	Chavez gold glove	Pepsi	15 000
28 July	MUG root beer day	Pepsi/MUG	All fans
14 August	Player figurine	Tide	15 000
15 August	Player bobblehead doll	Pepsi	15 000
28 August	Fireworks/wine festival	Chevron	All fans
29 August	A's school backpack	Pepsi	10 000
7 Sept	A's team photo	Oakland Tribune	20 000
11 Sept	A's visor	Farmers Insurance	10 000
12 Sept	A's T-shirt (breast cancer)	Comcast	10 000
2 October	Fireworks display	Meriwest Credit Union	All fans
3 October	A's team cards sets	Plumbers Local	15 000

Source: Oakland Athletics (2004).

The success in the USA, supported only by consistent use rather than empirical evidence, may be due to a set of different customer expectations and the tradition that country has of giveaway promotions in sport. The case study shows that almost every 'A's' game in the 2004 season featured a giveaway and highlights their understanding that one promotion will not necessarily result in repeat purchase. The dangers of such promotions are that they become an intrinsic part of the product and are therefore expected by fans. Therefore, if promotions are ceased or any one game promotion does not come up to expectation, there can be a detrimental affect. The case also demonstrates that the promotions on their own, without any advertising, would be of no use. Fans need to know that they get a giveaway at a particular game for the promotion to work.

Trade sales promotion activities

Customer sales promotions

The customer sales promotions activities above are in themselves an attractive incentive to intermediaries such as sales agencies. Anything that is likely to increase trade for an event's appointed ticket, corporate hospitality and sponsorship agencies is going to be welcomed. It is important therefore to inform these agencies of any customer focused sales promotion activity.

Sampling

Free samples of tickets, corporate hospitality and merchandise provide incentives and as a result can build stronger relationships with agencies and their personnel.

An agency that receives a direct experience of an event one year may not only feel rewarded but will also be better informed the next time they have to sell it on to their customers. The building of the relationship can also lead to a development of business with ticket agencies becoming corporate hospitality buyers. They may of course also become customers themselves and use an event for their own business-to-business activity.

Allowances

Allowances for intermediaries can come in the form of price discounts, additional product and special payment terms. Again these can be used to reward, develop and maintain relationships for further business.

Contests and incentives

An intermediary's sales personnel are a critical part of the relationship. If they are individually inspired by the event then results can be bettered. The careful management of rivalry and competition through the creation of contests can be used so that the sampling of the event above can be done more selectively and directed to those that are performing best.

Gifts

Samples that are necessarily event related can be used to provide intermediaries with incentives. This is also true for the distribution of gifts of other products and, as in most other industries the practice is very common with event managers. The advantage is that costs can be lower and the promotion can achieve other objectives such as communicating event information in order to make the sales process easier. Gifts are also an abused area of promotion, as the Olympics have demonstrated. The International Olympic Committee (IOC) saw fit to ban all gifts during the bidding process by prospective hosts to IOC voting members as the problem escalated in the 1990s. The distribution of 'pins' has also become a traditional Olympic promotion and, despite their inexpensive unit cost, they are used very effectively as they are much sought after. Coca-Cola have even recognized this phenomenon and associated themselves with Olympic pin kiosks and trading stations (IOC, 2002).

Merchandising, point of sale and training

Further support of the intermediary is essential if the relationship is going to work. Making merchandising and display material freely available to intermediaries may be a prerequisite depending on the nature of that relationship and the extent of the negotiating power of the event. There are clearly costs involved in the production of such materials and therefore in order to maximize the benefit, a key aim is ensuring that an intermediary provides highlighted and/or exclusive positioning over any other competitive products they may be handling. The provision of training is not a common requirement when appointing say ticket agency intermediaries, but any agreement with a sponsorship agency will necessitate pre-programme briefing, liaison and joint development of the sponsor roster.

Information

The provision of information in the form of selling and distribution instructions may be necessary and therefore an important sales promotion to intermediaries. For example, complex floor and seating plan copies, with full accompanying instructions, will be required by ticket sales agencies. The provision of manuals for the use of any event branding may also be pertinent. The intermediary will enjoy the benefits of the event logos, for example, but will benefit more from the use of sponsors' logos, especially if these are combined with joint promotions.

Joint promotions

The collaboration of event sponsors in providing gifts and samples to intermediaries can also be important. First, there is more to offer them and secondly, this can be a cost-effective route for the event to take as the gifts come free. Acknowledgement of the intermediary's details of sales procedures and contact points is an important element of this type of promotion. It can work for all parties involved. By agreeing with a sponsor to place a website address and telephone number in an advertisement in order to inspire sales will help promote the event, the sponsor and its relationship with the event, as well as the intermediary ticket agency.

Internal sales promotion activities

The same tools that are used for customer and trade focused sales promotion can be used internally by the event organization with its sales and other non-sales personnel. Information and training are key elements in terms of support, but incentive and motivational schemes are the drivers of sales performance. Contests can be used to create competition for rewards that are made directly to the employee. They can also be given the authority to distribute samples and gifts that can also help them instigate sales. The links with PR here are strong in that competition can be newsworthy and so employee of the month awards create internal news.

Sales promotion evaluation

Evaluation of all communications activity against overall marketing objectives is important for the purpose of feedback and there are a number of approaches when it comes to evaluation of sales promotion. Data on take-up rates for customer offers are readily available for some forms of sales promotion and data that relate any increases in sales to intermediary performance might also be used. Research can also be qualitative as well as quantitative in nature, with the assessment of sample target opinion and their thoughts on the ways in which certain promotions have or have not worked. This might reveal that an intermediary ticket agency provided improved and excellent service for example and that evidence together with data on its improved sales performance can provide feedback on how successful the support, training and materials were. Pre-testing is also important research for the IMC planning process as discussed earlier. However, as with a lot of evaluation, there are also a number of areas that are less objective. For example, the effects of displays and other forms of merchandising, the giving of gifts and sampling in particular, are difficult to relate to sales performance in anything other than inference.

Summary

Sales promotion can be an impressive tool and has consequently grown into a first choice for many events. Its cost effectiveness can in some cases be readily evaluated against objectives and achieve both short-term sales and long-term impact on an event brand. It is, however, totally dependent upon other communications tools if it is to work. On the one hand, it is a natural bed-fellow for advertising, public relations, personal selling, sponsorship and direct marketing but, on the other, it relies on these other forms of contact as communication vehicles. The greatest sales promotions cannot work unless target audiences are made aware of them.

Its flexibility as a key component of IMC also provides an indication of the attention required in sales promotion planning. Before any of the customer, trade and internal promotion tools can be selected, a systematic approach to sales promotion planning is required. Sales promotion options must be identified and evaluated alongside all other communication options for an integrated solution to marketing problems and opportunities. The selection of tools is therefore a considered choice of those options that work most effectively and cost efficiently alongside other forms of communication, for short-term sales results and long-term brand benefits.

Discussion points

- **Devise further consumer focused joint sales promotions for the Oakland Athletics based on the information given in Case study 9.1.**
- **By further studying Case study 9.1, determine how the Oakland Athletics might evaluate their promotional giveaway programme.**
- **Select one sales promotion implemented by an event of your choice. Identify the issues and opportunities the event may have faced in systematically progressing through the sales promotion planning process.**
- **Identify as many different customer focused sales promotion objectives and tools used as possible at events of your choice.**
- **Identify as many different trade focused sales promotion objectives and tools used as possible at events of your choice. Clearly identify the intermediaries involved.**

References

Boone, L. and Kurtz, D. (2002) *Contemporary Marketing 2002*. Thomson Learning.

Clow, K. and Baack, D. (2004) *Integrated Advertising, Promotion, and Marketing Communications*, 2nd edn. Pearson Prentice Hall.

Getz, D. (1997) *Event Management and Event Tourism*. Cognizant.

IOC (2002) *IOC Marketing Fact File: Salt Lake City*. IOC.

Laspadakis, A. (1999) The dynamic role of sales promotions. In *Marketing Communications: Principles and Practice*, Kitchen, P. (ed.). International Thomson Business Press.

Oakland Athletics (2004) www.oakland.athletics.mlb.com/NASApp/mlb/oak/schedule/promotions (accessed 16 June, 2004).

Pickton, D. and Broderick, A. (2001) *Integrated Marketing Communications*. Financial Times/Prentice Hall.

Shimp, T. (1997) *Advertising, Promotion, and Supplemental Aspects of Integrated Marketing Communications*, 4th edn. The Dryden Press.

Smith, P. and Taylor, J. (2004) *Marketing Communications: An Integrated Approach*, 4th edn. Kogan Page.

Chapter 10
Direct and Relationship Marketing

Objectives

- To appreciate the value of relationship building as an event communications objective
- To be aware of the development and relevance of the theory of relationship marketing to marketing communications
- To recognize the range of direct marketing communication tools that can be used to support relationship marketing
- To understand the use of database technology in undertaking direct marketing campaigns

Introduction

There is an increasing need to move towards personalized, individual communications with all stakeholder groups. This has been made possible through the developments in database and communication technology and is desirable due to the increasingly individual needs and expectations of today's consumer.

The main methods for communicating directly with customer groups include personal selling, direct mail, e-mail and telesales. These one-to-one two-way communication methods are often vital in the development of long-term customer relationships and in developing commitment, involvement and loyalty. The importance of customer relationship marketing is increasingly being recognized in events organizations and the focus of many marketing communications campaigns is to encourage the development of positive relationships with the various event stakeholder audiences. The focus of this chapter, therefore, is on the direct marketing communication methods which are most effective in achieving relationship marketing objectives for event organizations.

The relationship marketing paradigm

Definition and development

Relationship marketing can be seen as the natural development of a customer orientation. By focusing on customer and other stakeholder needs, characteristics and behaviour, an organization is in a stronger position to develop a mutually beneficial relationship with those customers. This 'relationship' increases the levels of involvement of both parties through shared interests and, if developed further, can lead to long-term loyalty and support.

Although the definitions of relationship marketing have proliferated with the increased academic research and writing in this field (e.g. Berry, 1983; Grönroos, 1990; Gummesson, 1996; Bruhn, 2003), the preferred definition for this text is,

relationship marketing is a marketing orientation that seeks to initiate and develop, close interactions with selected stakeholders for mutual value creation through cooperative and collaborative efforts (adapted from Sheth and Parvatiyar, 1995; Bruhn, 2003).

Relationship marketing is a move away from a focus on one-off transactions to an emphasis on customer retention. This is achieved through communicating the product's benefits rather than features, through higher levels of customer service and quality and through repeated and varied customer contacts. The goals of relationship marketing are longer term aiming to develop customer involvement, commitment, trust and loyalty. These goals require customers and other stakeholders to be empowered, to have valued inputs into the activities of the organization and to receive value in exchange.

The move towards relationship marketing has come about as a result of a number of social and technological trends. The increasing level of competition in most markets creates greater demands on organizations to differentiate what they offer in a meaningful and lasting way. This has led to many products and services being viewed by customers as homogeneous. Customers have increasing difficulty in differentiating between competing offerings and therefore demand higher levels of service and quality at all points of contact. Many stakeholder groups are looking for value over and above the product offering through engagement with the organization, its brand, its communications and its stakeholders. Organizations have realized that there are diminishing returns from one-off transactions and have started to recognize the 'life time value' of the customer. They have been able to facilitate this through the developments in information technology. Database advances, the Internet and telecommunications allow the organization and the customer better to understand each other and therefore develop repeated contacts and long-term relationships.

In considering the definitions of relationship marketing and the comparisons with what is now termed transactional marketing, the implications for marketing communications become clear. Relationship building requires personalization, interaction, many contact points and cooperation and collaboration. This suggests that the organization no longer initiates and controls the communication but that both parties create mutually beneficial exchanges. One-to-one communication methods will often be essential and a dialogue will need to be encouraged wherever

Table 10.1 Relationship stages and marketing communications

Relationship stage	Communication objective	Communication emphasis (for a concert venue)
Prospect *pre-relationship*	Build awareness, initiate contact	Mass media with direct response Sales promotions
First-time customer *developing relationship*	Encourage feedback, two-way dialogue	Post-purchase follow up through direct mail
Repeat customer *long-term relationship*	Personalize communication, increase involvement	Direct marketing using past purchase behaviour to personalize
Key customer, client *habitual relationship*	Build trust through regular personalized communication	Direct mail to offer loyalty rewards
Supporter *exchanges of greater value*	Encourage and reward commitment	Personal selling Corporate hospitality
Advocate *encourages others*	Encourage and reward commitment advocacy	Personal communication, involvement in 'communities', 'forums', special events
Partner *exchanges of greatest mutual value*	Regular exchanges allowing for high levels of mutual involvement	Involvement in internal communications, meetings, committees
Lapsed customer *relationship ended*	Encourage feedback and renewed interest	Offer opt-outs, confirm communication preferences

possible through the use of direct response and interactive media. The target audiences need to be empowered to initiate and drive communications to meet their needs. The trust and commitment needed in relationship building needs to be created through open and honest messages and credible media. These multiple points of contact needed require the careful integration of marketing communications allowing communication via a variety of methods to develop as the relationship develops. Examples of the relationship stages, along with the communication implications of each, are given in Table 10.1.

The importance and use of relationship marketing in events

Some event organizations are already starting to reap the benefits of sophisticated relationship marketing communication programmes and examples of these can be seen in the sports, arts and business event sectors. However, many event organizations remain product-focused and this leads to communication strategies aimed at encouraging an increased number of transactions rather than longer-term customer retention.

Bespoke events created for organizations require a relationship to develop even in a one-off transaction but there will be far greater benefits to both client and organizer if the relationship continues with future events as both parties will have a better understanding of each others needs and will be able to increase the mutual benefit of the relationship. This relationship is often supported through key account management where individuals within the organization are assigned to specific clients and can therefore develop a better understanding of their needs over the long term. This happens in many organizations involved in conferences for large corporate clients where an individual or small team is assigned to meeting the needs of each client organization.

Events aimed at businesses and other organizations often require personal communications with their clients from the onset in order to develop bespoke products and services and through these discussions a relationship can begin to be formed. However, it is post-purchase communications that can be the most influential in bringing about the transition from one-off customer to repeat customer (Curtis, 2001). Support for the client after the event in terms of evaluations and feedback given and received starts to build the trust and commitment needed. Post-event communications should therefore add value to the service provided rather than merely being used to push the next sale. For example, exhibitors at a trade exhibition will appreciate information on the amount of activity generated by the event, a breakdown of the numbers and types of attendees and feedback on the effectiveness of their stand. They in turn can provide feedback on the services received from the venue and event organizer, the benefits of exhibiting at the event and suggestions for improvement. If the event organizer initiates this post-event dialogue through the provision of useful information, the client will view the relationship as being mutually beneficial and worth pursuing. This will be far more effective than the standard issuing of direct mail offers for next year's event which, although offering some repeat purchase benefits to the client, is driven by the organizer's need to sell space.

Sports associations and clubs have learnt to use the inherent loyalty of fans and supporters to create better value relationships. This has been largely focused on the club providing value through additional information services (some free, some paid for) aimed at supporters. However, there has been less growth in the encouragement and facilitation of feedback from supporters to the club. This two-way communication is vital if supporters of the team are to be developed into supporters, advocates and eventually partners of the organization. Case study 10.1 illustrates how wireless technology has been used to enhance the relationship marketing efforts of a number of sports events.

The Rangers Football Club in Scotland has been using a variety of communication techniques over the last few years to build more meaningful and beneficial relationships with its supporters. At the core of their strategy is a centralized customer database integrated with the official website. The club encourages customers to register via the website in order to receive a variety of additional benefits. These include newsletters, access to exclusive player interviews, e-mail updates and newsflashes, competition entries and an attendance loyalty reward scheme. A greater depth of knowledge about their customers' behaviour is gathered through the use of smart cards containing microchip information storage. These are issued to season ticket holders and are swiped at turnstiles and whenever purchases are made. A further link to each customer has been created through a subscription SMS service which sends Rangers news and results direct to the subscriber's mobile phone along with Rangers related screensavers, logos and ringtones (Rangers Football Club, 2004).

These relationship marketing communications benefit the fans by providing them with more information on their club, by allowing for simpler and easier club contact systems, more suitable personalized season ticket packages and tangible rewards for attending. The club benefits through creating cross-selling opportunities,

Case study 10.1

Wireless Relations

There is increasing value being placed on the use of wireless technology for maximizing sports event customer revenues. The reason for this is its unique capacity for the development of relationships with large numbers of customers. How many other communications tools can deliver immediate and two-way channels between a sports organization and its supporters for example? This immediacy in timing of broadcast, consumption and reaction is directly attributable to the fact that those people who carry mobile phones tend to carry them at all times. As with many new technologies, however, there are few organizations that have even begun to exploit the potential. Those that are doing have benefited from enhanced customer relations and competitive advantage.

Fans can be encouraged into an interactive and direct relationship via the broadcasting of all kinds of services, SMS text alerts of up to the minute information, MMS action clips and competitions. One important factor to emerge out of the early use of such services is the critical timing of broadcast. Different services used at different times will have different responses. TWI Communications have found that broadcasts can be successful even while fans are at a football match if the content is linked and there is voting for favourite player performances for example.

The NHL (National Hockey League) in the USA has had similar success with most valuable player (mvp) awards. Fans can vote for their favourites by responding to prompts sent to their mobiles while they are at games. Results are accumulated across all games throughout the league so that both team and overall league outcomes can be reported back to each voter. The results are also posted to match day jumbotron screens for further linked communications. One of the key services in the NHL portfolio is the sending of alerts for last minute tickets that are available for matches, a service that most event organizers will want.

Use of wireless technology in this way is becoming increasingly popular because it has added new revenue streams. It is important for event organizations to understand why and how this is the case. Revenue is generated via the subscription charges that are applied to each service but, in order for these services to be adopted and then loyally and continuously used, there must be sport content, whether that be team, league or player related. The key connection is the fans' undying interest in feeding their passion with as much information as possible. The added benefit is that fans will feed that passion still further if they can interact, and the more interaction, the more the revenue. With this level of understanding an organization can also achieve competitive advantage.

The 2003 Rugby League World Club Champions, the UK's Bradford Bulls, provide its subscribed and mobile phone owning fans with a range of services to develop revenue directly and also event audiences. Pre-match anticipation is enhanced with the broadcasting of a minimum of three texts in the week prior to a game, for example content on player injuries and teams selections. The rates are £1.50 for five messages and this includes an automatic re-credit when the balance depletes. Subscribers have to unsubscribe but can do so at any time by text. The timing of these broadcasts is clearly important and critical if retention is to be achieved. The Bulls maintained that its subscription retention rate was at 88 per cent during 2003. The 'Bulls Mobile Match' service also offers what it calls snap polls on match days for pre-match team selection and post-match man of-the-match voting. The NFL (National Football League) in the USA launched a similar wireless service for the selection of the all-star teams for the end of season all-star game in October 2004 with each respondent getting an

NFL wallpaper free-of-charge. Following great success in 2003 when only a website-based on-line system was used for the same purpose (over 50 million votes were cast – fans could vote more than once) the NFL decided to offer a voting system that linked both on-line and wireless technology. In using these techniques to build customer relationships, the NFL was also generating significant revenue via premium rate charges.

Sports picture messaging started to emerge in 2004. Currently, the sending of video clips to mobiles is possible in Europe (though not in the USA), but that has not prevented still shot imagery being exploited. The advantages being that file sizes are smaller and download times are shorter and few phones have the technology to take video. Still pictures of a goal scorer, almost at the time he scored, will be gratefully received by sets of fans that did not make it to watch the game.

While developments in video technology will no doubt hastily ensure that still picture provision is only a short-term provision, transient services such as these are the nature of rapidly developing markets and the revenues are important for many event organizations. A still picture service provider, EMPICS, has estimated (following tests in early May 2004 at Manchester United and Arsenal of the Premier League and West Bromwich Albion and Nottingham Forest of the Football League), that the market could be worth up to £20 million in its first year. The forecast was that this technology would be used up until 2006.

The NHL predicted in late 2003 that there will be 456 million mobile phone users by 2007 and while they are one of the few event organizations that have so far begun to understand the magnitude of wireless technology, those that follow quickly will have much to gain.

Source: Hughes (2003); Sport and Technology (2004).

managing stadium capacity more efficiently and from a higher take up and repeat purchase of season tickets.

Although marketing *per se* has struggled for acceptance in many arts and cultural organizations, relationship marketing techniques appear more able to bridge the gap between the arts and business. The emphasis on one-to-one relationships and mutual exchanges fits better within the cultural sphere of arts events than the traditional marketing methods of sales and promotion (Collin-Lachaud and Duyck, 2002).

In the arts events sector the strategic trend over the last ten years has been towards audience development with many arts organizations and government agencies focusing their efforts and grants on encouraging new customers and developing new target markets. Although audience development is a valid objective, in many organizations this has been pursued to the detriment of audience retention. Communication aimed at new target markets has taken precedence over maintaining and deepening contacts with existing customers and therefore the opportunity to develop long-term loyalty and commitment is being lost (Rentschler et al., 2002). Building stronger long-term relationships through increased frequency and loyalty is a more cost effective method for filling auditorium seats than persuading new customers to attend as the required communication expenditure decreases as loyalty is built. Arts events can utilize box office data systems and front line staff to create personalized communications and subscription packages to encourage audience retention. Many venues and arts companies already offer membership schemes, 'friends of' opportunities and repeat attendance rewards.

The Arts Marketing Association (AMA) highlights the importance of the box office (staff and systems) for communications in developing relationship marketing for arts events, 'One-to-one contact with individual customers remains our best opportunity to try and introduce people to new events [and] nurture their relationship with us . . . We need to focus resources on this front line relationship with customers' (AMA, 2004).

Communication aimed at developing customer relationships will become increasingly important for all event types and for all stakeholders. The benefits to all parties of developing mutual understanding, trust and commitment are many. For the event organization operating in increasingly competitive markets this relationship provides a far greater sustainable competitive advantage than those created through service or price superiority. The maintenance of marketing relationships is particularly important for communications with sponsors and the media where a broken relationship can have severe financial and publicity implications.

Although these relationships are often easier to achieve in business-to-business event markets, due to the higher levels of personal contact, the use of technology and multiple communication contact points means that many consumer events can also develop successful relationship marketing strategies. So long as the event, the brand or the organization can inspire high levels of consumer involvement then an emotional and practical relationship can be developed. This may begin through repeat attendance and can then develop into loyal attendance, advocacy, volunteering and support, sponsorship and partnership. As many events are of a limited duration and occur at set intervals (weekly, monthly, annually), communication between event occurrences is of prime importance in encouraging repeated use and attendance. Therefore, relationship marketing communication strategies should not be concentrated solely on the build up to the event and for the event duration but should include post-event dialogue and continual contact between event occurrences. The Glastonbury festival (an annual event that runs over several days) illustrates this technique. The dedicated event website provides year round information, contact points and discussion and feedback opportunities maintaining contact with attendees and supporters at a geographic and temporal distance from the event itself. This creates and develops long-term user involvement with the brand rather than simply with the festival.

Although relationship marketing uses the tools of database marketing, cross-selling and loyalty rewards these are not sufficient to create real commitment, trust and interdependence (O'Malley and Tynan, 2000). Collecting customer information electronically provides an understanding of the behaviours and preferences of large target markets but can lead to the neglect of real qualitative communication with the customer base. Although the cross-selling of related products and merchandise can be used to personalize offers and add value, it can also be perceived as intrusive and pushy, tilting the balance of perceived value away from the customer. Loyalty scheme subscribers may become loyal to the scheme without developing real loyalty to the brand and will therefore brand-switch if they perceive other loyalty schemes as more beneficial.

Direct marketing

Direct marketing provides the personalized communication and direct response methods needed to develop successful relationship marketing strategies. Although any communications medium can be used to encourage a direct response, direct marketing is distinct in that it is targeted at identifiable individuals. In tracking customer contacts through a direct marketing database, organizations are better equipped to see their customers as individuals and to recognize them as being new prospects, repeat attendees or loyal customers. There is, therefore, a natural alignment between direct marketing and relationship marketing (Tapp, 2000). Indeed, it has been found that, although sales and fund-raising success is achieved through total general marketing effort, it is the breadth and uniqueness of the direct marketing techniques used that drive increases in season-ticket subscriptions (Arnold and Tapp, 2003).

Although direct marketing (and relationship marketing) involves many aspects of marketing strategy, this section will focus on the use of direct marketing in marketing communications. Direct marketing communications can be defined as any communication which is received personally and allows for an individualized response. There are, therefore, many media choices that can be utilized to transmit a direct marketing message such as direct mail, telemarketing, e-mail, SMS, personal selling, leafleting, wireless or mobile communications. However, direct marketing used as a strategic communication tool is more than just the medium of delivery. It involves the acquisition and retention of customers through the collection, analysis and strategic use of individual customer information. The customer database is therefore central to any successful direct marketing campaign and the use of direct response and personal contact provide the feedback necessary to improve the depth of information held in the database. From a customer information viewpoint, therefore, direct marketing can be self-sustaining and should grow in effectiveness and refinement the more it is used. Figure 10.1 illustrates the potentially virtuous circle of direct marketing activity.

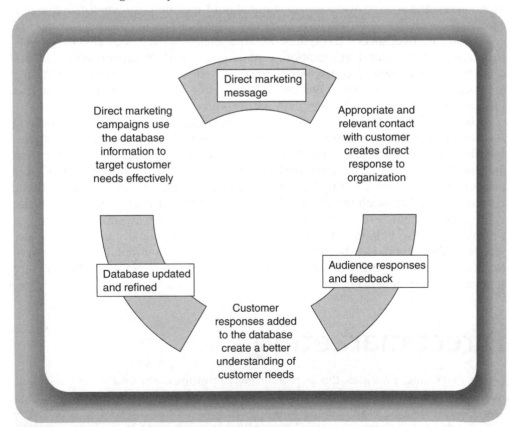

Figure 10.1 The virtuous cycle of direct marketing.

Direct marketing is one of the fastest growing areas in marketing communications as many organizations are switching a larger proportion of their budget away from mass media usage. Within direct marketing media, telemarketing has shown the largest increase with expenditure on this medium growing by 75 per cent between 2000 and 2004 (Smith and Taylor, 2004).

The reasons for the growth in direct marketing communication have been attributed to:

- The fragmentation of society in the proliferation of lifestyle options and an increase in individualism
- Proliferation of media has led to rising costs for mass communications and greater opportunities for personalized communications
- Audiences are more sophisticated in their needs and demand higher levels of personalized service and communication
- Audiences are empowered and are more likely to want to control the communication process through self-initiated contact
- Increasing levels of competition call for new ways of differentiating offerings
- An emphasis on cost effectiveness, measurability and control has created an organizational preference for more highly targeted and efficient communication methods
- The emphasis on customer retention and relationship building has led marketers to a greater use of direct marketing
- The continuing advances in database technology and computer capability alongside a reduction in the costs of processing
- The growth in information as a commodity has led to a proliferation of companies renting and selling highly specific lists for use in direct marketing campaigns (Tapp, 2000; Smith and Taylor, 2004).

Many of these trends are set to continue and, with the emergence of new media suitable for direct marketing use and the use of innovative and creative direct marketing messages, this communication method will undoubtedly increase in importance within the integrated communications mix of event organizations.

Direct marketing methods and uses

Media

The main media for direct marketing are:

- personal selling
- telesales
- mobile marketing
- direct mail
- e-mail.

Each of these will be discussed in turn.

Personal communication, or 'personal selling' as it is traditionally known, involves face-to-face contact with the customer and can be one of the most persuasive communication methods. Face-to-face contact is a vital aspect of many business-to-business communication strategies and is particularly useful in developing relationships with client organizations. In personal communication rapport and mutual understanding can quickly develop between the individuals involved and as a consequence this relationship is then transferred to the buyer and seller organizations.

Due to the high cost of personal contact this method is not used to build awareness or initiate interest but as a follow-up method to create preference, conviction and a purchase decision. Preferably, personal contact is made only after the customer has requested it as a result of being exposed to other marketing communications. Personal selling has been most often used for high involvement, complex or high value products such as bespoke events, larger event bids and sponsorship development. The method should, however, be incorporated into the communications mix of any event where employees come into contact with target audiences in order to ensure that all points of contact are used and are putting across a consistent message. Box office staff, for example, can be better trained and informed to provide relevant offers, additional services and information to customers. Stewards, ticket collectors, guides and security staff can all contribute to communications with customers and help to develop ongoing relationships.

An understanding of the value of key customers in terms of their current usage, frequency, spend and their potential future value is critical in determining the amount and type of personal contact they should receive. For example, it may be that a business customer who frequently purchases corporate boxes at the venue will respond well to personal contact and through this medium could be developed, at a later stage, into a sponsor or partner. However, for lower spending customers and larger target markets personal contact will not be the most cost effective direct marketing method.

Telesales is a less costly alternative to personal selling and can therefore be used to communicate with larger target audiences. Telephone contact can provide similar advantages in terms of person-to-person contact, immediate responses and flexibility, with the added benefit of speed of implementation and without the costs incurred in personally visiting a client. Telesales, however, can be seen as intrusive and is viewed with suspicion by many recipients. As the use, and misuse, of this medium grows, consumers and businesses are less likely to respond positively. This again highlights the importance of permission-based marketing that is well targeted at interested audiences.

Direct mail accounted for 14.3 per cent of advertising expenditure in the UK in 2003 (Direct Marketing Association, 2004) and is a rapidly growing medium. The success of direct mail is largely dependent on the mailing list used to reach the target audience. As success is usually measured in response rates then a well defined, up to date list of potential customers is vital. For example, the Museum of Modern Art in New York used a combination of subscriber lists from other New York cultural organizations, rented lists of upmarket lifestyle magazine subscribers and rented lists of upmarket mail order buyers to target a direct mail membership campaign. These targets matched the characteristics of current Museum members in terms of income, lifestyle, buying habits and geographic location. As the objective was to encourage new memberships, the message was presented in a visually appealing manner to position the Museum as fun, dynamic and unintimidating, using the broad appeal of the Mondrian exhibition. The campaign generated sufficient response to cover the cost of the campaign plus 25 per cent additional revenue, but had the extra benefit of attracting new customers, some of whom, through membership renewal, would become loyal customers (Wittkoff and Cobb, 1996).

As well as a focused mailing list, it is important to ensure that the message sent is as relevant as possible to the recipient. This will entail personalizing the mailing wherever possible to the needs of sub-segments within the total mailing list. For example, a US direct mail campaign aimed at generating support for the training of athletes for the Special Olympics in 1998 adapted the mailing for each target state. The adaptations used the fact that different events were taking place in different states at different times. Localized information included the number of athletes competing, the location of the Games and the names of 'home town' athletes. This more personalized information was made immediately visible to the recipient through an additional envelope window (Wheatley and Nocco, 1998). The localization of the campaign helped to develop an increased level of involvement from the recipients making it easier for them to equate their support/donation with a feeling of personal ownership of the Games.

Handing out leaflets and leafleting are also often classified as direct marketing communication methods and are techniques often used for communicating localized consumer events. However, these often have more in common with mass communication than personalized communication as the message is standardized and the targeting is limited to locations. The main benefits of this technique are that they do not require a database or list of targets and that they provide some level of personal interaction. Leafleting can be very useful in encouraging impulse attendance at events and is often used for this purpose in locations and times close to the event itself. The impact of leafleting can be greatly enhanced by combining this method with some form of ambient media communication or promotional event. The Leeds based nightclub, Evolution, targets the student population of the city by combining a mock student demonstration with the issuing of flyers for its club nights. 'Student-types' are seen holding placards outside the universities and student unions as though they are protesting a political issue. The placards include the word 'Evolution', easily mistaken for revolution at a distance and, once the passer-by's attention has been gained, they are more willing to accept the flyer promoting the club. The use of the 'mock demonstration' provides the extra impact needed in an overcrowded, competitive market and makes good use of the interests and characteristics of the target market to overcome some of the problems of leafleting as a direct marketing method.

Electronic direct marketing includes the use of mobile phone SMS and video messaging as well as e-mail. These were discussed in Chapter 6 and are growing in use in many areas. The use of mobile phone messaging for direct marketing is dependent upon the population's adoption of both the mobile phone itself and the use of messaging. This has occurred to differing degrees around the world with some of the highest usages being in Scandinavia and Japan. In the USA, the percentage of the population owning mobile phones is surprisingly small and the use of text messages has not achieved the same rates of usage as in Asia and Europe (Rettie and Brum, 2001). This is partly due to the nature of the industry with less standardized services and fragmented coverage, but is also due to cultural differences. An immediate spoken two-way conversation appears to be preferred by Americans ('why type it when you can say it?'), while a more private, silent correspondence is preferred in many situations in Asia and Europe ('why let others hear your business?').

Both e-mail and SMS provide the advantages of speed of implementation and response and message flexibility. Messages sent direct to mobile phones have the added advantage of reaching the target regardless of their location and can even be triggered by location to enhance their relevance. Organizations prefer to receive direct e-mail rather than direct mail as it can be dealt with more efficiently. The message can be easily forwarded if addressed to the wrong employee, can be deleted quickly if irrelevant and can be responded to quickly if of interest. However, as the relationship with the event organizer develops, either through repeat purchases or as the potential customer moves through the decision-making process, e-mail will no longer be sufficient and needs to be supported by personal contact via phone or visit.

Many consumers now also prefer to be contacted by e-mail rather than home phone or mail. E-mail is seen as less intrusive and pressuring than telesales and prevents the doormat clutter created by direct mail. The same material, as in letters, brochures and programmes, can be sent by e-mail at a fraction of the cost, although this can add to the perceived intangibility of the events product. Event customers may be happy to receive offers and announcements by e-mail but would prefer to have a hard copy of the event programme and physical tickets as opposed to e-tickets.

The reduced costs and increased implementation speed of electronic direct marketing will undoubtedly lead to a continued rise in the use of these media in event communications. However, they will always need to be supported by and fully integrated with the wider mass communication methods and non-electronic personal contacts. Examples of the organizational and consumer uses of direct marketing are given in Table 10.2.

Messages

The form of the message transmitted via direct marketing is dependent on the medium used, the target market and the objectives of the campaign. The aspects of message development which are unique to direct marketing are the use of personalization and the importance of the initial words and images viewed, read or heard by the recipient. These first impressions will largely determine whether or not the message elicits any further attention or whether the recipient hangs up, or deletes or bins the communication. For example, in direct mail the size, style and shape of the envelope and the format of the address can be readily interpreted by the target as either a bill, personal correspondence, unsolicited direct mail, requested direct mail. This initial perception will determine whether or not the letter is opened, when it is opened and the attitude of the recipient when opening it. Colchester Arts Centre, in the UK, has overcome some of these mail conventions to create unusual direct mail campaigns aimed at increasing attendance at their music and comedy nights. Their campaigns have used paper bags instead of envelopes, bank notes and polystyrene used as postcards and scrunched up letters to create an intriguing bulging envelope (Roberts, 2001). These campaigns not only overcame the consumer's inherent resistance to direct mail but created a positive attitude to the organization through the apt use of humour.

The subject line and the sender's name for e-mail direct marketing are the equivalent to the direct mail envelope. These will determine whether the e-mail is opened and read immediately, whether it is left to disappear down the page, or whether it is immediately deleted unread. The sender needs to be a recognized and accepted

Table 10.2 Uses of direct marketing methods

Direct marketing method	Organizational stakeholders	Consumer stakeholders
Personal contact	Ongoing relationship building with key clients, sponsors and the media	Communication via customer service staff to enhance experience and offer additional relevant products
Outbound telesales	Initial contacts with organizational clients. Retention/repeat purchase encouragement. Used to gain permission for personal contact	Post-event communication. Target frequent attendees to offer additional benefits, memberships, for example
Inbound telesales	Cross-selling and relationship building through customer service	Cross selling and relationship building through customer service
Mobile/SMS	Not appropriate for organizational clients unless specifically requested	Sales promotions, offers, cross-selling at the event. Provide relevant valued information to enhance experience. Viral marketing to build awareness
Direct mail	Can be used for initial contact for organizational clients if well designed and targeted and supported by telesales	Can be used as initial contact although more effective for reminder, retention, repeat purchase objectives
E-mail	Same as direct mail but needs previous permission, opt-ins. Useful for repeat business development in larger target markets	Very effective for repeat purchase encouragement when recipient has opted for contact via this medium

source and should ideally include an individual's name as well as the name of the organization. The organization's name will help recipients remember that they gave permission for this communication and will reassure them of its validity. The subject line needs to entice the reader in ensuring them of the relevance of the content and with the promise of something of value. For example the New York City Opera uses subject lines such as 'DIALOGUES at City Opera: Order now and save 25%!'. The limited time offer is clear from the start drawing the recipient in and both the subject line and the sender's name reassure the reader of the source of the message. Even consumers who have actively opted-in, subscribed, registered or given permission to be contacted may have forgotten they have done so and may therefore need reassurance early on in the message. The New York City Opera does this through the use of their organization's name in the subject field.

In the case of outbound telesales, many consumers are now experienced in recognizing a sales call from a personal call even before the caller has started speaking. This can be based on the delay on answering caused by automatic dialling or the use of international call centres or the quality of the sound or even the time of day the call is made. These issues may be difficult to overcome in large-scale campaigns but highlight the importance of the caller's opening statement in negating some of the scepticism which the respondent may already feel. The opening statement should always include an explanation of who the caller is and why they are calling, with some reassurance, whenever possible, that the recipient has requested or given permission for the caller to contact them in this way.

Once the e-mail or letter has been opened and the phone has not been put down the main body of the message can be communicated. Research among arts audiences found that it is not the medium (phone, mail, e-mail) or format (fact sheet, newsletter, leaflet, letter) that makes the difference but the message. 'The medium just delivers, the format just presents but it's the message that persuades' (Dunnett and McIntyre, 2001). However, the format and presentation will affect the recipient's initial levels of attention and interest and will need to draw them in to the content of the message. For telesales the format will be based on the tone, accent and attitude of the caller. In e-mail communications the format choices are wider with the use of text, graphics, video, file attachments and web links. Direct mail has an even wider range of possibilities as physical items (samples, CDs, merchandise, gimmicks) can be included along with text and graphics. Direct mail can also make use of three-dimensional mailings, for example, through pop-up displays, or fold and build inserts.

The Sadler's Wells organization (which includes three London theatres) has used direct e-mail successfully to generate repeat ticket sales. The format of their campaign is a monthly newsletter or e-bulletin with the content split into easily identifiable sub-sections to widen the appeal and allow for easier scan reading. The e-bulletin is targeted at previous attendees and is personalized through use of the recipient's details and by being sent from a named individual. They also always include the name of the theatre in the subject line. The use of the e-bulletin format allows the organization to keep in regular contact with its target audiences and therefore develops an ongoing and anticipated relationship. This format also prevents the simple replication of existing printed material by focusing on fresh, up-to-date information giving the e-mails a 'must read now' feel. The news value is further enhanced by the inclusion of offers, deals, competition entries and links (de Kretser, 2001).

For telesales the success of the message is determined by the pre-call preparation in terms of knowing and anticipating the needs of the recipient. The immediate feedback received in using the telephone as a medium allows the caller to empathize with the recipient, creating the opportunity to increase the personalization of the message as the conversation develops. The key structure of an outbound sales call according to Dixon (2001) is:

- prepare beforehand so that you have the relevant information to hand
- have a brief opening script detailing who you are, your organization and the purpose of your call
- engage the recipient by asking them about themselves
- make your offer or request
- negotiate depending upon their response, personalize the offer
- confirm what you have discussed and what has been agreed
- close the conversation by assuring them that you value their time and that you still 'like' and appreciate them even though they may not have agreed to anything
- administer the outcomes of the call by doing what you said you would do.

The more successful telesales calls are those which are not tightly scripted and therefore allow for the development of a natural interaction. In events the cost of telesales compared to the revenue from ticket sales means that this method is likely to be used for key stakeholders only and, in particular, to communicate with potential sponsors, corporate clients, members, donors and season-ticket holders and should therefore be structured accordingly. The relationship with these customers is one that can be developed over the long term and, therefore, it is important that they do not feel pressured or punished for a failure to comply at this stage. The call can be used to establish their future needs and to open a dialogue rather than generate an immediate agreement of support.

In addition to the format and main content of the message, direct marketing communications also require other elements if they are to work successfully. For direct mail items their needs to be a response mechanism suitable for the target audience and the kind of response being generated. A prepaid envelope or card may be appropriate to encourage responses. Pre-prepared clear and simple forms with tick box responses can encourage involvement and ease of response for such things as requests for further information, to be included in the programme mailing list, to order tickets, to donate funds, to be contacted by telephone or to take part in a sales promotion. As well as a written response, which should always be included, it is useful to offer the alternatives of phone, e-mail and website. This not only encourages additional responses but also indicates the communication preferences of those individuals for future use. Similarly, although the response to telesales is immediate, it is often worth asking at the close of the call how that individual would prefer to be contacted in the future. This helps meet their needs and also provides permission for future communications.

Responses to e-mails can be encouraged via a direct e-mail reply to the sender allowing for an individualized dialogue to take place or the responses can be limited through the use of online forms and website links. Direct e-mails aimed at organizations are usually more successful in encouraging a response if they allow the recipient to respond directly. However, if this is the case, it is important to have estimated the likely response and to ensure that the responses can be dealt with once they have been received. The expectation is that the e-mails will be responded to within twenty-four hours and if this is not met then the recipient's interest will have moved elsewhere. For larger consumer campaigns it is often more efficient to direct the responder to website links that provide response options. These may include online purchasing, event programme details, requests for further information and 'frequently asked questions'. The organization can then automate much of the administration and ensure that all requests are dealt with effectively. It is also important again to include other contact options through the provision of phone numbers and addresses.

To gain greater reach for direct mail campaigns it may be possible to include a viral element which will encourage information to be shared or passed on. E-mails are easily forwarded to the recipient's friends and colleagues and therefore the inclusion of something unusual, entertaining, humorous or of value can encourage the spreading of the message. This can be achieved subtly through jokes, games, graphics or can make use of special offers, competitions and freebies. Another option is to ask the respondent to 'recommend a friend' who may find the information of interest. In some instances it may be appropriate to reward the recipient with additional offers if they make a recommendation or if their friend responds to the offer.

Encouraging a wider audience through direct mail is harder to achieve but can be encouraged by the inclusion of more durable items. This may simply be a venue programme or brochure, a number of vouchers for discounted tickets or branded free gifts such as pens, CDs and key rings.

Opt outs and permission renewals

The final aspect to include in all direct marketing, regardless of media used, is the opportunity for the recipient to opt out. In a telephone call this can be a final question asking if they can be contacted again or how they would like to be contacted in the future. For direct mail items the response mechanism should include a tick box offering the option to be removed from the mailing list or to change the method of contact and for e-mail a clearly visible link or instruction on how to opt out of further e-mails is needed.

Although offering the opportunity to opt out of the list will reduce the number of contacts available to the organization, the benefits will outweigh this loss. Those that opt out are doing so for a reason, lack of interest, wrongly targeted or their situation has changed and are therefore not valid prospects. The opt out helps to 'clean' and maintain a focused and valid list of prospects. Secondly, those that choose not to opt out are giving permission for the organization to continue contacting them and are confirming their interests in the material they are receiving. They may not be purchasing as yet but they are live prospects who may do so in the future. Thirdly, a clearly offered opt-out helps to build trust with the recipients and reduces the appearance of direct marketing as junk mail, spam or high pressure sales. Finally, it ensures that the organization is complying with many of the increasingly stringent laws and regulations governing the use of personal information.

For example, the New York City Opera e-mail campaign to its past customers has clearly defined click through buttons, below the graphic, offering the following options:

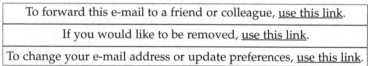

| To forward this e-mail to a friend or colleague, <u>use this link</u>. |
| If you would like to be removed, <u>use this link</u>. |
| To change your e-mail address or update preferences, <u>use this link</u>. |

These are additional to the links provided in the main body of the message offering additional information of the performance being promoted, on future performances and to buy tickets.

Marketing databases

In the discussion of the methods and media that are available for direct marketing communications it becomes clear that the success of these campaigns is largely determined through well-defined targeting and the use of personalized information. The list or database of contacts is therefore vital and can be used not only to underpin other communication methods but also to aid the development of other aspects of the organization's marketing strategy (product development, marketing research and pricing structures).

The marketing database is therefore much greater than a list of direct marketing contacts. It is central to the marketing information system and can be used to integrate many of the areas of marketing research and intelligence (Wood, 2004).

The database is built by the gathering of information at points of contact with customers and potential customers. This information can be gained through purchase transactions, requests for information, participation in sales promotions, registration on websites, memberships, complaints and 'recommend a friend' schemes. It is important when gathering the information explicitly to ask for permission to use it in order to contact that individual in the future. For new start-up organizations or those with small current customer contacts the database can be supplemented by bought-in lists. These can be purchased or rented from one of the many list brokers and can be highly targeted in whom they include. Lists purchased from specialist agencies should only include those who have given permission for their information to be passed on, however, bought-in lists will never be as accurate or focused as the organization's own database.

Timezone, for example, an Australian video entertainment centre chain, used direct mail to increase the demand for their children's group birthday parties. The campaign used the company's existing database built up from the collection of party guest details and sales promotion entrants. The detail within the database allowed personalization of the campaign through eight variable text options depending on age, store catchment zone and state. The mail out included two fold and die cut material to highlight the state of the art nature of the video game venues to attract the child audience. Mailouts aimed at parents stressed the quality and full service aspect of the product and incorporated direct response options through mail and telephone. The targeting was refined further by focusing on children who were soon to have a birthday and parents who would be potentially planning a birthday party. This resulted in a 13.5 per cent response rate (Fudge and Lucas, 1996).

The amount of detail collected on each contact can, therefore, help to produce a highly targeted and personalized campaign and, as responses are recorded and added to existing data, the patterns of behaviour and preferences can also be iden-tified. The database needs to be constantly updated with live information and cleaned of out-of-date or dead information. As well as basic contact details and demographics it is vital to record the customer's 'recency' (when did they last make contact), 'frequency' (how often are they in contact), 'value' (spend, support) and 'products' (what services have interested them) (Donovan, 2001).

The more detailed the information collected the more effectively it can be used. For example, the Mariners US Major League baseball team use membership swipe cards to record the purchase activities of their ticket holders. They can therefore track their buying habits at the game and have used this information to place appro-priate food and merchandise stands close to those fans that purchase these types of products. Similarly, fans who purchase a particular type of merchandise are e-mailed with offers of similar products. Although this use of database information may be seen as more pushy than relationship building in its focus on cross-selling, the Mariners also ensure that their customer service staff have the customer's history when processing an order transaction. This means that they can recognize and deal with any complaints during this moment of personal contact helping to forge future positive relationships (Hogan, 2001).

Direct marketing and consumer protection

A study of consumer's views of direct marketing found that they were largely sceptical of such activity and that this scepticism was largely due to their concerns regarding privacy, control and relevance (Evans et al., 2001). Indeed, as consumer concern grows regarding the way organizations collect and use personal information, this information exchange is becoming one of the most significant issues confronting business in the information age (Fletcher, 2003).

In many countries consumer information and privacy protection is becoming more stringently enforced through revised laws and regulations. However, those organizations which have already recognized that loyalty and long-term relationships are built through consumer trust have been proactive in developing and prominently displaying their privacy policies, in using opt-ins for further contacts and making opt-outs easy to select. These organizations were seeking customer permission long before there was any legal requirement to do so and in this way have gained a competitive advantage over those that continued to use personal information in a less scrupulous manner.

To overcome some of the continuing concerns of consumers regarding direct marketing Fletcher (2003) suggests that organizations must:

- always obtain permission to gather information
- make opt-ins the norm
- recognize that individual privacy preferences exist and treat customers accordingly
- recognize that there is a differing perceived value balance between privacy losses and benefits gained
- reward partners with honest and believable dialogue as opposed to prizes or monetary rewards
- actively display and adhere to privacy policies and encourage consumers to look for these.

Event marketers using direct marketing communications must therefore not simply comply with consumer information protection legislation but should actively use their ethical and sensitive handling of customer data as a competitive advantage in developing trust and loyalty.

Summary

Although direct marketing communication can be used to develop initial awareness, to disseminate sales promotion offers or to move respondents to purchase action, this method is most effectively used to further develop relationships with existing customers. These individualized methods which offer direct response and feedback offer the opportunity to provide the level of contact needed by organizational event clients as well creating a more personalized communication relationship with larger consumer target markets. Although the cost of direct marketing is higher in terms of overall reach than many mass media methods, the cost per response is lower. This is due to the more precise targeting of the message, the impact of a personalized message and the ability to generate an immediate response.

Direct marketing can be achieved through the use of several media and through a variety of methods but, to be successful, it needs to be targeted accurately using the detailed information gained through the development of a comprehensive customer database. The message delivered needs to be clear and persuasive and the format needs to be innovative enough to cut through the existing direct marketing clutter. Direct marketing is rarely successful as a stand alone method and needs to be integrated with mass media use, web marketing and sales promotion.

The use of any personal information needs to be handled sensitively and with regard to the individual contact's privacy requirements. Permission should always be gained for the gathering and use of any such information.

Discussion points

- 'Relationships are more important than ticket sales.' Discuss this statement with reference to the arts, sports and business event sectors.
- Obtain two examples of direct marketing material from the events industry. Critically evaluate the material in terms of targeting, personalization, format and message.
- How would you obtain, develop and maintain customer information for a database for non-ticketed events?
- Investigate the legal requirements governing consumer personal information use in two countries of your choice.

Useful websites

The UK Direct Marketing Association. [www.dma.org.uk]
The US Direct Marketing Association. [www.the-dma.org]
The Institute of Direct Marketing. [www.theidm.com]
The Direct Mail Information Service. [www.dmis.co.uk]

References

AMA (Arts Marketing Association) (2004) Relationship marketing and customer care. www.a-m-a.co.uk

Arnold, M.J. and Tapp, S.R. (2003) Direct marketing in non-profit services: Investigating the case of the arts industry. *Journal of Services Marketing*, 17 (2), 141–160.

Berry, L.L. (1983) Relationship marketing. In *Emerging Perspectives on Services Marketing*, AMA (ed.). AMA, pp. 25–28.

Bruhn, M. (2003) *Relationship Marketing: Management of Customer Relationships*. Pearson Education.

Collin-Lachaud, I. and Duyck, J.-Y. (2002) Relationship marketing as a paradigm for festivals: A case study of the Francofolies of La Rochelle, France. *International Journal of Arts Management*, 4 (3).

Curtis, J. (2001) The weakest link? *Marketing Business*, April, 38–40.

De Kretser, H. (2001) E-mail. *Journal of Arts Marketing*, 2, 17.

Direct Marketing Association (2004) www.dma.org.uk (accessed October, 2004).

Dixon, D. (2001) Planning a telephone campaign. *Journal of Arts Marketing*, 2, 12–13.

Donovan, J. (2001) Planning a direct marketing campaign. Using direct mail. *Journal of Arts Marketing*, 2, 7–9.

Dunnett, H. and McIntyre, A. (2001) Direct marketing. *Journal of Arts Marketing*, 2, 18.

Evans, M., Patterson, M. and O'Malley, L. (2001) The direct marketing–direct consumer gap: qualitative insights. *Qualitative Market Research: An International Journal*, 4 (1), 17–24.

Fletcher, K. (2003) Consumer power and privacy. The changing nature of CRM. *International Journal of Advertising*, 22 (2), 5–20.

Fudge, I. and Lucas, V. (1996) Party-zone. Direct Marketing Association. WARC.

Grönroos, C. (1990) Relationship approach to marketing in service contexts: The marketing and organizational behavior interface. *Journal of Business Research*, 20 (1), 3–11.

Gummesson, E. (1996) Relationship marketing and imaginary organizations. A synthesis. *European Journal of Marketing*, 30 (2), 31–44.

Hogan, J. (2001) Seattle Mariners building loyalty with CRM in the lineup. 18 December 2001. www.searchCRM.com (accessed October, 2004).

Hughes, R. (2003) Expanding the fan experience with wireless applications. A paper delivered by the NHL Director of New Business Development at *Sport Media and Technology* 2003, 13–14 November, New York Marriot Eastside, New York. Street and Smith.

O'Malley, L. and Tynan, C. (2000) Relationship marketing in consumer markets. Rhetoric or reality? *European Journal of Marketing*, 34 (7), 797–815.

Rangers Football Club (2004) www.rangers.premiumtv.co.uk (accessed October, 2004).

Rentschler, R., Radbourne, J., Carr, R. and Rickard, J. (2002) Relationship marketing, audience retention and performing arts organization viability. *International Journal of Nonprofit and Voluntary Sector Marketing*, 7 (2), 118–130.

Rettie, R. and Brum, M. (2001) M-commerce: The role of SMS text messages. *COTIM-2001 Proceedings: From E-commerce to M-commerce*. Karlsuhe.

Roberts, A. (2001) An unconventional mail. *Journal of Arts Marketing*, 2, 11.

Sheth, J.N. and Parvatiyar, A. (1995) Relationship marketing in consumer markets. Antecedents and consequences. *Journal of the Academy of Marketing Science*, 23 (4), 255–271.

Smith, P. and Taylor, J. (2004) *Marketing Communications: An Integrated Approach*, 4th edn. Kogan Page.

Sport and Technology (2004) www.sportandtechnology.com. Arksports (accessed October, 2004).

Tapp, A. (2000) *Principles of Direct and Database Marketing*. Pearson Education.

Wheatley, J. and Nocco, G. (1998) Special Olympics summer games campaign. Direct Marketing Association. WARC.

Wittkoff, S. and Cobb, B. (1996) Mondrian boogie-woogie membership campaign. Direct Marketing Association. WARC.

Wood, E.H. (2004) Marketing information for impact analysis and evaluation. In *Festival and Events Management: An International Arts and Cultural Perspective*, Yeoman, I., Robertson, M., Ali-McKnight, J., McMahon-Beattie, U. and Drummond, S. (eds). Butterworth-Heinemann.

Section Three
Events as Communications Tools

Goodbye for now. Panasonic (Matsushita Electrical Industrial Co.) was a sponsor at the 2004 Olympic Games in Athens. The brand has been a Games sponsor since 1984 and has developed the relationship to a position where it now supplies the Games with television, audio and video technology. Its use of this outdoor media here was in central Athens at the end of the Olympic Games and in time for the subsequent Paralympic Games. The advertisement was a part of Panasonic's strategy to exploit its Games sponsorship rights and was intended to portray the close association and long-term relationship the brand has with the Olympic movement as an IOC TOP Sponsor. (Picture courtesy of Brian Masterman, 2004.)

For this section the perspective changes to the one held by those organizations that are looking to use events for communications purposes. Three main event communication vehicles are considered.

Promotional events are created for a specific marketing purpose. They are produced to launch, showcase and demonstrate products and also develop awareness for corporate image. Chapter 11 considers the use of such events by marketing and public relations agencies as well as those firms that create and produce on an in-house basis.

While it is a young industry, sponsorship has grown quickly into a valuable communications tool. The extent of that value is not yet fully evidenced and so Chapter 12 covers the critical factors for the successful selection and development of sponsorships by sponsors and the case for further exploitation and evaluation in order to get closer to more objective measurement.

Corporate hospitality can be spectator as well as participation led. Tickets for calendar events are still the most popular but the creation of tailored activities is growing. Chapter 13 considers how entertaining can build both internal and external relationships for the development of future sales and image.

Promotional Events

Corporate Sponsorship of Events

Corporate Hospitality

Chapter 11
Promotional Events

Objectives

- To recognize the growing importance of events as a communications tool within a range of sectors
- To appreciate the use of events within the disciplines of experiential marketing and cause-related marketing
- To explain the variety of events available to support marketing communications
- To understand the benefits and drawbacks of using promotional events within the communications plan

Introduction

It can be argued that all events promote something. This may be the sponsor's brand, the event organizer's services, the caterer's business, interest in the sport being played, sales of the artist's recordings, further business for the funeral director or popularity of the host. This inherent ability of events to communicate with specific target audiences is now being more widely recognized by a variety of organizations leading to the increasingly innovative use of events as a vital element of the communications mix. All types of organizations, public and private sector, non-profit and profit making, operating in many different industries can benefit from the inclusion of some form of promotional event within their communications plan.

The use of events for promotion has grown alongside the emergence of lifestyle marketing. Lifestyle marketing simply involves matching the offering to the consumer's lifestyle. In order to do this, the offering needs to be tailored to the needs of small target markets and the communication of the offering needs to fit into each target market's lifestyle characteristics. Promotional events are therefore ideal as they can be highly focused and can relate directly to the audience's leisure, shopping and work activities (Schreiber and Lenson, 1994).

Promotional events are often used to develop and build relationships with specific target customers and are therefore closely related to direct marketing and personal selling. They can also be used to generate media interest and can therefore be incorporated into public relations campaigns. There is also a clear connection between promotional events, event sponsorship and corporate hospitality. These areas are covered in other chapters within this text and, therefore, this chapter will focus on defining promotional events and giving an overview of the different types of events that can be used as promotional tools. The importance of events within the emerging area of experiential marketing will be considered, as will the importance of events within cause-related marketing. The many benefits of using events for marketing communication are discussed alongside the drawbacks associated with these methods.

The events covered will be limited to those aimed at external stakeholders rather than events used for internal marketing purposes. These externally targeted events encompass a wide range of differing formats such as corporate charity events, product launch events, sales/sampling/trial events, trade shows and exhibitions, road shows, conferences, publicity/media events and stunts and many others.

Definitions and types of promotional event

The term 'promotional events' is used in several different ways, both within the academic literature and among practitioners. In its widest sense it encompasses any event-related form of promotion and therefore includes sponsorships, corporate hospitality, media invites and tickets as rewards or prizes in sales promotions. This wider remit is more correctly termed 'event marketing', but its usefulness as a category for communication methods is in doubt as it pulls together widely differing tools which are used in very different ways.

It is more useful to distinguish promotional events from these other aspects of event-related promotion and focus solely on those events whose primary objective is the promotion of a product, brand, organization or idea. Defining promotional events in this way excludes communication or promotion opportunities linked to an event if the event has been developed for another purpose. Therefore, the sponsorship of a sports tournament and the purchase of corporate boxes at the theatre would not constitute promotional events.

The event itself is therefore developed in order to communicate something about the product, brand, idea or organization with a specific target audience. Although this appears to be a straightforward delineation, there are many instances where the primary objective of the event is not so clear cut. Corporate interest can be the driving force behind the creation of a non-promotional event in order to create a suitable sponsorship vehicle. For example, Tennents Lager alongside DF Concerts created the 'T' in the Park festival in order to improve their image with a particular demographic group. Similarly Coca-Cola spearheaded a 'street cred' games competition in Scotland to give them valuable exposure to an opinion leading target market and through this enhance their credibility. The event was a product in its own right but was developed for Coca-Cola in order to gain entry into a new market dominated by a local soft drink supplier, Irn Bru. On a larger scale, many national and regional governmental bodies have created events for the main purpose of showcasing their city or region to a national and international audience of prospective tourists (Van Gessell, 2000). In these cases there is dedifferentiation between the product (the event) and the promotions' vehicle and the event becomes an extreme example of self-liquidating promotion in that the attendees are paying to be exposed to the organization's brand. Although these types of corporate created events clearly demonstrate the perceived value of events as a medium for communicating brand image, they are not included in this chapter as they are more akin to sponsorship than to promotional events.

There is also a distinction to be made between promotional events and events used for corporate hospitality. Although corporate hospitality may often use existing events as a form of entertainment and reward for clients, there is a growing trend towards creating events for the specific purpose of corporate hospitality. The difference between these and promotional events is in the objectives. Corporate hospitality events are most often used to reward existing clients, to foster and develop relationships and to create a social occasion. For this to happen they need to shy away from overt promotion of the organization's brand and products and focus solely on the entertainment and social aspects of the event. Promotional events, on the other hand, overtly promote the brand with a view to encouraging awareness of the product, involvement with it and, ultimately, changes in purchase behaviour. Relationship building may also be an objective, but the key difference between promotional events and corporate hospitality events is the focus on brand-building rather than the focus on client entertainment.

A useful further narrowing of the definition of promotional events is to focus on those events where the audience is more than a spectator. Promotional events should, therefore, involve some level of participation or interaction (Cunningham and Taylor, 1995). This may be at a fairly low level such as visitors to a trade exhibition interacting with exhibitors or can be highly participatory as in test drives for car retailers. Although there are examples of promotional events which are non-interactive, it can be argued that these will be far less effective as they are not using the advantages that events have over many other types of medium. A product launch which merely presents information to an audience may as well be done via direct marketing or mass media advertising if it does not make use of audience interaction and create involvement with the product through some form of participation.

Based on this discussion, promotional events can be defined as:

any event whose primary purpose is the promotion of a brand, product, idea or organization and which achieves this through the encouragement of audience involvement.

Events and experiential marketing

Experiential marketing focuses on the use of the six senses (smell, vision, taste, touch, hearing and balance) in developing emotional attachment to the brand (McCole, 2004). The shift is away from a focus on customer satisfaction to creating an ongoing emotional involvement achieved through bringing the brand alive through a unique experience (Schmitt, 1999). This experience can be any form of interaction but can be achieved most easily through created events. The emotional attachment developed through affecting the six senses during an event produces a relationship with the brand which can be sustained in the longer term. Many large organizations that have seen a decline in the effectiveness of traditional media are switching spend to 'customer experiences'. For example, Coca-Cola's CEO states that 'experience-based, access-driven marketing is the next frontier' (NZ Marketing Magazine, 2003). Pepsi-Cola have also been steadily switching their budget away from traditional media to non-traditional methods such as events (Schreiber and Lenson, 1994).

The use of events within experiential marketing creates a 'brand bubble' around the participants, ensuring that their involvement is not diluted by the myriad of other marketing communications that they are normally exposed to (Brown, 2001). Brand experience events cut out this clutter and allow the participant space and time to assimilate and become attached to the brand.

Experiential marketing, however, involves more than events within its strategy. Brown (2001) suggests that there are three stages to a brand experience. First, the target audience need to be 'invited' to take part, or take an interest in an experience. This invitation may use traditional mass media or direct marketing to maximize awareness of the experience. Secondly, there is the experience itself, the moment in time when the responding audience are emotionally engaged with the brand. As this needs to be personal and interactive it can creatively use direct marketing techniques, sales promotions, websites and, of course, events. The final stage is to make the most of the experience for participants and non-participants through public relations, integrated media campaigns and follow-up marketing. This 'milking it' stage is vital if maximum return or effect is to be gained from what is likely to be a relatively small (in terms of participants) and possibly expensive communications 'experience' campaign.

For the experience to have the most effect it should make use of unusual settings, timings and activities and, in this way, should incorporate the use of ambient media. The more out of the ordinary the experience is the more it will generate word of mouth and media interest. This is particularly suitable in markets where information overload and cynicism has led to the filtering out of many communication messages and where credibility is given to less obvious, underground or 'off the wall' campaigns. However, many mainstream companies are already making good use of these techniques. For example, Asda supermarkets have used their car parks to host drive-in movies and through this experience have brought attendees emotionally closer to the brand.

Experiential marketing is a relatively new development in marketing thinking but is rapidly being accepted by many organizations. Whether the business is a museum, library, shopping mall or car manufacturer, simply producing a good quality product at a fair price is no longer good enough. Customers now expect a compelling experience which they cannot get elsewhere (Kirsner, 2002). This has important implications for the events industry as promotional and media-related events are an integral part of successful experiential marketing. There is no better way to create an emotional experience for a target audience than through a unique event which engages, involves, entertains and educates the customer while exposing them to the brand.

Events and cause-related marketing

The effectiveness of promotional events can often be enhanced through the inclusion of a cause-related theme or charity partner. Cause-related marketing refers to organizations gaining commercial benefit from their support of charitable causes and this can be achieved through many communications tools. For example, sales promotions can include a percentage of the price paid in the form of a donation, sponsorship can be provided for non-profit museums, arts and educational institutes and public relations can gain significant media coverage with stories of charitable donations and fund-raising activities. Events, however, provide an ideal vehicle for cause-related communications as they are already frequently used as fund-raising vehicles by many charities and can readily combine this activity with very positive brand exposure. A promotional event, therefore, which provides a unique and entertaining experience for the participant while also making them feel good about themselves and the organization through their support of a charity or good cause can be even more effective.

However, customers are becoming more sceptical of cause-related efforts (Arnott, 1994) due to their misuse by some organizations and the generally held belief that companies should give to charities without expecting a return. Indeed, there is anecdotal evidence to suggest that the rise in cause-related marketing has led to a significant decline in organizational philanthropy, that is, companies will no longer support causes if there is no immediate benefit to their bottom-line. This feeling suggests that a move away from charity-related sales promotion, where donations are directly related to sales, towards events with carefully chosen cause-related themes and partners will be better received.

Promotional event development

The decision to use promotional events within the communications mix should be based upon thorough research to ascertain whether or not they are suitable for the organization's target markets and if they will have the desired effect within the budget available. Once the decision to go ahead has been made clear, objectives need to be set for the event or events which fit within and complement the organization's overall communication objectives. These should include target numbers for attendance and include subcategories for specific attendee types. More importantly, however, are measurable communication objectives such as those relating to attitude or behavioural changes for those attending. These may be set in terms of the percentage aware of the brand, preferring the brand, associating certain characteristics with the brand or can be focused on desire for further contact or information, intention to purchase, or willingness to recommend the brand.

Once objectives have been set, the target audiences need to be clearly defined. As promotional events tend to have limited numbers of participants, target market identification is vital. Those that attend need to be the best prospects in terms of the objectives. This may mean selecting opinion leaders who will further spread the word, customers who have already shown interest and are likely to make a purchase decision at the event or new customers who have not yet been exposed to the brand. A useful combination is to combine existing 'happy' customers with new potential customers at the event. The 'happy' customers are then used as advocates for the brand adding more credibility to the promotional message.

A thorough understanding of the characteristics and preferences of the target audiences is necessary before the creative process can begin. The event concept needs to use this customer understanding to create events which fit with the brand's overall positioning strategy and communications campaign but also to provide a unique and engaging experience for the targeted groups.

Integration and coordination with the other communications tools are vital to ensure a consistent message and to deliver the invitation to attend the event. The invitation needs to be sent via a range of media and needs to be repeated several times up to the day of the event. For example, if prospective attendee details are known, telesales can be used to follow up interest and a 'see you there' reminder can be sent just before the event (McIntosh, 2004). Informing the target market that the event is happening using a range of well-targeted media to reach the desired audience can also ensure that the event has a wider reaching impact than simply those that attend.

During and after the implementation of the event, increased value and effect can be achieved though the use of public relations, websites and sales promotion. These can help to involve non-participants, to encourage post-event interest in the brand and create an interest in future events. For example, data gathered during the event can be used for future direct marketing campaigns, competitions related to the event can form the basis of wider reaching sales promotions and aspects of the event can be translated into web content. The event itself can generate media interest in a number of ways, for example, through its success, its uniqueness, cause-related aspects or celebrity involvement.

It is imperative that each promotional event is evaluated thoroughly against the objectives set. The evaluation should include an assessment of the event itself but should mainly focus on its communication effects. Participants may have had a great time at the event with this having little or no effect on their attitude to the brand. Evaluating the communication effects will involve tracking participants after attendance to ascertain attitude and behavioural changes and word of mouth generated and will also include measurement of the wider effects achieved through additional publicity and other related activities. The evaluation of the event's effectiveness may be carried out by the organization itself, the event management company or creative agency involved in the event or by independent researchers, but it needs to be thorough, systematic and, above all, objective if it is to be of use in planning future campaigns.

A summary of the promotional events planning process is given in Figure 11.1. This process relates to the planning of the event from a communications perspective, a more detailed planning process for event management generally can be found in Masterman (2004).

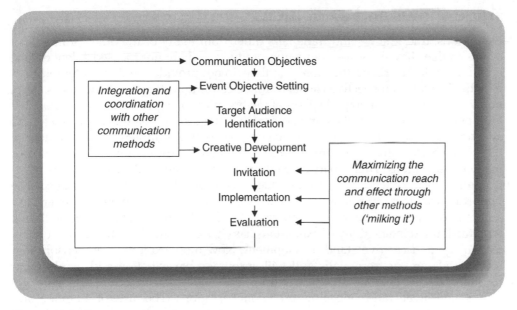

Figure 11.1 The promotional event process.

Promotional event types

There is currently very little discussion of events as communication tools in much of the marketing communications literature. Those authors that do include events tend to limit their use to sponsorship, media events for public relations and exhibitions and trade shows (Shimp, 1997; Pickton and Broderick, 2001; Smith and Taylor, 2004). However, as has been seen in the discussion of experiential marketing and through anecdotal evidence from event management companies, the range of events used for marketing communication appears to be growing rapidly as does the proportion of communications budget being spent on them.

Promotional events range from manufacturing plant open days to health promotion road shows, from international trade shows to product sampling in shopping malls. What all these events have in common is their ability to promote a brand to a focused group of customers through an interactive experience.

These events are often difficult to categorize because of their diversity and the continuous innovation and creativity in the industry. One possibility is to group them by attendee type into those aimed at the media (press conferences, publicity stunts), those aimed at intermediaries (e.g. product launches to retailers), those aimed at organizational customers (e.g. components exhibitions) and those aimed at consumers (e.g. car retailer test drive days). However, there are many events which target all these groups. For example a product launch event may be run initially for the press, then for retailers and then to selected members of the public and a motor show will attract organizational buyers, the media and end customers. Rather than categorize this type of event, therefore, a selection of the most common types will be discussed to give an overview of the range of choices available for this increasingly popular communication method.

Trade shows and exhibitions

Exhibitions, trade shows and trade fairs differ from many of the other promotional events in that they showcase competing products and are not focused solely on one brand. It could be argued therefore that they do not provide the desired 'brand bubble' that insulates prospective clients from the communications of competitors. Also, many exhibitions are merely displays of the organization's product and therefore the level of interaction and participation can be low, suggesting that the involvement and attachment obtained through a participatory experience is limited. However, despite these drawbacks exhibitions remain an important part of the communications mix for many organizations. This is partly due to tradition in some industries and the negative impact of not attending, but is also due to many benefits which can be gained. The opportunities offered through the bringing together of a large number of buyers and sellers in one place are many and outweigh the disadvantages of competitor clutter. Also the limited interactivity of exhibitions has changed with the introduction of new technology and creative stand development. Now most exhibitors will ensure that their stands are far from static and will encourage participation and involvement through product demonstrations and trials, interactive screens, competitions, giveaways and lively and engaging brand ambassadors. The use of humour and entertainment can work as well for industrial products as for consumer products. For example, Hepworth Building Products caused a stir at the IWEX exhibition (International Water Exhibition) in 1994 where their stand used life size blow-ups of naked ground workers holding the new Hepworth water pipe product and the opportunity for stand visitors to have their photos taken behind similar cardboard figures with face cut outs. The creative idea was to represent the pipe's benefits of being durable, strong, light and leak proof by using the analogy with a condom. A risqué humourous campaign aimed at the end-user, the ground worker, which generated unprecedented press coverage, stand footfall and most importantly sales presentation opportunities with product specifiers (Pringle and Paton, 1996).

Exhibitors may choose to use exhibitions for a number of reasons, including to generate sales leads, make appointments, make sales, generate publicity, launch new products, undertake marketing research, gather competitor intelligence, improve corporate morale, improve corporate image.

An example of some of the benefits offered by exhibition use is provided by The Water Africa 2003 North Exhibition held in Cairo. The exhibition's target market for attendees is the geographic regions of Europe, Africa, Middle East, Arabian Gulf, North and South America and Asia and these visitors represent a range of organizations and roles listed as:

- water industries and services companies
- academic institutions
- consulting firms
- water industry business leaders
- corporate environmental managers
- finance and investment professionals
- government officials and decision makers.

The benefits for exhibitors are given as (Ace Events, 2002):

- meet key buyers
- tap into new markets

- form strategic partnerships
- gain access to investment capital.

This exhibition clearly demonstrates one of the main benefits of exhibitions – their ability to concentrate the majority of the industry sector's key players in one place. This allows exhibitors to have personal interaction with a range of useful contacts (buyers, suppliers, partners, investors) in a far more cost effective way than through sales calls or other direct marketing methods.

The range of reasons for exhibiting goes some way to explaining why many organizations are unable or unwilling to assess the effectiveness of their spend on exhibitions. Objectives are rarely set for what should be achieved and success is measured simply on stand visitor numbers, business cards collected or sales made on the day. The expense and commitment required in exhibiting, along with the often high profile nature of the event, means that careful planning is required which begins with objective setting and ends with evaluation. Pickton and Broderick (2001) suggest an eight-stage planning process starting with clear and precise objective setting followed by systematic and informed exhibition selection. The third and fourth stages are planning staffing for the stand and determining the support promotions needed. The next stage is the creative aspect of stand layout, content and design. It is also vital to plan for follow-up activities and therefore, stage six is ensuring that resources and expertise are in place to make the most of contacts made during the exhibition. Finally, the logistics of exhibiting need to be arranged and plans put in place for evaluating the activity after the exhibition has finished.

Exhibitions can provide the organization with a well-defined target market accessible for the duration of the exhibition in a concentrated location. For example, Avon in the USA exhibited at twenty exhibitions aimed at women across the country, reaching an audience of 500 000, distributing thousands of samples and generating at least 60 000 sales leads (Schuverer, 1999).

A carefully chosen exhibition which reaches the desired target market, along with a well-designed stand providing an interactive experience for visitors, can be a highly effective promotional tool for both consumer and business markets. The setting of well-defined objectives for the exhibition and the evaluation of the success of exhibiting that is then measured against these objectives is vital if a return on investment is to be proven.

The value of exhibiting also needs to take into account the cost or likely effects of not exhibiting, which may include negative publicity, assumptions of financial problems as well as lost opportunities. It is also useful to consider the effectiveness gains or losses in spending the exhibition proportion of the communications budget elsewhere.

Corporate cause-related events

The use of charitable causes and worthy partners can greatly enhance participation rates and increase the perception of the value and credibility of the event. It can also help to generate press interest and coverage. For example, in 2002 Unilever Canada launched a three-month programme of events called 'Sunlight National PlayDays' which took place at a variety of locations throughout Canada. These promotional events formed part of their wider 'Go ahead. Get dirty' campaign. The campaign had two cause-related partners in the International Association for the Child's Right to Play and the Canadian Parks and Recreation Association (Ramage, 2002). These partners provided the expertise and local organization for the events as well as valuable credibility and a positive caring image for Unilever. The events incorporated the cause-related partners within their theme, therefore ensuring that the partnership was seen in a more positive, less calculating, light. Similarly the sponsors of the event were well matched and included Crayola and Little Tikes (Go ahead. Get dirty, 2002). The objectives were to achieve exposure to the Unilever Sunlight brand through prominent signage and the use of the logo and to encourage product trial and preference via 'brand ambassador' distributed free detergent samples and information to encourage website visits. Overall the PlayDays events aimed to achieve 200 000 'brand touches' (Ramage, 2002).

This type of event is seen as beneficial to the community in providing free, fun, educational activities for children during the school holidays and through this perception the participants become more receptive to the brand. An event which provides tangible benefits for the participants other than a few giveaways is more likely to result in a more favourable attitude to the brand or organization that has provided it.

Product launch events

Events to launch new products to a market vary in type and size. For example, some may be aimed at a large consumer market and therefore require a series of coordinated events across a wide geographical area along with substantial mass media support. Others may choose to launch their new product at a trade show or exhibition ensuring that their stand receives customer, intermediary and media interest. For some products a smaller event may be sufficient if there are a few key stakeholders who can be readily brought together. This may be a media launch relying on the publicity generated to spread the word to the target audience or it may involve launching the product to the potential distributors or retailers. This was the case for Gillette who launched its new female shaving product to its distributors through a high impact event (see Case study 11.1).

Product trial and sampling events

A variety of organizations use events to encourage trial of their product among non-users or to encourage further purchases from existing customers. These include demonstrations and samplings presented in supermarkets, shopping malls and other locations where a large footfall of the desired target market can be reached. For example, the Avon Mall Tour visited a number of shopping malls within six US regions enabling 12 000 women to interact with their beauty products through product demonstrations and trials (Schuverer, 1999). Indeed, consumer products such as Avon, Tupperware, Virgin Vie and Ann Summers focus on product trial events as their main form of communication with the end customer. Their representatives, agents or distributors are recruited from their target markets and are encouraged to hold parties or events within their homes to offer friends and acquaintances the opportunity to try, feel, use the product, to interact with it in an experiential setting. The success of these events is based on the credibility of the host (someone known to the attendees), the informality and comfort of the setting (a home) and the social aspect of the event encouraging trial and purchase through fun, entertainment and peer pressure.

Service products can also be offered for trial through special events. Restaurants will host special, themed events at reduced prices or through invitation only to encourage new customers to attend and through an enjoyable and memorable

Case study 11.1

Gillette Group UK: Venus Trade Launch

In 2000, Gillette approached marketing and events agency, Line Up Communications with the specific purpose of creating a new product trade launch. The task was to support overall marketing communications with a launch to UK retailers of the new women's shaving system, Venus, so that it could hit shelves in March 2001. The objectives were as follows:

- Build credibility of Gillette's understanding of women
- Counter preconceptions (Venus was not just a cosmetically altered version of Gillette's successful Mach3 men's razor)
- Accommodate buy-in across broad trade audience
- Generate real excitement
- Achieve 60 per cent distribution among major accounts by April 2001.

The Line Up Communications solution was an event, staged in two UK locations (North and South England), for multi-audiences as well as for two key accounts, Boots and Superdrug. Their concept was an experiential journey through the Venus production story and the vehicle a custom-built environment. This journey began in 'the white room' and depicted how Gillette researched shaving needs and began its product design process. The journey then continued through a futuristic tunnel and on into a main presentation area. This area consisted of individual booths and product tables for each retailer in order to

promote a tailored relationship. Giant models of the razors were then revealed alongside actual products for inspection.

The result was a trade launch that Gillette considered to be its most successful ever; 95 per cent distribution was achieved among major accounts within nine weeks of the launch and 79 per cent volume share of the women's razor market was achieved by May 2001.

Source: Line Up Communications (2003, 2004).

experience, repeat business and positive word of mouth. Corporate and promotional event agencies successfully use their own events as samples for prospective clients. For example, human resource managers from target industries are invited to sample, through participation, a team-building event or motivational seminar to encourage them to purchase a similar event for their employees. In order for this type of product trial event to work there must be sufficient benefit in attending other than the trial itself. This may be easy to achieve in some cases such as restaurant special events, but may be more difficult for business buyers. For example, the human resource manager attending a sample motivational event will need to justify their time away from the office through, perhaps, skills gained, information learned or contacts made as well as the consideration of the product on offer.

Land Rover vehicles have used country pursuit themed events at stately homes to offer customers the chance to test drive their vehicles while taking part in other country living type activities such as croquet and archery (Gofton, 1998). This type of product trial event showcases the product in a setting which is contingent with the product's desired image and the target market's aspirations. The event also provides sufficient additional benefits to encourage participation. Due to, perhaps, this match between target market, product and event, the level of participation and the perceived value of the event, research conducted for Land Rover found that 78 per cent of participants were more likely to purchase a vehicle after attending such an event (Smith, 1997).

Product trial events can be used successfully to enter relatively large new target markets. For example, Tequila Don Julio, the number two tequila brand in Mexico, wanted to improve its market share in the USA where it was ranked fourth. To do this they identified that they would need to target 25–54-year-old males with a sub-market of 30 per cent Hispanic. In order to do this their promotions company created the Tequila Don Julio Legends of Latin Music Series and staged it in five cities and in carefully selected venues where the clientele met the required demographic (MacMillan, 2003b). The event clearly related the product type to the music genre and encouraged sampling and purchase in a 'natural' environment. An association was made in the attendee's mind between the smooth, sexy, fun aspects of the music and the product itself, achieved through participation.

Road shows

Road shows or touring promotional events can reach pockets of wider target markets at a relatively low cost and can also build interest through anticipation and accumulating media coverage. A road show has aspects of 'the carnival coming to town' in that news of it can travel from one location to the next before the actual event.

A good example of the anticipation factor in road shows is provided by General Motors' Chevrolet brand use of this type of event. General Motors used the long association between the Chevrolet and rock and roll music (there are 200 songs to date with lyrics that mention Chevrolet) to create a touring exhibit of music memorabilia from the 1950s to the present day. The target market was the over fifties age group who grew up with rock and roll and the exhibit was brought to them by an eighteen month long tour of Chevy sponsored events at music venues across the USA. Visitors to the twenty metre long trailer were encouraged to participate through a number of activities including strumming along to the guitar greats. Alongside the 'Rock & Roll Tour' vehicle various classic and newly launched Chevrolet cars were displayed (MacMillan, 2003a). The event made use of existing associations between a music genre and the vehicles in order to reach a specific demographic group. The exhibit itself generated plenty of publicity and further leveraged Chevrolet's sponsorship of Nascar and figure skating.

Publicity and media events

Although public relations are covered in detail in Chapter 5, it is worth discussing here the importance of promotional events for generating media interest and coverage. All promotional events, whether exhibitions, product launches, road shows or charity related, will have some aspect that is newsworthy and this should be taken advantage of to encourage favourable media responses. However, there is also the possibility of creating a promotional event with the primary objective of generating media coverage, 'buzz' or word of mouth. This can be readily achieved through the use of celebrities, controversy, shock or humour, but can also be based on more 'real' aspects such as business success, cause-related activities or innovation.

The soft drink, Tango, themes its television advertisements using 'you've been tangoed' and features a variety of improbable situations where characters are immersed in orange soda. They have enhanced this campaign through one-off publicity events where similar situations are performed unannounced in public areas.

Red Bull, the energy drink, uses its 'gives you wings' message to host regular events where the public are encouraged to design, create and race 'flying machines'. These events generate substantial publicity as well as involving participants and spectators in the brand.

A further example of a well-integrated promotional event campaign that generated large amounts of favourable publicity is the promotion of milk in the USA. The highly successful 'milk moustache' advertising campaign for National Fluid Milk Processor Education Program Board and Dairy Management Inc. was enhanced by a 'Better Bones Tour' involving five 'Milk Mustache Mobiles' visiting over 400 locations to offer free bone-density screening tests. The tour also included educational materials, community service support, expert spokespeople and giveaways plus a photo studio to snap participants with their own milk moustaches. The combination of education, value and fun led to 17 000 bone-density tests, 70 000 people photographed with milk moustaches and, due largely to this, 262 million media impressions (Bozell Inc., 1999). The use of the overarching 'milk mustache' theme used the impetus of the already successful mass media campaign to add fun and interest to what could have been a very clinical and off-putting educational campaign.

Open days and site tours

Bringing prospective and existing customers to the 'home of the brand' for an event can create a far more intense and memorable experience and can be far more cost effective to stage. However, the event has to provide sufficient value to the visitors to justify their effort and cost in attending. This need to provide a reason to come often means that this type of event is aimed at audiences who have already shown an interest in the product through previous contact with the company. They are likely to be in the evaluation and purchase decision stage of the decision-making process and attendance at the event is used to encourage actual purchase. For example, many educational establishments host open days for prospective students, their families and friends, recognizing the variety of people involved in the decision. These open days will typically involve presentations on the college and the courses, tours of the facilities, sample lessons and interaction with existing students. For example, the Open University hosts regular open days described as, 'an interesting and fun-packed day, combining demonstrations of high-tech learning facilities with hands-on activities for all age groups' (The Open University, 2002). These open days combine information sessions with entertainment and opportunities to socialize for existing students, new students and their families. They are used to develop loyalty and commitment among their audiences, an important aspect when considering that many Open University students will study over many years. The events help by making attendees feel part of a learning community, by rewarding their commitment and by encouraging them to take up opportunities for further study.

Similarly, manufacturing organizations will invite existing customers and prospects as well as suppliers and partners to view their facilities in the form of plant or factory tours often combined with sales presentations and corporate hospitality. Many manufacturers also now include an interactive 'factory tour' on their websites providing a virtual visit for those who are unable to attend and therefore extending the benefits of this type of event to a wider international audience. In some cases these virtual events are replacing the physical plant tour due to the perceived costs, inconvenience and competitor misuse aspects of the tour. However, these do not provide the opportunity for one-to-one interaction, relationship development and a unique and memorable experience.

Manufacturers whose products are aimed at consumer markets have achieved increased effectiveness by evolving what were once simple factory tours into visitor attractions. For example, Cadbury's chocolate in the UK have developed Cadbury World which still includes a factory tour but focuses on interactive activities, theme-park style rides and of course the opportunity to buy and consume their products. Hershey's Chocolate World in Pennsylvania describes their experience as, 'interactive chocolate fun for everyone and a shopper's paradise for anything and everything Hershey's' (Hershey's, 2004).

A further example is Guinness in Dublin who used the popularity of their factory tour and tasting sessions and the growth in young male tourists to Dublin to develop the Guinness Experience, now one of the most popular attractions in the city. These types of factory experience not only immerse visitors in the brand and provide the opportunity for purchases but also provide additional income streams. The promotional event has become a valued product in its own right and can therefore have a charge. The entrance fees, therefore, contribute to the cost of the experience and in many cases provide substantial profit. In Australia, tourism within several regions is encouraged through many such 'factory experiences' including the Big Pineapple, the Ginger Factory and the Big Banana with several whole towns over theming themselves around the major produce of the region. Distilleries in Scotland offer similar experiences.

Benefits of communicating through promotional events

The wide variety of types of promotional event available means that they can create a range of benefits within the communications mix that cannot easily be achieved as cost effectively elsewhere.

One of the main benefits is the ability of an event to get a small group of people together in a controlled environment. This makes them ideal for relationship building due to the level and intensity of interaction and personalization that is possible. Events can be used to create new relationships or to develop further relationships in order to retain existing customers (McDonnell and Gebhardt, 2002).

The precise targeting opportunities offered by promotional events make them a highly effective communications tool. This type of event audience tends to be targeted through grouping people according to their values, enjoyment, personality type and social group (McCole, 2004) rather than simple demographic and geographic characteristics. This makes the targeting more meaningful and creates groups that have a resonance with the brand. As Flynn (1998) states, event marketing has become important and compelling because it is the doorway to highly segmented lifestyles.

In a world filled by competing promotional messages, events offer the opportunity to create a protected, clutter-free environment in which to deliver a single brand message. This makes the message far more memorable and if it has been delivered in a unique, creative and entertaining manner then the participants are likely to develop a preference for the brand and ultimately a change in purchase behaviour.

Events provide participants with the opportunity to interact with the brand creating an 'all senses' tangible experience rather than simply a visual or aural contact. This tangibility, created through sampling, testing and interaction, has a higher impact on the audience and also reduces the risk associated with a purchase.

A final advantage is the ability of promotional events to reach an audience which is far wider than those who attend or participate. This is achieved directly through the event via publicity generation and word of mouth and also through the integration of other communication methods. Creative events are an ideal way of seeding a word of mouth viral campaign and therefore creating an anticipatory buzz. Murphy's stout achieved this very successfully through their 'Sisters of Murphy' campaign which included the unannounced entrance of three provocatively dressed women ('the Sisters') into pubs and bars buying Murphy's for the clientele.

The effectiveness of promotional events coupled with the overuse of other communication methods will undoubtedly lead to a rise in the use of these techniques in a variety of industries. The challenge will be to continue to keep them innovative, unique and of value for the participants.

Disadvantages of using promotional events

One of the pitfalls to be wary of when developing promotional events is that the creativity of the event may overshadow the brand itself. However, this is less likely than in other media where many messages are competing for the same attention.

At the event the brand can be promoted relatively subtly and still be guaranteed exposure and attention due to the focus insulated nature of the experience.

A further perceived disadvantage is the amount of budget a promotional event may entail in order to influence a relatively small target audience. However, this is offset by the impact and effectiveness of a well-designed and targeted event ensuring a return on the investment. Also, as mentioned earlier a wider audience can be reached through word of mouth and integrated use of other communication methods.

There are also opportunities to augment the budget for an event through charging a fee for attending. This will only be possible if the audience's perceived value of the event is greater than the fee charged and if the promotional nature of the event is seen as secondary to the entertainment received. A further way to subsidise the event is through sponsorship. Complementary brands can be invited to have some involvement through sponsorship-in-kind or through direct payment. This may work well if the sponsors are carefully selected and do not overshadow the primary brand. The Sunlight example discussed earlier shows how this type of partner can enhance the event through their use of Crayola and Little Tikes as sponsors. However, a variety of sponsors will detract from the main brand and will negate the advantage of the 'brand bubble'. The event itself will become cluttered with brand messages vying for the audience's attention and will therefore be far less effective at promoting the organizing brand's interests.

Summary

Promotional events are an important and underused communication tool which will undoubtedly rise in popularity as organizations search for newer and more effective ways to reach promotional message saturated audiences. The variety of events available means that they can be used in a number of ways for new and existing customers, to develop awareness through to encouraging purchase. Their effectiveness is due to their use of the participant's 'experience' to create a memorable and high impact brand image. Promotional events showcase the brand in a tangible, interactive manner and, most importantly, do so while insulating the participants from competing messages. However, promotional events can only be successful if they are fully integrated with the rest of the communications mix as they need to be promoted in their own right through mass media, websites and require the use of other tools such as sales promotion, public relations and direct marketing to leverage the most value from them.

Discussion points

- Discuss the reasons why 'experiential marketing' is growing in importance. What, If any, are the differences between this concept and traditional marketing?
- Consider Case study 11.1 and identify how Gillette could extend the use of promotional events to launch Gillette Venus to the consumer market.
- Find and discuss examples of the innovative use of exhibition space at trade fairs. How can exhibitors make their stands more interactive and therefore more effective?

References

Ace Events (2002) Water Africa 2003 North Exhibition. www.ace-events.com/WA03NRx.htm (accessed November, 2004).

Arnott, N. (1994) Marketing with a passion. *Sales and Marketing Management*, January, p. 71.

Bozell Inc. (1999) Making milk cool through media neutral marketing. *The Advertiser*, August.

Brown, S. (2001) Torment your customer (they'll love it). *Harvard Business Review*. October 2001, pp. 83–88.

Cunningham, M.H. and Taylor, S.F. (1995) Event marketing: State of the industry and research agenda. *Festival Management and Event Tourism*, 2, 123–137.

Flynn, J. (1998) The new challenges of event marketing. *The Advertiser*, August.

Go ahead. Get dirty (2002) www.goaheadgetdirty.com (accessed November, 2004).

Gofton, K. (1998) Best use of live events. The Marketing awards for relationship marketing. *Marketing*, 20, 10.

Hershey's (2004) Hershey's Chocolate World. www.hershey's.com/discover/hcw/asp (accessed November, 2004).

Kirsner, S. (2002) Experience required. *Fast Company*. www.fastcompany.com/learning (accessed October, 2003).

Line Up Communications (2003) Case history. Gillette Group UK, New product trade launch. Industry lecture series, UK Centre for Event Management, Leeds Metropolitan University, January, 2003.

Line Up Communications (2004) www.lineup-communications.co.uk (accessed October, 2004).

MacMillan, C. (2003a) Chevy rocks and rolls. *Promo Magazine*, February. www.promomagazine.com (accessed November, 2004).

MacMillan, C. (2003b) A word from the roadies. *Promo Magazine*, February. www.promomagazine.com (accessed November, 2004).

Masterman, G.R. (2004) *Strategic Sports Event Management*. Butterworth-Heinemann.

McCole, P. (2004) Refocusing marketing to reflect practice: The changing role of marketing for business. *Marketing Intelligence and Planning*, 22 (5), 531–539.

McDonnell, I. and Gebhardt, S. (2002) The relative effectiveness of special events as a promotional tool: A case study. Conference proceedings. *Events and Place Making Conference*. UTS, Sydney, pp. 389–417.

McIntosh, M.H. (2004) Marketing events: What works, what doesn't. *Marketing Profs*, November. Available from www.marketingprofs.com (accessed November, 2004).

NZ Marketing Magazine (2003) Think again: Why experiential marketing is the next big thing. *NZ Marketing Magazine*, September, pp. 8–15.

The Open University (2002) About open day. www.open.ac.uk/open-day (accessed November, 2004).

Pickton, D. and Broderick, A. (2001) *Integrated Marketing Communications*. Pearson Education.

Pringle, H. and Paton, S. (1996) Hepworth Building Products – the launch of Hep_30 'How naked ground workers worked?' *Advertising Effectiveness Awards*. Institute of Practitioners in Advertising. Available from www.warc.com

Ramage, N. (2002) Unilever calls kids into the Sunlight. *Marketing Magazine*, 107, 2.

Schmitt, B. (1999) *Experiential Marketing: How to get Customers to Sense, Feel, Think, Act and Relate to your Company and Brands*. The Free Press.

Schreiber, A.L. and Lenson, B. (1994) *Lifestyle and Event Marketing – Building the New Customer Partnership*. McGraw-Hill.

Schuverer, L. (1999) Break through the clutter: Create your own events. *The Advertiser*, August.

Shimp, T.A. (1997) *Advertising, Promotion and Supplemental Aspects of Integrated Marketing Communications*. Dryden.

Smith, D.S. (1997) A new angle on car sales. *Marketing*, 26 June, pp. 27–30.

Smith, P.R. and Taylor, J. (2004) *Marketing Communications: An Integrated Approach*. Kogan Page.

Van Gessell, P. (2000) Events: Outstanding means for joint promotion. *Event Management*, 6, 111–116.

Chapter 12
Corporate Sponsorship of Events

Objectives

- Identify corporate sponsorship objectives
- Examine the development of sponsorship as a fully integrated marketing communications channel
- Understand the corporate sponsorship decision-making process
- Analyse the importance of sponsorship as an innovative corporate marketing communications tool and its capacity for return on investment
- Identify the key factors in making corporate sponsorship a success
- Consider contemporary and ethical issues in sponsorship and how will they impact on sponsorship decision making

Introduction

This chapter focuses on how sponsors utilize event sponsorship to achieve their communications objectives. The intention is to follow the line taken in Chapter 8, where sponsorship was discussed from an event management perspective with a focus on a strategic approach to developing event sponsorship programmes and how event communications can be developed as a result. Here the discussion considers the importance of event sponsorship as an integrated corporate communications tool from the sponsor's perspective.

Event sponsorship has developed into a sophisticated form of contact and communication from humble beginnings. What was once little more than an opportunity for advertising and corporate hospitality in the 1970s is now a way of achieving a number of marketing and corporate communication objectives. Event sponsorship is now used to drive sales as well as develop favourable brand associations and awareness, promote corporate awareness and develop internal and community relations. This chapter will identify how objectives are set ultimately to achieve a return on investment.

Sponsorship objectives are then considered via the identification of the sponsorship decision process, the information required in order to make decisions and the methods by which that information is gained and evaluated. There are three key factors for sponsors in making sponsorship successful: the necessity to exploit event rights, the role sponsorship needs to play in integrated marketing communications and the need for sponsors to evaluate sponsorship in order to improve future performance. These are all essential considerations and each one is considered in turn.

Finally, this chapter turns to some of the issues for sponsorship and considers ambush marketing and some of the current ethical issues that impact on decision making. While the approach is from the sponsor's perspective, event managers can also begin better to understand how to build sponsorship programmes from the points covered.

Sponsorship objectives

The use of sponsorship and events as communications tools is not new. History shows that events were used for political purposes in the times of the Roman Empire, with gladiatorial contests being underwritten by the wealthy ruling class in order to gain popularity and gain social standing and office (Head, 1988). Indeed, the political intent behind the holding of a 'Minus' (games) at election time became such a problem that, in 63 BC, the Roman Senate banned their staging by anyone in a two-year run up to an election. At a later point, second level magistrates (praetors) were limited to two games with a maximum of 120 gladiators each during their terms of office (Grant, 1975; Connolly, 2003). The capacities of the venues of the times, such as the Colosseum at 50 000 people and the Circus Maximus at 250 000, made many events powerful communication tools. In ancient Greece, too, there were both sporting and arts festivals that were underwritten with the intent of improving the sponsors' social standing (Sandler and Shani, 1993). In more recent times one of the earliest event sponsorships in modern sports is recorded as being that of the England cricket team's 1861 tour of Australia, catering company Spiers and Pond being the sponsors concerned (Gratton and Taylor, 2000). Coca-Cola is listed as a sponsor at the first modern Olympic Games, in Athens in 1896 (IOC, 2004). Kodak was involved too, but both their involvements were essentially limited to advertisements in the official programme. At the 1928 Olympic Games in Amsterdam, however, Coca-Cola acquired product sampling rights and has developed its relationship at each Games ever since in order to get to the level of sponsorship it has more recently enjoyed at the 2004 Games in Athens (Stotlar, 1993; Pitts and Stotlar, 2002). At the 2002 Winter Games in Salt Lake City, Coca-Cola had the non-alcoholic beverages sponsorship rights, was the presenting sponsor of the Torch Relay, produced Coca-Cola radio and ran a pin-trading centre (IOC, 2004). Corporate sponsorship as we have come to regard it today as a marketing communications tool, however, did not develop until the 1970s (Meenaghan and Shipley, 1999). Only since then has sponsorship been used to achieve marketing objectives.

On deciding if sponsorship is a viable communications tool, sponsors have a number of achievable objectives that would appear to make the decision easier. The IOC itself lists the building of brand equity and awareness, brand repositioning, driving revenue, enhancing internal relations, showcasing products and services, retaining competitive advantage by keeping other sponsors out and demonstrating altruism as the reasons why its 'TOP' sponsors associate with the Olympic Movement, (IOC, 2004). Mullin et al. (2000) add to that list, the development and reinforcement of public awareness of the company. Other objectives include post-merger identity building and enhancing financial sector confidence (International Marketing Reports, 2002). Milne and McDonald (1999) differentiate between objectives for short- and long-term sales revenue and include exposure and image enhancement of both the company and brands.

Some commentators provide categorizations for sponsorship objectives. Shank (2002), for example, maintains that there are two main categorizations. First, direct sponsorship objectives that are concerned with short-term impact on consumption behaviour via a focus on increasing sales. Secondly, indirect sponsorship objectives that lead to desired goals of enhancing sales via methods that are more difficult to attribute. In contrast, Pope (1998a) provides three category levels of objectives, corporate, marketing and media led plus a fourth area, personal objectives, where management interests might be reason enough to undertake sponsorship. He argues, quite rightly, that individual personal reasons cannot be corporately justified. The origins of early corporate sponsorship do though derive from such decisions and while they are not unheard of in certain contemporary cases, objectives are now more generally designed for return on investment (Meenaghan and Shipley, 1999; Pitts and Stotlar, 2002).

The various sponsorship objectives that are considered achievable can be categorized as follows.

Direct sales development

A more contemporary and not insignificant event sponsorship objective is the driving of sales. Events offer practical mechanisms for selling and because evaluation is a simple process of accounting for sales because of the event, this objective is being implemented by an increasing number of sponsors. These are therefore considered direct sales because they can be directly attributable to the sponsorship. Without the sponsorship of the event, the sales would not have occurred.

Various kinds of consumer products can lend themselves very well to event environments, especially when there is simultaneous consumption. Food and drink manufacturers, for example, have long been setting the standards as official suppliers at all kinds of events, none more so than the Wimbledon tennis championships as mentioned in Chapter 8, with six official drinks sponsors of one sort or another. With sufficient audience numbers, direct sales at events can be significant. For example, the Tennents beer brand, the oldest and number one selling lager in Scotland, has been the title sponsor of 'T in the Park' since 1994. In 2004, the music festival attracted over 52 000 on each of two days and was able to sell beer to those music fans on an exclusive basis.

Brand awareness development

In contrast, brand awareness development objectives are less tangible. It is difficult to confirm, for example, that sales have resulted from an increase in awareness and that they are therefore directly attributable to an event sponsorship. A sponsorship can be implemented, market share monitored and seen to increase, but because there are other variables, the increase can, at best, only be indirectly linked to the sponsorship. The intervention of other factors such as carry-over effects of past advertising and promotions, changing economic conditions and market entry or exit of competing businesses, for example, can all have a variable effect (Bennett, 1999). The use of market research can reveal a clearer picture, however. The use of consumer survey instruments, for example, can capture a depth of perception of the awareness, whether it was sponsorship driven and what links there may be with sales behaviour for a more reliable evaluation.

For market penetration, sponsorship is used to increase recognition of a brand within existing target markets and develop greater sales to existing and/or sales to new customers. Aiming to get the same customers to buy in greater volume is also attempting to increase consumer loyalty, an objective that ranks high among corporate decision makers when assessing the value of a sponsorship's properties. In the IEG/Sponsorship Research (2004) annual survey of corporate sponsorship decision makers, 79 per cent and 71 per cent of respondents made awareness and increased brand loyalty, respectively, as the two most important reasons for taking a sponsorship on. Coca-Cola, in its sponsorship of the 2003 Houston's Livestock Show and Rodeo, achieved incremental store presence and volume sales by offering incentives to distributors and consumers in 'push and pull' style sales promotions. Activities included coupons on 400 000 event themed '18-packs' of Coca-Cola that gave price discounts on co-sponsors merchandise. Sales grew by 67 per cent on 2002 sales. However, these sales cannot be directly attributed to the sponsorship even if they could be used as a measure against other activities in order to determine the extent of its success. Puma sold just 15 000 tennis rackets in 1984, agreed sponsorship terms with Boris Becker while he was rising to the height of his sport and when the player later won the Wimbledon championships in 1985 the manufacturer's sales grew to 150 000 rackets (Pope, 1998b). These examples demonstrate the allure of sponsorship while still not fully explaining or confirming that it was a direct cause of the improved sales performance.

Sponsorship is also used to try to develop brand awareness with new target markets and for market development strategies. Extending brand equity into similar but new markets, or stretching it into dissimilar new markets may be assisted by well-chosen sponsorships. Nike sponsor Manchester United Football Club and one aspect of their sophisticated partnership strategy is to penetrate new markets in new territories. One of these is the US soccer market and Nike has used its sponsorship of Fox television soccer programming, its website, advertising and local team sponsorships to try to develop new business with this burgeoning opportunity. Its sponsorship of Manchester United is supported by utilizing other forms of communication including the club's website, exclusive match coverage on the Yes television network (USA) and when the club tours and plays in summer US soccer tournaments as it did in both 2003 and 2004. This example demonstrates how sponsorship can be used to launch new products into new territories.

Another role for sponsorship is as a tool for increasing market knowledge and thereby the further enhancement of market position. Events offer sponsors ideal opportunities in the form of event functionality (see Chapter 8) whereby a sponsor's products and services can perform valuable, or more construed roles and functions and thus help the event. In assisting the event to function, the objective is then to use that functionality to showcase the sponsor's products to target markets. This might involve seeing the products in a new light or adding new knowledge. Amis et al. (1999) maintain that image, reputation and awareness are resources from which competitive advantage may be derived and sponsorship is an effective tool by which image might be altered. They consequently propose that sponsorship be used to secure, sustain and redevelop market position.

This same functionality can also reinforce or revitalize brands to existing markets but in so doing achieve competitive advantage and thereby indirectly affect sales performance.

External corporate awareness development

Sponsorship can also be used by those organizations that are seeking to position or re-position themselves corporately. In 1993, Allied Domecq entered into an $8 million sponsorship of the Royal Shakespeare Company (RSC) with the objective of rein-venting its corporate image. The organization identified that because it was per-ceived as a conglomerate of individual trading companies rather than one single entity, it was losing competitive advantage. Its portfolio of alcohol brands of Canadian Club, Beefeater Gin and Courvoisier Cognac, together with its outlets of Dunkin Donuts and Baskin Robbins, lacked an identifiable personality and, as a result, the organization was falling behind its competitors. A sponsorship was designed that would gain an identity for Allied Domecq. It included principal spon-sor status rights and exposure to target markets via venue branding, joint media relations projects, corporate hospitality and tickets and print acknowledgements. The Allied Domecq name was used throughout in order to increase awareness.

Similarly, awareness through sponsorship exposure can position a new corporate merger/takeover. An event offers opportunities for launching new organizations because they can be newsworthy and have wide target reach thus giving relatively quick and integrated solutions to a problem of how to inform but not spend too much time in transition.

Event sponsorship can also provide an organization with access to wider public awareness of its mission and values. This kind of exposure can be critical in times of hardship and in response to adverse public perception. Equally, it can be used to enhance public perception. For example, Merrill Lynch, as part of its sponsorship of the education programmes at the Weill Music Institute at Carnegie Hall in New York, leveraged its rights with magazine advertising that was targeted at chil-dren and focused on the benefits of learning music (*The New York Times Magazine*, 2004). It did not miss the opportunity to display its website address but there were no references to any products or services.

A further corporate objective is the development of financial relations such as with investors, lenders and the financial markets. Financial relationships can be addressed via sponsorships in order to defend market status and performance by demonstrating future intention. Nabisco International demonstrated this in the 1980s when the conglomerate was vulnerable and ripe for takeovers. Its sponsor-ship of the ATP Tour and title end of season championship events utilized the group name rather than those of its individual brands for a wider corporate message.

Sponsorship of government projects and events can enhance key relationships that can lead to new business or bear influence on future performance. This can occur at all levels of government. The early involvement of sponsors in support of bids for events that have been initiated and underwritten by national governments are common examples, but partnerships between local municipal councils and the commercial sector are also well practised. The West Midlands Local Government Association in the UK has a number of initiatives where it seeks the support of the commercial sector. For its exhibitions and conference event projects it has recruited such sponsors as British Gas, Fujitsu and Zurich Municipal, for example (WMLGA, 2004).

Corporate hospitality has long been a cornerstone of sponsorship rights and continues to be so. In the IEG/Sponsorship Research (2004) annual survey it was ranked the highest desired rights element with 77 per cent of respondents indicating that it was a part of their programmes. The entertainment of key customers and the development of business-to-business relationships can be well facilitated by event corporate hospitality, but the communications with those customers can be greatly enhanced if the host is also providing event function and is seen more widely at the event because of an integrated set of sponsorship benefits. Business relations can be for both corporate and brand objectives.

Sponsorships can be used to communicate with target publics as well as target markets. Local communities are key target publics for all organizations and events offer vehicles by which the company might offer a wide reaching philanthropic arm. Community involvement, as opposed to an arm's length approach, is important for such activities if they are to be viewed credibly and event sponsorship can offer suitable solutions for such. A good example is provided by the Bank of Ireland and its sponsorship of the 2003 Special Olympics' 'Host Town' programme in Ireland. The initiative was developed to build local community support for the Games all around Ireland and was used by the sponsor for similar reasons. For three years prior to these Games for people with learning disabilities, the focus was on recruiting towns into the programme. By the time the Games opened in June 2003, 177 towns were active with signage and associated events. The Bank of Ireland played a significant part with 85 per cent of the towns having a bank representative on their local committees. The sponsor also ran a national television campaign that promoted the programme and featured bank employees. In Kilkenny of Callan, a small town of 1400 people, the bank manager instigated the committee so that the community could apply and participate as a host town. In so doing the town played host and housed a Games delegate from the Ivory Coast (Business 2000, 2004). The whole exercise was designed to create goodwill on a local basis where involvement could be implemented, but at the same time achieve this in nationally significant numbers.

Internal relations development

Employees are a key target public and sponsorships offer all kinds of vehicles by which to develop internal communications. Sponsorship of an event can create goodwill via an involvement with the employees' community as well as become a theme for employee team-building activities. Allied Domecq's sponsorship of the Royal Shakespeare Company included one-year free memberships for all its UK employees and the creation of an internal newsletter dedicated to the sponsorship with performance information. It expanded the latter with benefits to all its 70 000 employees worldwide (Charity Village, 2004). Flora, the margarine brand, has implemented similar internal activities that are focused on its sponsorship of the London Marathon.

Competitive advantage

Competitive advantage can be gained by achieving any or all of the above objectives, but there is one further potential aspect for gaining the upper hand. A key event can mean a sponsor can attempt to achieve a number of the above objectives and because sponsorship benefits are predominantly negotiated, even if not offered, on exclusive terms, a sponsor also manages to keep its rivals out of such opportunities. The IOC, as stated earlier, is clear that one of its TOP sponsorship attributes is the objective of defence strategy. Defence being the best form of attack in this case. Of course, this does not necessarily keep rivals away from the platforms that sponsorships create for ambush marketing. In developing competitive advantage through sponsorship, sponsors need to recognize that they are setting themselves up for retaliatory competitor activity and therefore have to be capable of defending that position. The feasibility of this should be ascertained before the sponsorship is undertaken and particularly when assessing future sponsorship costs. The willingness and capacity for a sponsor to exploit their sponsorship is key.

Whatever the objective or combination of objectives, the focus is on a return on investment through mutual benefit. It is that which now drives sponsorship evaluation and so the focus now turns to how these objectives can best be achieved?

Sponsorship decision making

It was noted earlier that sponsorship is not a new communications tool. As a marketing activity and its use for commercial gain, however, it is a recent development. As recently as 1970, there was little in the way of event sponsorship with market spending totalling only £4 million (Meenaghan and Shipley, 1999). Since then, however, there have been steep increases on a worldwide basis, particularly in the two largest growing sectors of Europe and the USA. In 2002, Mintel (2002) has estimated that the UK sponsorship market alone was valued at £798 million, with sports sponsorship significantly dominating that market at £440 million. Broadcast, arts and community-based sponsorships follow at £195 million, £105 million and £58 million, respectively. The growth in the UK over the last twenty years alone has been by over seven and a half fold. On a worldwide basis, sponsorship expenditure reached a high of US$34 billion in 2003 representing a 32 per cent increase in spending since 2000. The forecast for 2005 showed a slowing of that rate of growth but still a rise in spending to US$43.1 billion (Sponsorclick, 2004). Significantly, this is a figure that represents the amount of spending on sponsorship fees only. The amounts that are spent on exploiting sponsorship rights are not included as such data are seldom available. It is therefore not difficult to understand the significance of Mintel's (2002) summary for the future of sponsorship in the UK. It reports that the last ten years have seen great changes including increased spending as a result of greater churn as sponsors seek shorter lasting deals. It also reports that while there is an increase in opportunities as rights owners segment and create more fragmented sponsorships, the need for continued and increased use of sponsorship as a fully integrated communications tool and the exploiting of rights in order to maximize success are becoming increasingly critical.

With such high spending in the industry the emphasis on a return on sponsorship investment has never been so significant. The decision to sponsor at all is therefore where accountability starts. The essential question is, will sponsorship perform better than all the other marketing communications available? A process is required in order to ensure that sponsorship is well chosen and does provide this return.

Pitts and Stotlar (2002) propose a process that is made up of four key stages. The first stage addresses the need for sponsorship to be integrated into wider communications activity. The second provides a set of steps for review and selection in order to arrive at an appropriate sponsorship and the third is concerned with implementation and exploitation. The final stage is evaluation. Their final three stages provide a route through the decision-making process once the decision to sponsor has been made. The first stage, however, does not acknowledge the need for an assessment of whether sponsorship can provide the most effective and efficient communications solution. Gratton and Taylor (2000), for example, note that sponsorship activity is below 5 per cent of total marketing expenditure for most firms. One view they offer is that sponsorship is a part of the profit-maximizing behaviour that is undertaken when the risk and uncertainty of revenue response to advertising expenditure indicates other strategies should be used. This is wholly an economic perspective and does not consider the wider range of sponsorship objectives, but it serves the point that it is at least one of the assessment criteria by which sponsorship decisions should be first considered. Their example of tobacco manufacturers being restricted over time in their choice of communications by law, serves well in that advertising has been a banned activity in many countries and motor racing and snooker sponsorships in particular were alternative avenues for the achievement of image building marketing objectives.

The attraction and subsequent growth of sponsorship has been due in no small terms to its apparent ability to offer effective and efficient alternatives to advertising, although the lack of objective evaluation of this has clearly held back the further penetration of sponsorship into the communications mix as the Gratton and Taylor (2000) 5 per cent share figure indicates above. Sponsorship may offer more cost effective returns than advertising but this is by no means comprehensively accepted. Thwaites (1995) reports that sponsorship may even be considered by many customers to be advertising. There is one aspect that sets sponsorship aside, however and that is that part of its effectiveness may be derived from the perception that event sponsorship has third party credibility. A sponsor is buying into a ready-made image, albeit an image they have hopefully researched and deemed a worthy fit. They are thereby borrowing and integrating an image that is ostensibly endorsing the sponsor in return. The decisions to sponsor and then which sponsorship to select, are clearly critical and certain information is required in order reliably to make these decisions. The information required has been categorized into the following criteria.

Customer potential

The sponsor needs to determine whether the event has mutually attractive target markets. Reaching the same target market segments is ostensibly a prerequisite for sponsorship choices but, in order to determine the extent to which they are an attractive proposition, the sponsor requires detailed segment profiles and the size of target market that can be reached. This selection procedure is essentially a demographic and psychographic based exercise.

Exposure potential

The extent of the target market reach can be evaluated by considering all of the potential points of exposure. Depending on the type and scale of event, this can involve the size and numbers of live event audience, recipients of event communications and viewers, listeners and readers of event broadcasting and reporting. In addition, it is also dependent upon the size and amount of target markets reached via the sponsor's own exploitation. This can often come down to the question of how newsworthy the event and sponsorship is going to be. However, considering a wider set of available sponsorship objectives, other questions will not only pertain to whether the sponsorship will reach the right target markets in sufficient numbers, but also will this be with the right message. This highlights the need for thorough and early exploitation planning in addition to an assessment of the rights on offer. For an accurate assessment of the potential reach of a sponsorship, a sponsor will therefore need to have determined the total amount and quality of potential target market reach prior to any decision to go ahead with that sponsorship.

Distribution channel benefit

Some sponsors require sponsorships that provide distribution channel benefits in order that their target market reach can be achieved. Those sponsors with wholesale operations, for example, will look for ways in which they can provide sales promotion 'push' in order to incentivize those that are at the selling end of their distribution chains. The incentive is something the distributor can either benefit from directly or pass on to their customers in turn. The idea is that they are 'pushed' in order to produce more sales (Pickton and Broderick, 2001; Boone and Kurtz, 2002). For example, a sponsor can use their event as an incentive by setting sales targets, that when achieved, gain the distributor event tickets and invitations. Alternatively, the sponsor can allocate tickets to their distributors for them to reach end-on customers more effectively. Either way, the distributor is incentivized to perform better and the event is the catalyst.

T-Mobile, the mobile telecommunications company, was an 'official partner of UEFA Euro 2004' and so that they could exploit their rights they devised a push and pull strategy in the UK. The end-user promotion involved free downloads, texting, call minutes and exclusive event content packages while they incentivized key retail partners like Carphone Warehouse with event-related sales incentives and graphics/point of sale in order to gain prime space on the front of their magazine and in their stores.

Advantage over competitors

All of the above factors also add up to the capacity for a sponsorship to offer a sponsor competitive advantage. In successfully reaching target markets and providing incentives for distribution channels, sponsors can gain competitive advantage via their communications efforts. This is an additional consideration when assessing sponsorship opportunity. The capacity for sponsors to prevent competitors from benefiting from a sponsorship opportunity needs to be evaluated not just in terms of what competitors are being denied. A consideration of the platform that is being created for the competition to exploit is also required. This platform, referred to more commonly as ambush marketing, is discussed later in this chapter. The strategy should always be to undertake the sponsorship if it is right but to ensure that there is potential for sufficient protection from ambush tactics and capacity for adequate exploitation of the rights while making that decision.

Resource investment

An obvious consideration for the sponsor is the amount of resources the sponsorship will require. This not only involves finance that is available at the right time for sponsorship fees but also finance for any provision of services and product. This is also linked to the early assessment of exploitation of the rights and the determination of not just how target markets are going to be reached but how much that will cost.

Characteristics and fit

The event and the sponsorship opportunity have either an established or an emerging brand image. The important question for any sponsor is whether this image and its characteristics are something that will provide a positive or negative effect on the sponsoring brand. This is referred to as 'sponsorship fit'. Milne and McDonald (1999) refer to 'Schema congruity theory' in order to ground this concept. They proffer that a schema is a preconception that has been developed through experience and that consumers maintain such for individual brands. They believe that when a sponsor associates with an event, consumers assess the congruency between the two and that when the two share perceptual characteristics there is an increased likelihood of congruence. This can result in a closer acceptance of the association between sponsor and event. The aim then is to find a suitable 'fit' and Milne and McDonald (1999) sought to test their hypothesis that the 'matching' of sponsor and event characteristics, or personalities as they suggest, is critical. Their research indicated that not only would a good match enhance the image of a sponsor's brand, a poor match would damage it. Their conclusions were that while demographic based criteria (mutual target markets) might be successful in the goal of increasing target market awareness, the achievement of image enhancement objectives is better served by selecting matching image characteristics (fit). Meenaghan and Shipley (1999) support this and, indeed, go further to propose that because a sponsorship message is inextricably bound up with the attributes of the event, any incongruity would be perceived very confusingly by an audience.

The credibility of the event rights owner is clearly an important issue when it comes to sponsorship fit. The ability of an event owner to organize and deliver the rights as agreed is a key area of concern for a sponsor and something they should be keen to explore prior to any decision. In many cases the profile of the owning body is inextricably linked to the event itself and so evaluation of them is simultaneous. Even though the sponsorship of the Royal Shakespeare Company (RSC) by Allied Domecq was undertaken in order to enhance corporate awareness for example, it was based on a 'fit' between the latter's international alcohol and restaurant brands and the international fame and repute of the theatre production company (Charity Village 2004). The highly perceived reputation of the RSC is arguably garnered as much by its ability behind the scenes as it is on the stage.

Identifying tried and tested event owner ability is of course that much easier when there is a history to examine. The identification of a good fit between a sponsor and an organizing body is more difficult when the event and/or the owners are new. A series of unknown variables disrupts the decision-making process and it will often come down to a close examination of the individual event managers concerned. The London 2012 Olympic bid team identified for example that its proposed event, and the future sponsorship and funding of that event, would be better served by not continuing with an American chairperson. Barbara Cassani, having been recruited to the job in 2003, was replaced in mid-2004 by British ex-athlete Lord Sebastian Coe amid fears that anti-American feeling post the Iraq war would stand against them (Kelso, 2004; Mackay, 2004).

The media impact of event sponsorship in terms of audience size and demographics is readily and commonly evaluated, just as with conventional advertising. However, the measurement of image perception has been rare, with few studies of personality attributes for sponsorship purposes conducted and more trust given over to 'informed' judgements (Meenaghan and Shipley, 1999). The value of the fit and the achievement of image-related sponsorship objectives are clearly important and so a more objective approach to the identification of good fit between event and sponsor is deserved. An advertising message is a controlled communication involving designed and bought media space. Sponsorship, on the other hand, is reliant on the image of the event and is thus a critical element in its success. The sponsor therefore has a duty to consider an objective route in its determination of which sponsorship to select.

What of the nature of the images and perceptions of events that can be sought by sponsors? Meenaghan and Shipley (1999) conducted research that revealed that sport in general is seen as healthy, young, energetic, fast, vibrant and masculine. Mass arts are also seen as young, accessible, friendly, current, innovative but commercial. High-brow arts on the other hand are seen as elitist, sophisticated, discriminating, serious and pretentious. This research considered these categories generically and not as individual sports, mass or high-brow arts, but it is the adopted research methods that should be of most interest. Consumer focus groups were required in order to acquire sufficient knowledge and this should serve as an indication of the level of research to which sponsors need to aspire.

Sponsorship process

A full process for sponsorship decision making that encapsulates all of this information acquisition is offered in Figure 12.1. The process can be divided into three key stages: a) organizational marketing decisions, where marketing planning is aligned with organizational objectives; b) sponsorship selection decisions, where the process is founded in research, targeting and evaluation to determine if sponsorship offers effective and efficient marketing solutions; and c) sponsorship implementation, involving the planning, execution and evaluation for feedback that will aid future decision making and the development of a sponsorship relationship. The proposal is that sponsorship should always be a consideration when determining the communications mix.

Key factors for sponsorship success

There are three further factors that sponsors need to consider. First, in order for the sponsorship to be successful, the rights need to be exploited. This is achieved via the development of communications that leverage the bought rights but are at a cost over and above any fees paid for those rights. Secondly, these communications need to be integrated into the overall marketing communications that are planned for the pertinent product or service. These two factors are clearly linked. Thirdly, all sponsorships should be evaluated (Masterman, 2004). Amis et al. (1999) maintain that a successful sponsorship is achieved when a sponsor has developed a distinctive competence in implementing sponsorship. The sponsorship decision process should therefore be indicative of all the elements of timing and knowledge that will be required to achieve that competency. However, there is no substitute for experience and analysis that is then used to feedback into the system in order to improve. Continuous and post-event evaluation of sponsorship, against the objectives set for

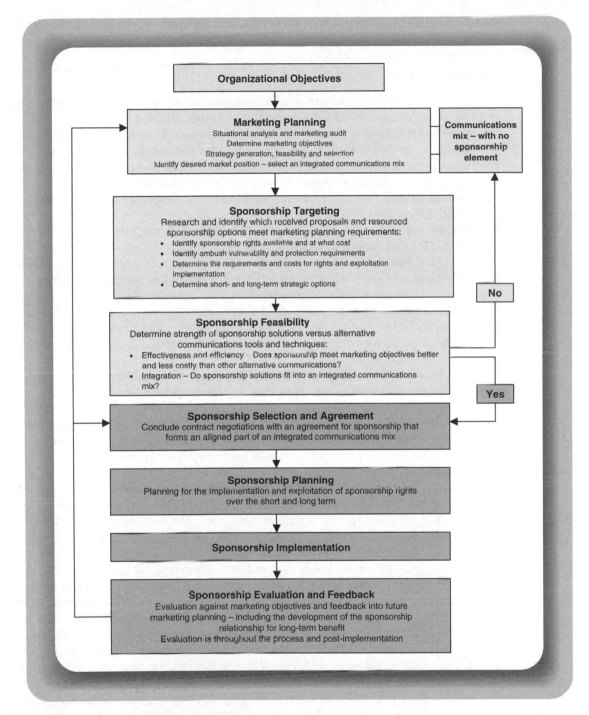

Figure 12.1 Sponsorship planning process. Process for the planning of sponsorship in corporate integrated marketing communications.

it, by both the event and the sponsor enables feedback for improved future performance. Each of these factors is now discussed in turn.

Exploitation

The importance of the exploitation of a sponsorship through the leveraging of the rights was introduced in Chapter 8 and the key points there make relevant reading in support of this chapter. There the focus was on how the exploitation of a sponsorship by a sponsor can have positive results for the event; in the form of event promotions that are over and beyond what the event does for itself and that they are also at the sponsor's expense. It is important here to inculcate that there is a mutual benefit and that without exploitation sponsorships are less likely to be as successful (Otker, 1998). The effectiveness of a sponsorship is reliant on support advertising and promotions that leverage the rights (Meenaghan and Shipley, 1999; Mintel, 2002). The findings of Thompson and Quester (2000) also support this. They indicate that the effectiveness of sponsorship is directly related to the degree to which sponsors are willing to exploit their rights. However, they do maintain that there is little empirical evidence to show to what extent exploitation is necessary. They claim there is no optimal level and, indeed, how can there be generic guidelines for a level of communications activity when the required amount of exploitation can only be determined according to the unique circumstances of each individual sponsor.

Case study 12.1 considers some of the leveraging implemented by American Express in its exploitation of its status as the founding and lead sponsor of New York's Tribeca Film Festival.

The examples chosen to exemplify exploitation in Chapter 8 are discussed in order to highlight the benefits to events and so here are three very different examples of how and why event sponsors have leveraged their rights.

The sponsors at UEFA Euro 2004 were very active with mainstream mass communications in support of their status with the event. In addition to T-Mobile, an example used earlier, Motorola, Coca-Cola, Adidas, Canon and Mastercard all implemented television and print advertising on a pan-European basis. The latter used its advertisements to drive consumers to its website for event ticket competitions by offering a competition that could only be accessed on-line.

Flybe, the discount airline headquartered in Devon in the UK, is a sponsor of local football club Exeter City FC. To mark the 90th anniversary of the Brazil national team's first competitive football fixture, which was against Exeter, Flybe created the Brazil Festival. Legends of former Brazil teams played at Exeter's St James Park and in order to attract media coverage pre-event, ticket promotions were distributed to the printed news media whereby readers could win a trip with Flybe airlines to the event. The event was the newly devised catalyst for gaining national exposure from the relatively less profiled sponsorship of a lower league football club.

The third example shows how a sponsorship can be designed for mutual benefit but demonstrates unusual and innovative forms of contact. Jaguar cars provided products for the film 'Oceans 12', the not too dissimilarly titled sequel to 'Oceans 11', that starred George Clooney, Brad Pitt, Matt Damon and Julia Roberts. In return, the film producers, Warner Brothers, took the unprecedented step of sponsoring the two Jaguar Formula 1 cars and race team for the 2004 Monaco Grand Prix. It was unusual in many ways, not least because it was a one-off sponsorship for the one race. Exploitation of the rights included using the stars of the film in televised

Case study 12.1

American Express: Tribeca Film Festival

The Tribeca Film Institute, created by Jane Rosenthal and Robert De Niro in Manhattan, New York, staged its first Tribeca Film Festival in 2002. The 2004 Festival featured 150 feature films, documentaries and other events in 17 Tribeca (triangle below Canal street) locations with over 350 000 people attending. The Festival's own communications programme consisted of television, radio and print media public relations, promotions and advertising. A number of media partners were also acquired and a tiered sponsorship programme was created. The sponsorship programme had three levels: Friends of the Festival consisting of donors and sponsors-in-kind, 14 signature sponsors including Budweiser, General Motors and Sony, and founding and lead sponsor, American Express.

American Express sponsorship objectives included brand and image awareness and sales. Their exploitation of their rights as founding sponsor, which included acknowledgement as the official card of the Festival, consisted of the following:

Websites

The American Express site incorporated pages that offered Festival information, wireless alert promotions (ticket sales, film information and screening times), photograph opportunities, ticket purchasing and map locations that were all providing event functions. As a result they were able to showcase products and services in order to develop brand image. There were also member credit card exclusive offers (see below) to help develop customer loyalty and card activation opportunities in order to develop new customers. Maps and information about the sponsor's client restaurants in the Tribeca area were also featured in an attempt to support and drive sales.

The Festival site offered American Express card members the exclusive opportunity of purchasing tickets for the whole Festival, via their card, 4 days ahead of all other ticket sales in an effort to drive sales for both sponsor and the event.

Various other mechanisms were used to drive people to use the linked sites including the following communications tools.

Print news media

Various local magazines and distributed newspapers were used for bought advertising space. A series of advertisements were designed and linked to the Festival that utilized a 'film poster' theme. All advertisements carried the flash acknowledgement 'Official Card of the Tribeca Film Festival'. Some advertisements carried special sales promotions.

Once such promotion was entitled 'The man with the golden card', again utilizing a film poster theme, and offered a season ticket for the most-in-demand films as part of a package that also included food and beverage and free gifts. The offer was promoted as a 'Gold Card Event Special Offer' in order to grow brand awareness and collect market data for future targeted activities.

Billboards and fly-posters

Utilizing the same themed poster designs, billboard space was bought around the edge of the Tribeca area. Fly-posting was utilized in a wider catchment area and in locations where film posters would normally be found. The consistent use of one set of designed themes helped to ensure integrated activity.

Other print: 'A Walking Tour of Film Locations'

The sponsors created new Festival foldout maps that located all event venues, but also identified where featured film shooting was done for those films, for example Barney Greengrass Restaurant where Meg Ryan dines in 'You've Got Mail'. This event function was intended to develop brand image.

Source: *The Village Voice* (2004); *Downtown Express* (2004); *The L Magazine* (2004); American Express (2004); Tribeca Film Festival (2004).

walkabouts on the race qualifying day and extensive print and photo media activity across Europe. The televised elements were boosted with the use of race team clothing, pit garage signage and the cars themselves all featuring the name and logo for the film.

The importance of exploitation is reflected in the industry. The IEG/Sponsorship Research (2004) annual survey revealed that 77 per cent of sponsors spend additional monies to leverage their sponsorship rights. Alarmingly though, this figure was higher at 87 per cent in 2003. The sponsorship decision makers that were surveyed in 2004 listed corporate hospitality, internal communications, advertising, public relations, Internet tie-ins and sales promotion as the top six forms of sponsorship leverage.

Integration

The sponsorship decision-making process in Figure 12.1 acknowledges the important role that sponsorship should play in an integrated communications mix by ensuring that sponsorship options are fully developed and then considered alongside other forms of contact in order to determine the most effective and efficient set of message channels. While sponsorship is always an option worth assessing it is not necessarily always going to be a solution. However, if and when it is, it is important that it is only one part of an integrated marketing communications effort. This is especially the case when there is increased spending on exploitation. The communications that are implemented to leverage the sponsorship rights need to be integrated with all other communications activities for the sponsoring product/service. Failure to do so limits the success achievable as messages become dysfunctional and then diluted when they are acting in different ways and are at cross-purposes (Pickton and Broderick, 2001; Boone and Kurtz, 2002).

The common failure in developing a communications mix is to distinguish between techniques and see sponsorship, advertising, public relations and direct marketing as separate components (Fill, 2002). The approach uses all forms of brand or corporate contact as message channels (Shimp, 1997) and that is where there is a potential problem area in sponsorship. The growth of the industry has long seen the emergence and development of separate sponsorship agencies and the monitoring of their agenda, operation and implementation of sponsorships is critical if they are to be an integrated component. The more external agencies there are at play in the activation of marketing communications the more the potential for dysfunction (Shimp, 1997; Kitchen, 1999; Fill, 2002) and so communications management with a global view is paramount, especially in the light of market reports that indicate that this is now a key growth issue for sponsorship (Mintel, 2002).

The focus for integrated marketing communications is to affect the behaviour of its audience. This requires more than influencing brand awareness and instigating action and so there is more of a focus on a return (Shimp, 1997; Kitchen, 1999). This could be in the form of sales, and so as sponsorship develops as a fully accepted and integrated communications tool (Tripodi, 2001), the demands on it for such returns will increase, again highlighting the importance of exploitation strategies.

The toiletries manufacturer PZ Cussons recognized that exploitation was going to be critical in its sponsorship of the 2002 Commonwealth Games. It utilized its soap brand 'Imperial Leather' in an approach that steered clear of the typical 'official' sports sponsorship status by first ensuring that all its agencies, BDH/TBWA, Biss Lancaster and Mediaedge:cia worked together to identify all opportunities. These included national television and regional outdoor and print campaigns, event signage, the use of celebrity and former athlete Sally Gunnell in engineered public relations, sampling and hospitality for key trade clients. In addition, ten million packs of soap carried promotions and the brand was functionally used in the event via ambient forms of contact such as event venue washrooms (Hawtin, 2004).

Evaluation

Evaluation methods are discussed in sufficient detail in Chapter 8 and while they are intended as tools for the event manager, they apply equally to the sponsor.

It is apparent that there needs to be a justification of evaluation in the industry as it is not a widely practised exercise (Hoek et al., 1997). Dolphin (2003) asks if this is because the true cost of sponsorship is difficult to determine. Another reason for not conducting evaluation, particularly post-event evaluation, is that it requires resources that event managers are keen to devote to their next event. A longer-term view is clearly required and the cost of evaluation needs to be included in the event budget because it is clear that a lack of evaluation can hinder success. In an industry where the bottom line is a return on investment, this can only derive from appropriately set objectives. Measurement or evaluation is against objectives (Tripodi, 2001) and if evaluation is both iterative and end-on, the results can be fed back to help improve future performance. For example, evaluation can be critical for identifying and then recruiting/renewing sponsors (Thompson and Quester, 2000). Those sponsors that fail to set clear objectives or fail to evaluate against those objectives, are also more likely to experience shorter and less successful sponsorship relationships (Pope and Voges, 1994).

In addition to these three critical factors, there are also contemporary and external forces at play that can impact on sponsorship decision making. Some of the more pertinent ones are considered next.

Ambush marketing – fair game?

Since the early 1990s ambush marketing has emerged and grown into a considerable issue for the events industry. The key concern for event managers has always been the threat to sponsorship value and that sponsors will consequently pay less, but now there is the expense of meeting sponsors' expectations so that their sponsorship rights will be protected from ambush tactics. The greater the threat of ambush, the harder the job of recruiting sponsors becomes. The threat to sponsorship value is a concern for sponsors too, of course, and if they are exploiting their rights they are in effect creating new platforms for their competitors to compete.

Sponsors have done a good job in portraying their ambushing competition as employers of unscrupulous tactics. This is supported to some degree by those commentators that see event ambush marketing as the tactics of those companies that seek to associate with an event without paying any sponsorship fees (Kolah, 1999). There is another view, that free markets are fair game. Considering that so far, most event ambush marketing has not been illegal, the opposite view is that it is just active and competitive use of marketing communications. Dare we say, even innovative use of marketing communications. The sponsor has created a market position and its competitors see this as a legitimate opportunity to direct a competitive campaign. Indeed, Gratton and Taylor (2000) refer to Nike as a company that positions itself as anti-establishment and that ambush marketing tactics fit very well with that stance. A stance the company consistently appears to take.

The increasing danger for events is that more companies may decide that ambush tactics are more successful and do not then become or continue as event sponsors. The signs are there. According to Performance Research Europe (2002) their research demonstrated that Nike achieved higher recall in fans attending UEFA's Euro 2000 football championship than many of the sponsors. When fans were asked to identify sponsors from a list, the brewer Carling and Nike both featured and yet they were not event sponsors. Nike recorded 71 per cent recall while sponsors Mastercard (56 per cent), JVC (48 per cent) and Fuji (48 per cent) were some way behind. Adidas, the sportswear manufacturer and event sponsors for the sportswear sponsorship category, also recorded less recall at 70 per cent. The most frequently recalled television advertisers during the event were Nike (18 per cent), Adidas and Carling (both 5 per cent).

The snack brand Pringles, owned by Procter and Gamble, was formerly a sponsor of UEFA and Euro 2000, but used ambush tactics at UEFA's Euro 2004 Championships. They contracted a number of players and the use of their image on-pack. The players could not be seen in their national team shirts without authorization from their national associations and club shirts would not have had the same effect and would have required similar permissions. The players were therefore depicted on-pack wearing different coloured plain shirts. For example, Ruud van Nistelrooy, the Dutch striker, was shown in an orange jersey that was only one pantone number away from the colour of the national team strip he wore in the event itself. The deal was deemed to be worth £2 million with the beneficiaries including the 12 players and the players' agents, but not UEFA, the host nation and event organizers, the Portuguese Football Association or the national Government. The event was pretty much 'fair game' to a number of non-sponsor brands throughout Europe. The Absolut vodka brand distributed promotional postcards on a pan-European basis one month out of the tournament. On one side of the card there was the tag line 'Absolut kick-off' together with a representation of the actual tournament competition draw, team-by-team, group-by-group and depicted in the shape of the brands distinctive bottle shape. There was no reference at all to Euro 2004 as Absolut were not an event sponsor. Their perceived association with the event though was all too clear. Again, the concern for the organizers is a devaluing of their product in the eyes of paying sponsors.

In addition to the use of advertising commercials in ambush tactics, the acquiring of television broadcast sponsorship was once an opportunity in the 1990s. The latter has for the most part been eradicated by major events in their attempts to police ambush marketing. By negotiating with broadcast partners prior to their approach to sponsors, events have been able to secure combined rights of broadcast and event sponsorship for their eventual sponsorship programme.

One of the areas that has proved difficult for events to protect is the use of individual or team sponsorship as a way of infiltrating events. The sponsorship of one sports team or an individual player by a sportswear manufacturer and then that team competing in an event that has a different sportswear category sponsor is actually not policed at all. Indeed, in some cases the event offers sponsors a take-it-or-leave-it set of rights. To continue with football and in particular Nike, the FIFA World Cup currently has an official sportswear manufacturer in Adidas and readily accepts that it cannot prevent Brazil from competing and often doing very well in the competition while wearing its Nike sponsored team kit. This will be the case for the 2006 FIFA World Cup in Germany. The company also widely used its television advertisement that featured Brazil and Portugal in Nike team kit and throughout Europe and the build up to the UEFA Euro 2004 Championships. The official sportswear sponsor for this event was again Adidas.

The standard rights package for the 2006 FIFA World Cup event includes ambush marketing protection (FIFA, 2004). FIFA maintain that profiting from the popularity of their event, without making any financial contribution directly to it or the game of football, undermines the integrity of the event and its marketing programme and also the interests of football worldwide. The international governing body has developed a worldwide 'Rights Protection Programme' that focuses on the prevention of illegal use of trademarks and associations with the event. When it comes to attempts at stopping companies buying advertising billboards outside event stadia then the prevention is quite simple. The space has to be booked, well in advance and used by official sponsors as part of their exploitation. This is certainly one way of ensuring sponsors exploit their rights. In an unprecedented move to protect potential sponsors of the New York 2012 Olympics, NYC2012 secured the majority of the outdoor media that would be available in New York City for 2012 and it did this prior to making its bid and not knowing if it would host the event or not. This amounted to 95 per cent of the 600 000 advertising signs (billboards, transport, street signage) available. To achieve this it had to negotiate a price with commercial suppliers eight years in advance (NYC2012, 2004).

Indeed, strategies of defence are now becoming the norm at this level. Exploitation of rights is now not only a requirement in order to make sponsorship work, but also to keep competitors away from the communications platform.

Other sponsorship issues

There are perhaps even clearer ethical issues in event sponsorship. These are issues that border between the innovative and what is socially acceptable. For example, the use of sponsorship by tobacco manufacturers has moved on from an acceptable to a banned form of their marketing communications.

Hock et al. (1997) report that alcohol has also caused ethical concerns because of its potentially negative effects on society. Alcohol and sport, in particular, remains a potent combination and exposure to young fans continues unabated. The production of replica team jerseys that carry alcohol brand names is one such example. The exploitation of the young as endorsers is more recent. Across the USA there are many young skateboarders that have been given products bedecked in logos in return for the placement of stickers. Of more concern perhaps are those youngsters that have been given contracts. In 2003, one such 6-year-old skateboarder had sponsors in Jones Soda, Lego and Termite and had appeared on several national television programmes (Talbot, 2003). In the same year, a three-and-a-half-year-old boy, Mark Walker, had a contract with Reebok that furnished him with his own website address (markwalker.reebok.com, 2004). On that website Mark played basketball and could be heard to say that he was the future of basketball and the words, 'I am Reebok'. The ethics are not clear here, but the communications decisions by Reebok were. They were exploiting a sponsorship and in many ways innovatively. The question asked in this chapter is not whether this is ethically correct, but what are the factors that govern marketing decision making. Reebok removed the site in April 2004 and of concern to them was the content of their message, its reach, its perceived value and whether their objectives were being best met.

The exploitation of one's personal rights for sponsorship also presents some interesting new dilemmas. As branding becomes an increasingly imaginative and innovative exercise, it appears to get closer to that ethical line of what is and is not socially acceptable. Transparent speed-skating suits that reveal commercial brands and logos that are painted on the body may be innovative until banned by the governing body. Body billboarding in boxing, however, has moved on to the use of commercially related tattoos and moves by television broadcasters to get it banned (Christie, 2002; Masterman, 2004). The ethics are complex because, not only is tattooing a debatable issue, so is the move by media to play a part in the governance of sport. The latter is of concern in all areas of event management. As sponsorship revenues increase so do the expectations of sponsors and, with the emphasis clearly on sponsorship for a return on investment, the power of the media grows. The sponsor needs to be concerned too, because the more that the integrity of the arts, music, sport and rights holders in general are affected, the less the power of corporate sponsorship as a marketing communications channel.

Summary

This chapter complements Chapter 8 in that together they complete the event sponsorship picture by presenting two perspectives and approaches – those of the event and those of the sponsor. While the sponsorship relationship is mutually beneficial and often regarded as a partnership, it is still a business relationship and there will always be two agendas. Here the emphasis has been on the objectives that are now commonly sought by corporate sponsors in the event industry. These objectives can be summarily divided into four categories: direct sales objectives, brand awareness, external and internal corporate awareness. A fifth category links them all. By achieving any or all of these a sponsor can be gaining competitive advantage not least by shutting rival companies out of the opportunity.

The process by which sponsorship decisions are made is critical for the achievement of these objectives, but it is not a process that begins with the decision of whether to sponsor or not. The sponsorship decision-making process is only one aspect of marketing planning and sponsorship is therefore only one of a series of choices for marketing communications channels. A number of key areas of information are required throughout the process in order to support decision making and these include identification and size of the target market any sponsorship will reach, whether there is appropriate 'fit', how distribution channels can be provided with incentives, where competitive advantage can be gained and the extent and type of resources that will be required. These questions are answered by following a process that is comprised of three key stages. The first stage is concerned with organizational marketing planning where marketing plans are initiated and aligned with corporate objectives. The second stage researches, targets and evaluates sponsorship opportunities against other channels and contact points in an effort to ensure that marketing communications are integrated. Sponsorship only then becomes a choice of contact if it is an effective and efficient alternative. The final stage is concerned with the planning, execution and then evaluation of the sponsorship.

There are three factors that are critical for success: exploitation, integration and evaluation. Exploitation, consisting of additional communications activity that is over and above the sponsorship rights, is required as rights are generally insufficient on their own to achieve sponsorship objectives. These communications also need to be an integral part of the sponsor's overall marketing plans in order to have the greatest effect. Evaluation, the third factor, is not commonly conducted by many sponsors but is nevertheless essential for future decision making.

There are a number of contemporary issues that are worthy of note because they are key for future sponsorship decision making. In particular the emergence and development of ambush marketing has had such an impact that now certain sponsorship rights packages are expected to contain inbuilt ambush protection. A key part of the sponsorship decision-making process is also to consider the platform that a sponsorship will create for rival brands to compete for market advantage. With such intense competition and increasingly high sponsorship spending, the sponsorship market has been led to innovative, though sometimes ethically debatable, branding activities in the continuous quest for competitive advantage. The lengths to which sponsors will go to reach target markets are testament to this. With such market conditions the corresponding and increasing expectation for sponsorship is that it has to be accountable and be a return on investment.

Discussion points

- Consider the exploitation implemented by American Express at the 2004 Tribeca Film Festival in Case study 12.1 and identify further exploitation opportunities that might be undertaken for future events.
- Select a sponsored event and identify the objectives for each sponsor. Critically analyse how each of these objectives was met by identifying target markets, message content, choice of communications channels and how the strategies could be improved.
- Select an event sponsor and sponsorship that you consider to be both innovative and integrated. Discuss the extent to which an integrated marketing communications approach has been the key factor in the achievement of sponsorship objectives.
- Select one key issue that you feel is impacting on the sponsorship industry and discuss its implications on future corporate sponsorship decision making.

References

American Express (2004) www.americanexpress.com (accessed 9 May, 2004).

Amis, J., Slack, T. and Berrett, T. (1999) Sport sponsorship as distinctive competence. *European Journal of Marketing*, 33 (3), 250–272.

Bennett, R. (1999) Sports sponsorship, spectator recall and false consensus. *European Journal of Marketing*, 33 (3), 291–313.

Boone, L. and Kurtz, D. (2002) *Contemporary Marketing 2002*. Thomson Learning.

Business 2000 (2004) Case study: Bank of Ireland. Sponsorship of the Special Olympics: A partnership approach. www.business2000.ie/cases (accessed 26 April, 2004).

Charity Village (2004) www.charityvillage.com/cv/research (accessed 11 May, 2004).

Christie, J. (2002) New meaning to bottom feeders. *The Globe and Mail*. 23 January. www.sportsethicsinstitute.org/sports_marketing_ethics (accessed 28 March, 2003).

Connolly, P. (2003) *Colosseum: Rome's Arena of Death*. BBC Books.

Dolphin, R. (2003) Sponsorship: Perspectives on its strategic role. *Corporate Communications: An International Journal*, 8 (3), 173–186.

Downtown Express (2004) Special Section: Tribeca Film Festival. 16 (49), 30 April–6 May.

FIFA (2004) www.fifa.com/en/marketing/partners (accessed 12 May, 2004).

Fill, C. (2002) *Integrated Marketing Communications*. Butterworth-Heinemann.

Grant, M. (1975) *The twelve Ceasers*. Barnes and Noble Books.

Gratton, C. and Taylor, P. (2000) *Economics of Sport and Recreation*. E & FN Spon.

Hawtin, L. (2004) Imperial Leather: A winning performance. Admap, April. World Advertising Research Centre.

Head, V. (1988) *Successful Sponsorship*, 2nd edn. Director Books.

Hoek, J., Gendall, P., Jeffcoat, M. and Orsman, D. (1997) Sponsorship and advertising: A comparison of their effects. *Journal of Marketing Communications*, 3 (1), 21–32.

IEG/Sponsorship Research (2004) 4th Annual Sponsorship Decision-Makers Survey. IEG Sponsorship Report, Sample Issue. IEG.

International Marketing Reports (2002) www.im-reports.com/Sample3 (accessed 15 April, 2002).

IOC (2004) *2002 Marketing Fact File*. IOC.

Kelso, P. (2004) Why Cassani had to call time, gentlemen, please. *The Guardian*, 20 May.

Kitchen, P. (1999) *Marketing Communications: Principles and Practice*. International Thomson Business Press.

Kolah, A. (1999) *Maximizing the Value of Sports Sponsorship*. Financial Times Media.

Mackay, D. (2004) The urgent promotion of Britain's double gold medallist. *The Guardian*, 20 May.

Markwalker.reebok.com (2004) www.markwalker.reebok.com (accessed 28 April, 2004).

Masterman, G. (2004) *Strategic Sports Event Management: An International Approach*. Butterworth-Heinemann.

Meenaghan, T. and Shipley, D. (1999) Media effect in commercial sponsorship. *European Journal of Marketing*, 33 (3), 328–348.

Milne, G. and McDonald, M. (1999) *Sport Marketing: Managing the Exchange Process*. Jones and Bartlett Publishers.

Mintel (2002) *Sponsorship Report*. Mintel.

Mullin, B., Hardy, S. and Sutton, W. (2000) *Sport Marketing*, 2nd edn. Human Kinetics.

NYC2012 (2004) *2012 Olympic Bid Document: Theme 7, Marketing*. NYC2012, p. 127.

Otker, T. (1998) Exploitation: The key to sponsorship success. *European Research*, 16 (22), 77–86.

Performance Research Europe (2002) British football fans can't recall Euro 2000 sponsors. www.performanceresearch.com (accessed 9 October, 2003).

Pickton, D. and Broderick, A. (2001) *Integrated Marketing Communications*. Pearson Education.

Pitts, B. and Stotlar, D. (2002) *Fundamentals of Sport Marketing*, 2nd edn. Fitness Information Technology.

Pope, N. (1998a) Overview of current sponsorship thought. *Cyber-Journal of Sport Marketing*. www.ausport.gov.au/fulltext/1998/cjsm/v2n1/pope21 (accessed 29 April, 2004).

Pope, N. (1998b) Consumption values, sponsorship awareness, brand and product use. *Journal of Product and Brand Management*, 7 (2), 124–136.

Pope, N. and Voges, K. (1994) Sponsorship evaluation: Does it match the motive and the mechanism? *Sport Marketing Quarterly*, 3 (4), 38–45.

Sandler, D. and Shani, D. (1993) Sponsorship and the Olympic Games: The consumer perspective. *Sport Marketing Quarterly*, 2 (3), 38–43.

Shank, M. (2002) *Sports Marketing: A Strategic Perspective*, 2nd edn. Prentice Hall International.

Shimp, T. (1997) *Advertising, Promotion and Supplemental Aspects of Integrated Marketing Communications*, 4th edn. The Dryden Press.

Sponsorclick (2004) www.sponsorclick.com (accessed 10 June, 2004).

Stotlar, D. (1993) Sponsorship and the Olympic Winter Games. *Sport Marketing Quarterly*, 2 (1), 35–43.

Talbot, M. (2003) Play date with destiny. *The New York Times Magazine*, September 21.

The L Magazine (2004) The Film Issue. II (08), 28 April–11 May.

The New York Times Magazine (2004) The earlier they start. Merrill Lynch advertisement. 28 March.

The Village Voice (2004) XLIX (17), 28 April–4 May.

Thompson, B. and Quester, P. (2000) Conference paper. Evaluating sponsorship effectiveness: The Adelaide Festival of the Arts. *Australian and New Zealand Marketing Academy Conference*, November–December, 2000. Visionary marketing for the 21st Century: Facing the challenge.

Thwaites, D. (1995) *Welcome to the Pirana Club*. November 12, 46–50.

Tribeca Film Festival (2004) www.tribecafilmfestival.org (accessed 9 May, 2004).

Tripodi, J. (2001) Sponsorship – a confirmed weapon in the promotional armoury. *International Journal of Sports Marketing and Sponsorship*, March/April.

WMLGA (2004) www.wmlga.gov.uk/sponsorship (accessed 25 May, 2004).

Chapter 13
Corporate Hospitality

Objectives

- Identify achievable objectives for event corporate hospitality
- Examine the use and success of event corporate hospitality as a fully integrated marketing communications tool
- Identify the critical factors in making event corporate hospitality a success

Introduction

So what is so important about corporate hospitality? Is corporate hospitality just simply the inviting of guests to an event with the intent of developing business? The issue for communications decisions is that in practice, corporate hospitality has long been used by hosts to entertain guests of varying degrees of importance, but without any evaluation, and therefore justification, of why. There is no doubt that corporate hospitality is indeed a valuable marketing communications tool, but as such, it needs to be strategically selected, implemented and then evaluated alongside and against other tools.

In order to assess the importance of corporate hospitality it is necessary to consider a historical perspective of how it has emerged and the role it plays in the events industry today. It has been around for some time and is a forerunner to the emergence of event sponsorship as we know it today, but its history demonstrates a lack of strategic use and even abuse of corporate funds for unjustified expense. This chapter will consider how it has grown from these beginnings into a legitimate marketing communications option.

The focus of this chapter moves on to how, in practice, organizations use corporate hospitality and how these events and activities might otherwise be used as vehicles to achieve marketing objectives. The identification of how corporate hospitality is used as a communications tool by the organizations that utilize it, also helps to demonstrate the level of understanding that the providers to the industry need to attain, including, of course, event management organizations.

Event organizers need to understand why and how corporate hospitality can achieve a client's marketing objectives so that they can meet their customers' needs. In order to demonstrate how corporate hospitality can be a valuable communications choice, the chapter will discuss the critical factors for success: integration, strategic planning, the setting of objectives, facilitation of quality points of interaction, evaluation and management approach.

The emergence of corporate hospitality

Over the last decade there have been considerable changes in the perception of corporate hospitality. The industry itself has worked hard in order to improve a once tarnished image, so that today there are signs that corporate hospitality is seen as a valuable choice of marketing tool. In particular, there are signs that corporate hospitality can be successfully integrated into customer relationship management (CRM) strategies (Mintel, 2002). However, this is only a relatively recent perspective and, in order to identify the reasons for the issues that still exist with corporate hospitality today, a closer look at how it has emerged is required.

There is no need to go too far into the history of corporate hospitality to find examples of firms creating guest lists that were based on personal rather than organizationally justified reasons. This is a key issue for corporate hospitality. It was frequently used as a way of entertaining guests but not stakeholders. The second issue is that even when key stakeholders were invited, the exercise was not an integrated part of any strategic marketing plan. It was often a decision taken by individual managers or departments and, even where corporate hospitality activities were linked to marketing objectives, there was little planning for the development of key relationships and virtually no evaluation in order to assess whether those objectives were being met.

In the 1980s, in the UK, there was plenty of evidence of guests being invited to events by host organizations for non-marketing reasons. For example, the invitation of clients was viewed by many hosts as something they gave as a reward for previous business. However, as there was no plan to develop this opportunity for further business, the process was not serving a marketing purpose. For corporate hospitality to be used for marketing purposes it would need to be incorporated into a marketing plan in a way that it might achieve marketing communications objectives.

World Championship Tennis Inc (WCT) organized considerable corporate hospitality for its annual Nabisco Masters Doubles Championships in the 1980s. The event was staged at the Royal Albert Hall in London and that afforded them the use of three tiers of velvet lined corporate boxes. With over 100 boxes and seven sessions of tennis, this event accommodated over 5000 corporate guests. One of their biggest corporate hospitality clients was from the packaging industry. Having been a loyal corporate hospitality buyer for a number of years, the opportunity to convert this client into a sponsor arose after the 1987 event. On taking the sponsorship for the 1988 event, however, the client continued to run its corporate hospitality programme independently. Apart from typically demonstrating how sponsorships used to be developed out of corporate hospitality, this example also shows how the integration of such activities for the achievement of marketing objectives was an issue.

The sponsorship was entrenched in the development of new packaging business and yet the numbers of hospitality invitations that went to personal rather than corporate contacts was much larger. The hospitality remained a separate activity as far as this sponsor was concerned.

The lack of evaluation of corporate hospitality by those that buy it has been and remains a key issue. Tony Barnard (2003) of the Corporate Event Association (CEA) in the UK remarks that while there has been growth through the considerable use of innovation in recent times, there continues to be a lack of measurement, despite the clear need for such. He maintains that evaluation is predominantly restricted to feedback from guests as a measure of enjoyment. Similarly, thank-you letters have been used for the same purpose. There is little evidence of the use of evaluation that links back to objectives and nor is there consistent evidence that marketing objectives are even being set. The CEA (2004) advocates that benchmarks and performance criteria are established just as they would be for any other tool in the communications mix. In particular, there is evidence of corporate hospitality budgets being cut when an evaluation, if carried out, might have indicated that continued use was worthwhile.

There was clearly little understanding of how corporate hospitality might be used to achieve business development objectives in its earliest uses and the emergence of a different perception was aided in the UK by the forming of the CEA in 1988. At the time there was consistently poor press concerning the use of hospitality budgets at major sports events and a code of conduct was deemed appropriate by like-minded organizations selling and creating hospitality. The result was a body that has worked hard at establishing corporate hospitality as a credible communications choice. This work included a change of name, from the Corporate Hospitality and Event Association to the CEA. This was an attempt to introduce greater focus and standards and combat poor public and media perception. This poor perception of corporate hospitality did not arise just as a result of poor use by hosts however. Activity providers have also been guilty of selling hospitality packages without ever fully understanding how their customers might use them for marketing purposes.

This poor perception has derived from a use of corporate hospitality as a reward. The reward was for those guests that the hosts considered themselves close to and, although that would include customers, the reward was for past dealings. There may have been hopes founded in new business from such invitees but there was little proactivity in order to achieve that. Invitations then became an expected part of the supplier–customer relationship and a new word for corporate hospitality emerged. Being invited to go to the races, the sky-box, the clay-pigeon shoot and the opera became known as going on a 'jolly' and while these events were fun and may have got an invitee to 'like' or think more pleasantly about their hosts, there was nothing strategic about it from a communications standpoint. When hosts also despatched personally derived invitations, it is no wonder that questions arose as to whether corporate hospitality was merely executive indulgence (Bennett, 2003).

The corporate hospitality industry

Nevertheless, the corporate hospitality industry has grown. It has also grown to the extent that for Mintel (2002) and their market reports, there is a need to classify the corporate hospitality industry into three distinct sectors: spectator sports, cultural/ arts events and participatory activities (including sports and the arts). The largest sector is spectator sports and contributes approximately half of the total value of the industry (Key Note, 2000; Mintel, 2002) and was in growth between 1999 and 2001. Cultural/arts events have also experienced growth, although the greater rate of growth of both spectator sports and participatory activities meant that they did lose market share.

The largest growth has not been in the use of the traditional 'big ticket' events but in participatory events, which grew by 40 per cent between 1997 and 2001. These are events that are generally created for the sole purpose of entertaining guests and, as they can incorporate more involvement and therefore result in greater impact, an alarm bell is already ringing for those that manage regular sporting and culturally based calendar events that depend upon corporate hospitality as a key revenue stream. The reasons for this growth in participatory events was due to a demand for more greatly differentiated entertainment, especially as costs for established corporate hospitality destinations such as the Henley Regatta (rowing), Royal Ascot (horse racing) and Glyndebourne (opera) had risen to unaffordable heights for many organizations. Buyers of corporate hospitality also needed more differentiation in order to attract the attention of those clients they wanted to invite. Other factors for this growth include the emergence of more proactive and adventurous client organizations and requirements that were shifting towards more hands-on and 'new' experiences. As a result, corporate hospitality also became less of an elitist activity. It possibly started in the UK in the late 1980s/early 1990s with the emergence of clay pigeon shoots in particular, mainly because they retained an air of exclusivity and privilege and because they were relatively inexpensive to stage. Activities such as driving vehicles, including racing cars around tracks, off-road and blindfolded then followed. Parties at stately homes, hot air balloon flights, treasure hunts around cities were then developed and then, more recently, themed entertainments including battling with armoured vehicles and paintball weaponry. Some agencies offer fuller services that include tour operations. This move towards the provision of an 'experience', as opposed to 'hospitality', is again something that is of concern to some event organizers in the industry and yet it is an opportunity for others.

The consequence is an industry with a diverse set of players. Any organization can use corporate hospitality, but the supply side of the industry can be categorized: owners or managers of hospitality activities that are part of events; organizations that create and sell their own purpose-built activities; venues; suppliers of associated services and goods such as caterers; and there are also management agencies that acquire and/or create hospitality activities either on behalf of sellers and/or buyers. The focus here in this chapter is on the use of corporate hospitality as a communications tool and Key Note (2000) reported a major restructuring of the industry between 1998 and 2000 that bore influence on the choices of event hospitality. Demand from client organizations for greater differentiation and provision of marketing solutions, often on an international scale, led to mergers between some of the larger players and provision at higher profiled spectator events. At the same time that left opportunities for smaller more specialized providers to enter the market with fashion-sensitive solutions. The result is a highly fragmented and competitive industry and a plethora of choice.

A review of what client organizations are buying from these suppliers reveals that traditional high-profile spectator sports events remain the top preferences, with football drawing the largest numbers of corporate hospitality guests according to

Key Note (2000). Conversely, Mintel (2002) places golf days as the most popular, followed by football, horse racing, theatre/opera and rugby union via its analysis of research of 250 large to middle-sized UK hospitality client organizations.

Identifying market values is difficult if internal corporate hospitality data are required, but for external activities, data are readily available for the UK market via a number of sources. The total UK market was valued at £676 million in 2001 by Mintel (2002) and they forecasted an estimated drop to £649 million for 2002. There had been growth every year since 1997, but the impact of the terrorist attacks on the USA on 11 September 2001 was expected to have affected the business. Significantly, earlier forecasts made by Key Note (2000) and by MAPS (1998), both obviously prior to the attacks, predicted continued growth to £834 million and £998 million for 2003 respectively. Key Note (2000) predicted a growth between 2000 and 2003 of 12.5 per cent for the market overall but with the spectator sports sector growing at the greatest rate of 18 per cent. Retrospectively it is now easier to see that this was a sector that was hard hit by the economic downtown as a result of the attacks. Two factors took effect. Many organizations banned international travel and/or cut expenditure on hospitality that seemed somewhat out of place under the circumstances. Mintel (2002) notes that there were signs of upturns for the second quarter of 2002 and comments that this demonstrated that the corporate hospitality industry was strong enough to come back from such impacts. As a consequence it predicts a steady 22 per cent growth in 2002 terms between 2002 and 2006 (7 per cent real growth after the effects of inflation). Its forecast for 2006 values the UK corporate hospitality industry at £793 million.

Despite previous growth, the size of the industry in monetary terms and a realization that corporate hospitality is potentially a valuable communications tool, the 'old' view is still prevalent. Alarmingly, there remain examples of the choice of entertainment being at the behest of chief executives (Cobb, 2003). It is important then that there is a clear understanding in the industry of exactly what corporate hospitality is if the traditional perception is finally to be extinguished. Mintel (2002), for example, describe it as the use of events or venues by a business to entertain associates, clients and potential clients. This is perfectly satisfactory, as organizations do not have to buy hospitality packages from events or venues, they can also create their own activities and manage them either at their own or hired venues. However, the definition refers to associates while not making it clear if this includes employees and, in any case, specifically excludes the internal use of entertainment activities for its purpose of producing its market report. In looking at the events industry as a whole, however, internally derived events are tools that are used to achieve internal marketing objectives and for an integrated marketing approach where internal marketing is key, it is therefore important to consider that all uses of activities for entertaining can be described as corporate hospitality. The CEA (2004) certainly includes employees in its categorizations for the industry. Meanwhile, Bennett (2003) considers corporate hospitality to be the provision of opportunities at events (or via activities) that enable organizations to benefit from the entertainment of clients, prospective clients or employees at that organization's expense. Bennett's (2003) definition does however exclude two key aspects. Suppliers are a category of guest that consistently receive invitations and should therefore be included in any definition. It should also be noted that clients could be distributors as well as end-user customers. It is also generally accepted that corporate hospitality is for business-to-business clients only but, it should be noted that provided the host deems them so, key consumers might also be worthwhile invitees. For example, the car industry consistently invites what it considers as key consumers to be entertained at all kinds of activities. Industry practice would appear to demonstrate that corporate hospitality is in fact being used to affect the whole of the customer value chain (Porter, 1985). For example, inbound logistics, operations, outbound logistics, sales and marketing and service, can all be affected through the entertainment of suppliers, employees and customers. Corporate hospitality might therefore be more comprehensively described as those activities that are utilized at an organization's expense to enable that organization to benefit from the entertainment of its clients and distributors, prospective clients and distributors, suppliers or employees.

The next step is to understand why and how corporate hospitality can be used as a marketing tool in order to achieve that benefit.

A marketing tool

The idea of rewarding is still an important factor according to Bennett (2003). He refers to the study of corporate hospitality, which is predominantly practitioner based from sources such as marketing trade magazines and associations rather than academic, as being closely tied to the theory of 'liking'. He proposes that because social psychology studies have demonstrated that 'liking' is known to encourage commitment and that people will like someone or some organization that has rewarded them, the principle of providing someone with a good experience can initiate 'liking' and the beginnings of a relationship. He builds this case further with psychological research that has established that individuals are inclined to like those that praise or flatter them and with social psychology study findings that demonstrate that simple forms of close proximity also have the capacity to enhance 'liking'. Further, he reveals that some investigations have led to claims that behaviour that enhances a 'liking' for someone else, can result in positive reciprocity. Bennett (2003) proposes that corporate hospitality, because of its capacity to bring people together in close proximity, to promote individual interaction for numbers of hours at a time, and to provide high levels of guest attention, can enhance 'liking'. He concludes that being able to offer rewards in the form of good experiences via corporate hospitality can form the base for potentially closer relationships that may bring future positive responses.

Bennett's (2003) own exploratory study of client organizations provided results that demonstrated that most organizations that use corporate hospitality seek to develop relationships with existing rather than potential clients. His analysis showed that corporate hospitality was normally viewed as a tool for retaining and developing existing business and not so much for winning new business from new or former customers. Clearly, reward was a factor and the key objective for most was to develop the relationship for further business.

Unfortunately, there are few other academic-based research studies to call on, but there are contrasting view points in practitioner-led marketing literature (Irwin, 2002) and from the Mintel (2002) report. In the latter, the findings contrast with those of Bennett (2003) when it comes to which target customers will be most successfully reached via corporate hospitality. It reports the findings of a survey undertaken in 2000, of 250 corporate hospitality client organizations conducted by NOP on behalf of Sodexho Group, an independent supplier of corporate hospitality and catering services. In those findings, the key benefit of hospitality was the building of relationships with potential customers. Repeat business from existing customers was acknowledged as being insignificant. However, the report also highlights that client organizations are tending to have fewer guests at events with higher staff-to-client ratios indicating that they are looking to develop relationships and personal selling. It concludes that there is a growing understanding that corporate hospitality can help develop long-term relationships and that many organizations demonstrate a 'Customer Relationship Management' (CRM) approach with a view to maximizing the life-time value of their invited guests. There is therefore an anomaly here. Life-time values are concerned with relationships that are continuously developed, over the long term, and necessarily, after the first sale, with existing customers.

The indications are that most corporate hospitality suppliers are aware of these objectives. Many use them on their websites in order to attract custom. Some suppliers offer consultation as part of the service so that specific client needs and requirements can be met. Motivaction (2004) in the UK has a 17-year history of building events to suit client corporate entertaining needs. While it does have generic activity 'solutions' already available, for example 'Director' and 'Synergy' are themed activity events that have been used with several clients, each client is consulted so that the locations, timings, guests lists and specific objectives are considered and built in. Sportsworld, also based in the UK, does something similar but with established pursuits such as golf and motor driving days. The requirements of the two clients in Case study 13.1 were met with the use of consultation and research. Conversely, like many other suppliers, Sportsworld also offers standard packages for sailing, polo coaching, theatre and wine tasting with an approach that very much leaves it to the client to decide if the activities will meet their objectives for entertaining or not. The Washington Redskins in the USA have an interesting approach with their website-based sales of executive and owners club suites. They claim that these are an effective way of entertaining clients or employees because it is proven that such activities can maintain relationships with existing clients and develop relationships with potential clients (Washington Redskins, 2004). While they indicate that their hospitality team will work with prospective customers to achieve specific needs, they do not offer actual evidence of what they refer to.

It would appear that there is agreement that the value of corporate hospitality, as an integrated tool, would appear to be in its capacity to build relationships, but not on which target customers, existing or new, it has the most effect. What is clear is that further research into corporate hospitality objectives is required.

There is one further issue to consider, the question of who is making the decision to use corporate hospitality. Bennett's (2003) study demonstrates that decision making lies predominantly within the domain of marketing, public relations or sponsorship departments. Few of his respondent organizations reported a multidisciplinary team decision and of those that did there was always a marketing department member involved. He concluded that corporate hospitality is viewed and used as a marketing communications tool. Irwin (2002) concludes that the fact that decisions are now coming from marketing departments demonstrates that organizations do see the significance of corporate hospitality from a marketing perspective. However, this does not mean that corporate hospitality is necessarily being considered as an integrated communications tool. A closer look at Bennett's (2003) findings shows that only 55 per cent of the respondent organizations agreed or strongly agreed that corporate hospitality was fully integrated into their marketing communications strategies.

Case study 13.1

Sportsworld Group

Sportsworld Group is an event management organization based in the UK with separate divisions offering services across the full extent of the events industry, including the organization of congresses and conferences, incentive travel, corporate entertainment and hospitality. The following cases demonstrate how even traditional activities such as golf and driving days need a researched and tailored approach if they are to achieve corporate objectives.

Post Office

The Group was contracted to provide two regionally based golf days for the Post Office – one in the South and one in the North, for 30 people each, in September 2003. The objectives were to develop relationships with existing suppliers and customers.

The choice of locations involved research and guest travel criteria was high on the list of key considerations. The selected golf courses were The Buckinghamshire in Denham, Buckinghamshire, 18 miles from central London, and the Camden Park Golf and Country Club in Cheshire. The programme for a full day included breakfast, lunch and dinner, and commemorative gifts and prizes that incorporated the Post Office branding. The golf involved competition in different 'Texas Scramble' and 'Stapleford' formats, but also accommodated for those who preferred coaching because research into the requirements of the guests had identified that a number would prefer non-competitive activities. The teaming-up of players was constructed in liaison with the client so that key senior personnel could partner appropriate guests in order to achieve relationship development.

Procter and Gamble

Procter and Gamble required a series of regional events to be used in connection with a 'push' strategy and, in particular, with an incentive scheme aimed at distributors. The target for early 2003 had been to sell three months worth of product in two months and those that achieved that would be rewarded with invitations to a participation event.

The challenge for Sportsworld was a fixed price per head budget and the need for a number of regional events. Through research of the distribution network, six locations were used between May and June and 720 guests were entertained. The task was also made difficult due to the fact that guests would remain unknown until well after the programme was designed and so profiles of potential guests had to be devised in order to determine the right activities. A series of motor sports days at six race tracks was designed and promoted through the distribution network well in advance to maximize the effect of the incentive scheme.

To maximize attendance, events were coordinated on Saturdays and included off- as well as on-track driving. The days included three meals, prizes, awards, safety training, instruction and Sportsworld ensured a smooth running event with at least two event managers at each site. This enabled carefully selected Procter and Gamble executives to focus on their guests.

The results proved successful for the client with over 75 per cent of distributors achieving their targets and feedback from those that participated enabled Procter and Gamble to plan the same programme for 2004.

Source: Sportsworld Group (2004).

Critical success factors

In such a highly fragmented and competitive industry, the pressure is on suppliers to meet ever-rising client organization expectations. In meeting those expectations, the industry as a whole also needs to rise to the occasion. For example, from the supplier side, greater spending in the industry by client organizations has led to an increase in the numbers of providers that, in turn, has meant an increase in competition just to retain, let alone win, business. Concurrently, from the user side, the increases in spending should lead to a greater requirement for accountability. While it is clear that this is beginning to happen, it is by no means widespread. Corporate hospitality needs to be evaluated just like any other business tool. Therefore, both users and suppliers, in order to achieve their marketing objectives via corporate hospitality, need to consider a number of critical factors.

Integration

If corporate hospitality has the capacity to build relationships via the use of events that create close proximate environments, enhance interaction and 'liking', then it is an option for one-to-one marketing activities. However, the extraction of new business directly from such environments would be perceived very poorly and would countermand the development of any relationship, and so the options need to take a longer-term perspective. It is unlikely that the entertainment of a corporate guest will, on its own, achieve the longer-term objectives the hosts might have and so other communications tools need to be used alongside. A successful approach for the use of corporate hospitality therefore uses it in combination with other tools in an integrated effort (Mintel, 2002; Bennett, 2003).

Strategic planning

In times of economic downturn it has been regularly observed that organizations cut corporate hospitality budgets. Indeed, there is a strong argument from a public relations perspective that there should be discontinuance if there are redundancies involved. However, in such times, the marketing effort can make all the difference for sales and possibly even for positive image and so the strategic use of corporate hospitality in an integrated marketing communications effort may be required. In a study by Flack (1999), 60 per cent of respondent organizations indicated that they would continue their corporate hospitality expenditure for the next five years, even if there were a recession. Bennett (2003) remarks that the willingness to continue under financially difficult times clearly demonstrates that corporate hospitality is being used strategically.

Assessing whether the use of corporate hospitality can play a part in the integrated marketing communications plan begins with an identification of whether those who would be invited are a good fit for the overall strategy. This requires research in order to pinpoint and then target guests and, at the same time, to identify the most appropriate activities for those guests in order that objectives might be achieved (Irwin, 2002). The setting of specific corporate hospitality objectives that are aligned with the overall marketing objectives is clearly essential (Irwin,

2002; Bennett, 2003). Tailoring activities to an organization's precise brief is perhaps one way of aligning more exactly to objectives. Similarly, finding out what your guests might want is one focus for research that can help lead to the setting of achievable objectives.

Objectives

Placing objectives near to the end of the chapter may appear counterproductive, but there was a need first to understand that there is no common or justified view of what corporate hospitality can achieve. As discussed earlier in this chapter, there is some agreement in it having the capacity to assist in the development of new business, but disagreement on whether that comes predominantly from either new or existing clients.

Bennett (2003) proposes that the setting of specific objectives for corporate hospitality is essential. The need to identify this as a critical factor, he maintains, is required because it is not so widespread within the industry. Sixty-two per cent of the respondents in his study said that they set specific objectives, but that still leaves over a third that did not. Results from his study indicated that organizations predominantly set objectives for increasing sales and from existing rather than new customers; 79 per cent directed invitations mainly towards existing rather than potential customers. Gaining new customers was also an objective but did not receive as high a priority. Conversely, the NOP study, as reported by Mintel (2002), saw few respondents indicating that repeat business and retention was a high priority, (7 per cent), although another 21 per cent stated that they used corporate hospitality as a reward for existing business. New business was similarly placed in the results as the number one objective, but it was to be gained from building relationships with potential customers.

Most organizations are concerned with developing internal relations with their employees. Among a number of ways that are used to achieve this is the use of corporate hospitality. Events can provide entertaining ways of communicating, motivating, team building and rewarding staff. The CEA (2004) states that even here there are organizations that adopt ill-prepared decisions when it comes to the choice of activity. With research, the CEA claims that an organization can increase loyalty in the company, improve inter-staff relations and also improve morale if it makes the appropriate selections, but can also do much damage if it makes the wrong ones. The key is to identify what the staff would like to do and sometimes a more objective perspective is required. Too many organizations, and even individual senior executives will make that choice and they will make it independent of the desires of their employees. The use of specialist event organizations can help remedy this. Their view can remain objective and if they are briefed they can also tailor activities to requirements. In 2004 Motivaction worked with a major computer manufacturer to produce a unique team-building solution. A virtual event was created for 360 of the firm's staff across 16 countries. The challenge was to engage and stimulate this number of people, simultaneously in one event, but without them leaving their offices. The objective was to demonstrate that by working together, despite geographical, cultural and time differences the team could be stronger, more efficient and effective in reaching its goals. Motivaction (2004) used their 'Emaze' game, run on-line, with a competition between teams that required them to meet various challenges that were specifically created around researched staff demographics. The client declared it an innovative success.

Bennett (2003) reported two other key objectives resulting from his study – developing corporate image and winning back former profitable customers. Mintel (2002) also adds increasing product awareness as a one further objective. One integrated approach to increase product awareness is through sponsorship programmes where target customers, such as invited corporate hospitality guests, get to see the organization's products showcased in action. For example, watching products in action as they play their role in providing a functional element of an event – tennis balls, computer mainframes, wireless communications and medical services are all different products or services that might be seen, in action, at events (see Chapters 8 and 12). The historical links between corporate hospitality and sponsorship are close. Thirty years or so ago, when the sponsorship industry was in its infancy, many sponsorships involved sets of rights that were predominantly made up of corporate hospitality packages. Even today, corporate hospitality rates by many sponsors as the foremost required set of rights. As reported in Chapter 12, an IEG/Sponsorship Research (2004) annual survey of corporate sponsorship decision makers ranked it the highest desired set of rights; 77 per cent of respondents indicating that it was a part of their sponsorship programmes. There are also opportunities for some host organizations to showcase their products within the environs of the hospitality facilities they use, whether they are a corporate box, marquee, or banqueting room. The host's food and beverage products if they manufacture them can of course be consumed and all manner of other manufactured products may be given as welcome or departing gifts. The selection and/or design of a bespoke set of hospitality activities that enables this showcasing is clearly an optimum strategy for any corporate hospitality user.

The creation of events in order to promote products is of course widespread and naturally these events include mechanisms for showcasing products. While this is covered in more depth in Chapter 11, it is important to note that corporate hospitality can also be incorporated into these events too. Using the car industry as an example, car manufacturers have clearly looked to develop the idea of entertaining key customers. There is the traditional route of showcasing products at car shows and rewarding key customers with hospitality on exhibitions stands. In addition, there are now invitations to go to days out at the track and the factory and experience extended hospitality. Lotus Cars in Norfolk own their own track for just such purposes.

It is also important to note that a lot of hospitality is directed at suppliers. Offering hospitality to those key suppliers that can have an effect on costs, and therefore efficiency and effectiveness, is as important to some organizations as directing corporate hospitality at customers. Case study 13.1 demonstrates how the Post Office entertained both suppliers and key customers at purpose built entertainment events, for example.

A lack of research does inhibit the identification of objectives, however, in considering and acting on the critical factors above it is possible to achieve the following objectives via the use of corporate hospitality:

1 *Develop new business*: using corporate hospitality to help build existing relationships via reward, close proximity interaction and the dissemination of information for a better understanding of the organization so that further new business can be acquired.

 Using corporate hospitality to redevelop former relationships via close proximity interaction and the dissemination of information for a better understanding of the organization so that new business can be acquired.

Using corporate hospitality to initiate and then develop new relationships via close proximity interaction and the dissemination of information for a better understanding of the organization so that new business can be acquired.

2 *Develop product awareness*: using corporate hospitality to develop product awareness via the dissemination of information and in the exploitation of opportunities for showcasing the product to guests.

3 *Develop corporate image awareness*: using corporate hospitality to initiate or enhance an awareness of a corporate image via the dissemination of information for a better understanding of the organization.

4 *Develop internal relations*: using corporate hospitality to develop internal awareness and understanding of corporate image and objectives via reward and the dissemination of information.

5 *Develop supplier relations*: using corporate hospitality to initiate and/or develop new supplier relationships via close proximity interaction and the dissemination of information for a better understanding of the organization for enhanced efficiency and effectiveness.

Points of interaction

The choice of activity is as critical a decision as who to invite. The two tasks go hand-in-hand because the choice of activity has to be an exact fit for each guest in order to achieve objectives. From the market reports (MAPS, 1998; Key Note, 2000; Mintel, 2002) it is clear that spectator sports are still the top choices. To know if these are the right choices, again there should be more evaluation. The established 'big ticket' events are also still high on that list, although the use of participatory and tailored activities is growing (Mintel, 2002). There are two key factors in making the selection. Innovation plays a part, but that does not necessarily mean that a regular guest has to have new every time. The continued use by many guests of their invitations to the 'big ticket' events is an indication of that. The first factor comes from an enhanced knowledge of the guests to be invited. Organizations need to research the entertainment needs of their guests and then after the activities or event, evaluate whether those needs were met. The second factor is ensuring that the point of close proximity interaction can meet the organization's objectives. It needs to be of a sufficient length of time, with the right ambience that enables the effective use of relationship development skills. This will also necessitate the selection of the right people to host the activities, which may or may not require training, but will certainly need a cohesive understanding among that team of the objectives that are to be achieved (Bennett, 2003). This further explains that this is a carefully planned element of a strategic programme.

Evaluation

The question of whether corporate hospitality is an effective and efficient choice of communication is a difficult one for user organizations. There is not enough research to justify that it works or indeed what objectives it works for.

The growth of its use, however, would suggest that organizations assume that it works, but while all organizations would agree that assumption is not enough for decision making, there is little evidence of them trying to remedy that when it comes to the evaluation of corporate hospitality. The MAPS (1998) report for example, showed that two-thirds of hosts did not evaluate the effectiveness of their activities and while the Mintel (2002) report actually disagrees, stating that almost every organization it surveyed performed some form of measure, it still concludes that there is a need to develop more sophisticated techniques for the measurement of outcomes and ultimately the justification of corporate hospitality expenditure. For example, its respondent organizations used measures that were limited to the use of informal feedback from guests who indicated the level of their enjoyment of the activity, verbal observations of guests on the day, thank-you letters and subjective views from managers as to the level of relationships with guests.

Bennett (2003) refers to the difficulties of performing evaluation. His study reported the use of similar informal techniques with 34 per cent relying on guest feedback and 23 per cent on informal managerial estimates of the amount of business the hosting of the activities generated. For the latter type of evaluation there is the difficulty of attributing new business that is acquired some time on in the future. The fact that time has lapsed, and it could be years, means that other factors could have affected the decision. This is why corporate hospitality must be used as an integrated tool so that it does not stand-alone and so that other communications can continue to build the relationship over whatever time period.

Evaluation is a critical factor for the successful use of corporate hospitality for two reasons. First, its selection as one of the tools in each particular communications programme needs to be justified. Identifying if other tools would have been more effective and efficient is the required focus for the evaluation here, but appropriate techniques for this job are so far proving an elusive find. Certainly more formal feedback might be recommended. For example, the use of more evaluation feedback sheets that are designed to work in tandem with the evaluation of other communications tools that are being utilized to target these guests is more effective. This leads to the second reason why evaluation is critical. The evaluation of corporate hospitality is in fact only one part of the evaluation of the overall integrated programme. Therefore, while the single evaluation of the hospitality activities on their own may not be enough to measure whether objectives have been met, the wider ranging evaluation of the communications programme as a whole, hospitality included, is a more effective approach to evaluation against marketing objectives.

Management

There are two basic choices for the management of corporate hospitality – in- or out-of-house. In recent years the decision-making process has been impacted by the speed with which client organizations want their hospitality and consequently the supplier agencies have gained business. There are few organizations that have sufficiently experienced and/or trained event managers and the infancy of event management as a choice in higher education is testament to that. As a consequence, there are few organizations that will create and then manage external corporate hospitality programmes in their entirety. For many there is an agency involved somewhere along the line and therefore the choice for many is how much of the job is to be out-sourced.

The extent to which corporate hospitality and event management organizations supply, varies according to the level of service they provide, therefore there may also be more than one supplier for any one hospitality activity. The importance of monitoring, coordination and evaluation, as with any other outsourced service, will therefore rise as more providers become involved. Even with one supplier providing a complete hospitality programme it is clear that the host organization needs to manage its requirements. Clearer criteria for engagement, as per the other critical factors above, can make the job an easier one for those that have that job and while it has been the case, in the past that this has been the job that someone 'ends up with', there are indications that this is now being led by marketers.

For those organizations that are intent on managing events themselves there are now increasing numbers of trained and certificated event managers available. The development of event management in higher education, as a result of demand from industry, together with an emerging body of academic research and literature, is of major benefit to all those users of corporate hospitality and the management choices they have to make.

Summary

The development of corporate hospitality as a valuable marketing tool is arguably not yet fully mature. From simple beginnings, where invitations to corporately paid-for activities were derived from as many personal objectives as they were organizational objectives, the industry has come a long way. In the early stages of the growth of sponsorship, corporate hospitality provided many of the rights, and today it is still the number one choice of preferred rights. The industry is consequently large with a number of objectives sought by those organizations that are forecasted to spend up to nearly £800 million in 2006, in the UK alone (Mintel, 2002). Yet, these organizations have little credible evidence that these objectives are being met. The growth of the industry has been on less than solid foundations considering the lack of research, objectives setting and evaluation of results. Organizations somewhere in their decision making are making the assumption that using corporate hospitality can develop business prospects via the development of customer relationships, corporate image and product awareness, and internal relations. While these objectives are achievable, with an integrated marketing communications approach that researches and then strategically uses the opportunities, the important issue for every user of corporate hospitality, and the industry at large, is to what extent these objectives are being met. To answer that there is a considerable requirement for organizations to accept the need and devise the know-how for reliable evaluation.

Discussion points

- Identify an appropriate corporate hospitality activity for the organization you are currently employed by, or one you are sufficiently familiar with, and demonstrate your understanding of the critical factors for its success.
- Given the information in Case study 13.1, how would you organize the corporate hospitality activities for the Post Office and Procter and Gamble next year?
- Your organization is going through a slump in sales, has lost market share and is considering reducing its workforce. Given that you are working with an organization that has an integrated marketing communications approach, identify, in detail, how corporate hospitality might be used to assist the overall strategy for business development. Identify all of the issues you will need to deal with and how you will deal with them.

References

Barnard, T. (2003) Measure it or lose it – How to maintain your entertainment budget. *Marketing Business*, April.

Bennett, R. (2003) Corporate hospitality: Executive indulgence or vital corporate communications weapon? *Corporate communications: An International Journal*, 8 (4), 229–240.

CEA (2004) www.cha-online.co.uk/about.htm (accessed 28 September, 2004).

Cobb, R. (2003) Let me entertain you. Special Report. *Marketing Business*, April.

Flack, J. (1999) Slump action. *Marketing Week*, 4 March, 57–59.

IEG/Sponsorship Research (2004) 4th Annual Sponsorship Decision-Makers Survey. *IEG Sponsorship Report*. Sample Issue. IEG.

Irwin, R. (2002) Coming of age: Corporate Hospitality. *Marketing Business*, April, pp. 21–23.

Key Note (2000) Corporate Hospitality. Market Report, Executive Summary 2000. www.keynote.co.uk/kn2k1/10778_03//doc_19.htm?uni=1096437499 (accessed 29 September, 2004).

MAPS (1998) Corporate Hospitality. Market Report, July. www.the-list.co.uk/acatalog/mp74008.html (accessed 29 September, 2004).

Mintel (2002) *Corporate Hospitality*. Market Report, June. Mintel International Group Ltd.

Motivaction (2004) www.themotivactiongroup.co.uk (accessed 1 October, 2004).

Porter, M. (1985) *Competitive Advantage: Creating and Sustaining Superior Performance*. Free Press.

Sportsworld Group (2004) www.sportsworld-group.com/swg/casestudies (accessed 1 October, 2004).

Washington Redskins (2004) www.redskins.com (accessed 1 October, 2004).

Section Four

Ensuring Future Success

Attack is the best means of defence. Nike placed its giant replica footballs in key cities all over Europe prior to and during UEFA Euro 2004. The ball here is in Prague. This type of innovative ambush tactic, aimed at the event and its sponsor Adidas, is increasingly being used and is a concern for all event organizers and sponsors. This particular tactic demonstrates the level to which event communications need to go if they are to be successful. (Picture courtesy of Trish Coll, 2004.)

Ensuring future success is a necessary consideration for all in the events industry and this section considers the two key factors that are involved. The first, management control, ensures that day-to-day operations are managed to achieve objectives and that evaluation is undertaken in order to assist in future decision making. Chapter 14 considers the implementation, evaluation and control for marketing communications.

An increased usage of evaluation and feedback will help to professionalize and develop the events industry. Decisions for the next event will also be that much more informed. However, decisions are affected by external factors that are out of the organization's control and so, in order to make successful decisions, the second key factor is an awareness of the trends for the future and the industry at large. The last chapter therefore identifies some of the current thought on future implications for communications in the events industry.

Implementation Evaluation and Control

Trends and Forecasts

Chapter 14

Implementation, Evaluation and Control

Objectives

- ■ To consider the methods used for communications budget allocation and negotiation
- ■ To explain the process of communications plan implementation and the importance of internal marketing within this process
- ■ To emphasize the necessity of ongoing measurement and evaluation of communications activity
- ■ To understand the range of methods needed for measuring and evaluating marketing communications
- ■ To recognize the importance of ongoing evaluation for control purposes

Introduction

The management of the communications plan over the planning period is a vital aspect of the integrated marketing communications process and includes implementation through scheduling and resource allocation, measurement and evaluation and control. Ensuring the effectiveness of communication strategies is only possible if their impacts are measurable and can be regularly evaluated against the objectives set to ensure that the plan is meeting its aims. It is imperative that event marketing communicators understand the importance of this ongoing measurement and the variety of methods and data sources needed including operational data as well as the scanning of the external environment and direct research of customers. This data gathering helps to inform the development of future communication plans as well as providing control data to allow for adaptations in the current plan. The process of setting and adhering to a budget is an integral part of marketing communications planning and is closely related to the issues of measurement and control. The focus of this chapter is therefore on the importance of continuous monitoring of the plan in line with the budget, objectives and the implementation schedule. The areas of budget setting,

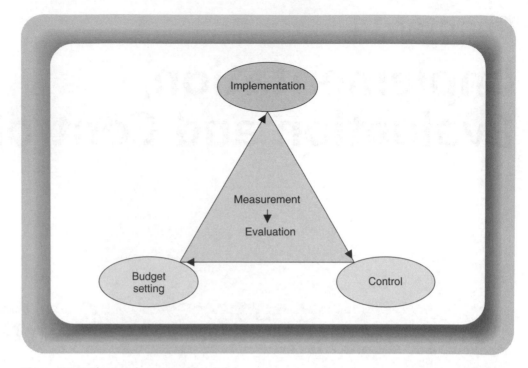

Figure 14.1 The implementation cycle.

implementation and control will be discussed along with an overview of the methods used in measuring and evaluating communications effectiveness and efficiency.

The process for implementing, evaluating and controlling the plan is illustrated in Figure 14.1, which shows the importance of measurement and evaluation to the three functions of implementation, control and budget setting.

Setting the communications budget

It could be argued that the budget should be set prior to the communications plan being determined as the budget available will be a constraining factor to be considered when developing the objectives, target audiences, methods and media. However, a communications plan which is soundly based on the information gathered in the situation analysis will have taken into account the resources of the company while considering and selecting the best course of action for the organization in terms of its marketing communications. Therefore, the budget required should be made available or at least be available for negotiation based upon what the plan will achieve.

There are many different methods for deciding an appropriate amount to spend on marketing communications and the selection of these is largely based upon the organization's operation in terms of profit making or non-profit making, funded through sales revenue or funded through donations, grants, government support and also by the organizational structure, functional roles, experience and general philosophy. For example, a customer-oriented event organization will view the communication budget differently from one that is product or profit oriented, with the former focusing on what is needed to achieve the desired effect on customers and the latter focusing on what can be afforded or what will give the best return.

The functional discipline of the organization's owners or managers will also affect the communications budget. A finance/accounting managerial style may lead to less spend on communications with a focus more on the bottom line (profit) and a marketing-led firm will push for more to be spent on communications in order to be competitive. It is often necessary, therefore, to prove to others in the organization that money allocated to marketing communications is worthwhile and produces a tangible return.

Measurement and evaluation of the communications plan is, therefore, necessary to justify the budget and as a basis for further budget negotiation as well as for control and information purposes.

According to Gullen (2003) communications budget-setting methods can be grouped into five types.

1 Inertia based (last year's budget, last year's budget plus or minus a percentage). This is appropriate if the market is stable and objectives are similar to previous years.
2 Business based (what's affordable, percentage of last year's sales). These methods treat communications purely as a cost without considering the return on investment. A commonly used figure is 10 per cent of projected sales for next year.
3 Media based (cost of media plan, cost of plan to achieve objectives). These methods depend on the appropriate briefing of the media agent and are particularly useful when the communications focus is on generating consumer 'pull'.
4 Competition based (match competitor, share of voice). It is advisable to monitor competitor spend on communications and build this into the benchmarking process. However, simply matching or bettering their spend may not achieve the same results as each firm's situational context is different.
5 Dynamic based (objective and task, experimentation, market modelling). Judging the amount needed based on what needs to be achieved is inherently the most logical approach but is also the most difficult as it requires estimates of the effect given a certain expenditure. This may use past data, competitor or other organizations' experience or statistical modelling using econometrics and response-curve analysis. The required analysis time can be off putting, however, the results can pay for themselves through improved communication return on investment.

The communications budget should, therefore, be based on a realistic assessment of the costs that are likely to be incurred in achieving communication objectives rather than on an extrapolation of past expenses or a percentage of past sales. This assessment may be based on previous experience if similar events or campaigns have been run before and evaluations of these are available or the assessment can be based on the activities of similar organizations and campaigns using competitor benchmarking to estimate the likely budget spend needed to achieve certain communication objectives. As many events are unique, take place infrequently and/or are one-offs then there will often be few past data on which to base the budget decision. A version of objective and task budget setting is therefore needed and this can be developed through competitor information, experimentation and 'feel'. The imperative for all companies is to ensure that a database of information (both within-company and information on competitors) is built up and can then be used to enhance the budget-setting process in the future (Fill, 2002).

Although the objective and task method is the ideal, in many organizations the budget will simply be handed down from 'on-high' and is therefore unlikely to be optimum for the task in hand. This often means that, whichever methods are used, after the budget has been set it may be necessary to revisit the objectives to ensure that they are still achievable within the financial resources available and, if not, the plan may need to be amended and the budget reallocated.

A further consideration in budget setting is the allocation of the communications budget between the various products or events within the organization's portfolio. It is not possible in these cases merely to determine the overall budget required to meet general communication goals. More complex modelling is required to ensure that an appropriate allocation is determined (Dyson, 2002) for each service offered, each event being produced or each venue used. Although, it is common practice to allocate budget on a strategic business unit (SBU) or brand basis, it can also be appropriate to base budget allocation on stakeholder groups or target audiences. For example, an organization producing a range of festivals may determine that 20 per cent of the budget is required to attract sponsors, 25 per cent is needed for the local community, 30 per cent is needed to attract national tourists, 15 per cent is allocated to media relations and 10 per cent is used to attract participants. The appropriateness of this method is largely determined by the timing of the events within the portfolio and whether or not they run consecutively or contiguously.

Examples of budget allocations are given in Table 14.1. The table illustrates how the budget allocation can be refined using a number of criteria. For example, if 40 per cent of the budget is allocated to achieving brand awareness then this can be achieved for both exhibitions shown using a variety of methods and may be targeted mainly at the new exhibitors. For costing purposes it would be possible, therefore, to say that 10 per cent of the budget spent on direct marketing is used to develop brand awareness in the new exhibitor target audience for Exhibition 1.

Table 14.1 Hierarchical budget allocation

Allocation by objectives (%)		Allocation by event (%)		Allocation by target audience (%)		Allocation by communication method (%)	
Increase brand awareness	40			Previous exhibitors	30	Direct marketing	25
		Exhibition 1	60			Print advertising	25
Encourage trial	30			First-time exhibitors	40	Public relations	10
		Exhibition 2	40			Website	15
Increase preference	30			Attendees	30	Sales promotion	25

Although this level of refinement is useful for cost allocation, it does not necessarily fit well with the idea of integrated marketing communications where the overall effect is of more importance than each individual component. For example, all of the communication methods are likely to have some effect on brand awareness, preference and trial in all target audiences for both events.

Implementing the communications plan

The communications strategy and tactics developed through the planning process can be translated into operational or implementation activities. Therefore, setting objectives becomes achieving objectives, effectiveness becomes efficiency, doing the right thing becomes doing things right, designing the plan equates to executing the plan and of course committing resources becomes using resources. These operational aspects are equally important to the original formulation of the plan.

The importance of implementation can be demonstrated through Bonoma's (1984) discussion of the four possible combinations of strategy and implementation. A plan with good strategic fit to the organization and the external environment, which is well implemented, will lead to success. A plan with poor strategic fit that is implemented well will lead to poor performance but this will be recognized, due to suitable monitoring, in time to make changes. A good strategy that is implemented badly can lead to trouble as the fault may initially be blamed on the strategy. Finally, an inappropriate strategy which is badly implemented will lead to failure as the strategic fault may not be noticed due to the poor implementation. This highlights the need to get the implementation right but also the importance of measurement, evaluation and control. Only through these processes can mistakes or unforeseen circumstances affecting the strategic fit be recognized and dealt with.

The reasons why the communications plan may be implemented badly vary but, if recognized, can be avoided. It may be that those who devise the plan do not have sufficient understanding or experience of the difficulties faced by those responsible for implementing the plan. This can happen in larger organizations where implementation is delegated from above without sufficient consultation and can also occur when there is a lack of understanding between a client and their communications agencies. Measurement and judgement on short-term factors can also badly affect implementation as this can lead to demotivation and erroneous adjustments to the plan. Resistance to change is a common difficulty facing those trying to implement something which is different from previous plans. Staff often feel more comfortable with existing ways of doing things and will be sceptical of new ways. Plans that lack detail in terms of timing, scheduling and roles and responsibilities required to achieve goals are likely to fail due to poor implementation. Individuals need to understand their responsibilities and feel able to undertake them. Implementation may therefore also require the identification of training needs.

Many of these potential dangers in plan implementation can be overcome through internal communication. Communication with other areas of the organization and with agencies is the realm of internal marketing and is a vital aspect of successful integrated marketing communications.

This internal communication begins during the plan's development through consultation and through keeping interested parties involved and informed and becomes critical when the plan is finalized and needs to be implemented. The communications plan needs to be marketed to others within the organization in order to gain their support, cooperation and enthusiasm. The goals within the plan need to be viewed as shared goals and the methods for achieving them need to be understood and appreciated by those who will be involved in implementing them.

The way in which this internal communication takes place is dependent on the organization's size, structure and culture. It is likely that those closely involved in implementing the plan will be included at an early stage ensuring that they understand their roles and responsibilities and that they receive sufficient training and skills development to enable them to do the job. This will be done through personal communication and consultative meetings. Those with a lesser involvement can be kept informed through less personal communication such as presentations, newsletters or the intranet. The key is to ensure that the whole organization understands what is to be achieved and supports these goals. Some understanding and appreciation of the methods to be used by those not directly involved helps ensure a shared purpose. The participation, involvement and empowerment of the operational staff who will implement the plan is crucial and this process can be started by using their knowledge, experience and expertise in the early stages of the planning process.

The main roles of the communications planner are organizing, initiating monitoring, and controlling and will, therefore, involve communication with a range of other organizations and individuals who can aid and support these roles including the other functional areas of the organization, subordinates and superiors, distributors, customers, agencies and consultants. Internal marketing of the plan is therefore vital to ensure that all parties involved understand what is to be achieved and their role in achieving it.

Table 14.2 gives an example of a document which could be used for internal marketing of the communications plan. This form of document summarizes the activities to be undertaken, giving an indication of the reasons why they have been chosen and an overview of when each activity will take place. Figure 14.2 provides a form for use in detailing how communications messages will be disseminated and can be used for internal and external communications.

The practical components of the implementation process encompass a range of areas and include:

- the action programme (the decisions and actions needed to implement the communications plan, responsibilities and timetable for these tasks)
- organizational structure (formal ties, lines of authority and communication)
- decision and reward system (formal and informal procedures that guide a company's activities such as planning, information gathering, budgeting, recruiting, training and control)
- human resources (skills, motivation, personal character)
- managerial climate and company culture (shared set of beliefs and values and the way management work together).

Table 14.2 An implementation plan summary for a local theatre

Media		Reach	Frequency	Impact	Timing	Vehicle
Word of mouth	Information sessions with volunteers, facilitators, targeted information sharers to pass along current information about all events	Extensive	Weekly	High	Month 1	Internal education sessions on corporate mission and event programmes
	Board member evangelism	1 new corporate member per board member	Every 3 months	High	Month 2 (following board member information session)	Board members will speak with people in their circle, about the current events. They can contact a targeted information sharer
Public relations	Public relations kit (press packet)	Media Local National Trade	Quarterly	Significant	Prepare by month 3	A folder with current press releases (as appropriate), fact sheet (mission, programme synopses), 100-, 50- and 25-word summaries. Pack ready to assemble and mail to press as requested
Digital	Website	Main attendee target audience. Existing and new customers	Continuous	Varies with use. Low for browsers, high for bookers	Develop months 2–4. Launch month 5. Continuous updating	Interactive site with on-line booking facility, regularly updated content and useful links
	Electronic version of the event programme	Opted-in customers requesting this format	Monthly (or more frequently as programme updated)	Moderate	Begin month 6	E-mailable brochure consisting of short snippets with separate content to encourage people to visit the site and other resources

Table 14.2 (*Continued*)

Media		Reach	Frequency	Impact	Timing	Vehicle
Events	Ensure presence at community events within catchment area	Local community and community groups	As events occur	Moderate	Summer	Information stand displaying events and encouraging participation as volunteer, sponsor, attendees
Direct marketing	Telesales	Corporates	Every 6 months	High	Month 3	Benefits of corporate sponsorship and hospitality
	Brochure and offer letters	Opted-in audience from database	Every 6 months and as offers available	Moderate	Month 2	Offers and information to encourage increased attendance and loyalty
Advertising	Local papers	Thirty mile radius of venue	Weekly	Low	Month 1	Focus on events occurring each week. Awareness within attendee catchment zone
	Local radio	Fifty mile radius of venue	Weekly	Low	Month 1	Focus on events occurring each week Awareness within attendee catchment zone

Marketing communications dissemination plan for: Activity name here

Item description:

Objective:

Associated items:

Dissemination methods summary

Area (For example: Wales)	Stakeholder Title (For example: current attendees)	Item Name (Message to be conveyed)	Dissemination Method (For example: postal, e-mail, personal contact, advert)	Delivery Method (For example: 3rd party mail house, e-mail list, exhibition, magazine)	Timing (Development time and delivery schedule)	Comments (Additional materials required)

Figure 14.2 Pro forma for a dissemination plan.

For many organizations within the events industry it will not be possible to create, produce and implement the communications campaign in-house. A range of specialisms, expertise and experience is required and also a considerable investment in time. For many organizations this will mean using communications agencies to undertake some or all of the campaign development and implementation. The selection of the right agency or agencies, therefore, becomes one of the main tasks of the campaign planner and will have a great impact on the success and integration of the campaign. Selecting the right agency or agencies should be a formalized and disciplined process as the agency chosen will be one of the organization's key suppliers in that they can have an immediate and long-lasting effect on business success. A relationship needs to be developed between the event organization and the agency based on professionalism, trust and confidence underpinned by a carefully drawn up legal contract. The relationship should be one of partnership and will require close working practices with a clear delineation of roles and responsibilities and understood expectations. Friction that often develops through the creative ideas of the agency not seeming to match the client's communications problems can be best solved through detailed pre-testing and research to give reassurance and confidence. Where the client and the agency work together to develop appropriate metrics and measurement systems the better chance there is for a harmonious relationship and a fuller understanding of how the communications work (Admap, 2004).

If a number of different communication methods are chosen it may be necessary to appoint a number of specialist agencies and, therefore, integration and consistency of message become more difficult to achieve. In many cases it is better to appoint an agency that can provide or at least manage the whole campaign. This may mean that they outsource aspects to other agencies but that they maintain overall control and in this way can ensure the required integration, consistency and complementarity and also manage the complex scheduling and implementation aspects (Figure 14.3).

However, although organizations recognize that control over the whole promotional process achieves greater synergy, there is not always agreement over whether this control should be put in the hands of an agency or managed in-house. Those that opt to maintain control themselves usually do so as they feel that agencies lack the expertise in the supporting areas of database marketing, marketing research and information technology (Abatt and Cowan, 1999). These client perceptions are now increasingly being dealt with through the emergence of agencies that can provide the supporting research, measurements and metrics and who work closely with the client's own marketing team in order to ensure that the communications decisions are based upon the best information available. This is further proof of the need for agency–client relationships to be at a partnership level where information can be shared in an atmosphere of mutual trust and commitment.

Research by Blueprint Communications using Association of National Advertisers (ANA) members found that most believed that integration could not be achieved through a 'holding company' agency but needed to be client led with the organization facilitating the process by bringing together the various agencies for a briefing and ensuring that all understand the total business plan (Shelton and O'Gorman, 2004). Creating opportunities for open communications internally and externally helps improve the IMC process along with centralized control over the brand message.

Successful integration requires customer insight, planning processes, consistency in execution and trust to encourage open collaboration between the client organization and the various agencies employed.

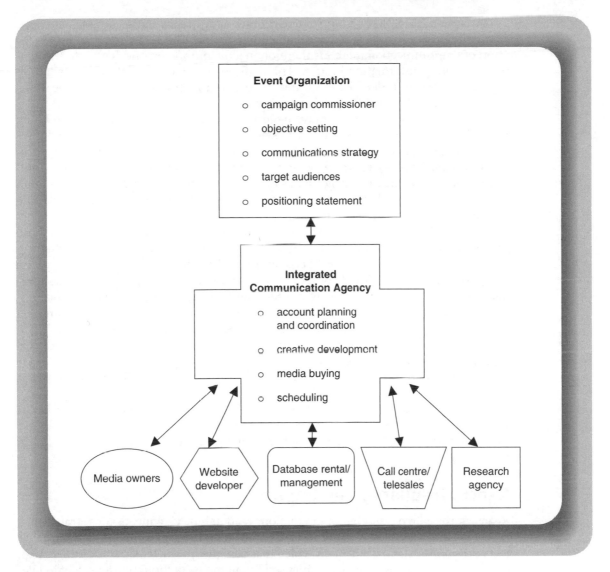

Figure 14.3 Communication agency as the coordinator.

Measurement and evaluation

This phase of communications is often neglected and this omission is often compounded within the events industry where the planning focus quickly moves on to the next event. A lack of evaluation of the event itself is common and therefore evaluation of the communications methods used for the event is even less likely to occur. However, this is a dangerously short-term view as it is only through objective and systematic measurement and evaluation of the actions taken in the plan that the organization can understand whether it has met its goals and can learn from the experience, therefore improving competitive advantage in the future.

The earlier discussion relating to budgeting and implementation stresses the need for these decisions to be based on reliable information. The measurement and evaluation of communication methods therefore needs to draw on and feed into the central marketing information system. This will ensure that a variety of information sources is used in order to get a fuller picture and integration of communications with the rest of the marketing mix variables.

Eadie and Kitchen (1999) strongly suggest that measurement and evaluation in the form of research should take place in all stages of the campaign, from problem definition research, strategy definition research, through to creative development research, execution and then effectiveness testing and finally in-market evaluation. The result of each of these evaluation stages feeds into the next stage or suggests a return to an earlier stage. The whole process is circular with the problem definition process at the start of the next campaign being informed by the results of prior evaluations.

It is relatively easy to undertake the pre-campaign testing and evaluation as these can be done under controlled conditions. However, the final stages of evaluating the campaign once it is in-market becomes more difficult as isolating the effect of the campaign and its individual components from other factors operating on the market is notoriously difficult and will affect the validity of any evaluation findings. This is, perhaps, why many in-market measurements focus only on the tangible aspects of exposure – reach and direct response. The intermediate effects of each communication component can be measured such as campaign recall, brand perception and awareness, but the effect on behavioural and attitudinal changes is far more difficult to attribute to a particular aspect of a communications campaign (unless related to direct response).

The communications campaign needs to be evaluated for effectiveness (most effect), efficiency (least waste) and economy (least cost). These factors relate closely to the impact, reach and frequency of the campaign's media components in relation to the target audiences.

Reach, frequency and impact

Reach is measured in terms of circulation, readership, viewing figures, traffic-hits, mail-outs, attendance and many industry bodies and research reports regularly collect and publish standard data on which to assess media reach (e.g. JICNARS, BARB, CAA, TGI, BRAD[1]). Rating points are used for all media (although extensively in television where they are known as TVRs) and combine measures of reach and frequency.

Frequency measures the average number of times a member of the target audience will be exposed to the message and is measured in opportunities to see (OTS) or hear (OTH). Although normally calculated for each element of the campaign, in an integrated campaign it is useful to assess the total number of exposures or 'brand contacts'. In some media many exposures may be needed to gain the desired effect (such as radio, outdoor), whereas those with higher impact (such as promotional events, cinema ads, dramatic ambient media) may require fewer.

It is therefore necessary to consider impact alongside reach and frequency. Impact is related to getting the message noticed and is more intangible in terms of measurement. To assess impact, which is created through a combination of the

---

[1] BRAD – British Advertising Directory; BARB – Broadcasters' Audience Research Board; CAA – Cinema Advertising Association; JICNARS – Joint Industry Committee for National Readership Surveys; TGI – Target Group Index.

creativity of the message, the medium chosen to deliver it and the timing and frequency of exposure, then qualitative techniques are needed alongside simpler quantitative measures.

Rating points are a calculation of reach multiplied by frequency, for example, reach measured in a percentage of the target market exposed to the communication multiplied by the OTS or OTH for that medium. A full-page advertisement in a music/lifestyle magazine aimed at 15–20-year-old males may reach 30 per cent of that target market with each advertisement. If the advertisement is placed in the magazine for three months then there are three opportunities to see it (OTS). This therefore gives this aspect of the campaign ninety gross rating points (GRPs). However, this does not mean that 90 per cent of the audience has been exposed as each 30 per cent may have seen the advertisement more than once. The measure gives an average rating only but is useful in providing standard figures which can be compared across media, although a higher GRP does not necessarily imply that a campaign is better than those with a lower GRP as this depends on other factors. A further refinement can be used which is to take account of the impact of each medium and use it as weighting. This is achieved by multiplying the GRP by a relative impact score.

An additional factor in media evaluation is, of course, the cost. This is often compared in cost per thousand (CPT), so that the reach of the medium is taken into account. Although these are CPT figures, they are often provided by the media owner and so it is more reliable for the campaign planner to calculate them by basing the figure on target audience rather than total audience reached. It is calculated by simply dividing the cost of the item of marketing communication by the number of members of the target audience reached and then multiplying the answer by one thousand.

The factors of reach, frequency, impact and cost should all be evaluated prior to making media choices, but should also form the basis for evaluating the media after the campaign. It is necessary to consider if objectives have been met in terms of reach and frequency and whether or not the media had the expected impact. On this basis decisions can be made on whether the best media were selected and the best media mix chosen for the budget spent.

Measuring campaign effect

The measures discussed above relate solely to evaluating the media used. In addition, it is also necessary to measure the combined effects of method, media and message on the target audience. The overall effects of the campaign can be measured through application of the following criteria:

- *Relevance* – was the message appropriate and clear in purpose?
- *Clarity* – was the message coherent and easily understood?
- *Credibility* – was the message believable and trustworthy?
- *Response* – what was the registered impact of the message?
- *Satisfaction* – was the audience satisfied with the communication?

Techniques that can be used include post-testing using focus groups to assess effectiveness once the external factors of competing messages and environmental influences have been added to the campaign effects. These can provide very detailed rich data of use in fine-tuning the existing campaign and for improving future developments.

Surveys can be used to produce a snap shot of recall, recognition, likeability and behavioural intentions. These, however, are of most use if they can be compared to some form of normative data gathered from previous campaigns or benchmarks.

'Pre-post' longitudinal research collects data at regular intervals from a panel before, during and after campaigns so as to infer changes in behaviour related to the communications effect. These can be useful in proving a return on investment and in depicting the longer-term effect of marketing communications. They are limited, however, in providing reasons for behavioural changes in that they do not explain how the effects are occurring. They are, therefore, of limited use as an input to the creative process but can be used successfully in forecasting and predicting likely behavioural effects.

Tracking studies also use a longitudinal methodology but take samples rather than using a panel. The focus of tracking studies are the cognitive processes triggered by the campaign in terms of recall, message internalization, brand awareness and attitude, and purchase intention. These can be very resource intensive but provide the most comprehensive and reliable data for campaign evaluation. In order to defray some of the costs, syndicated tracking surveys are offered by some agencies where the costs are shared between a number of different participating organizations.

Due to the often relatively large investment in communications, it is important to ensure that all elements of the campaign are tested before, during and after the campaign itself. The variety of methods used to measure communications effectiveness are summarized in Table 14.3. Likeability tests have emerged as an important and most reliable predictor of sales success (Fill, 2002) and are used to measure the 'likeability' of the marketing communication (advertisement, sales promotion, website, direct marketing material) rather than the likeability of the product, brand or organization. Although there is a significant link between communication likeability and purchase behaviour, there is a far stronger link between likeability of the product and purchase. There are many instances where the audience may like the advertisement considerably but would not consider buying the product. Therefore, this type of test needs to be combined with research into brand image, brand preference and brand liking.

Although it is also important to evaluate each component of the communications mix in an integrated campaign, it is often difficult, if not impossible, to separate the effects of each component. Evaluation should therefore include the overall effects of the campaign in line with the communication objectives. If these have not been achieved or have been exceeded, it is then possible to investigate each component in order to try to determine where the particular weaknesses and strengths lie. Reach and ROI (return on investment) based measures can be combined to assess the individual components and also to track the longer-term branding impacts (Mandese, 2003). However, it needs to be clear that any return on investment measures need to include cognitive, emotional and aspirational effects as well as those relating to behavioural changes.

Hayman and Schultz (1998) recommend a move away from measuring ROI to a focus on ROCI (return on customer investment) and evaluate target audiences or key customer groups. They recommend that this is measured using consumer panels and that longitudinal data are collected covering a number of years. The type of data collected should include attitudinal and behavioural information that is converted to income flows for comparison with the investment received. What results is information that is clearly linking communication investment to specific customer groups and a measure of the effect of that investment on their behaviour and therefore ultimately the profit of the organization. This is a useful technique for the focusing of budget allocation on to target audience needs and for the justification of communication expenditure through quantifiable results.

A holistic approach to marketing communications research is recommended by Archer and Hubbard (1996) where the focus for research efforts is on the tracking of the overall communication effects so that the following questions can be answered:

- how well are target audiences being reached and involved?
- what messages are consumers receiving about the brand?
- what are consumers doing?
- what would they prefer to do?
- why would they prefer to do that?
- what is hindering or helping them?

A holistic system should also measure short-term tactical effects as well as longer-term strategic ones and cover both above and below the line communications. Many of these questions can be answered through the adaptation of a fairly standardized survey used as the basis for repeated tracking of these effects. HI Europe (2004), a marketing communications research agency, suggests that this should include the following:

- screening questions
- brand equity questions
- unaided and aided brand awareness
- aided recognition
- usage and purchase intent
- aided awareness of brand and competitor brands
- copy point recall
- brand imagery.

Individual communications evaluation and measurement

Although there are many measurements and evaluation methods which are suitable for the majority of communication methods, it is also necessary to recognize methods which are particularly suited to specific methods. An overview of some of these methods related to each communication technique is given in Table 14.3.

For example, sales promotions will usually include some form of direct response or call to action mechanism. It is therefore relatively easy to measure the behavioural effects of this type of communication through directly attributable incremental sales, redemption of voucher, offer take ups and participation rates. Similarly, direct marketing methods, due to their interactivity, can incorporate a measure of success in terms of, for example, the number of leads generated, the quality or length of the relationship developed, or a direct behavioural response in terms of tickets booked, sponsorship obtained or willingness to be contacted again.

Advertising effects are not so easily attributable to behaviour and are therefore more often measured in terms of reach, likeability and general awareness and attitude. The attitudinal and behavioural changes taking place during an advertising campaign can be measured but cannot necessarily be associated with the advertising itself as other elements of the campaign will also be affecting the target audience.

The problems associated with measuring and evaluating the effect of corporate hospitality as a communications tool often stem from a lack of clear objectives for this method. If the objectives set have been done so realistically then they will be

Table 14.3 An overview of measurement and evaluation techniques

Communication method	Pre-test	During and Post-test
Advertising	Concept testing Focus groups Consumer juries Dummy vehicles Test markets Theatre tests Physiological measures	Enquiry test Recall test Recognition tests Tracking studies Likeability tests Copy point recall
Sales promotion	Concept testing Focus groups Test markets Dummy vehicles	Redemption Sales Enquiries Leads Direct responses Contact data collected
Direct marketing	Concept tests Copy/script tests	Enquiries Sales Contact data collected Opt-ins Copy point recall Pass-ons
Personal selling	Script tests Dummy runs	Sales Sales per visit Sales per lead No. of pitches Invitations to bid
Sponsorship	Brand 'fit' tests Focus groups	Equivalent media cost Brand awareness changes Brand preference Brand image changes Tracking studies
Corporate hospitality	Concept testing	Likeability Corporate image changes
Promotional events	Concept testing Focus groups Brand 'fit' tests	Contacts/opt-ins Attendance figures Sales Trials Media coverage Likeability Brand awareness Brand preference Word of mouth
Websites/on-line	Usability tests	Usability Hits, click-throughs Registrations Sales Opt-ins

Continued

Table 14.3 (*Continued*)

Communication method	Pre-test	During and Post-test
Public relations	Focus groups Consumer juries Journalist audits	Press cuttings Equivalent media cost Media evaluation Tracking studies Journalist audits

measurable. For example, a simple measure may be the number of invitees taking up the offer of hospitality. However, this does not prove effectiveness of the method itself but only the attractiveness of the offer. As corporate hospitality is often aimed at rewarding existing customers and strengthening relationships, the effects need to be measured through attitudinal research rather than behavioural.

The development of a variety of metrics to evaluate websites and other online marketing techniques has spawned a specialist industry in its own right. The focus is no longer simply on the highly quantifiable measures of user behaviour such as click through rates (CTR) and cost per click (CPC) but on developing more qualitative measures which assess effectiveness from the users' point of view rather than the technical ability of the website. The wealth of quantitative data available through a variety of software tracking systems now needs to be supplemented with qualitative measures focusing on attitudes, perceptions and motivations. There also needs to be more pre-campaign measurement to anticipate consumer action rather than simply measuring it when it occurs (Goodwin, 2004).

Many of the desired outcomes of promotional events can often be measured during and immediately after the event. This may be in terms of attendance, participation and enjoyment or more specifically brand related in terms of number of exposures, product trials or related requests for information, website visits and sales promotion take-ups. The longer-term effects on participants need to be measured through tracking studies, focusing on attitude and behaviour changes as a result of event participation.

Public relations effectiveness can be measured at two levels. First, the functional level of the amount of publicity generated usually measured in equivalent advertising costs but, as discussed in Chapter 5, there are considerable flaws in this approach. Secondly, the effects on stakeholder attitudes and perception of corporate image where research can be used which directly relates the exposure to media commentary and the attitude to the company and can be done at a local, national and international level. The lower investment needed in public relations often leads to a neglect of evaluation, but this tool's effectiveness should not be overlooked. With objective measurement it is possible to show that a small relative increase in budget spend on public relations can lead to large gains in attitudinal and behavioural changes in a range of stakeholder audiences.

For event organizations the measurement of sponsorship effectiveness is doubly important. First, to measure the effect of their own organizations' sponsorship of an event and secondly, and more importantly, perhaps is to measure the effectiveness of their sponsors' spend. This second area is vital to provide a full service to sponsors, to show return on sponsorship investment, to understand the promotional potential of the event and to provide evidence for use in future sponsorship pitches and negotiation. Sponsorship effectiveness can be measured in a number of ways. Many companies attempt to associate increased sales with sponsorship exposure, however, isolating the effect of sponsorship when used alongside other communications elements is prone to error and overestimations. A simple and commonly used method is to calculate the amount of equivalent media value, but this is increasingly receiving criticism as it fails accurately to measure effects on the audience. More suitable is some measure of the communication effects through cognitive impact and using consumer perceptions. These effects can be measured through one-off measures or more usefully through longitudinal tracking studies and involve a variety of cueing questions to ascertain sponsorship awareness (Tripodi, 2003).

As can be seen from the discussion above, although some attitude and behaviour changes can be directly associated with a specific communication method, it is difficult to isolate the effect of each. For integrated marketing communication campaigns, therefore, it is more appropriate to measure the overall effects in terms of attitudes to the event, organization and brand and the effects on preference and purchase behaviour. Evaluation of the individual components should not be overlooked but should concentrate on the more easily attributable measures of reach, exposure and impact.

Control

Control is the process of using measurement and evaluation of marketing communications strategies and plans to monitor, and take corrective action if needed, to ensure that communication objectives are achieved.

The principles of control are that often the variances spotted are caused by a few small areas rather than the whole plan. Control should focus on those areas where there is the greatest opportunity for influence. Control is most important at the point of action and therefore, managers need the means to effective control which are, first, adequate data and secondly, the appropriate authority and responsibility.

In order to control the marketing communications plan it is necessary to specify the feedback data required, collect the data through whichever methods are most appropriate, evaluate the data against the staged communication objectives and budget allocations and then take corrective action. This process therefore requires continuous tracking, monitoring and, where necessary, reassessment and adjustment of the communications strategy. The units for control analysis need to be broken down to ensure that problem areas can be identified. This may mean ensuring that each communications method and medium is evaluated separately but should also include a breakdown of the overall communication results for each target audience, each event, each distribution channel or each venue.

The control of the marketing communications plan takes place at a number of levels. At the highest level there is strategic control which focuses on whether or not the organization is pursuing its best opportunities. This requires the scanning of the external environment alongside monitoring the effects of the communications implementation and being willing to adjust the plan if new opportunities arise. Efficiency control concentrates on the usage of the budget and assesses whether or not expenditure is being wasted or would be better reallocated elsewhere. Finally, effectiveness control assesses the plan based on whether or not the expenditure and action is having the desired effect. Case study 14.1 illustrates how effective control is only possible if measurable objectives have been set for the marketing communications implemented.

The Barnes Exhibit

This event took place between September and December 1994 and involved the exhibiting of one of the finest collections of post-impressionist paintings to come to Toronto, Canada. The collection consisted of Renoir, Cézanne, van Gogh, Picasso and Monet paintings and was owned by the prestigious Barnes Foundation (founded by Dr Albert Barnes). The venue, the Art Gallery of Ontario (AGO), set ambitious targets of 50 000 pre-sold and 500 000 total tickets and in so doing, identified the need for a dedicated communications plan.

Situation analysis

Consumer research was undertaken in order to establish ticket pricing, opening times, attendance forecasts and possible buying motivation factors.

This research revealed a very low awareness of Dr Barnes and the Foundation and only marginal awareness for the artists even when prompted. Separately run AGO member and non-member focus groups also revealed a low awareness of the Foundation and moderate interest in the artists. The research also revealed an anxiety of whether genuine pictures would be shown and perceptions of intimidation both from the gallery and art in general. The AGO was also not considered a top Toronto attraction.

Objectives

Measurable targets were set at 500 000 tickets to be sold, 10 per cent of which were to be pre-sold prior to the event. In addition, the extra onus of achieving 42 000 room nights at Toronto hotels was set (a Government stipulation).

Strategy

The creative task was to produce communications that would increase awareness and build excitement in the gallery, the artists and the event. There was a nine-month period in which to achieve it.

Research assisted decisions determined ticket prices at CN$15 and opening times of 11 hours per day from 17 September to 31 December, 1994.

In order to simplify the message, the campaign would focus on the event and created the title, 'The Barnes Exhibit'. The title was kept deliberately short for variable use in print advertising, transport, television, direct marketing and public relations. A further control was set for the 50 000 pre-sold tickets of three-months in advance. In order to be able to measure performance, a four-stage strategy with controls was devised:

- *Educational stage*: generate interest and build awareness about the event, the artists and the significance of Dr Barnes. A sense of urgency was to be created with a 'limited time only' effect.
- *Pre-launch and launch stage*: intense activity in the four weeks leading up to the event. Word of mouth had to create public anticipation.
- *Sustaining stage*: use of testimonials during the event to enhance the experience of the event. In addition, tactical advertising would be utilized for key holidays, Sunday evening and same-day ticket promotions and to counter sold-out rumours. This stage in particular

required flexibility and the capacity to respond which, in turn, required constant use of performance indicators.
- *Countdown stage*: generate interest right through to the end of the event.

A budget of CN$1 million was set and of that, 70 per cent had to be spent out of metropolitan Toronto as part of the agreement with the Ontario Government to ensure this was a province-wide campaign. The communications were executed as follows:

- *News media advertising*: small mono advertisements were placed in various sections of key newspapers such as the *Toronto Star* (non-AGO traditional target audience), *Globe and Mail* (primary target audience) in April, May, June and July. Three advertisements were run each week, but every insertion had a changed headline and a ticket number. The numbers allowed sales to be tracked for effectiveness. No actual art was depicted in the advertisements so as not to alienate and increase the anxiety revealed in the research.
- *Transport and television advertising*: consistent design was used to emphasize the visual aspects of the event with colour and art in advertisements that were run from August in the pre and launch stage.
- *Direct marketing*: this was an important element for the out-of-Toronto reach. The primary targets were travel agents and hotels within a day's drive (Ottawa, London, Kitchener, Montreal, Buffalo, Syracuse, Detroit, Chicago and Cleveland). A brochure was produced and sent to members of out-of-town galleries that had provided mailing lists.
- *Public relations*: centred on launch week with a 'must-see' theme. By this time the pre-sales target had already been exceeded with a total of 250 000 tickets pre-sold, but the planned activities were still executed in order to maintain the momentum.

Results

The 'Barnes' became a must-see event by exceeding its budgeted targets. In all, 597 000 tickets were sold, almost 20 per cent up on budget and the pre-sales were five times the original target of 50 000. An added benefit was the increase on average merchandise sales at CN$12 per person.

Post-event research by the Ontario Government evaluated that 60 per cent of event attendees were from outside of metropolitan Toronto and that the 42 000 hotel room nights target was exceeded.

The importance of setting measurable targets for the evaluation of performance are highlighted in this case.

Source: Addison et al. (1995).

The control function is therefore vital in ensuring that a poorly designed or implemented plan is identified as quickly as possible and that corrective action is taken. This relies on a continual flow of pertinent information on which to measure the success of the plan against the objectives and the changes in the external environment and the authority and ability to adjust the plan accordingly. The control system is illustrated diagrammatically in Figure 14.4.

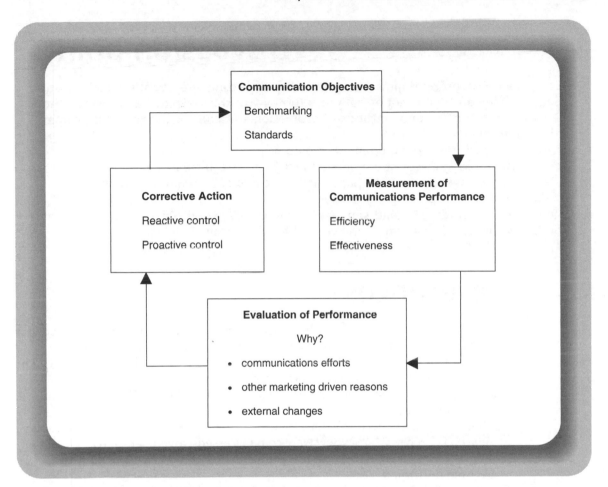

Figure 14.4 Marketing communications control system.

Summary

It can be seen that information in the form of measurement and evaluation of that information against clearly defined objectives is needed to underpin and support the budgeting, implementation and control aspects of marketing communications planning. Although these are not the creative or perhaps exciting elements of event communications they are, nonetheless, vital to success and should not be overlooked. Time and resources should be allocated to these tasks in the early planning stages to ensure that they are undertaken appropriately.

The use of internal marketing and internal communications is vital if the plan is to be implemented smoothly and effectively, making use of the resources and expertise available and ensuring that all those involved understand their roles and responsibilities and the overall aims and objectives of the plan.

Once in the process of being implemented all the components of the communications plan as well as the plan's overall effects need to be monitored, measured and evaluated at regular intervals. These evaluations will then be used to form the basis of control decisions which may lead to adjustments to the plan and therefore suggest the need for in-built flexibility and the recognition of contingencies.

Discussion points

- Compare the appropriateness and practicality of setting the event's communication budget based on 10 per cent of last year's turnover or the 'objective-and-task' method.
- Discuss the measures and methods of evaluation suitable for the following communication methods:
  - PR generated through an opening ceremony
  - an early booking discount e-mailed to last year's exhibitors
  - an advertisement in the local paper giving details of a community festival
  - the website of a sporting association.
- Consider Case study 14.1 and summarize the link between objectives, implementation, measurement, evaluation and control for the Barnes Exhibit.

References

Abatt, R. and Cowan, D. (1999) Client–agency perspectives of information needs for media planning. *Journal of Advertising Research*, November/December.

Addison, E., Comelia, F., Satterthwaite, A. et al. (1995) Art Gallery of Ontario: The Barnes Exhibit. www.warc.com (accessed 13 October, 2004).

Admap (2004) Choosing and using agencies. *Admap*, May (450), 19–20. Available from www.warc.com.

Archer and Hubbard (1996) Integrated tracking for integrated communications. *Admap*, February, 22–26. www.warc.com (accessed November, 2004).

Bonoma, T.V. (1984) Making your marketing strategy work. *Harvard Business Review*, 62, March–April, p. 72.

Dyson, P. (2002) Setting the communications budget. *Admap*, November (433), 39–42. Available from www.warc.com.

Eadie, D.R. and Kitchen, P.J. (1999) Measuring the success rate: evaluating the marketing communications process and marcom programmes. In *Marketing Communications: Principles and Practice*. International Thomson Business Press.

Fill, C. (2002) *Integrated Marketing Communications*. Butterworth-Heinemann.

Goodwin, T. (2004) Measuring the effectiveness of online marketing. *Journal of the Market Research Society*, 41 (4).

Gullen, P. (2003) 5 steps to effective budget setting. *Admap*, July (441), 22–24. Available from www.warc.com.

Hayman, D.W. and Schultz, D.E. (1998) Connecting the dots: From ROI to ROBI to ROCI. Measuring returns on marketing communication investments. *Advertising Research Foundation Workshop*, October. Available from www.warc.com.

HI Europe (2004) Marketing communications research. www.hieurope.com (accessed July, 2004).

Mandese, J. (2003) Media ink: Media planning's new crossroads. *Admap*, December (445), 8. Available from www.warc.com.

Shelton, D. and O'Gorman, R. (2004) Advertisers disappointed with marketing integration. *The Advertiser*, February, 48–51. Available from www.warc.com.

Tripodi, J.A. (2003) Cognitive evaluation. Prompts used to measure sponsorship awareness. *International Journal of Market Research*, 45 (4), 435–455.

Chapter 15
Trends and Forecasts

Objectives

- To consider the current and future trends in the events industry
- To appreciate the changes occurring in the market place
- To discuss the developments in marketing practice and theory
- To understand the likely effects of these and other changes on marketing communications methods and media

Introduction

Marketing communications within the events industry must continuously evolve as the industry and the market place change. These changes in event products, customer preferences, competitive forces, market types and locations, along with changes such as technological advances and economic ups and downs, create an operating environment that is highly dynamic. It is necessary, therefore, for event organizations to understand and take account of these changes in any long-term planning.

Predicting the future, of course, is never an exact science and various contrasting scenarios may be forecast by different experts and interested parties at different times. However, by using past trends and present indications it is possible to be fairly accurate in a number of areas. For example, population changes can be predicted, as can general economic cycles. Using these data along with informed estimates of other trends can create the edge needed for long-term success in an industry. The events firm that successfully predicts and anticipates future customer needs can gain considerable competitive advantage through innovation to meet those needs, whether this be in the products and services it offers, or through the way it communicates those offerings.

In order to plan for future communications strategies it is, therefore, useful to recognize some of the trends occurring in a number of related areas. This chapter will focus on the areas of the events industry (structure, size and types of events), the marketplace (customer types and preferences), developments in marketing theory and practice and finally, the methods and media used for marketing communications.

Trends in events

One of the major trends that appears to be continuing in both consumer and business markets is the move towards smaller, more narrowly focused events. In the exhibition industry past data and current predictions show that these events are becoming more specialized, diversified and more targeted. However, this also means that they are increasing in number. Where a number of exhibitions' content complements each other and they aim for the same target audience, they are increasingly running alongside each other or operating as shows within shows (Keynote, 2004a). This trend increases the scope for trialling new shows and also increases the opportunity for partnerships between venues, organizers and exhibitors. Similar trends can also be seen in the conference/convention sector where there are fewer attendees at each conference but an increasing number of conferences and meetings being held.

As consumer society becomes more individualistic and mass media tends to be viewed as less of an instrument for creating or reinforcing socially acceptable behaviour, target markets will become more and more fragmented. This can already be seen in musical tastes, clothing and entertainment choices. This may signal the demise of the global appeal of music performers and the mass crowd mega-venue type pop concerts that have dominated the last ten years. Individualism will be demonstrated by attendance at smaller specialized, art, music or even sports events or through larger festivals where individuals can pick and mix from a variety of entertainment on offer.

However, the increased number of such events needs to be managed and targeted carefully or the already information and decision overloaded consumer will be further confused by the proliferation of choices. This can already be seen in areas of the exhibition industry where the sheer number of events related to a particular manufacturer's industry prevents them from choosing one to exhibit at. This can also be seen in the increasing number of smaller sporting events, tournaments and competitions which lead to a possible dilution of participants and spectator overload, confusion and hence avoidance.

This continued growth in the number of small firms in the industry offering specialist services suggests that outsourcing of more services will become the norm and that the role of the event organizer will evolve into one of acting solely as the coordinating agency.

The move towards smaller events of all types is not solely driven by the move towards individualism and customization, but is also likely to be related to increased levels of anxiety, insecurity and pessimism in society. These feelings, fuelled by world events, changes in social structures and media coverage, are likely to increase the perceived risk levels involved in attending a large event at a conspicuous venue. This may be one of the factors contributing to the decline in sports event attendance, although a more influential factor is the increased availability of home-based spectating through media broadcasts.

The use of home based or other personalized ways of accessing sports events has already increased dramatically and is set to grow further through wider accessibility of pay-per-view and interactive television and the Internet. These viewing methods allow tailored match choices, player focus and even camera angle selection providing a spectator controlled experience. The growth in viewing via these methods will undoubtedly change the dynamics of the marketing of the event, in that the main audience are likely not to be those that physically attend and therefore their experiences will need to be managed differently. Despite these changes, interactive television has positive implications for consumer choice and audience building as well as revenue creation through advertising, sponsorship and merchandising (Mintel, 2003).

Although web broadcast coverage of sports will increase with its acceptance with broadband technology, it is unlikely to be taken up to the same extent as interactive television due to the social setting of the television versus the computer. As technologies converge and the Internet is accessed via the television or at least from the living room of the home then this will be a more viable means of broadcasting sports events.

The definition of events as products and services in their own right will become more difficult to ascertain as the traditional distinctions become blurred. This dedifferentiation is prevalent in many areas as industries converge and as consumers and sponsors demand more from the event experience. There is already a merging of the roles of event sponsor and organizer and overlaps between customer and suppliers. These roles were once defined by supply and demand and financial transactions, but are now more likely to be based on mutually beneficial partnerships. The venue may be paid in exchange for its space or may pay a fee to the performer. The event itself along with its attendees may be 'bought' as a product by television programmers. Although this trend offers more opportunities than threats for event organizations, it does suggest that traditional ways of doing business may need to change and that the 'product' is viewed as widely as possible in order to take advantage of these opportunities.

Perhaps a more controversial issue related to this dedifferentiation is in the creation of events for commercial purposes. This is not necessarily new, but does appear to be becoming more prevalent as brands seek newer ways to interact with their target audiences. These commercially created as opposed to naturally evolved events can be seen occurring in many tourism strategies around the world where a festival or cultural event has been developed to boost visitor numbers and attract business tourism. However, the longer-term efficacy of these is yet to be proven. The music industry has also seen an increase in the number of sponsor created tours and the growth in commercial sponsors seeking out new talent to get in before the competition. In the future, it is likely that commercially focused interest will start at an earlier stage in the 'manufacturing' of bands or performers to embody the brand image needs of a particular sponsor. This is already the case with commercial content in an increasing number of television programmes created with the increasing use of product placement.

This move to a greater brand involvement in the music industry will be fuelled by the decline in worldwide recorded music sales (Mintel, 2004a) which, in turn, has led to a lack of support by record companies for artists' tours. It will, therefore, no longer be financially viable for record companies to instigate and finance the tour leaving the live music industry reliant upon an increase in commercially created tours that provide sponsorship platforms. The commercial need may, therefore, replace the previous objections by artists who complained that sponsorship was an infringement of artistic integrity.

The growth in corporate social responsibility and cause-related marketing is also leading to the corporate sector's increased involvement in the music, arts and sports sectors. This may take several forms, for example, Jaguar Cars commissioning local artists to create a sculpture of a jaguar, Manolo Blahnik shoes being displayed in the artistic space of the Design Museum or the creation of street sports tournaments by Coca-Cola. Although this is undoubtedly beneficial in terms of financial support and exposure for the art form or sport, it also can be seen as overly controlling in the desire for the corporate partner to receive something tangible in return.

The controversy with these commercially created events, therefore, relates to the potential erosion of artistic integrity and the move away from the philosophy of 'art for art's sake'. Whether the event is music, visual arts, culture or sport based, from the audience and the participants' perspective there will always be the need for honesty in the core product. Events are the means to showcase artistic ability, sporting prowess and cultural heritage and this inherent integrity of the product may become tainted through commercially supported overly commodified events.

A further example of dedifferentiation related to events is in the retail sector. 'Retailtainment' is a phenomenon which, although not new, is set to grow as retailers compete, not on the goods they stock, but on the experiences they offer. Shopping and event attendance will become merged as malls and shops become venues for a wide range of relatively small events. This merging of retail and entertainment will be needed in order to compete with the convenience of online shopping and can already be seen in many of the large malls in South East Asia and the Middle East which encompass water parks, theme parks and other forms of entertainment. This is one area where the events industry will see substantial growth as other industries seek to satisfy their consumers' need for new and more stimulating experiences while undertaking other necessary and more mundane activities. This consumer multitasking need and ability will increase as consumers' perceptions of free time diminishes and can already be seen, for example, in developments in in-car entertainment systems, in-store dining and business tourism. The conference and exhibition industry has seen a growing trend towards the combining of a business trip with a tourist/holiday experience as attendees seek to make the best use of their time and money. This trend has implications for client choice of conference location in that they will no longer necessarily be solely basing this on practical issues of cost, accessibility and convenience but on the interest of the location and the entertainment available. The conference organizer may, therefore, be chosen on their ability to provide these additional services as part of the package.

Research undertaken by the MICE Research Unit (2004) at Bournemouth University has identified that the UK conference and meetings industry needs to respond to the challenges of an increasingly competitive global marketplace in order to remain competitive in the future. They suggest that there is a need to upgrade conference venue infrastructure and invest in new products alongside human resource development. The industry will also need to embrace and utilize fully new technology to facilitate the organization and delivery of conferences. This will become a key competitive tool and those organizers embracing online booking and registration systems, electronic tracking or tagging of attendees and new ways of measuring exhibitor performance and lead generation will provide greater attendee and exhibitor benefits.

With the increasing internationalization of the industry and the opening up of new markets in Eastern Europe and Asia marketing communications may be better focused on raising the profile of the UK conference and meetings industry overseas and on lobbying government to support funding and investments. This suggests that competing conference organizers and venues should form partnerships, affiliations and consortia in order to create a UK brand and grow the overall market by targeting non-UK businesses rather than focusing solely on their own business. This is a strategy that has worked well in the closely related tourism industry.

In addition to increasing international competition, there will be a growth in other venues offering conference facilities. This can already be seen as sports and entertainment venues diversify into the conference sector to make better economic use of their facilities. Although the number of conferences is likely to grow, we have seen that the size of each is diminishing. Economies of scale will therefore be more difficult to achieve suggesting that, for both exhibition and conference organizers, revenues from sponsorships will grow in importance. This will also be true for other event organizers who move from large scale events to a larger number of small events.

Consumer trends

The consumer trends that will impact on the event industry include a wide range of issues including the ageing population, the new behaviours of generation Y and changing family structures. However, it is the impact of increasing exposure to information that will create the most challenges.

The constant bombardment of commercial messages and other information sources is unlikely to diminish as newer ways are found to communicate with audiences regardless of location or time. This exposure to information is likely to lead to information overload in the older generations who have not been equipped to handle it and can lead to the desire to simplify and retreat into the familiar. This may manifest itself in increased levels of brand loyalty and a reliance on infomediaries to provide, order and filter information. These agencies already provide a service to consumers unable to manage information overload. For example, tripadvisor.com provides all types of travel information in one site and allows easy price comparisons between online flight and hotel retailers. Consumer events will need to support their customers in handling information through clear communications that are always permission based. The growing use of online agencies to handle ticket sales rather than individual websites is also likely to increase.

The younger consumer and particularly generation Y, or 'the millennials', have been brought up in a world of media choice and feel at home in and in control of the information environment (Geraci and Nagy, 2004). For this generation, the problem is not information overload but decision overload. This generation, who have been exposed to more than 20 000 commercial messages each a year for the last fifteen years, has far more choice in all areas of life than any generation before and also has the information available on which to make those choices. However, the time and effort required in decision making creates a growing desire for simplification and escapism. This may result in a less risk taking mentality where new experiences are only embraced if the risk has been lowered. This will lead to a greater reliance on peer groups, opinion leaders and word of mouth to recommend and reassure consumers on untried products. The job of marketing communications, for these well informed marketing savvy consumers suffering decision overload, is to persuade them to make up their minds rather than persuade them which brand they should buy (Proctor and Kitchen, 2002).

A further consequence of the information age is the growing mistrust young and old consumers have in handing over information to organizations. The overuse and abuse of personal information has made the public far more suspicious of information use and more aware of its value to companies. Organizations collecting and using customer data will therefore need to provide reassurance on the use of the data in terms of the benefits and value they will give in return.

Internet use and online shopping in particular is growing rapidly on a worldwide basis and is set to continue as Internet penetration increases and shoppers are further reassured over security issues. Britain presently has the highest rates of Internet shopping (33 per cent) followed by Australia (25 per cent), the USA (18 per cent) and Germany (18 per cent) (Cooke and Carter, 2004). The number of people purchasing tickets on-line has grown considerably and this growth is set to continue as more event organizations provide this function on their websites or make their tickets available through e-agencies. Business-to-business on-line purchases are showing little growth, however, and may remain an area where traditional methods are preferred in the final decision stage.

As the millennials are currently at the start of their lives as consumers, it is worth further understanding this segment of today's market as many of their traits will affect how they behave as older consumers over the next twenty years. Syrett and Lammiman (2004) highlight five characteristics found in 18–24 year olds. These are intimacy (in relationships over the Internet), loyalty (to personal networks not brands or employers), awareness (of social issues, need honesty and openness, spot hypocrisy), balance (between work and personal life, 24/7 lifestyles) and risk (embrace change, open, flexible and mobile).

This age group already have and will continue to develop an intolerance of unwanted intrusion. They are empowered by their understanding of the media and will select when and what they want to be exposed to. To reach this group communications need to be amusing, entertaining or disarmingly direct and need to bring messages to them in the places where they congregate. On the Internet, at music venues, snowboarding contests, college, for example. Millennials are likely to become increasingly anti-globalized and are aware of social issues and injustices related to the products they buy. Cause-branding will become increasingly important, as will the need to disassociate the brand from unethical practices. Events, therefore, will need to communicate what they are against as well as what they stand for and support and will have to choose partners and sponsors who represent the same values.

This generation are avid Internet users and are the major drivers behind Internet usage exceeding television viewership for the first time in 2003 in the USA (Syrett and Lammiman, 2004). Termed as the 'digerati' by Spero and Stone (2004), these young people inhabit a digital domain where they develop personal relationships, play, learn and consume. Their media prowess allows them to multitask, using more than one medium at once. However, they still rely on traditional media as the pointers for on-line activity and will visit websites recommended in fashion magazines and radio programmes. This generation view new media as more than just tools but also as image enhancers and eschew the use of these by the older generation.

To reach this generation and to build up a long-term relationship with them event communicators need to help them to discover the brand through the new media of their choice. They should not be bombarded by the message but need to be allowed to choose it on their own terms. These experience hungry, time poor younger markets require short, sharp communications which offer something unusual or extraordinary and they will respond positively to humour, irony and unvarnished truth.

Event communications will need to tap into these characteristics and recognize that communicating with the millennials will be increasingly via electronic means. In order to have credibility, the message source (organization or media) will need to be accepted as part of their personal network and as such will rely heavily on viral techniques. This generation's ability to bond at a distance can be used in marketing communications to create relationships with the brand which once established can be long lasting.

The older, or 'grey', consumer will become an increasingly important target market for events as the populations of many countries contain an increasing number of over 55s. This group are not homogeneous and the subgroups within this age range will need to be understood. Many will work for longer and may still have grown up children living at home. Returning to the parental home is becoming increasingly common as fewer people are marrying and cohabiting or having children until later in life and property is increasingly difficult to afford for single people. This means that these older consumers are not necessarily the time rich segment they once were and their income is still being used partly to support their children. Many will use the Internet for work and leisure and this will be one of the key communication tools to reach this target segment, however, as the focus turns to the older 'silver surfer' issues of sight, hearing and dexterity will need to be considered. The use of SMS and other mobile phone techniques will not necessarily be suitable.

These relatively time rich older markets will provide potential growth markets for many types of events. This generation's concerns for health, vigour and prolonged vitality means that they will be more active in their leisure and social pursuits than before, accessing a variety of out-of-home activities rather than in-home entertainment. These older consumers want brands they can trust and are positive towards relationship-building communications that provide reassurance and commitment.

However, events aimed at this target market must also recognize that these audiences are loyal but ageing. For example, classical music concerts, opera and ballet will struggle to maintain audience levels without attracting younger audiences as well. This needs to be addressed through product, venue and communication innovation without alienating the existing core market.

A more generalized view of the new consumer can be described in postmodernist terms. Postmodern consumers are seen as 'restless, cynical, world weary, self-obsessed hedonists demanding instant gratification and ever increasing doses of stimulation . . . and a moronic inferno of narcissists cretinized by television' (Lasch, 1978; Callinicos, 1989; cited in Brown, 1994: 6). This less than complementary view nevertheless points out some important trends. Today's consumer desires new and exciting experiences and only has a limited time in which to experience them. Their empowerment and confidence in media understanding allows them to be more individualistic and less socially constrained. The postmodern consumer can be seen more positively as a liberated, confident individual who will no longer give their valuable time to marketers' messages unless they are being entertained, amused or educated in a way that suits them and at a time they choose.

Events will need to be developed which more flexibly meet the needs of these consumers in terms of times, locations and content. Booking tickets far in advance is likely to become a thing of the past as audiences make more impulse purchases. The use of events as promotional tools will increase as an effective method of communicating with these customers in a way that provides value in the promotion itself rather than through actual brand usage.

The increased levels of anxiety in society and the perception of social decline are also trends to be aware of. The perception that we are worse off than we used to be, although a myth (Cornish and Flatters, 2004) and a yearning for the 'good old days' can be utilized in communications messages through references to traditional values, the family, and a simpler, healthier life.

Blackburn (2004) suggests future segmentation or 'mindset' groups could be usefully based on the handling of anxiety. These mindset groups would be applicable for event audiences if research shows that they are susceptible to anxiety and if the business is influenced by these mindsets. The first of the four groups are the 'super choosers' who individually confront their anxiety or change the cause of it. This group demonstrates very little brand loyalty and will switch readily. To be successful with this group the brand needs to be in front of them and needs to be seen as a servant to them. For example, event tickets booked through lastminute.com would be typical of their behaviour. 'Solution seekers' group with others to avoid or escape anxiety. They look for positive belief brands and require communications that focus on familiar, friendly, family images. They favour events with a clear cause-related theme or community experiences. 'New ragers' use social behaviour to confront or change anxiety causes. This group distrust and reject conventional marketing in favour of word of mouth. A strong socially responsible brand image is needed for the events they attend and viral communications methods and public relations are the most effective tools. Finally, 'simplifiers' find their own individual ways of avoiding or escaping anxiety. This is done by sticking to brands they know and the simplification of choices through ruthless filtering of information and spur of moment decisions. Short simple communications are most effective with this group who also respond well to information filtered by infomediaries.

Marketing trends

A number of areas of development within marketing mirror the changes taking place in the market place. Relationship marketing has emerged to meet the consumer's need to be more than a passive recipient of marketing offerings. Relationship marketing offers the customer involvement and participation in the whole marketing process through the development of commitment, mutual trust and ultimately partnership. Related to this development are the areas of partnership and affinity marketing where the focus is not on developing a buyer/seller relationship but on creating and maintaining mutually beneficial partnerships with a variety of stakeholders. These marketing methods are particularly suitable in areas where there is no clear definition of who is the customer and who is the supplier. For example, the relationships between the event producer and sponsoring organizations or the relationship between venue owners and exhibition organizers are appropriate for partnership marketing.

The characteristics of the postmodern consumer have also been incorporated into developing marketing practice through a variety of ideas (Brown, 1993; van Raaij, 1993; Firat and Ventakesh, 1995). The postmodern preference of consumers for hyperreality can be seen in so called 'landscapes of consumption' where a different reality is created. This can be seen in the development and design of theme parks, shopping malls and leisure complexes and can easily be incorporated into a variety of events. Consumers are looking for a larger than life reality that also fits their location and time availability. This may be an 'Eastern Bazaar' theme used in a western shopping mall or the sights and sounds of a Caribbean carnival in the local high street.

A further aspect of postmodern marketing is the idea of reversed production and consumption. This manifests itself both in the increased link between consumption and brand image and in consumer involvement in the marketing process. Consumers can be seen as customizers and producers of self-images at each consumptive moment and their individuality and empowerment is encouraged as they become partners in the production, creative and marketing processes of the organization.

This consumer individuality means that consumers will be far more likely to alter their self-image frequently by switching products that represent images in order to free themselves from boredom and the need to conform. Due to the chameleon-like nature of these consumers traditional segmentation criteria will no longer be as valid. Communicating with selected audiences and stakeholders will take on a new dynamic importance and will necessitate a highly creative approach to marketing and corporate communications in terms of the messages and images deployed (Proctor and Kitchen, 2002).

The use of juxtaposition and pastiche can already be seen in a variety of marketing communications and in brands. These are as a response to the consumer's desire for new and unusual experiences, subtlety and humour. Unclear and deliberately vague advertisements and the use of contradictions can lead the audience to create their own interpretations allowing scope for imaginative consumer participation.

Other areas of postmodern marketing include the recognition that consumers are losing traditional commitment and brand loyalty as a consequence of anti-foundationalism, a lack of belief or trust in the traditional pillars of society. However, they respond well to openness and candour and can develop a lasting liking (if not loyalty) for brands and organizations that display these qualities. The desire for new forms and styles constantly to recreate self-image requires a dynamic of continuous communication of new images associated with the brand. In this climate it is, therefore, difficult to maintain a consistent unchanging brand image through which loyalty could be developed. What is required is an emphasis on brand image for the entire portfolio maintained as fresh up-to-date images. This move from line branding to corporate branding should focus on the three areas of brand personality, identity and image. Brands that have personalities and optimism, a trait associated with a youthful personality, is one aspect that should be portrayed in the brand. Virgin, Orange and Nike have all successfully managed an optimistic brand image. The attractiveness of these brands, which implicitly or explicitly express an optimistic vision, is due to them offering a more positive vision of the consumer's future (Landell-Mills, 2004).

Brown (2001) suggests that the postmodern consumer, in fact, is not looking for a relationship with an organization but is looking to be surprised by them. It may be that, in the continuing anxiety caused by information and decision overload, consumers would rather withdraw from the process and sit back and be sold to. Retro marketing refers to marketing as it was 'in the good old days' but with the twist of marketers 'teasing, tantalizing and torturing' their consumers (Brown, 2001). The move towards this form of marketing comes as a result of consumers who no longer want a 'relationship' where they are pandered to but marketing they can enjoy. It is also argued that a customer focus inevitably leads to stagnation in the marketplace and a lack of creativity and innovation. Manifestations of retro marketing can be seen in products that, at least in appearance, relate back to a previous era. The relaunched Beetle, for example, the 1950s styling of fridges, the use of 1970s football strips and retro events such as Masters series in golf and tennis. However, 'retro' is not simply in the products but also in the marketing methods. Brown (2001) suggests the acronym TEASE in that consumers want marketers to use 'tricksterism, entertainment, amplification, secrecy and exclusivity'. They want to enjoy, rather than suffer, the marketing communication process. Retro marketing is seen by the consumer as a way to simplify choices as a result of too much information and apparently endless, yet in reality undifferentiated, choices. In some ways retro marketing is a backlash against the very information based analytical methods of relationship marketing and overcomes some of the consumers concerns regarding privacy and intrusion. Retro marketing also encompasses experiential marketing in that the 'TEASE' methods are all about consumer involvement and experience and should also encompass viral techniques to give the secrecy and exclusivity needed.

This style of communication has worked very successfully for Lush, the handmade cosmetics company (www.lush.com). Their direct mail, catalogue, website and signage are all created to give an honest yet inherently attractive view of their products and the company. The use of old style fonts, hand drawn illustrations and good and bad product reviews create interest and liking in keeping with the company's image of quirkiness and openness. The successful television advertising campaign for Ronseal also has a retro feel in its simplistic *'it does what it says on the tin'* message. Posters and leaflets for events ranging from snooker competitions to club nights aimed at younger markets have recently started to use 1950s style images and fonts.

Event communications would do well to follow some of these techniques, especially in those sectors, such as small music venues, where there is a proliferation of very similar communication methods such as the overuse of flyers. Certainly, many of the sports events with long traditions but dwindling audiences could benefit from this type of communications campaign, although it may be more suitable for NBA, NFL and MLB teams in the US than for more austere bodies such as the International Olympic Committee. The desire for retro methods could, of course, turn out to be a short-lived fad and may not be suitable for all event and audience types, but it is based on the continued consumer belief that things were better in the old days and brings in the honesty, openness and entertainment required by the jaded audiences of the future. It certainly opens up opportunities for promotional events and event sponsorship that can apply these techniques to enhance the promoter's products. For example, the relating of the brand to better past times may be readily achieved through the sponsorship of existing or created historical or cultural events. This has already been successfully achieved to a certain extent through 'masters' events which use stars from past times.

Communication trends

The changes in the events industry, in the marketplace and in marketing practice will create opportunities for new innovative communications methods and media as well as help to refocus communications messages.

One of the major changes is the continuing growth of the Internet as a medium for communicating on a variety of levels with many different target audiences. Research by the European Interactive Advertising Association shows that the Internet now represents 10 per cent of European's media consumption (cited in

Dobson, 2004). Magazines account for 8 per cent, newspapers for 13 per cent and television still has the largest at 41 per cent. However, the amount of time spent viewing television is being reduced as people spend more time on the Internet. The study also found that users of the Internet are engaged with the activity, whereas television is used to help them relax. Add to this the view that television is cluttered with advertisements and it appears inevitable that online promotion is set to increase.

Despite the increasing use of the Internet by event customers and the number and sophistication of event websites, the amount of actual advertising on-line is not growing at the rates initially expected. This is due to several factors including the annoyance of such advertisements to the user, the complexity of advertising options and technology for the client, the uncertain reach and the current lack of creative use shown by advertising agencies (Keynote, 2004b). However, the medium needs to be seen not as a direct replacement for television advertisements but as a subtler medium for enhancing brand image. Internet advertising needs to fit with the consumer's desire to choose when to view commercial content rather than forcing the advertisements upon them as they browse. This can only be achieved through content that is of interest and value and increased levels of interactivity.

The Internet is not the only medium bringing about changes in the use of traditional 'above-the-line' advertising. Print, television and radio advertising are all likely to diminish in terms of importance as other methods better meet the needs of the future consumer. Advertising is already seen as far less influential than e-mail, guerrilla marketing, sponsorship, direct mail, events and exhibitions (Campaign, 2003). There is also a gradual slowing and decline of advertising supported media as a percentage of time spent with media. However, time spent with these types of media is still increasing but each medium is now competing with more media as consumers increasingly multitask (Mandese, 2004).

Developments in telecommunications and the further convergence of this industry with computing and the Internet will lead to greater marketing communication opportunities. One prediction is that information technology will allow data to be stored as personal memories. These multimedia memories will be used as diaries or albums and will be created through the use of mobile phones and intimate data and stored elsewhere (Spero and Stone, 2004). These data can be supported and tapped into by organizations that are able to gain the trust and loyalty of the future consumer.

Another area of growth is likely to be in the appearance of WiFi hotspots and thus the provision of a new sponsorship medium.

The digitization of television, radio and publishing has already led to lower costs and the emergence of many more channels of communication. The convergence of television, publishing, IT and telecommunications will also create opportunities for cross-media synergies. These abundant media opportunities already mean that there is no longer a shortage of supply. Space is therefore cheaper enabling smaller event organizations to use media that have traditionally been out of their reach (Blackman, 2004).

Some of the new marketing communications models of the future related to digitization and the Internet are likely to include: micro advertising using highly targeted digital television; one-to-one communication using personalized advertisements sent via digital set-top decoders; portal advertising using portals such as MSN, AOL, Yahoo; affiliate advertising using the websites of others for referrals; cross-marketing alliances between brands promoting each others goods and services using the interactive nature of the Internet; in-programme/event promotion using product placement and sponsorship; and advertising which appears as the user searches the digital television programme guides (Keynote, 2003).

The growth in direct marketing techniques will also be linked to the Internet and interactive television as consumers become used to using these media to request event and entertainment information and make ticket purchases and bookings directly. These techniques will increasingly be used to reach global microsegments of customers.

Although information technology and telecommunications will continue to have the largest impact on marketing communications of the future, other changes are occurring in the communications industry. The industry, like the media, is becoming more fragmented with many media and method specialists and agencies appearing to manage and integrate the use of these outsourced specialists. This can create a complex structure with many levels between the company, the creatives and the target audience. A possible consequence of this is a move back to simpler in-house created communications.

The trends that can already be seen in the youth market in terms of their media expertise will become a general society trait. The target audience will therefore, be no longer passive recipients but actively searching, creating and experiencing participants. The image of the event itself is likely to be increasingly dependent not just on the functions it serves, but on its contributions to self-image and to levels of happiness and feeling good. There will therefore be a greater need to pay attention to design with communications that appeal to the mindsets of event customers and stakeholders.

Many of the future consumer's characteristics along with media fragmentation, levels of anxiety and increasing competition will lead to a distrust, disinterest and boredom with many communication techniques. Individualized messages which emanate from trusted sources, such as peer groups, will increase in importance leading to a rise in the use of created word of mouth campaigns using viral and experiential marketing methods. Mintel (2004b) found that 57 per cent of respondents looked to word of mouth as the main source of information on live performance events, although local newspapers (54 per cent) and the Internet (37 per cent) were also vital media sources.

The dedifferentiation discussed earlier can also be seen in the convergence of advertising and entertainment. As the only marketing communications the consumer of the future will see are the ones they choose to see, marketers need to create and own the content of promotional vehicles rather than 'sneaking in' with product placement, sponsorship and celebrity endorsement. This can be achieved by creating television programming, movies, magazines, books and events. Examples of this can already be seen in reality shows and lifestyle magazines developed by advertisers in order to showcase client's products and in the creation of music, sports and arts events as sponsorship or cause-related communications vehicles. This trend will mean that the medium is owned by the client's brand not the media company's brand and as such will provide a potential additional revenue stream. For example, a sports team could create and market sports lifestyle magazine as an extension of its merchandising but reaching a far wider audience. This is more than a 'fan' or corporate magazine and includes more generic rather than solely branded content but enhances the brand through its association with the magazine. A festival may create a range of specialist music magazines which enhance the brand through the value of its content meeting the needs of many target segments. There are of course implications for artistic integrity but Generation Y tend to be more accepting of commercial involvement in a range of products if this is done sympathetically and openly (Cheyfitz, 2004).

Promotional events organizations will also be able to take advantage of this trend by extending the range of services offered to their clients. However, any development in this area needs to be undertaken with integrity to the event content if audiences are not to be alienated by an overcommodification of their experience.

Summary

What emerges from the discussion above is a changing landscape for both the events industry and marketing communications. These changes are driven by consumer trends that manifest themselves in issues such as increased anxiety, cynicism, the desire for new experiences and the increasing move towards individualism. This is already resulting in the event product changing through moves towards a larger number of smaller events in both consumer and organizational markets.

These more targeted events will be able to communicate with target audiences using a variety of media with an emphasis on digital media, the Internet and mobile telecommunications. These in turn will allow audiences to access the marketing message when they choose to so long as they are made aware of these opportunities through the subtler methods of viral and experiential marketing and the use of ambient media. The key to being accepted is to become part of the audience's personal network and this will require a focus on trust building, honesty and openness.

The convergence of several industries and the increasing use of events as a promotional tool will inevitably lead to greater competition for existing event organizers, however, it will also create opportunities for new product development and ultimately growth within the sector.

The future looks bright for event industry players who are in tune with their customers and creative in their communications.

Discussion points

- Discuss the implication of the future trends for a large-scale event of your choice. Suggest developments that could overcome any threats and take advantage of any opportunities.
- What marketing communication message, methods and media would be most appropriate for promoting a snowboarding contest to postmodern fourteen to eighteen year olds?

References

Blackburn, D. (2004) Dealing with the decade of anxiety. *Market Research Society Conferences*. Available from www.warc.com.

Blackman, C. (2004) Paying the price: The future for Europe's media sector. *Foresight*, 6 (5), 292–301.

Brown, S. (1993) Postmodern marketing: Principles, practice and panaceas. *Irish Marketing Review*, 6, 91–100.

Brown, S. (1994) Marketing as multiplex: Screening postmodernism. *European Journal of Marketing*, 28 (9), 27–51.

Brown, S. (2001) Torment your customers (they'll love it). *Harvard Business Review*, 79 (9), 82–88.

Campaign (2003) PR more influential than above-the-line ads. *Campaign*, 24 October.

Cheyfitz, K. (2004) Goodbye media commercial, hello commercial content. *Admap*, April (449). (Available from www.warc.com.)

Cooke, S. and Carter, P. (2004) Online shoppers around the world. *TGI Global Consumer Barometer*, October (9). (Available from www.warc.com.)

Cornish, C. and Flatters, P. (2004) Bringing reality to the dream – the myth of decline. *Market Research Society Conferences*. (Available from www.warc.com.)

Dobson, C. (2004) Changing fortunes for Internet advertising. *Admap*, March (448). (Available from www.warc.com.)

Firat, A.F. and Ventakesh, A. (1995) Liberatory postmodernism and the re-enchantment of consumption. *Journal of Consumer Research*, 22, 239–267.

Geraci, J.C. and Nagy, J. (2004) Millennials – the new generation. *International Journal of Advertising and Marketing to Children*, 5 (2). (Available from www.warc.com.)

Keynote (2003) *Advertising Agencies MA*. August.

Keynote (2004a) *Exhibitions and Conferences*. April.

Keynote (2004b) *Internet Advertising*. October.

Landell-Mills, W. (2004) What 'the future' means for brands. *Admap*, May (450). (Available from www.warc.com.) pp. 47–49.

Mandese, J. (2004) This is the end, my friend, the end-user. *Admap*, September (453). (Available from www.warc.com.)

MICE Research Unit (2004) Future trends and issues affecting the UK meetings and convention industry. Bournemouth University. //icthr.bournemouth.ac.uk/mice/pubs.htm (accessed November, 2004).

Mintel (2003) *Sport and the Media – UK*. May. Mintel International Group.

Mintel (2004a) *Music Concerts and Festivals – UK*. August. Mintel International Group.

Mintel (2004b) *Leisure Promotion – UK*. January. Mintel International Group.

Proctor, T. and Kitchen, P. (2002) Communication in postmodern integrated marketing. *Corporate Communications: An International Journal*, 7 (3), 144–154.

Spero, I. and Stone, M. (2004) Agents of change: How young consumers are changing the world of marketing. *Qualitative Market Research: An International Journal*, 7 (2), 1853–1859.

Syrett, M. and Lammiman, J. (2004) Advertising and the millennials. *Young Consumers*, 5 (4).

van Raaij, W.F. (1993) Postmodern consumption. *Journal of Economic Psychology*, 14, 541–563.

Appendix

Figure 7.3(a) Means-end chain theory. Artwork courtesy of ICEP Portugal 2004 (**See page 145**).

Figure 7.3(b) Means-end chain theory. Artwork courtesy of ICEP Portugal 2004 (**See page 145**).

Figure 7.3(c) Means-end chain theory. Artwork courtesy of ICEP Portugal 2004 (**See page 145**).

Author Index

Subject Index